21世纪旅游英语系列教材
教学资源库网址:http://zlgc.sicnu.edu.cn/

旅游学概论（双语）
（第二版）

An Introduction to Tourism Principles

(Second Edition)

主　编　朱　华
副主编　王雪霏　朱　红　刘汇明

图书在版编目(CIP)数据

旅游学概论(双语)/朱华主编.—2版.—北京:北京大学出版社,2012.8
(21世纪旅游英语系列教材)
ISBN 978-7-301-18734-0

Ⅰ.①旅… Ⅱ.①朱… Ⅲ.①旅游学—双语教学—高等学校—教材 Ⅳ.①F590

中国版本图书馆CIP数据核字(2012)第193950号

| 书　　　名：旅游学概论(双语)(第二版)
| 著作责任者：朱　华　主编
| 责 任 编 辑：李　颖　刘　爽
| 标 准 书 号：ISBN 978-7-301-18734-0/H·3116
| 出 版 发 行：北京大学出版社
| 地　　　址：北京市海淀区成府路205号　100871
| 网　　　址：http://www.pup.cn　新浪官方微博:@北京大学出版社
| 电 子 邮 箱：zbing@pup.pku.edu.cn
| 电　　　话：邮购部 62752015　发行部 62750672　编辑部 62754382　出版部 62754962
| 印　刷　者：天津和萱印刷有限公司
| 经　销　者：新华书店
| 　　　　　787毫米×1092毫米　16开本　19.5印张　470千字
| 　　　　　2009年5月第1版
| 　　　　　2012年8月第2版　2023年5月第5次印刷
| 定　　　价：45.00元

未经许可,不得以任何方式复制或抄袭本书之部分或全部内容。
版权所有,侵权必究
举报电话:010-62752024　电子邮箱: fd@pup.pku.edu.cn

第二版序

旅游学是一门新型学科。由于旅游研究多学科的性质，我国旅游教育工作者对旅游学科认识不同，高等院校的旅游课程体系差异较大，教材建设相对落后，影响了旅游人才的培养。为此，教育部要求全国高等院校积极开展双语教学，特别是在学科建设、教材建设相对落后的专业率先开展双语教学课程建设，力争在较短的时间内缩短与国外教育的差距，为我国培养一批具有竞争力的高素质旅游管理人才。

2010年11月，我赴瑞士参加国际旅游休闲学术会议，访问了瑞士国际酒店与旅游管理学院（HTMi），聆听了该校本科生课程，参加了MBA研究生课程的教学，深受启发，瑞士旅游高等院校的案例教学给我留下了深刻印象。2012年2月，应美国旧金山州立大学（San Francisco State University）和波士顿大学（Boston University）的邀请，我赴美讲学，再次感受到欧美旅游教育的先进理念和教学方法。

《旅游学概论》（双语）第二版借鉴了欧美旅游专业教学理念和教材编写方法，结合中国高等教育实际，重新设计了教材体例，提供了课文导读、阅读分析、案例矩阵；新增了教学要点、关键术语、知识链接、案例教学指导、网上测试和中英文教学案例，进一步完善了教学资源库和网络课堂 http://zlgc.sicnu.edu.cn/，为教师编写了电子教案、制作了多媒体课件，提供期末考试样题二套。

在此，我要感谢瑞士国际酒店与旅游管理学院 Lan R. J. Larmour 校长，他为我提供了颇有价值的旅游教学案例，"奔跑在瑞士山川的'黄金列车'"案例正是我和众多游客在瑞士旅游的真切体验。我要感谢美国旧金山州立大学休闲、公园与旅游系 Patrick T. Tierney 教授和美国波士顿大学 Robert P. Weller 教授，在美的学术交流和教学研讨提高了我对旅游教育的认识，拓展了我的学术研究视野，为《旅游学概论》双语教材的编写不仅提供了写作资料，更重要的是提供了符合旅游学科建设和教学的写作思路。

《旅游学概论》双语教材是我国高等院校旅游管理专业双语教学多年探索和实践的总结，也是我国旅游管理专业建设和旅游教育国际交流阶段性的成果。教材的出版将减轻我国高等学校旅游管理专业双语教学成本，提升我国高等院校双语教学质量，为我国培养更多的具有国际视野、通晓一门外语的高素质旅游人才。

国家双语教学示范课程《旅游学概论》主持人
朱华教授
2012年6月22日

前　言

　　《旅游学概论》2008年被教育部正式立项，成为我国高等院校旅游管理专业第一门国家级双语教学示范课程。2009年5月，根据教育部国家双语示范课程建设的要求，《旅游学概论》双语教材由北京大学出版社出版，是我国高等院校旅游管理专业第一部自编双语教材。《旅游学概论》（双语）第二版内容更丰富，版式更加合理，呈现以下特点：

　　1. 结构严谨，以雷柏尔模型（Leiper's Model）为框架，将旅游活动置于旅游模型之下观察学习，建立起符合旅游管理专业学科体系的教材结构，避免了一般旅游学概论教材结构松散的弊病。

　　2. 英语课文语言朴实、流畅易懂，符合大二、大三学生英语阅读水平，解决了原著难读难懂的问题；

　　3. 导读帮助学生理解英文课文，是课文内容科学的阐释和有益的补充，提高了学生对原文的理解；

　　4. 中英文案例类型丰富，典型实用。教材既有国外典型旅游案例，也有中国本土旅游案例，富有启发性，有助于案例教学；

　　5. 每一章有旅游扩展知识和中英文参考文献，帮助学生了解中外旅游学者前沿研究成果，增强学生的自主学习能力和研究水平。

　　6. 建立网络课堂，提供网络化教学平台。师生可以利用丰富的网络资源开展教学，利用网络教学平台课内、课后互动，提升教学质量。

　　参加《旅游学概论》（双语）第二版编写的作者有：朱华、王雪霏、吴其付、李文汇、黄文、李婵、朱晓霞、李晨、王砥；还有第一版的作者朱红、刘汇明、游佳、李峰、何畅、张黎、代敏、陈然。四川师范大学旅游管理专业本科生，特别是中瑞（3+1）联合培养项目的学生在教学过程中提出了宝贵建议，研究生何碧云参加了校对和编写。

　　《旅游学概论》（双语）教材的编写得到我国高等院校旅游管理专业同行、欧美学者的建议和帮助，参考了众多中外旅游专家的著作、论文，在此谨向他们表示衷心的感谢。教材内容多，涉及管理学、经济学、行为学、心理学、自然科学、人文历史等学科，加之英文写作难度较大，不当疏漏之处在所难免，敬请各位专家和读者指正。

　　北京大学出版社出版的《旅游学概论》（双语）教材是我国高等院校双语教学取得的最新成果之一，凝聚了大家的智慧与汗水。我们相信，有众多旅游教育者和广大旅游从业人员的共同努力，我国一定会在本世纪内完成旅游产业的转型升级，实现从世界旅游大国到世界旅游强国的历史性转变，中国旅游和旅游从业员的发展前景会更加美好。

《旅游学概论》（双语）教材编委会
2012年6月22日

案例教学指南

一、案例教学目的

旅游案例讨论的目的,在于让学生深刻理解旅游基本原理,运用旅游理论分析问题和解决问题,特别是解决我国旅游发展实践中出现的各种难题。通过案例教学,学生应当具备以下能力:发觉复杂现象中的潜在问题;系统分析问题结构,并进行推理、归纳;正确判断案例不同问题,并提出一套完整的解决方案。培养独立思考、分析问题、解决问题的能力是旅游案例教学的主要目的。

二、教学案例类型

旅游管理教学采用的案例一般分为三类:一是问题评审型,即案例给出了问题和解决问题的方案,让同学评价是非得失;二是分析决策型,即不给出方案,要求同学通过讨论分析给出决策方案;三是发展理论型,即通过案例印证理论或发现新的理论生长点,深化并完善理论认识。

三、案例分析要点

1. 仔细阅读案例,研究案例背景和案例相关资料。
2. 寻找案例中隐含的信息,挖掘案例中的各种问题。
3. 寻找运用各种原理和分析的工具。
4. 对案例中的观点进行充分的论述和推理,并提供相关材料和证据。
5. 对各种建议和方案进行优先性排序,确保实施框架和步骤的可操作性。
6. 提出具有充分论证和材料证明的建议和解决方案。

四、案例教学步骤

案例教学的过程一般分为以下五个步骤:

1. 阅读案例、准备资料。老师课前准备所要讨论的背景资料,布置教学案例,让学生充分利用网络资源和图书资料收集相关信息。

2. 分组讨论、头脑风暴。教师仔细聆听小组讨论,充分掌握讨论的重点议题,并适时提出自己的观点,但不做任何结论。

3. 课堂发言、陈述观点。每个小组要为发言的角色预先定位,并选派一位同学陈述分析案例。教师要控制发言人的时间,让每个小组都有发表意见的机会。

4. 教师总结,升华认识。老师针对每个小组的发言点评,指出精彩和不足之处,进行概况性的总结,但应当包容不同的观点,结论应当多为开方式的结论。

5. 写出书面报告,课堂演讲。学生要将课堂讨论的内容加以整理上交,内容一般分为四个部分:个案所提供的事实经验(Fact)、个案分析适用的理论依据(Theory)、个案问题的解决方案(Solution)、个案讨论所归纳出的共通性观点(Generalization)。一份好的书面报告,必须是打字、装订、格式整齐,显示撰写者的用心和重视。如果时间允许的话,可择优让学生在下一次课堂上陈述自己的案例分析报告,让大家共享案例教学的成果。

旅游教学案例

案例一	以成都市为中心的四川旅游
案例二	马罗卡岛的大众旅游
案例三	旅游需求的增长与变化——以佛罗里达中心地区为例
案例四	云南民族村主题公园如何走出困境
案例五	奔跑在瑞士山川的"黄金列车"
案例六	Amadeus：全球旅游分销
案例七	中国旅游市场出现旅游批发商
案例八	盖特威饭店的经营管理
案例九	时运假日旅行社的市场营销
案例十	周庄古镇生命周期研究
案例十一	旅游对上海经济的影响——基于投入产出模型的研究和评价
案例十二	野三坡旅游发展跟踪调查
案例十三	旅游环境容量的测算——以四川省宜宾地区为例
案例十四	萨尔茨堡旅游资源的开发和保护
案例十五	生存还是毁灭：大堡礁海洋公园的未来

相关理论和问题

1. 旅游系统(Tourism system)
2. 旅游流(Tourist flow)
3. 旅游口岸城市的功能(Functions of the tourist port city)
4. 旅游空间布局(Spacious layout of tourism)
5. 可自由支配收入和时间(Disposal income and time)
6. 小规模旅游与大众旅游(Small-scale tourism and mass tourism)
7. 生态旅游(Ecotourism)
8. 旅游的可持续发展(Sustainable development of tourism)
9. 家庭生命周期和生活方式(Family life cycle and life style)
10. 消费者行为(Consumer behavior)
11. 旅游需求弹性(Elasticity of tourism demand)
12. 旅游需求价格曲线(Price curve of tourism demand)
13. 旅游的真实性(Authenticity of tourism)
14. 旅游商品化(Commercialization of tourism)
15. 虚拟的真实(Virtual reality)
16. 旅游感知和旅游体验(Perception and experience of tourism)
17. 旅游交通成本(Transport cost of tourism)
18. 旅游时空和交通优化(Time & space of travel and optimization of transport)
19. 旅游距离抗阻(Resistance of the travel distance)
20. 旅游环境(Travel environment)
21. 旅游信息化(Tourism informatization)
22. 旅游电子商务(E-commerce of tourism)
23. 目的地管理系统(Destination management system)

24. 旅行社分类和组结构（Categories and structures of travel agencies）

25. 旅游上游企业与下游企业（Upstream and downstream enterprises in tourism industry）

26. 旅游产业链（Tourism industrial chain）

27. 旅游产品销售渠道（Sales channels of tourism products）

28. 营销信息和营销环境（Marketing information and marketing environment）

29. 目标市场选择和定位（Choice and positioning of the target market）

30. 营销计划和控制（Marketing plan and control）

31. 企业竞争战略（Corporate competitive strategy）

32. 旅游市场调查（Investigation of tourism market）

33. 分销渠道（Distribution channels）

34. 市场细分（Segmentation of the markets）

35. 营销组合—4Ps（Marketing mix—4Ps）

36. 目的地生命周期（Destination life cycle）

37. 目的地承载力（Destination bearing capacity）

38. 旅游乘数效应（Multiplier effect）

39. 收入漏损（Revenue leakage）

40. 投入产出模型（Input-output model）

41. 企业伦理（Corporate ethics）

42. 示范效应（Demonstration effect）

43. 东道主与客人关系（Relation between host and guest）

44. 环境容量（Environmental capacity）

45. 旅游环境平衡（Tourism environmental balance）

46. 环境审计和保护（Environmental auditing and protection）

47. 旅游资源开发（Tourism resource development）

48. 旅游规划（Tourism planning）

49. 替代旅游（Alternative tourism）

50. 旅游法规（Tourism law）

51. 景区管理（Management of tourist resorts）

案例相关问题矩阵

	案例1	案例2	案例3	案例4	案例5	案例6	案例7	案例8	案例9	案例10	案例11	案例12	案例13	案例14	案例15
1	√	#	√	#	√	√	#	#	√	√	#	√	#	√	√
2	√														
3	√														
4	√														
5		√													
6		√								√		#		#	#
7												#	#	√	√
8		√		√						√		√	√	√	√
9															
10		√					#	√	√	√	#	√			
11		#	√									#		#	
12		#	√											#	
13				√						#		#			
14		√		√						√		√			#
15				#											
16		#		√	#					√		#			
17	√				√										
18	√			√									#	#	#
19	√		#	√											
20		#		√	#						#		#	√	
21						√									
22						√									
23						√									
24							√		√						
25							√	#	#	√					
26							#	#	#	√					
27						√	√	#	√						
28						√	√	#	√						

	1	2	3	4	5	6	7	8	9	10	11	12	13
29			#		#	√	√	√					
30					#	#	√	#					
31						#	√	√					
32			#										
33					#	#							
34			#			√	#	√					
35			#			√	√	√					
36								√		#	√	√	√
37		√	#		#			√		#	√	√	√
38								√			#		
39								√			#		
40								√					
41										#			#
42								#		#			
43		√		√				√			√	√	√
44		#	#		#			√		#	√	√	√
45					#						√	√	
46					#								√
47					√			√		#	√	√	
48	√				√			√		#	√	√	
49		#									#	√	
50												√	√
51		√	#	#				#		√		√	√

√为主要相关；#为一般相关。

目 录

Contents

Chapter 1   Tourism System
第一章　旅游系统 1

　Part I   Text
　第一部分　课文 2
　　☞ Tourism System　旅游系统

　Part II   Guided Reading
　第二部分　课文导读 7

　Part III   Case Study
　第三部分　案例研究 9
　　☞ 以成都市为中心的四川旅游

　Part IV   Reading Box
　第四部分　阅读与分析 11
　　☞ Travel in Singapore　新加坡旅游

　Part V   Additional Know-how of Tourism
　第五部分　旅游知识扩展 14
　　☞ 1. 旅游功能系统
　　☞ 2. 吴必虎旅游系统

　Part VI   Further Readings
　第六部分　课外阅读 18

Chapter 2   The Rise and Evolution of Tourism
第二章　旅游的兴起和演变 20

　Part I   Text
　第一部分　课文 21
　　☞ The History of Mass Tourism　大众旅游发展史

　Part II   Guided Reading
　第二部分　课文导读 26

1

Part III　Case Study
　第三部分　案例研究 28
　　☞ 马罗卡岛的大众旅游
Part IV　Reading Box
　第四部分　阅读与分析 30
　　☞ Thomas Cook　托马斯·库克
Part V　Additional Know-how of Tourism
　第五部分　旅游知识扩展 33
　　☞ 1. 现代大众旅游的构成
　　☞ 2. 旅行社与大众旅游
Part VI　Further Readings
　第六部分　课外阅读 36

Chapter 3　Demand for Tourism and Consumer Behavior
第三章　旅游需求与消费者行为 38
Part I　Text
　第一部分　课文 39
　　☞ Demand for Tourism and Consumer Behavior　旅游需求
Part II　Guided Reading
　第二部分　课文导读 45
Part III　Case Study
　第三部分　案例研究 47
　　☞ 旅游需求的增长与变化——以佛罗里达中心地区为例
Part IV　Reading Box
　第四部分　阅读与分析 50
　　☞ Resistance of the Travel Distance　旅游距离抗阻
Part V　Additional Know-how of Tourism
　第五部分　旅游知识扩展 54
　　☞ 1. 旅游需求和旅游者需求
　　☞ 2. 旅游需求的特点
Part VI　Further Readings
　第六部分　课外阅读 57

Chapter 4　Tourist Attractions
第四章　旅游吸引物 59
Part I　Text　第一部分　课文 60
　　☞ Tourist Attractions　旅游吸引物
Part II　Guided Reading
　第二部分　课文导读 65
Part III　Case Study
　第三部分　案例研究 67
　　☞ 云南民族村主题公园如何走出困境

Part IV　Reading Box
第四部分　阅读与分析 69
☞ Virtual Reality　虚拟的真实

Part V　Additional Know-how of Tourism
第五部分　旅游知识扩展 72
☞ 1. 影响民族文化真实性的因素
☞ 2. 舞台的真实性

Part VI　Further Readings
第六部分　课外阅读 75

Chapter 5　Mobility and Tourism Transportation
第五章　移动性与旅游交通 77

Part I　Text
第一部分　课文 78
☞ Mobility and Tourism Transportation　移动性与旅游交通

Part II　Guided Reading
第二部分　课文导读 84

Part III　Case Study
第三部分　案例研究 86
☞ 奔跑在瑞士山川的"黄金列车"

Part IV　Reading Box
第四部分　阅读与分析 88
☞ Passenger Transport　旅客交通

Part V　Additional Know-how of Tourism
第五部分　旅游知识扩展 91
☞ 1. 旅游交通运输市场细分
☞ 3. 旅游交通优化战略

Part VI　Further Readings
第六部分　课外阅读 93

Chapter 6　Information Technology and Travel Industry
第六章　信息技术与旅游业 95

Part I　Text
第一部分　课文 96
☞ Information Technology and Travel Industry　信息技术与旅游产业

Part II　Guided Reading
第二部分　课文导读 101

Part III　Case Study
第三部分　案例研究 103
☞ Amadeus：全球旅游分销

Part IV　Reading Box
　　第四部分　阅读与分析 106
　　　　☞ Management of Tourist Destinations　旅游目的地管理
Part V　Additional Know-how of Tourism
　　第五部分　旅游知识扩展 109
　　　　☞ 1. 旅游目的信息系统
　　　　☞ 2. 信息通讯技术与旅游目的地营销
Part VI　Further Readings
　　第六部分　课外阅读 112

Chapter 7　Tour Operator
第七章　旅游经营商 113
Part I　Text
　　第一部分　课文 114
　　　　☞ Tour Operator　旅游经营商
Part II　Guided Reading
　　第二部分　课文导读 120
Part III　Case Study
　　第三部分　案例研究 122
　　　　☞ 中国旅游市场出现旅游批发商
Part IV　Reading Box
　　第四部分　阅读与分析 124
　　　　☞ Tour Wholesalers in North America　北美的旅游批发商
Part V　Additional Know-how of Tourism
　　第五部分　旅游知识扩展 127
　　　　☞ 1. 批发旅游经营商
　　　　☞ 2. 专业媒介者
Part VI　Further Readings
　　第六部分　课外阅读 129

Chapter 8　Accommodation and Hotel Chain
第八章　住宿与饭店连锁 131
Part I　Text
　　第一部分　课文 132
　　　　☞ Hotel Management　饭店管理
Part II　Guided Reading
　　第二部分　课文导读 136
Part III　Case Study
　　第三部分　案例研究 138
　　　　☞ 盖特威饭店的经营管理

Part IV　Reading Box
　　第四部分　阅读与分析 141
　　　　☞ Hotel Chains　饭店连锁
Part V　Additional Know-how of Tourism
　　第五部分　旅游知识扩展 145
　　　　☞ 1. "金钥匙服务"
　　　　☞ 2. 饭店管理职能
Part VI　Further Readings
　　第六部分　课外阅读 147

Chapter 9　Distribution of the Tourist Product
第九章　旅游产品的分销 149
Part I　Text
　　第一部分　课文 150
　　　　☞ Distribution of the Tourist Product　旅游产品分销
Part II　Guided Reading
　　第二部分　课文导读 155
Part III　Case Study
　　第三部分　案例研究 158
　　　　☞ 时运假日旅行社的市场营销
Part IV　Reading Box
　　第四部分　阅读与分析 161
　　　　☞ The Marketing Approach for Tourism Products
　　　　　旅游产品的营销方法
Part V　Additional Know-how of Tourism
　　第五部分　旅游知识扩展 165
　　　　☞ 1. 营销渠道成本
　　　　☞ 2. 旅游中间商
Part VI　Further Readings
　　第六部分　课外阅读 168

Chapter 10　Destination Life Cycle
第十章　目的地生命周期 170
Part I　Text
　　第一部分　课文 171
　　　　☞ Destination Life Cycle　目的地生命周期
Part II　Guided Reading
　　第二部分　课文导读 177
Part III　Case Study
　　第三部分　案例研究 179
　　　　☞ 周庄古镇生命周期研究

Part IV　Reading Box
第四部分　阅读与分析 182
☞ Destination in Decline　目的地的衰落
Part V　Additional Know-how of Tourism
第五部分　旅游知识扩展 186
☞ 1. 旅游目的地形象的形成
☞ 2. 旅游目的地系统的功能分区
Part VI　Further Readings
第六部分　课外阅读 188

Chapter 11　Economic Costs of Tourism
第十一章　旅游的经济成本 190
Part I　Text
第一部分　课文 191
☞ Economic Costs of Tourism　旅游的经济成本
Part II　Guided Reading
第二部分　课文导读 197
Part III　Case Study
第三部分　案例研究 199
☞ 旅游对上海经济的影响——基于投入产出模型的研究和评价
Part IV　Reading Box
第四部分　阅读与分析 203
☞ Dependency on Tourism Industry
　—A lesson from the Caribbean Island of Antigua
　对旅游的依赖——加勒比海安提瓜岛的教训
Part V　Additional Know-how of Tourism
第五部分　旅游知识扩展 207
☞ 1. 旅游外汇漏损
☞ 2. 旅游卫星账户
Part VI　Further Readings
第六部分　课外阅读 210

Chapter 12　The Socio-cultural Impact of Tourism
第十二章　旅游的社会文化影响 212
Part I　Text
第一部分　课文 213
☞ The Socio-cultural Impact of Tourism　旅游的社会文化影响
Part II　Guided Reading
第二部分　课文导读 218
Part III　Case Study
第三部分　案例研究 221
☞ 野三坡旅游发展跟踪调查

Part IV　Reading Box
第四部分　阅读与分析 223
☞ Irridex　旅游愤怒指数
Part V　Additional Know-how of Tourism
第五部分　旅游知识扩展 227
☞ 1. 旅游与文化变迁
☞ 2. 旅游与民族认同意识
Part VI　Further Readings
第六部分　课外阅读 229

Chapter 13　Environmental Impact Assessment of Tourism
第十三章　旅游环境影响评估 231

Part I　Text
第一部分　课文 232
☞ Environmental Impact Assessment of Tourism　旅游环境影响评估
Part II　Guided Reading
第二部分　课文导读 237
Part III　Case Study
第三部分　案例研究 239
☞ 旅游环境容量的测算——以四川省宜宾地区为例
Part IV　Reading Box
第四部分　阅读与分析 242
☞ Carrying Capacity　承载力
Part V　Additional Know-how of Tourism
第五部分　旅游知识扩展 245
☞ 1. 累积效应
☞ 2. 旅游环境容量
Part VI　Further Readings
第六部分　课外阅读 248

Chapter 14　Utilization and Conservation of the Tourism Resources
第十四章　旅游资源的利用与保护 250

Part I　Text
第一部分　课文 251
☞ Utilization and Conservation of the Tourism Resources
　　旅游资源的利用与保护
Part II　Guided Reading
第二部分　课文导读 257
Part III　Case Study
第三部分　案例研究 259
☞ 萨尔茨堡旅游资源的开发和保护

Part IV Reading Box
第四部分　阅读与分析 263
　　☞ National Parks　国家公园
Part V Additional Know-how of Tourism
第五部分　旅游知识扩展 266
　　☞ 1. 旅游资源的定义
　　☞ 2. 旅游资源的移动性
Part VI Further Readings
第六部分　课外阅读 268

Chapter 15 The Sustainable Tourism
第十五章　可持续发展旅游 270
Part I Text
第一部分　课文 271
　　☞ The Sustainable Tourism　可持续发展旅游
Part II Guided Reading
第二部分　课文导读 276
Part III Case Study
第三部分　案例研究 278
　　☞ 生存还是毁灭：大堡礁海洋公园的未来
Part IV Reading Box
第四部分　阅读与分析 280
　　☞ New Tourism　新旅游
Part V Additional Know-how of Tourism
第五部分　旅游知识扩展 284
　　☞ 1. 替代旅游
　　☞ 2. 可持续旅游的几种名称
Part VI Further Readings
第六部分　课外阅读 287

Reference 289

参考答案（见课件或电子教案）

Chapter 1 Tourism System
第一章 旅游系统

Learning objects：学习目标

- Understand the important role of tourism system in the study of tourism 了解旅游系统对于学习旅游的重要作用
- Describe the fundamental structure of the tourism system 陈述旅游系统的基本结构
- Observe the tourist flow and industry within the system from the perspective of O-D Pair and N-S pair 从客源地与目的地、供给与需求两个方面观察旅游流和旅游产业在系统中的活动
- Discuss the external factors that influence tourism and are influenced by tourism 讨论外在因素对旅游的影响以及旅游如何影响这些外在因素
- Understand the industrial distribution in the tourism system 了解旅游产业在旅游系统中的分布情况
- Appreciate the multifunctional Singaporean tourism with a perspective of the tourism system 以旅游系统为视角观察多功能的新加坡旅游

Ability goals：能力目标

- Case Study 案例分析以成都市为中心的四川旅游
- Reading Box 阅读分析 Travel in Singapore 新加坡旅游

Part I Text
第一部分 课文

Tourism System

【教学要点】

知识要点	掌握程度	相关章节
Leiper's model 雷柏尔模型	重点掌握	本课文是绪论，与其他章节是"纲"与"目"的关系，与课文所有章节相关联，学习教材其他章节应以本文为"纲"，作为指导整个教学的框架。
spatial movement of tourism 旅游的空间移动	重点掌握	
push and pull forces in tourism system 旅游系统中的推力和拉力	一般了解	
definition of the tourist 旅游者的定义	重点掌握	
categories of tourism 旅游的类型	一般了解	
distribution of tourism sectors in the tourism system 旅游产业在旅游系统中的分布	一般了解	
external or environmental systems 外部或环境系统	一般了解	

  Tourism happens when people travel from their residence to the destinations and when they enjoy the beautiful landscapes or the historical interests there. A tourist has to leave his residence for a certain destination by means of transport or by himself. The **spatial movement** from his residence to the destination plays an important role in realizing his travel desire. What is more, in a sense, a tourist consumes the tourism product while he or she produces it simultaneously, so his or her activities will influence the overall quality of the tourist product.[1]

  As mentioned above, the spatial movement is very important and worth our attention. Moreover, it is necessary to provide an organizing framework in order to study the tourism. To do so, we have adopted **Leiper's model**, which was suggested in 1979 and adapted in 1990 (Figure 1).[2] In the model, he points out three aspects of the tourism—tourist, the tourism sectors and the geographical elements.

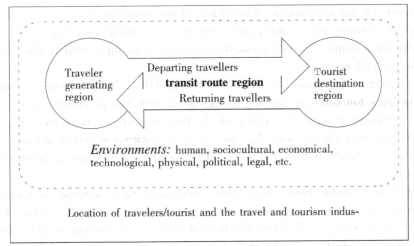

Figure I Leiper's model

1. Geographical Elements

Leiper outlines three geographical elements in his model:
(a) Traveler-generating region;
(b) Tourist destination region;
(c) Transit route region.

The traveler-generating region (or origin region), refers to the place where tourists come from. It is the generating market, which stimulates and motivates travel.

The transit route region includes both the short period of travel from their origin region to the destination and other places on the way that tourists may stop to visit.

The tourist destination is one of the most important elements in the whole tourism system. It emphasizes what suppliers can do for tourists. Of course, this includes not only the physical equipments which are crucial to attract tourists, but also the management and service which are helpful to enhance its images and motivate the visit. In other words, the tourist destination functions as a **"pull" factor** in the market and provides an area for most of the tourism activities.[3] It attracts different kinds of tourists through the attractions and the quality of management and service.

The tourist destination region is where tourists can realize their temporary goal of travel and go through a memorable tourism experience. The destination provides tourists with attractions of various types and planning and management strategies should be carried out in order to secure the tourist satisfaction. So, it is the core of the tourism.

2. Tourist

After studying the geographical elements of the tourism system, you may understand that the spatial movement from the traveler-generating region through the transit route to the destination region. It is an essential and indispensable part of the tourism experience.

The following are to be considered to define a tourist:
- traveling for pleasure, for health, etc;
- traveling in a representative capacity of any kind;
- traveling for business or meeting relatives and friends;
- arriving by a sea cruise, even when they stay for less than 24 hours;

The following are not to be regarded as a tourist:
- a person arriving to work for the company in the country;

- a person coming to establish a residence in the country;
- a person living in one country and working in adjoining country;
- a traveler passing through a country without stopping, even if the journey takes more than 24 hours.

There are different types of tourism such as holiday, business and common interest tourism. **Business tourism** can further be classified into the incentive travel, conference tourism and business travel. According to the time a tourist takes, we can also classify tourist activities into two kinds: 1. day trips or **excursions** which do not involve an overnight stay; 2. tourism which often refers to journeys or stays at destinations for at least 24 hours.[4]

Now you are probably clear about what the distinct characteristics of tourism are and what a tourist is expected to experience in order to travel. The tourist plays an important role in the tourism system. Without the tourist there is no tourism in the world, not to mention tourism product, tourism industry or their impacts on the destination. It is worthwhile to study the tourist—the **demand side of tourism**. Some factors may have an influence on the tourism demand. They are economic, social and cultural factors.

3. Tourism Industry

The tourism industry refers to the businesses and organizations that help to promote the tourism product. According to Leiper, various industrial sectors can be located in different places. In the traveler-generating region, we can find travel agents and tour operators. In the destination region, we can find attractions and hospitality industry and in the transit route region, we have the transport sector.

The tourist, as the tourism subject and located in the traveler-generating region, is the **"push" factor** and gives impetus to the development of it.[5] The destination functions as the tourism object. It is the area in which various kinds of tourism products are delivered, such as the accommodations, restaurants, leisure facilities and other ancillary services. The **tourism intermediaries** help to connect the traveler-generating region and the tourist destination. They are the transport and the travel agents, tour operators, etc, who help tourists realize their travel desire and obtain a tourism experience worth memorizing.[6] You may find the distribution of the travel trade within the tourism system. (see Figure 2)

Categories	Origin regions	Transit regions	Destination regions
Travel agencies	◆	■	■
Transportation	●	◆	◆
Accommodation	■	◆	◆
Food and beverages	■	◆	◆
Tour operators	●	◆	◆
Attractions	●	◆	■
Merchandisers	●	■	◆

■Negligible ●Minor ◆Major

Figure 2   Distribution of travel trade within the tourism system

The **tourism industry** is primarily composed of travel trade, transport, accommodation and catering, as well as catering facilities and tourist attractions, etc.[7] Different sectors or companies to suit all budgets and tastes provide these products and services. The hospitality industry provides accommodation and entertainments for travelers. The tour wholesaler and travel agency sell and promote the products and services of the other sectors to travelers.

Now you may have a clearer idea of the tourism system. But we also should keep in mind that the tourism system is not an independent system. Its development relies on the support of other **external or environmental systems**, such as sociocultural, economic, political, physical, etc.[8] These systems are interdependent. For example, without agriculture, no one can supply food for restaurant; without the oil industry, no vehicle can move and help tourists realize their spatial movement. And the tourism system, in turn, is also important to the development of other systems. It may be seriously affected by some adverse factors. For example, the political issue that has existed between Cuba and the United States for many years has hindered the establishment of a tourism system as the origin or destination regions.

New Words

spatial	adj.	空间的
memorable	adj.	值得纪念的
framework	n.	参照标准,基准体系
indispensable	adj.	必不可少的,不可或缺的
generate	v.	引起,产生
incentive	n.	奖励
origin	n.	发源
wholesaler	n.	批发商

Key Terms

historical interests	历史名胜	"push" factor	"推动"因素
spatial movement	空间移动	incentive travel	奖励旅游
tour operator	旅游经营商	conference tourism	会议旅游
"pull" factor	"拉动"因素	business travel	商务旅游

Notes

1. What is more, in a sense, a tourist consumes the tourism product while he or she produces it simultaneously, so his or her activities will influence the overall quality of the tourist product.
   此外,从某种意义上来讲,旅游者既消费又同时生产这一旅游产品,因此,其活动会影响旅游产品的整体质量。

2. To do so, we have adopted Leiper's model, which was suggested in 1979 and adapted in 1990 (Figure 1).
   为了给大家一个系统的框架结构,我们采用了雷柏尔在1979年提出并于1990年修订的模型(图1)。

3. In other words, the tourist destination functions as a "pull" factor in the market and provides an area for most of the tourism activities.
   换句话说,旅游目的地在市场中起着拉动作用,并且为大部份旅游活动提供了场地。

4. According to the time a tourist takes, we can also classify tourist activities into two kinds: 1. day trips or excursions which do not involve an overnight stay; 2. tourism which often refers to journeys or stays at destinations for at least 24 hours.

根据旅游者所花费的时间，我们可以将旅游活动分为两类：1. 不过夜的一日游或短程游览；2. 至少要在目的地逗留 24 小时的旅游。

5. The tourist, as the tourism subject and located in the traveler-generating region, is the "push" factor and gives impetus to the development of it.
作为旅游主体的旅游者位于客源地，起着"推力"作用，促进旅游的发展。

6. The tourism intermediaries help to connect the traveler-generating region and the tourist destination. They are the transport and the travel agents, tour operators, etc, who help tourists to realize their travel desire and obtain a tourism experience worth memorizing.
旅游中介有交通、旅行社、旅游经营商等，它们有助于连接旅游客源地和目的地，同时帮助游客实现旅游愿望，获得难忘的旅游经历。

7. The tourism industry is primarily composed of travel trade, transport, accommodation and catering, as well as catering facilities and tourist attractions, etc.
旅游业主要包括旅游经营部门、交通、住宿、餐饮业，以及餐饮供应设施和旅游景点。

8. But we also should keep in mind that the tourism system is not an independent system. Its development relies on the support of other external or environmental systems, such as sociocultural, economic, political, physical, etc.
但是我们应该记住旅游系统不是一个独立的系统，它的发展依赖于其他外部因素或环境系统的支持，如社会环境、经济、政治、物质等。

Exercise

1. Fill in the blanks with proper words to complete the following statements.

| product | residence | attractions | "pull" |
| external | spatial | traveler-generating | destination |

(1) Tourism happens only when people travel from their _____ to the destinations and enjoy the beautiful landscapes or the historical interests there.

(2) A tourist will consume the tourism _____ the tour operator offers when they are traveling.

(3) The _____ movement from his residence to the destination plays an important role in realizing his travel desire.

(4) The tourist destination functions as a _____ factor in the market and provides an area for most of the tourism activeties.

(5) In the _____ region, we can find attractions and hospitality industry and in the transit route region, we have the transport sector.

(6) The tourist, as the tourism subject and located in the _____ region, is the "push" factor and gives impetus to the development of it.

(7) The tourism industry is primarily composed of travel trade, transport, accommodation and catering, as well as catering facilities and tourist _____, etc.

(8) The development of tourism system relies on the support of other _____ or environmental systems, such as sociocultural, economic, political, physical, etc.

2. Questions for discussion

(1) In Leiper's model, he points out three elements of the tourism system. What are

the three elements in the system? How does the system work?

_____

(2) Leiper outlines three geographical elements in his model. How do the three elements interact with each other?

_____

(3) Who can be considered as a tourist? Who.

_____

(4) Who cannot be considered as tourists? Give examples.

_____

(5) What are the "pull" and "push" factors? Why are they called so?

_____

(6) What are the main sectors in the tourism industry? Where are they located in the tourism system?

_____

(7) Tourism system is not an independent system and is influenced by external or environmental factors. Can you give some examples to illustrate how these factors influence the system?

_____

Part II Guided Reading
第二部分 课文导读

　　建立一种旅游研究的框架结构是非常重要的,这能帮助我们解决许多问题。本文采用了雷柏尔(Leiper)在1979年提出并于1990年重建的模型作为旅游研究的框架结构,并对其系统中包含的三个要素(地理因素、旅游者、旅游业)进行了详细的阐述。本文首先介绍了三个地理因素及其相互关联,客源产生地、旅游目的地和旅游交通系统的关系,怎样相互作用;其次,对旅游者进行定义和分类;最后,阐明了旅游业各部门在旅游系统中所处的位置。旅游代理商和经营商主要位于客源地,旅游景点和旅游接待业位于旅游目的地,旅游交通业大部分在交通线上。雷柏尔模型简明、实用,提供了研究旅游的有效方法,阐明了各要素之间的相互联系,对我们研究旅游现象具有提纲挈领的作用。

　　从系统理论角度来考虑旅游活动,旅游活动实际上是一个系统。旅游活动的发生涉及客源地(O=Origin)和目的地(D=Destination)两类场所,这两类场所大多数情况下是不重叠的,而是相距一定的距离,并且各自具有自己的运行规律;从空间角度观察,我们不仅需要对两者分别进行分析,还需要对客源地和目的地之间的相互作用进行诠释,包括客流从O到D之间的移动以及D对O的市场营销,地理学上称其为O-D对(O-D pairs)的研究;从市场角度观察,旅游活动涉及旅游者对旅游产品的需求(Need)和旅游企业、政府部门对市场的供给(Supply),经济学上称其为N-S对(N-S pairs)的研究;从旅游活动的运行过程观察,除了O与D两者内部的过程及两者之间的相互作用外,还涉及一些支持系统的运行。

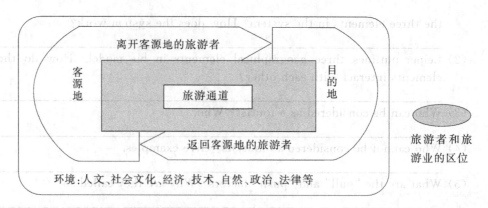

图1 雷柏尔旅游系统模型

从空间结构角度考察的旅游系统模型中,雷柏尔1979年提出、1990年予以修正的模型影响力较大。雷柏尔的模型包括旅游者、旅游业、客源地、旅游通道和目的地等5个要素,在结构功能和空间结构两个层面上讨论旅游系统。

在雷柏尔模型中重点突出了客源地、目的地和旅游通道3个空间要素,他把旅游系统描述为旅游通道连接的客源地和目的地的组合。旅游客源地是旅游者居住及旅行的始发地,而旅游目的地是吸引旅游者在此作短暂停留,进行观光度假的地方。旅游通道将客源地和目的地两个区域连接起来,且不仅仅指那些能够帮助旅游者实现空间移动的物质载体,同时也包括一些旅游者可能参观的地方。对照旅游功能系统模型可以发现,旅游通道同时也应该是一条信息的通道。一方面是市场需求信息从客源地流向目的地,另一方面是具有促销功能的目的地信息从目的地流向客源地。旅游通道的特征和效率将影响和改变旅游流的规模和方向。

雷柏尔同时也指出了旅游系统中的另外两个要素:旅游者和旅游业。旅游者是旅游系统的主体,在客源地和目的地的推拉作用下,旅游者在空间上进行流动。旅游业存在的意义在于通过其产品满足旅游者的旅游需求。从雷柏尔的模型可以看到,旅游业中的不同部门分布于客源地、目的地或旅游通道等不同的空间,为旅游者提供服务。虽然,雷柏尔重视旅游者和旅游业的空间属性,但是雷柏尔同样也强调供给与需求间的关系。他认为客源地的需求具有不稳定性、季节性和非理性等特点,另一方面旅游目的地的供给又是割裂的、刚性的。因此,旅游业是一个在供求关系上充满矛盾的产业。

在雷柏尔的模型中既可以看到旅游功能系统模型的影子(供给与需求的相互关系),又可以发现客源地和目的地的空间关系。因此,可以认为雷柏尔对旅游系统的分析是从两个层面着手的。第一个是结构功能层面,在这个层面上他强调供给与需求之间的关系。另一个是空间层面,在这个层面上,他强调客源地、目的地和旅游通道等空间要素的关系。应该说这两个层面是有联系的,后者(旅游空间结构)正是前者(旅游供求关系)的空间表现形式。

雷柏尔的主要贡献是把旅游功能系统投射到了地理空间上,他的模型对旅游空间结构的研究具有重要意义。首先,该模型深刻地揭示了旅游空间结构的本质含义,为旅游空间结构研究指明了方向,即任何有关旅游空间结构的问题最终都应归结为对旅游系统的研究;同时,雷柏尔的模型也为旅游地理研究提供了一个基本的研究框架,如对旅游空间相互作用的研究就可以在这个高度抽象的框架下进行;此外,雷柏尔的分析也表明了,在旅游系统的研究中,空间距离的摩擦(旅行成本)是必须考虑的因素。我们应当看到,雷柏尔的模型不仅对旅游空间结构的研究具有重要意义,同时对研究旅游市场、旅游产业、旅游经济、旅游影响,特别是为研究旅游供需关系提供了一个总体框架。

第一章 旅游系统

旅游知识测试

正误判断：请在正确的选题上划√，错误的选题上划×。

1. 雷柏尔的模型包括旅游者、旅游业、客源地、旅游通道和目的地等5个要素，重点突出了客源地、目的地和旅游通道3个空间要素。

2. 旅游活动涉及旅游者对旅游产品的需求（Need）和旅游企业、政府部门对市场的供给（Supply），地理学上称其为N-S对（N-S pairs）的研究。

3. 旅游活动的地理集中性不仅反映在全世界国际旅游活动的地区分布格局上，具体到某一个国家，旅游活动在该国各省（州、郡）及各城市间的分布情况，同样也呈现出这一特点。

4. 按照在旅游目的国停留的时间的长短，国际旅游活动划分为过夜的国际旅游和不过夜的国际一日游。

5. 旅游产业分布在旅游系统中的客源地、目的地和连接客源地和目的地的中转地。旅行社和饭店一般分布在旅游目的地。

Part III Case Study
第三部分 案例研究

以成都市为中心的四川旅游

分析要点

1. 简要概述成都的地理位置，并运用雷柏尔模型分析成都市在中国旅游市场中的地位和作用。
2. 成都在四川旅游布局中处在一个怎样的位置，它是如何影响整个四川旅游系统的？
3. 举例说明为什么说成都既是旅游目的地，又是旅游客源地和旅游中转地。
4. 成都作为一个四川旅游集散地和旅游目的地功能性作用怎样转换？有哪些优势和劣势？
5. "大成都旅游发展区"是怎样规划的？你认为有什么意义？

相关理论和问题

1. 旅游系统（Tourism system）
2. 旅游流（Tourist flow）
3. 旅游口岸城市的功能（Functions of the tourist port city）
4. 旅游空间布局（Spacious layout of tourism）

翻开世界地图，神秘的北纬30°线，贯穿了世界四大文明古国和众多奇观，成为世界各地旅游者的朝圣之地。同样位于这条神秘纬线上的成都，因其辉煌灿烂的古蜀文明和融汇古今的休闲文化，成为西方视野中的中国西部神秘之旅的窗口。聚焦中国地图，成都位于西部腹地，西有青藏高原，北有秦岭和大巴山，南有云贵高原，背靠丰富的旅游资源。在四川地图上，省会城市的地位让成都拥有完备的交通体系，发达的交通动脉横贯东西、纵通南北，使之成为旅游者西部之旅的必经之地。

察看四川旅游版图,如果以成都为中心,向南是峨眉山、乐山、蜀南竹海,向西有四姑娘山、康定、稻城亚丁,往北有九寨、黄龙……省内丰富的旅游资源成为支撑成都旅游业的后盾,也在一定程度上影响着成都旅游的发展和定位。据不完全统计,2005年至2006年,在来蓉的游客中,不超过四分之一的人只在成都做短暂停留,超过八成的境外游客只是将成都作为旅游的中转站……透过这一组数据,成都作为旅游"中转站"的形象清晰地凸显出来。在旅游业研究者的眼中,他们用"旅游中心城市"来定位成都。旅游中心城市同时具备旅游目的地和旅游集散地的两大功能,而从成都旅游业目前发展现状来看,其扮演的角色更倾向于后者。对成都作为旅游集散地的争论由来已久,纵然其背后有着诸多复杂的成因,但在决策者的眼中,"中转站"的独特角色更意味着旅游发展的契机和方向。

在早前出台的《四川省"十一五"旅游产业发展规划》中,将成都市打造成为"国际旅游城市"成为引人注目的亮点。一个"大成都"旅游区的概念正日渐成熟——以成都为圆心,一小时车程为半径,涵盖了成都市及其周边的乐山、眉山、资阳、德阳、绵阳、雅安、遂宁等8个城市。由此,峨眉山—乐山大佛、都江堰—青城山世界遗产旅游,成都—雅安大熊猫生态旅游,成德绵三国文化旅游,安仁古镇文化旅游,眉山三苏文化旅游,彭祖长寿文化旅游,陈毅故里红色旅游,李白文化旅游等省内的旅游资源都整合到了"大成都"的概念之中。这样的定位,无疑是看中了成都所具有的旅游集散地的功能。

不论是作为整合省内旅游资源、促进四川旅游发展的"发动机",还是面向世界的西部旅游门户,成都都摆在了旅游集散地的位置。然而,随着对成都本土旅游资源的进一步挖掘和"中国最佳旅游城市"落户蓉城,成都作为旅游目的地已不再是一个需要回避的问题。

随着我国取代意大利上升为世界第四热门的旅游目的地,四川省向亚洲重要旅游目的地大步迈进,旅游目的地的发展不仅是成都入境旅游市场的现实需要,而且也是发展现代服务业、带动经济社会又好又快发展的迫切要求。

在政策制定者的蓝图中,将成都打造成为旅游目的地已经有了清晰的脉络。随着"大成都"旅游区的建立,构建"中心商业游憩区、环城休闲度假旅游圈、一日游精品观光旅游圈"的发展格局已然形成,观光旅游、休闲度假、会展商务、康体娱乐等旅游成为发展的重点。而大成都旅游区的发展也被定位为旅游主题形象鲜明、产品特色突出、旅游设施完备、服务质量优良、入境旅游快速增长的旅游目的地。

2007年5月24日,由成都文化旅游发展集团、峨眉山管理委员会、九寨沟风景名胜区管理局签订的旅游目的地营销联盟正式启动。作为国内首家旅游目的地联盟,成都—峨眉山—九寨沟旅游目的地营销联盟的成立将节约旅游宣传成本,缩短游客旅游滞留时间,提高游客旅游效率,节省游客游览成都、九寨、峨眉三地的旅游费用。联盟将把日本和港澳台等国家和地区作为第一客源市场,并积极探索开拓印度等新兴旅游市场。这也是成都旅游业实践对旅游目的地发展取向的最新解读。

资料来源:四川省人民政府网站.从"中转站"到"目的地":成都旅游华丽转身. http://www.sc.gov.cn/lysc/lyyw/200706/t20070628_189111.shtml

Part IV Reading Box
第四部分 阅读与分析

Travel in Singapore

阅读分析要点

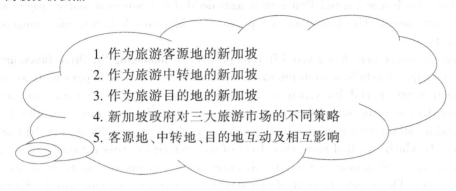

1. 作为旅游客源地的新加坡
2. 作为旅游中转地的新加坡
3. 作为旅游目的地的新加坡
4. 新加坡政府对三大旅游市场的不同策略
5. 客源地、中转地、目的地互动及相互影响

Singapore, the Southeast Asian city-state, is famous for its development as an origin region, a transit region and a destination region. Some people believe that Singapore has one specific position within the tourism system, but this belief has been now challenged and changed by Singapore's multifunctional status.

Singapore has developed as an important **origin region** because it is one of the four Asian "tiger" economies. In the early 1950s, there were almost no outbound trips in Singapore. However, Singaporeans now become the most frequent outbound tourists in the Asian countries. In 1996, it was reported that there were 3.3 million outbound trips. That is to say, each family has about one trip. Compared with 2.7 million outbound trips in Australia in the same year, each Australian family had only 0.15 trips. Two neighbors Malaysia and Indonesia help a lot to increase Singapore's higher position. Long-haul travel has also turned Singapore into the front ranks of inbound markets to countries such as Australia and New Zealand.[1] As a result, many **bilateral tourism systems** between countries have developed. Among these countries, Singapore becomes a major origin region.

Meanwhile, Singapore has developed as an important **transit region** because of travel on oceans. For a long time, it has been a vital link on the trans-shipment lanes. It functions as a link connecting Europe with eastern Asia. Although its position as tourist's oceanic transit stopover is no longer as important as it used to be, Singapore has now played a similar important role as an air transportation hub.[2] For instance, Australians traveling from Sydney or Brisbane to London usually have a regular and fixed stopover in Singapore. As of 1997, 68 airlines directly linked Singapore with 133 cities in 53 countries. In the same year, its Changi airport provided 172,672 flights and more than 25 million passengers. This airport was being expanded to provide 60 million passengers by 2004. This reflects Singapore's intentional plan to further strengthen its position as a main transit hub. A case in point is the negotiation of air services and open skies arrangements with over 90 countries.

Finally, Singapore has developed as a major **tourist destination**. Inbound traffic after World War II was very small and remained a level that could be ignored. However, with the outbound

flow, inbound tourists increased up to 7.3 million in 1996, or 2.2 arrivals per Singaporean family. In order to keep a comparable proportion with the arrivals in Singapore, Australia would have to accept 40 million inbound tourists per year. This is about ten times of the current volume. About 60% of all inbound tourists in Singapore declare that their main visiting purpose is vacation, although they may go shopping and have some activities on beach. Since Asian markets are the main inbound traffic for Singapore, if regional economy breaks off, it will affect its tourism sector. The financial crisis that happened in the late 1990s is one of the examples. During the mid-1990s, the Indonesian and Thai governments decided that outbound tourists pay more tax when they went abroad. This is another example to show how outside factors affect Singapore's tourism sector.

Singapore government has given different priority to **managing the three functions**. So far, it pays comparatively less attention to its outbound tourism, but it pays more attention to its transit function and its status as a final destination.[3] The economic impacts of inbound tourism explain why Singapore government emphasizes more on the transit function and its status as a final destination. As a result, during 1996 almost $13 billion was produced, which equalled more than 10% of the country's gross national product. To earn more income, Singapore's tourism planning and management has focused on some important plans. These include methods to attract tourists to visit and stay in Singapore much longer. The Singaporean government is also improving its basic systems and services. Meanwhile, to strengthen its image as a modern, safe and clean destination, it is also improving its downtown environment. Among Asian states, Singapore is a better example of a destination where its government has played an important role and involved more in managing and controlling its tourism sector.[4]

The origin, transit and destination functions of Singapore **affect one another** in various ways.[5] For example, since inbound tourists increased largely since 1994, outbound tourists also increased steadily during the same period. As a result, the balance between the inbound and outbound decreased (see Table 1.1). This has encouraged Singapore government to take more measures to increase more inbound tourists. Ironically, the increasing of inbound travel causes a further increasing of outbound travel.[6] Moreover, in order to attract more inbound tourists, Singapore government sets up more connections with other cities. Thus Singaporean residents get more places for their direct outbound travel. Such kind of mutual influence also exists between the transit and destination functions. Many inbound visitors have their first impression on Singapore when they have to stop over or have short trips during their transfer in Singapore. Similarly, in order to strengthen Singapore's position as a traffic hub, Singapore government has improved its international airport. This improvement attracts more and more tourists to come to visit Singapore and make Singapore an attractive destination for inbound tourists.

Table 1.1 Revenues of Singapore from 1992 to 1996

YEAR	INBOUND (US$ million)	OUTBOUND (US$ million)	SURPLUS (US$ million)
1992	5499	2489	3010
1993	6294	3019	3275
1994	7527	4076	3451

| 1995 | 8378 | 5039 | 3339 |
| 1996 | 7961 | 6139 | 1822 |

New Words

specific	*adj.*	特定的
intentional	*adj.*	有意的,故意的
multifunctional	*adj.*	多功能的
hub	*n.*	中心
bilateral	*adj.*	双边的
negotiation	*n.*	谈判,协商
lane	*n.*	航道,航线
comparatively	*adv.*	相对地,比较地

Key Terms

origin region	客源地	transportation hub	交通枢纽
transit region	旅游中转地区	inbound tourist	入境旅游者
destination region	目的地地区		

Notes

1. Long-haul travel has also turned Singapore into the front ranks of inbound markets to countries such as Australia and New Zealand.
   长距离旅游使新加坡成为诸如澳大利亚和新西兰等国首选的入境旅游市场。

2. It functions as a link connecting Europe with eastern Asia. Although its position as tourist's oceanic transit stopover is no longer as important as it used to be, Singapore has now played a similar important role as an air transportation hub.
   新加坡起着连接欧洲和东亚的作用。虽然其作为跨洋中转站的重要性大不如前,但作为航空交通枢纽,它仍然起着同样重要的作用。

3. So far, it pays comparatively less attention to its outbound tourism, but it pays more attention to its transit function and its status as a final destination.
   迄今为止,新加坡不太重视出境旅游,而更看重其作为中转站和最终旅游目的地的功能。

4. Among Asian states, Singapore is a better example of a destination where its government has played an important role and involved more in managing and controlling its tourism sector.
   新加坡政府对旅游业的管理和控制发挥了重要作用,在亚洲国家当中应当说起到了更好的示范作用。

5. The origin, transit and destination functions of Singapore affect one another in various ways.
   新加坡具有客源地、中转站和目的地的多种功能,它们以各种方式相互作用,相互影响。

6. Ironically, the increasing of inbound travel causes a further increasing of outbound travel.
   具有讽刺意味的是,入境旅游愈多,出境旅游也随之增多。

Topic discussion

1. Why does Singapore become a major regional transit hub?

2. Why does Singapore also become a major tourist destination? Explore the Web site to search for more information about Singapore.

3. How do the origin, transit and destination of Singapore interact with each other?

4. What are some of the management implications on these interactions? What are the consequences?

5. Which city in China is an origin region, a transit region as well as a destination region? why?

【即学即用】

With reference to the theory, information or research approach in the Reading Box, have a case study of the tourism system in your city. Make presentation of your study in Chinese or in English using PPT.

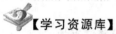
【学习资源库】

为了掌握本章更多的相关专业知识,请您登录 http://sicnu.edu.cn/,点击国家双语教学示范课程《旅游学概论》,进入网络学堂查询相关资料。

Chapter Review 本章小结

> This chapter has considered the important role of tourism system in the study of tourism and industry. It is very essential to observe the tourist flow and industry within the system from the perspective of O-D Pair and N-S pair. Of course, the external factors or environmental factors may exert an impact on tourism activity, but they are also influenced by tourism activity. Tourism activity falls into two categories: tourist activities and industrial activities. For this reason, we should know not only the tourist flow in the system, but also the industrial distribution in the system. The case study of the multifunctional Singaporean tourism shows the three elements of tourism system interact with each other and each element of the system is mutually influential.

Part V Additional Know-how of Tourism
第五部分 旅游知识扩展

【关键术语】

Tourism: the activities of persons travelling to and staying in places outside their usual environment for not more than one consecutive year for leisure, business and other purposes.

旅游:旅游是人们为了休闲、商务和其他目的,离开自己的常居环境、连续不超过一年的旅行和逗留活动。

Tourism industry: the sum of the industrial and commercial activities that produce goods and services wholly or mainly for tourist consumption. The range of businesses and organizations are involved in delivering the tourism product. It consists of those firms, organizations and facilities which are intended to serve the specific needs and wants of tourists

旅游业:完全或主要为旅游者消费提供产品和服务的产业和商业活动的总称,是各类旅游企业和旅游部门提供旅游产品的行业,由满足旅游者需要和愿望的企业、组织和设施组成。

Tourist: a person who travels temporarily outside of his or her usual environment (usually defined by some distance threshold) for certain qualifying purposes

- **Domestic tourist**: a tourist whose itinerary is confined to his or her usual country of residence
- **International tourist**: a tourist who travels beyond his or her usual country of residence
- **Outbound tourist**: an international tourist departing from his or her usual country of residence
- **Inbound tourist**: an international tourist arriving from another country
- **Stay over**: a tourist who spends at least one night in a destination region
- **Excursionist**: a tourist who spends less than one night in a destination region

旅游者:指因某种目的暂时离开他(她)惯常环境(通常由距离阈值定义)到其他地方旅游的人。分为:**国内旅游者**:通常指行程局限于惯常居住国家的旅游者;**国际旅游者**:指跨越惯常居住国去旅游的旅游者;**出境旅游者**:指离开惯常居住国的国际旅游者;**入境旅游者**:指来自其他国家或地区的国际旅游者;**过夜旅游者**:指在目的地至少停留一夜的旅游者;**短途旅游者**:指在目的地不过夜的旅游者。

Travel purpose: the reason why people travel; in tourism, these involve recreation/leisure, visits to friends and relatives (VFR), business, and less domestic purposes such as study, sport, religion and health

旅游目的:人们为什么出游?从旅游学角度上,旅游目的可以分为以下几类,即娱乐/休闲、探亲访友、商务、游学、体育旅游、宗教朝拜与健康医疗类。

Tourism system: an application of a system approach to tourism, wherein tourism consists of geographical components (origin, transit and destination regions), tourists and a tourism industry, embedded within an external environment that includes political, social, physical and other systems

旅游系统:是一种对旅游进行系统分析的方法,认为旅游包括地理组成部分(客源地、中转地、目的地)、旅游者和旅游业。旅游系统存在于外部环境之中,包括政治环境、社会环境、物质环境以及其他系统。

North-south flow: a common term used to describe the dominant pattern of international tourist traffic from the MDCs to the LDCs located mainly to the south of the MDCs

北南旅游流:一个用来描述国际旅游流向的常用术语,旅游流从较发达国家向主要是位于南部的欠发达国家流动是主要的流动模式。

【知识链接】

1. 旅游功能系统

最早从结构—功能的角度分析旅游系统的是规划学者 Gunn，他在 1972 年提出了旅游功能系统模型(Functioning Tourism System)，并在 2002 年加以修订。旅游功能系统模型的主要特点是：强调旅游系统的功能，决定旅游系统功能的系统结构和影响旅游系统结构的外部环境。旅游系统这一根本功能也会派生出其他的附属功能，即旅游系统会对上一级系统产生各种影响，如社会影响、经济影响、环境影响等。Gunn 的模型包括旅游人口、交通、吸引物、服务以及信息促销等 5 项。

在功能结构分析中，Gunn 在 2002 年提出的旅游功能系统模型是对旅游系统认识的一个飞跃。Gunn 的研究使我们认识到供求关系是旅游系统最基本的结构，吸引物、服务、交通等因素构成了旅游系统的子系统——旅游产业体系。Gunn 明确地指出供给与需求间的匹配关系是实现旅游系统功能的基础。这样，对旅游系统的分析关键就是对旅游产品供给和需求的分析。

在旅游系统中各组成要素是相互依赖、共同作用的。其中任何一个要素发生变化都将引起其他要素的变化。如果旅游者偏好发生变化、旅行成本或模式发生改变，开发了新的旅游资源，提供了新的服务，或者增加了新的促销，原来旅游系统的平衡状态就会偏移，系统中的其他要素也要发生相应的变化。这个模型的内在含义是：旅游功能系统有效运行的动力就在于"推"和"拉"两个作用，即旅游目的地通过营销环节把旅游者"拉"过来，市场借助于交通环节把旅游者"推"出去。

2. 吴必虎旅游系统

在 Gunn-Mill Morrison 模型的框架下，北京大学教授吴必虎提出了一个新的旅游系统概念模型(如图)。他把交通和促销合并成一个出行子系统。此外，他增加了一个支持子系统，包括政策法规、环境保证和人力资源。像我国这样的发展中国家，在旅游发展过程中，政府主导发挥了关键性作用，因此，增加支持子系统是有一定合理性的。

归纳起来，旅游活动可以被视为一个开放的复杂系统，研究该系统的特征及其在旅游开发、规划、经营、管理中的应用，就是旅游科学的核心任务。根据多年来对旅游业和相关现象的观察和分析，旅游系统构架应包括四个部分，即客源市场系统、出行系统、目的地系统和支持系统。

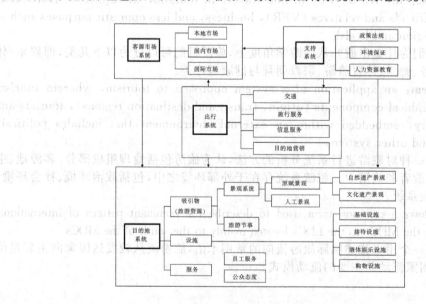

图 2　旅游系统(游憩系统)

旅游系统是动态的。外界环境会使旅游的供给或需求发生改变,并进一步通过供给与需求间的关系以及供给子系统中各要素的相互依赖关系,把这一变化传递到系统中的任何一部分。因此,考虑旅游系统的外界环境对于理解旅游功能系统的演化是至关重要的。影响供给的外部因素主要包括文化资源、自然资源、政府政策、竞争者、社区、企业家精神、劳动力、金融、组织领导能力等。对需求而言,可自由支配收入和可自由支配时间无疑是最重要的两个因素,而这两个因素又决定于全社会的劳动生产率。此外,人口因素、社会因素、政府的管制政策等也都是影响旅游需求的因素。

【小思考】

1. 研究城市旅游空间布局有什么意义?根据城市旅游空间布局的特点怎样开发城市旅游项目?

参考阅读:

城市作为旅游目的地,它不可避免地是区域旅游空间尺度的一个组成部分。城市旅游研究也应以空间为基本概念来探讨城市旅游产品的特性及其市场营销的方式。城市旅游具有多面性特征、多目标动机和多功能性质,城市是历史建筑、城市现代景观、历史文化见证的博物馆、美术馆、影剧院、完善的接待娱乐场所、体育运动等设施和活动的有机结合体,Jansen Verbeke(1988)把这些要素归为城市的主要元素。Basauli Umar Lubis(2003)认为城市旅游活动在空间上的集中表现与城市的3种分布状态有关:"主要吸引物",将游客吸引到城市中的旅游吸引物的位置;"次要吸引物",为游客提供支持、供给、娱乐等服务设施的位置;以及游客在城市中实际使用这些设施的空间分布模式。城市提供的多种功能和设施可以用于休闲娱乐目的,游客和当地居民都可使用,这些功能和设施构成了城市的全部旅游产品。城市旅游研究不能孤立地研究城市的某种要素,而应充分重视城市不同组成部分及在不同空间尺度上不同活动之间的整体协调。

城市旅游整体吸引力的形成模式如图1所示。卞显红(2003)对城市旅游空间结构进行了分析,认为城市旅游空间结构的构成有:旅游目的地区域、旅游客源地市场、旅游节点、旅游区、旅游循环路线及旅游入(出)通道等六大基本要素,并把城市旅游空间结构归纳为:单节点、多节点及链状节点等3种。

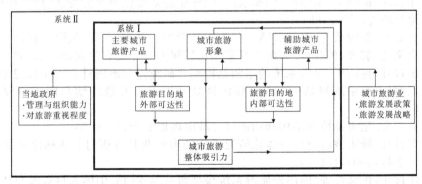

图1 城市旅游整体吸引力的形成模式
Figure 1 Formative model of urban tourism overall attraction

2. 你是怎样理解旅游流的?旅游流在旅游系统中有什么规律?

参考阅读:

在旅游系统中,客源地、目的地和中转地之间会形成旅游者的双向或多向流动。旅游流是由旅游者的旅游需求和旅游行为所引发的,也是满足旅游需求和践行旅游行为的空间过程,在这个过程中,旅游流各因子的经济行为、空间行为、文化行为和心理行为在旅游影响场的作用下,对旅游目的地产生一系列直接和间接的影响,并实现旅游目的地经济、社会、环境价值的增值和综合效益的最大化。旅游流系统对旅游影响驱动作用的强度、范围和特征是由各因子的流向、流量、流速、属性等特征决定的,其驱动作用是通过旅游流的各种行为进行的。

(1) 由于旅游流的经济行为,旅游货币流通过产业链流向旅游企业、当地居民、地方团体和地方政府,在信息场和经济场的作用下,引起旅游供求矛盾,促使当地居民增收致富,推动当地经济发展、空间格局演进和生态环境演变,从而引起旅游目的地社会经济的一系列变化。

(2) 旅游流的经济行为还伴随着旅游能流,如交通工具的废弃物、生活垃圾、排泄物等,在生态场的作用下,产生旅游生态影响。

(3) 在旅游流与当地居民进行直接和间接交流的文化行为中,旅游者所蕴涵的信息流在心理场和经济场的作用下,进行信息传播和扩散,促使旅游目的地社会文化发展和演化。旅游客源地的旅游需求信息,通过信息场传播到旅游目的地,旅游信息流在引力场、信息场和经济场的作用下,引起旅游目的地供给的变化。

(4) 旅游客流和旅游物流的空间行为在引力场的作用下,对环境空间产生一定的压力,引起自然与人文环境的变化。

(5) 旅游流的心理行为在心理场的作用下,影响着旅游动机、旅游需求、旅游消费、旅游体验以及与目的地的文化互动,其所蕴涵的信息在信息场、经济场和心理场的作用下,导致旅游供给内涵和形式上的变化,从而引起旅游目的地的一系列变化。

Part VI Further Readings
第六部分 课外阅读

如果您想进一步学习本章的内容,探讨旅游系统以及旅游系统对研究旅游学方法上的意义,建议您阅读以下学者的著作和论文。

一、中文部分

[1] 郭长江,崔晓奇,宋绿叶,韩军表.国内外旅游系统模型研究综述[J].中国人口·资源与环境,2007,(04).

[2] 吴必虎.旅游系统:对旅游活动与旅游科学的一种解释[J].旅游学刊,1998,(01).

[3] 李文亮,翁瑾,杨开忠.旅游系统模型比较研究[J].旅游学刊,2005,(02).

[4] 吴晋峰,包浩生.旅游系统的空间结构模式研究[J].地理科学,2002,22(01).

[5] 刘峰.旅游系统规划——一种旅游规划新思路[J].地理学与国土研究,1999,15(01).

[6] 吴人韦.旅游系统的结构和功能[J].城市规划汇刊,1999(6).

[7] 卞显红.城市旅游空间一体化研究模式的构建及其分析[J].桂林旅游高等专科学校学报,2004,15(06).

[8] 郭长江,崔晓奇等.国内外旅游系统模型研究综述[J].中国人口资源与环境,2007,(04).

[9] 李景宜.旅游系统市场竞争态及市场动态发展模型[J].经济地理,2002,(22).

[10] 旅游系统的空间分层拓扑结构研究[J].人文地理,2007,(05).

二、英文部分

[1] Wade L. Hadwen. Lake tourism: an integrated approach to lacustrine tourism systems[J]. *Annals of Tourism Research*, 2007, 34(2): 555—556.

［2］Greg Richards. Tourism attraction systems: exploring cultural behavior［J］. *Annals of Tourism Research*, 2002, 29(4):1048—1064.

［3］Neil Leiper. Industrial entropy in tourism systems［J］. *Annals of Tourism Research*, 1993, 20(1):221—226.

［4］Clare A. Gunn. Amendment to Leiper the framework of tourism［J］. *Annals of Tourism Research*, 1980, 7(2):253—255.

［5］Neil Leiper. Partial industrialization of tourism systems［J］. *Annals of Tourism Research*, 1990, 17(4):600—605.

［6］Neil Leiper. The framework of tourism towards a definition of tourism, tourist and the tourist industry［J］. *Annals of Tourism Research*, 1979, 6(4):390—407.

［7］Brian King. Tourism-a new systematic approach?［J］. *Tourism Management*, 1987, 8(3):272—274.

［8］Mill Robert Christie, Alastair M. Morrison. *The Tourism System*［M］. Englewood Cliffs, NJ: Prentice-Hall, 1985.

［9］Neil Leiper. Tourist attraction systems［J］. *Annals of Tourism Research*, 1990, 17(3):367—384.

［10］Neil Leiper. The status of attractions in the tourism system a reply to Clare Gunn［J］. *Annals of Tourism Research*, 1980, 7(2):255—258.

Chapter 2　The Rise and Evolution of Tourism
第二章　旅游的兴起和演变

Learning objects：学习目标

- Study the evolution of mass tourism and different phases with reference to the model of the tourism system 参照旅游系统模型,研究大众旅游的演进过程和不同阶段
- Interpret the definition of mass tourism and its characteristics 解析大众旅游的定义及其特征
- Discuss the importance of disposal income and disposal time for the emergence of mass tourism 讨论可自由支配收入和可自由支配时间对大众旅游兴起的重要性
- Understand the role of the Industrial Revolution on the rise of mass tourism 了解工业革命对大众旅游兴起所产生的作用
- Differentiate the Grand Tour and modern mass tourism 区分"大旅游"与现代大众旅游的不同之处
- Explain the reasons why Thomas Cook is regarded as the "father of early modern tourism" 解释托马斯·库克为什么被称为"近代旅游之父"的原因

Ability goals：能力目标

- Case Study 案例分析马罗卡岛的大众旅游
- Reading Box 阅读分析 Thomas Cook 托马斯·库克

Part I Text
第一部分 课文

The History of Mass Tourism

【教学要点】

知识要点	掌握程度	相关章节
definition of mass tourism 大众旅游的定义	重点掌握	本课文与第1单元、第3单元、第5单元、第7单元、第10单元、第12单元、第13单元、第15单元相关内容有联系。
disposal income and disposal time 可自由支配收入和可自由支配时间	重点掌握	
Grand Tour "大旅游"	一般了解	
the Industrial Revolution 工业革命	重点掌握	
development of tourism sectors 旅游产业的发展	重点掌握	
package holidays 包价度假	一般了解	
inbound and outbound markets 入境和出境旅游市场	一般了解	

Tourism is an ancient phenomenon that was evident in Egypt, Greece and Rome, as well as in China. Distinctive characteristics of tourism in the ancient times include its accessibility to only the small leisure class, the importance of religious as well as educational and health motivations, and the lack of any formal tourism or hospitality industry to serve travelers. Other features include the risky, uncomfortable and time-consuming nature of most travel, and the restriction of most travel to very few destinations. It was not until the 1960s that **mass tourism** began to develop in the economically developed countries, and later became popular in the world.

Mass tourism is the product of mass leisure. It refers to the large-scale packaging of **standardized leisure services** that are sold to customers at fixed prices. The main feature of the mass tourism is standardization. It provides a **package tour** that covers transportation, accommodation, guides, food and other goods and services. The travel is pre-paid, based on a strict time schedule, and the price is affordable because of the cheaper cost created through large customer volumes. Such features of mass tourism have been reflected in the international tourism industry of "BRIC" countries, such as in Brazil, Russia, India and China, as well as in other developing countries.

Disposable income

If people want to travel, they must first have money, especially the money at their own disposal. Such kind of money or income is called disposable income. Thus disposable income is one of the pre-conditions for tourists to travel. Without disposal income people cannot travel. Generally speaking, the demand for tourism is in accordance with people's personal income. The more people's income is, the higher their demand for travel. In fact, due to institutional changes in tourism, such as, cheaper air travel, package tours and holiday camps, tourism has become accessible to most people. Their demand for leisure and travel has improved as a result of increased disposable income. The emergence of mass tourism is largely due to the growing economics of the tourism industry. Great changes in transport technology, including by air, by land and by sea, have accelerated travel. So the costs for travel are reduced. All those have encouraged people to travel more. In return, economies of scale appear, and the cost for travel is further reduced. In addition, more and more travel agents appear and they are able to sell package tours at a comparably low cost. Because of falling costs, rising demand and the emergence of economies of scale, mass tourism has come into being.

Disposal time

Besides disposable income, people need leisure time in order to travel since travel needs free time. Thus leisure time is another pre-condition for tourists to travel. Without leisure time, people cannot travel. Statistics from the World Tourism Organization (1984) showed that between 1960 and 1980 the proportion of countries with more than 40 working hours fell from 75% to 56%.[1] Consequently, the number of people who can enjoy travel has been increasing.

From what we have discussed, we find that mass tourism relies on the growth of leisure time. However, it also relies on the **structure of free time**. That is, the structure of free time affects mass tourism. The lifetime distribution of leisure time plays an importance role in mass tourism. In the 20th century, the annual distribution of free time, especially **paid holidays**, has been an important factor in deciding the speed of mass tourism. The World Tourism Organization estimated in 1994 that all over the world there were 800 million workers receiving paid holidays. Two other factors also help increase the demand for tourism. They are the aging of the population and the increasing of people with disposable income.

Grand Tour

The emergence of mass tourism can be traced back to the great event called the Industrial Revolution in the 19th century. Travel before the Industrial Revolution was mainly for pilgrimages, for business or for official purposes. There was no private travel in the medieval period.

The word "tourism" came into the English language till the early 19th century. Its meaning could be connected with the idea of the Grand Tour which occurred from the 16th to 18th centuries. The Grand Tour was a popular activity among the British upper class, and most of them were property owner elite. In fact it was a tour of certain cities in Western Europe and was undertaken primarily for the sake of education and health. The travel time for such Grand Tour varied from several months to several years. Merchants or others also traveled for the purpose of business. During that period, most people hardly traveled beyond their village and nearest market town. That is why we take it for granted that the concept of leisure and holiday in the modern sense did not exist at that time.[2] The concept of leisure, in its modern sense, did not appear until in the most recent years.

Industrial Revolution

The Industrial Revolution began late in the 18th century, and it accelerated the rise of mass tourism. Lots of machines were invented to improve the productivity of the society. And new kinds of power were invented to move various vehicles such as trains and ships. Meanwhile, people had strong desire to explore the New World, and they wanted to have guidebooks and maps for their exploration. The publishing industry developed to meet this need. During this period the most outstanding change was the urbanization of the population. More and more people moved to towns, and the number of official governments, professions and managerial occupations increased. All those contributed to the creation of new purchasing power. People's demand for more recreational tour increased because of the rapid expansion of the middle class's wealth, the upgrading of the education level and the increase of leisure time. With the increase of travel, People's desire to know more about the places of interests and the wish to visit those places became stronger. Consequently, the popularity of the Grand Tour declined.

Hospitality industry

By the 19th century, people had the trend of travel for pleasure. With more and more people moving into towns, towns grew and expanded in a rapid speed. However, towns needed to find a way to provide people with enough accommodation. In order to meet this rising demand, lots of hotels and inns came into being and began to serve the increasing travelers brought by railways. The railways themselves played a very important role in stimulating a new type of hotel: **terminus hotels**. They were hotels at the terminal station of the railways. By train, lots of people could have long distance trips to far away coastal resorts and to enjoy the beauty and relax themselves on the beaches.

Between the 1920's and 1930's paid holidays and the increase of **private cars** became popular. They were two important factors which stimulated mass tourism. The growth of motel chains was another factor which stimulated mass tourism.[3] It laid a solid foundation for the emergence of tourism industry and it also provided necessary systems and services of accommodation. In the beginning, coastal resorts and spa resorts were the major destinations of the tourists. At that time in Europe there was also some special tourism operated at the coastal areas. Later on, artificial attractions rather than natural attractions became popular.

World War I (1914—1918) had a direct influence on the development of tourism since it emphasized the importance of the motorcar. Similarly World War II (1939—1945) confirmed that **aircraft** was for civil use. The car has deeply changed the nature of domestic tourism. Most families have stopped taking vacations by train which used to be their favorite means of transport. Instead they have used their private cars to extend their leisure for short holidays and day trips. Private cars provide tourism with such a special feature which public service transport cannot.

Travel regulations

In the 1960s tourism developed and people began to take package holidays or inclusive tours in large scale. It was growing popular, especially in Europe, from the northern industrial countries to the resorts of the Mediterranean. British people contributed a lot to the development of package holidays. Because of the easing of travel regulations and the growth of the international air travel industry, it was easier for mass tourism to develop.[4] Within Europe, foreign travel did not have too many financial, legal or practical barriers. Mass car ownership in Western Europe was one of the important pre-conditions for the mass international travel.

By 1970 tourism was no longer the market for the wealthy and the leisured. It had become a mass market. In developed countries, people got well-educated, had good salaries and had more disposable income. Thus they would regard holiday as an essential and inseparable part of their life. The whole world witnessed a considerable growth in **mass tourism** in the 1970's. Governments began to realize the important role of tourism in economy. They thought it was a key item in balancing payments. So the idea of package holidays spread rapidly all over the world.

A global industry

From the 1980's to 1990's Europe and North America functioned both as tourist generating regions and as destinations in the world and they are the centers of the world tourism.5 However, most of the people travel in their own countries. Statistics showed that **domestic tourism** was larger than **international tourism**. About two-thirds to three quarters of all tourism belonged to domestic tourism and only one-quarter to one-third belonged to international tourism.

In the late 20th and 21st century tourism industry has become a global industry. Such kind of globalization occurs because more people take part in the international travel and more countries aim at international travel. More and more tourists travel abroad as they have more disposal income. Europe, North America, Australia, Japan, China, India and the Middle East have become both **inbound and outbound markets** in the world. More and more destinations have been developed for the mass tourism.

From what we have described so far, we can conclude that mass tourism has appeared as a result of increasing world peace and prosperity. It has developed with reforms in transport, especially in aircraft technology, changes in labor legislation, especially paid holidays, and the development of the package tour. Social progress, especially in the 1960's and various reforms in transport and labor legislation help mass tourism reach its climax. Yet now mass tourism faces the new challenges for it has fostered many negative impacts on society and environments.6

New Words

accelerate	v.	加快,促进
institutional	adj.	惯例的,风俗的
disposal	n.	布置,处理
pilgrimage	n.	朝圣,朝觐
elite	n.	精英,杰出人物
proportion	n.	比例
globalization	n.	全球化
standardization	n.	标准化
barrier	n.	障碍物,屏障
legislation	n.	立法

Key Terms

mass tourism	大众旅游	paid holiday	带薪休假
package tour	包价旅游	Grand Tour	大旅游(旧时欧洲贵族在一些城市的旅游)
disposal income	可支配收入	inclusive tour	包价旅游
leisure time	闲暇时间		

Notes

1. Statistics from the World Tourism Organization (1984) showed that between 1960 and 1980 the proportion of countries with more than 40 working hours fell from 75% to 56%.

1984年世界旅游组织的统计表明,在1960年到1980年间,每周工作时间超过40小时的国家的比例从原来的 75% 下降到 56%。

2. That is why we take it for granted that the concept of leisure and holiday in the modern sense did not exist at that time.
这就是我们为什么理所当然地认为那时并不存在现代意义上的娱乐和度假的概念。

3. The growth of motel chains was another factor which stimulated mass tourism.
汽车旅馆连锁店的发展成为刺激大众旅游发展的又一个因素。

4. Because of the easing of travel regulations and the growth of the international air travel industry, it was easier for mass tourism to develop.
由于旅游法规的宽松和国际航空旅游业的发展,大众旅游也就更加便捷快速地发展起来。

5. Europe and North America functioned both as tourist generating regions and as destinations in the world and they are the centers of the world tourism.
欧洲和北美既发挥了世界上旅游客源地的功能,也发挥了世界旅游目的地的功能,成为世界旅游的中心。

6. Yet now mass tourism faces the new challenges for it has fostered many negative impacts on society and environments.
但是,由于给社会和环境带来众多的负面影响,大众旅游正面临诸多新的挑战。

Exercise

1. Decide whether the statements are true or false. If it is true, put "T" in the space provided and "F" if it is false.

(1) _____ Mass tourism refers to the large-scale packaging of standardized leisure services that are sold to customers at changeable prices.

(2) _____ The disposal income is the only pre-condition for tourists to travel because they could travel only when they have enough money.

(3) _____ Mass tourism relies on the growth of leisure time as well as the structure of free time.

(4) _____ The more time tourists have, the more travel propensity they have. The structure of free time has nothing to do with travel.

(5) _____ Travel before the Industrial Revolution was mainly for pilgrimages, for business or for official purposes.

(6) _____ The Industrial Revolution began late in the 18th century, and it accelerated the rise of mass tourism.

(7) _____ Between the 1920's and 1930's, two important factors which stimulated mass tourism were paid holidays and the invention of aircraft.

(8) _____ Mass car ownership in Western Europe was one of the important pre-conditions for the mass international travel.

(9) _____ In the late 20th century, there has been a globalization of the tourism industry.

(10) _____ Mass tourism fosters negative impacts on environment and positive impacts on the destination.

2. Question for discussion

(1) What are the differences between the Grand Tour and modern mass tourism?

（2）What are the major pre-conditions for people who can offer to travel?
_____

（3）What a role does transportation play in the development of mass tourism?
_____

（4）How did the Industrial Revolution speed up the rise of mass tourism?
_____

（5）What are the most important factors that stimulate the mass tourism?
_____

Part II　Guided Reading
第二部分　课文导读

　　大众旅游是大众休闲的产物。大众旅游是指将大规模的标准化休闲服务以一定价格出售给客户。标准化是大规模包价旅游最明显的特征。从需求角度看，旅游是一种消费行为，大众旅游就是大众消费。大众消费有两层含义，其一是指旅游成为一种普通大众（蓝领阶层）都能消费得起的产品；其二是指在各种旅游消费分类中（或旅游者人口统计中），具有明显数量和规模优势的那种旅游消费和旅游形式。从供给角度看，大众旅游就是以普通大众为目标市场，提供满足他们需要的、消费得起的旅游产品。大众旅游概念本身是相对的、动态的，上述第一层意思是指在近代出现旅游者阶层大众化的阶段，如工薪阶层的旅游消费开始成为主流。第二层意思是指在当前旅游市场中的大众化产品，如占市场份额较大的度假观光产品等。大众旅游存在和发展的前提就是廉价（Cheap）、便利（Convenient）、安全（Safe）和舒适（Comfort）。

　　本文阐述了大众旅游兴起的社会经济因素和历史演变过程，分析了大众旅游兴起的两个前提条件，即"自由支配收入"和"可自由支配时间"。是什么原因使小规模的精英旅游发展成为大众普遍参与的包价旅游呢？影响大众旅游主要的因素有哪些呢？

　　首先是旅游者的"可自由支配收入"，这是旅游产生的首要条件。众所周知，旅游和收入有着直接的关系，对假期需求的增长和个人收入的增加是成正比例的。只有人们的可支配收入增加了，旅游才可能成为现实。交通工具的技术革新促进了旅游费用的不断降低，这使得人们对旅游的需求快速增加，而这些又更进一步地扩大了经济的规模，减少了旅游的花销。由于越来越低的旅游费用，不断增长的旅游需求和经济规模的扩大，大众旅游终于得以形成。

　　第二，闲暇的时间也是影响人们旅游的重要因素。人们想要旅游就必须有"可自由支配时间"。根据世界旅游组织1984年的调查，在1960年到1980年之间，世界上平均每周工作时间达40个小时的国家从75%降到了56%。这说明越来越多的人拥有了参与旅游活动的时间。大众旅游不仅和闲暇时间的增加有关联，还和空闲时间结构有关系。空闲时间的分配和大众旅游有很大的关系，比如带薪假期对于20世纪大众旅游的兴起起了非常重要的作用。

　　综观旅游产生的历史，大众旅游的产生与社会经济发展的进程密切相关，是社会经济发展到一定时期的产物。旅游这个词直到19世纪才出现，不过旅游的概念与16世纪到18世纪的"大旅游"的内容有关联。18世纪的旅行主要是少数富裕的人所进行的一种活动，其目的主要是为了接受教育或出于政务目的。其他的旅行也是商人为了经商的需要而进行的旅行。绝大多数的人甚至很少离开他们生活的村庄或到附近的市场去。这就是现代意义上的休闲和假期在那个时代不存在的理由，也就是说休闲这个概念是在最近一段时间才产生的。

　　18世纪后半期，工业革命出现并促进了大众旅游的兴起。人们制造机械来提高社会的生产力，因此火车和轮船有了新的动力来推动。出版业的发展满足了人们探索新世界所需要的各种指南和地图。这个时期发生的最剧烈的变化就是人口大量城市化,这为旅游提供了新的购买力。中产阶级大量出现也是这个时期的一个重要特征,更高的教育程度、更多的休闲时间使得他们对娱乐的需求增加。由于人们对名胜古迹越来越感兴趣,16—17世纪的精英旅游渐渐失去了活力。

到19世纪,为娱乐而旅游的地位得到了巩固。人口城市化和城镇的增加使得酒店和旅馆也得到发展,他们不仅为当地游客也为乘火车来的外地游客提供服务。火车线路的延伸使得海滨旅游也成为可能,火车是住宿业向更遥远的地区发展的动因之一。到了19世纪20、30年代,两大因素影响着大众旅游的发展:带薪休假的增加和私家车的普及。汽车旅馆的增多也为住宿业的发展提供了条件。旅游目的地还是以海滨和矿泉疗养地为主。不久,人工的旅游吸引物受到人们的关注。

第一次世界大战后,汽车对大众旅游的兴起起到重要作用。汽车使内旅游的本质发生了根本性的变化,大多数家庭不再愿意选择火车作为度假的交通方式,汽车也让有车族能够在短假里或一日游中增加自己的休闲活动,而使用公共交通这种方式是不能实现的。同样的,第二次世界大战后喷气客机的发明确定了民用飞机在大众旅游的核心地位。到了20世纪60年代,旅游经营商大规模地使用包价旅游,特别是在欧洲。随着旅游政策的放宽,国际航空业的发展,大众旅游得到了空前的发展。

旅游再也不是有钱人的特权,这个时期的大众旅游得到了极大的发展,各国政府纷纷意识到了旅游对经济的重要作用,包价旅游的概念越传越广。到了20世纪后半期,旅游业出现了全球化。普通的劳动大众的旅游需求得到满足,旅游消遣不再为少数人所独享,旅游活动发展成为遍及全球的大规模的社会现象。由此可见,大众旅游的兴起与社会经济的发展是紧密相关的,"可自由支配收入"和"可自由支配时间"的增加是大众旅游兴起的必要条件,社会的进步和技术革新是推动大众旅游发展的重要动因。

大众旅游的出现使相当一部分人的旅游需求得到了满足,但是在旅游业取得快速发展的同时,旅游业给旅游目的地的经济、环境、文化、社会等方面带来的负面影响也日渐显现出来,一系列的生态和社会问题不断出现,旅游业健康发展所面临的问题更加严峻。人们开始质疑大众旅游是否有利于旅游业的长远发展,大众旅游对旅游的可持续发展带来严峻的挑战。

旅游知识测试

正误判断:请在正确的选题上划√,错误的选题上划×。

1. 众所周知,旅游和收入有直接关系,对假期需求的增长和个人收入的增加是成正比例的。

2. 历史表明,人类有意识的自愿外出旅行活动始于原始社会初期,并在封建社会时期得到了迅速的发展。

3. 旅游的概念与16世纪到18世纪的"大旅游"的内容相关。"大旅游"标志人类社会大众旅游的开始。

4. 1841年7月5日,英国托马斯·库克利用包租火车的方式,组织了一次从英国中部地区的莱斯特前往洛赫伯勒的团体旅游,这次团体旅游实际上就是单纯的休闲旅游。

5. 决定一个人旅游需求的家庭收入水平,指的是其家庭的可支配收入水平,或者更确切说是其家庭的可随意支配收入的水平。

Part III Case Study
第三部分 案例研究

马罗卡岛的大众旅游

分析要点

1. 马罗卡岛的大众旅游是在什么样的背景下产生的？
2. 马罗卡岛的旅游对整个岛屿的经济有何促进作用？
3. 大众旅游给马罗卡岛的水资源带来何种隐患？
4. 大量新建的酒店和旅游设施对马罗卡岛的海景造成了什么影响？
5. 你认为是大众旅游好，还是小规模旅游好？为什么？
6. 你对我国海南岛大众旅游发展现状有什么看法？如何以马罗卡岛为戒？

相关理论和问题

1. 可自由支配收入和时间（Disposal income and time）
2. 小规模旅游与大众旅游（Small-scale tourism and mass tourism）
3. 生态旅游（Ecotourism）
4. 旅游的可持续发展（Sustainable development of tourism）

　　马罗卡是西班牙贝里瑞群岛中的一个小岛屿。这里曾经是一个宁静、快乐、和平的海边小村庄。白色的沙滩、美丽的迎客松和橘黄色的胡姬花遍布岛上。20 世纪 60 年代以前，由于岛上闹饥荒，使一些世代生活在岛上的居民迁移出岛，留下的居民仅靠落后的农业和经济作物维持贫困的生活。60 年代后，一些冒险家、艺术家及好奇的游客发现了马罗卡岛。他们欣赏这里的自然风光、未被污染的海滩，以及封闭、平静、安全的环境，喜欢岛上依然保留着的世界最古老的文明。

　　70 年代初期，由于经济的不断发展，中下层人们的收入水平显著提高，马罗卡岛涌入大量游客。随着游客的不断增加，岛上建起了各类旅游设施。旅游景点也被开发利用，并且获得了令人羡慕的旅游收益。岛上继而新建了许多大众化的度假设施。其中有许多是外商投资的。马罗卡从一个不知名的小岛变成了大众旅游的目的地。旅游业在马罗卡岛占有重要的经济地位。岛上 80% 的国民收入来自旅游业；50% 的岛上居民在旅游业就业；旅游业所创造的大量就业机会使愈来愈多的外来人口不断涌入。迁入人口的数量超过了迁出人口的数量。岛上居民的收入水平不断提高。家庭拥有汽车的数量在西班牙位居首位，而失业率在西班牙最低。

　　1973 年，世界性石油危机使油价飞速上涨，提高了各类产品的成本，降低了游客的可支配收入。旅游业为了在危机中求得生存，要不断降低成本，从而降低价格。例如，建设廉价的住宿公寓替代正规的饭店客房，可以减少服务人员，降低人工费用；采用旅馆高层建筑技术，尽可能地在每平方米的面积上增加床位数，可以降低建筑成本。这使岛上的住宿设施快速增加，并且超过了游客增长的速度。在旅游接待能力供大于求的情况下，饭店的房价必然降低。这虽然导致了游客数量的增加，但却减少了游客的人均消费水平。

到80年代晚期,由于岛上的主要客源国英国发生了严重的经济危机,来岛的游客数量锐减,阳光海滩度假市场不断恶化。与此同时,马罗卡岛的旅游发展在经历了大众旅游所带来的繁荣后,进入了萧条期。岛上出现了由于过度旅游开发所造成的一系列环境问题。其中比较严重的问题之一就是地下水的过度消耗和水盐浓度的提高,从地下抽取净水的数量大大超过了从积蓄的雨水中获取净水的数量。众所周知,马罗卡岛是一个水资源稀缺的地方。岛上每个乡村人口的日用水量一般在140升左右;城镇人口的日用水量为250升;而每个游客的日均用水量为440升;一位住豪华饭店游客的日用水量竟高达880升。这其中包括浇灌饭店的绿地和花园,以及高尔夫球场、灌注游泳池、桑拿浴、大量洗涤布巾等用水。由于净水水位不断下降,海水随之大量涌入,使原有的净水资源被污染和代替。这不但严重破坏了岛上农业和园林的灌溉系统,而且还威胁着公众的健康。1993年,岛上每升净水的含盐量为1500毫克,高于正常含盐量的5倍。

地下水的过度消耗和水盐浓度的增加又造成了新的环境污染。岛上居民和游客越来越多地使用从外地运来的矿泉水和当地生产的纯净水,这一方面增加了交通运输量和汽油使用量,造成了温室效应;另一方面出售矿泉水、纯净水使用的塑料包装瓶又给垃圾的处理造成了困难。餐馆、咖啡厅和饭店大量使用昂贵、高度纯净水,每生产3升就需要10升的普通水,提取净化水后剩下的水不能饮用。因此又使地下水的消耗数量增加了3倍,最终使地下水消耗和水盐浓度的状况进一步恶化。

由旅游发展造成的另一个环境问题,是岛上垃圾的大量增加。由于马罗卡岛所处的地理位置,岛上需要的绝大部分产品须从内陆运来。这些产品在运输过程中使用大量结实的包装,仓储费用也远远高于船运费用。如果分流处理或重新加工使用废弃的包装材料,将进一步提高产品的成本。据统计,外来游客产生的垃圾比当地居民高出50%。在一所饭店经营的4年当中,垃圾的产出量增加了30%,而遗留在饭店客房里的垃圾增加了50%。

旅游开发造成最突出和最严重的问题,是岛上的自然风景遭到破坏。层出不穷的高层旅馆建筑破坏了岛上美丽的空中地平线。原有的金黄色海岸沙滩、大片的绿色沼泽和银白色的盐田都在层层叠叠的钢筋水泥中消失了。特别是在淡季,岛上饭店大部分空闲的时候,这里的景象更加荒凉。旅游设施的建设占用了大量的农田;岛上可防水的梯田逐级坍塌;频繁的暴风雨将大量的土壤冲进了大海;古老的田园风光被吞噬;岛上80%的海岸地带被占用;许多珍奇动物和植物濒临绝境。60年代马罗卡岛宁静、幽雅、安全的环境已不复存在。游客们再也享受不到令人陶醉的灿烂阳光、洁净的海水、蔚蓝的天空、秀丽的自然景观和宜人的气候。这个靠自然旅游资源生存和发展的小岛对游客的吸引力变得越来越小。

资料来源:即将被大众旅游所毁灭的马罗卡岛. 田里. 旅游经济学[M],北京:高等教育出版社,2002。

Part IV Reading Box
第四部分　阅读与分析

阅读分析要点

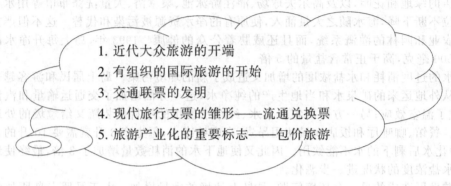

1. 近代大众旅游的开端
2. 有组织的国际旅游的开始
3. 交通联票的发明
4. 现代旅行支票的雏形——流通兑换票
5. 旅游产业化的重要标志——包价旅游

  Thomas Cook is regarded as the most suitable person who is related to the emergence of **modern and large-scale tourism**, although it takes another one and half century for tourism to develop into a global industry. Cook was once a Baptist preacher who was concerned about how to help the English working class to improve their moral standards.[1] Cook arranged for trains to take the workers to the countryside to take part in self-control meetings and Bible camps so that their spirit could be purified. The first trip started from Leicester to Lough Borough on 5th July 1841 and lasted just one day. However, it can be regarded as the **beginning of the modern tourism**. Gradually, more and more people took part in these short trips and the range of destinations became larger and larger. Of course, people took part in these tourism activities with completely different purposes.

  Thomas Cook set up the famous travel business Thomas Cook & Son and provided short trips from Leicester to London on a regular basis. In 1863, Cook organized the first international trip to the Swiss Alps, and in 1872, he organized the first tourism around the world. The destinations included British colonies of Australia and New Zealand. These trips were significant and considered as **the era of international tourism** for the two countries. Of course, such trips were just the privileges of the very wealthy as the common people could not afford them.[2]

  For the trips Cook dealt with all the matters concerning **connections, tickets, and timetables**. He also provided various services including currency exchange for trips abroad, the distribution of published travel guides and tour timetables. Moreover, he developed the idea of guided or Cook's tour. Consequently, his customers kept participating in the tours organized by Cook's company and never turned to other companies. These customers would share the joys of a Cook's Tour with their friends or relatives. In this way, an effective marketing program was finally built.

  Cook provided his customers with not only good service but also convenience at a **reasonable cost**. In those days, railways were owned by separate companies offering different schedules and fares. These railways were not connected with each other. They could be either short or long and could carry passengers near a city but did not pass through it. According to the specific arrangements of a particular journey, Cook connected all the tickets needed together—sometimes including the tickets of stage or steamer, and called this **Circular Ticket**.[3] For the unused tickets, he would credit back to the customers.

Another important concept introduced by Cook was the **Cook Coupon**. His customers could use these coupons to pay for meals and rooms at the hotels that joined the framework organized by Cook. In 1873, Cook introduced another idea—**Circular Notes** which can be considered as the original form of the traveler's check. Tourists paid cash for these notes and could cash them at hundreds of particular hotels. On one hand, tourists using these notes must patronize those establishments on Cook's list. On the other hand, it provided a safe and convenient means for tourists to carry and exchange money. At the beginning of this practice, there were only about 200 hotels on Cook's list. By 1890 when Cook's business began to be expanded to the global market, the number of participating hotels had reached nearly 1,000.

Cook organized the Great Exhibition in London in 1851. His arrangements best reflected his ideas of **reform in the tourism industry**. He supplied the 160,000 clients with:

- an all-round, pre-paid, one-fee structure that covered transportation, accommodation, guides, food and other goods and services
- organized journeys based on strict time schedules
- uniform products of a highly professional quality
- affordable prices, made possible by the economies of scale created through large customer volumes

The talent of Thomas Cook was mainly embodied in his application of the production principles of the Industrial Revolution for operations of tourism.[4] He provided a large number of commercialized package tours for which he set uniform standards and fixed time.[5] These **package tours** were a sign of the industrialization of tourism industry. While few people paid much attention to the development of attractions such as the seaside resorts, Thomas Cook first offered tourists such opportunities to travel and enjoy themselves there with low cost. As the railway, the steamship and the telegraph were invented, tourism could actually be expanded and tourism systems could be formalized. The adoption of these reforms made it possible for Thomas Cook to attract a large number of tourists, and to widen the range of destinations to an unusual level, a phenomenon that had never happened before. In other words, Cook helped to enlarge both the tourism market and supply to an extraordinary extent. Today, we can take it for granted that the package tour is one of the fundamental components of the modern tourism industry. Thomas Cook can be regarded as a pioneer in this industry.

New Words

Baptist	n.	浸信会教友
patronize	v.	光顾,惠顾
distribution	n.	分配,分销
pioneer	n.	拓荒者,开拓者
formalized	adj.	固定的
preacher	n.	说教者,布道者

Key Terms

currency exchange   货币兑换   traveler's check   旅行支票

Notes

1. Cook was once a Baptist preacher who was concerned about how to help the English working class to improve their moral standards.
   库克曾经是浸信会教友的布道者,他关心的是如何帮助英国工薪阶层提高他们的道德标准。

2. Of course, such trips were just the privileges of the very wealthy as the common people could not afford them.
   当然,这些旅行仅仅只是非常富有的人的特权,因为普通人是没有钱参加这样的旅行的。

3. According to the specific arrangements of a particular journey, Cook connected all the tickets needed together—sometimes including the tickets of stage or steamer, and called this circular ticket.
   根据某一特定行程的具体安排,库克将旅行中所需要的票全部结合在一起,有时还会包括剧院的戏票和船票,称之为联票。

4. The talent of Thomas Cook was mainly embodied in his application of the production principles of the Industrial Revolution for operations of tourism.
   托马斯·库克的才能主要体现在他将工业革命中的生产原理运用于旅游的运作。

5. He provided a large number of commercialized package tours for which he set uniform standards and fixed time.
   他提供了大量商业化的包价旅游,并制定了统一的标准和固定的时间。

Topic discussion

1. What is the initial purpose for Cook to arrange a tour to the countryside?

   _____

2. How did Cook organize a tour that most people could offer?

   _____

3. What is a Circular Ticket? In what way does it help organize Cook's trips?

   _____

4. What is a Circular Note? What is the significance for tourism?

   _____

5. Why is Thomas Cook regarded as the father of early modern tourism?

   _____

【即学即用】

With reference to the theory, information or approach applied in the Reading Box, have a case study of the package tour in your city. Make presentation of your study in Chinese or in English using PPT.

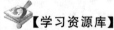【学习资源库】

为了掌握本章更多的相关专业知识,请您登录 http://sicnu.edu.cn/,点击国家双语教

学示范课程《旅游学概论》,进入网络学堂查询相关资料。

Chapter Review 本章小结

This chapter has discussed the importance of disposal income and disposal time for the emergence of mass tourism. It depicts the role of the Industrial Revolution on the rise of mass tourism, and differentiates the Grand Tour and modern mass tourism. Modern mass tourism has developed with increased disposal income and time. Besides, it has developed with reforms in transport, especially in aircraft technology, paid holidays and development of the package tour. Social progress, especially in the 1960's and various reforms in holiday entitlement and labor legislation speed up the development of mass tourism. Thomas Cook contributes a lot to modern mass tourism. He is regarded as the "father of early modern tourism".

Part V　Additional Know-how of Tourism
第五部分　旅游知识扩展

【关键术语】

Discretionary income：the amount of income that remains after household necessities such as food, housing, clothing, education and transportation have been purchased

可支配收入：扣除日常必需消费(如衣、食、住、行、教育等)部分后的剩余收入。

Leisure and recreation：Leisure refers to the time available to an individual when work, sleep and other basic needs have been met；the recreation is the pursuit engaged upon during leisure time.

休闲与消遣：休闲是一个人工作、睡觉和满足其他需求后所拥有的时间。消遣是在休闲时间寻求参与性的活动。

Demographic transition model（DTM）：an idealized process whereby societies evolve from a high fertility/ high mortality structure to a low fertility/ low mortality structure. This evolution usually parallels the phases of the development of a society

人口变迁模型(DTM)：社会由高出生率/高死亡率结构向低出生率/低死亡率结构演变的一种理想化过程。这种演变与社会发展的各个阶段相并行。

Push factors of tourism development：economic, social, demographic, technological and political forces that stimulate a demand for tourism activity by "pushing" consumers away from their usual place of residence

旅游发展推动因素：经济、社会、人口统计学、技术、政治等是"推动"消费者离开常住地、激发旅游活动的需求的动力。

Pilgrimage：generic term for travel undertaken for some religious purpose. Pilgrimages have declined in importance during the modern era compared with recreational, business and social tourism

朝圣：是出于某些宗教目的而旅行的通用语。随着现代旅游的发展,与休闲旅游、商务旅游和社会旅游相比,朝圣旅游的重要性已经下降。

Grand Tour：a form of early modern tourism that involved a lengthy trip to the major cities of France and Italy by young adults of the leisure class, for purposes of education and culture

大旅游：早期现代旅游的一种形式。有闲阶级中的年轻人出于教育和文化的目的在法国和意大利的主要城市进行的长途旅游。

Industrial Revolution：a process that occurred in England from the mid-1700s to the mid-1900s（and spread outwards to other countries），in which society was transformed from an agrarian to an industrial basis，thereby spawning conditions that were conductive to the growth of tourism-related activity.

工业革命：18世纪中期到20世纪中期，英国发生工业革命（随后传播到其他国家）。这一时期实现了从传统农业社会向现代工业社会的重要转变，为旅游相关活动的发展创造了条件。

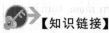
【知识链接】

1. 现代大众旅游的构成

现代大众旅游由以下几个部分组成。

现代交通。发展快速交通是现代旅游业的第一要务。以机场和高速公路为代表的现代交通带给人们史无前例的流动自由。快速交通缩短了旅游的时空距离，降低了旅游成本，增加了旅游的可进入性，旅游者的文化飞地（cultural enclaves）获得了技术上的可能。旅游者的文化飞地以机场和高速公路的出入口为依托，并随着它们的延伸而延伸。文化飞地能为大众旅游者提供有效的安全保护与交往缓冲。因此，只有大量游客的存在才能引致更大量大众旅游者的到来。

旅游团与导游。旅游团与导游是现代旅游业的标准形式。旅游团是一种具有四重筛选机制的制度：其一，是对组团范围的筛选；其二，是对经济能力的筛选；其三，是对闲暇能力的筛选；其四，是对旅游趣味的筛选。这四重筛选使旅游团趋于同质化，加之导游的主持与中介，旅途既表现得高度民主又具有极大的社会身份与文化身份安全性。而以旅游团集体的力量，加之导游的主持、中介与代理，又保障了与接待地交往的质量与安全。

商业饭店。商业饭店是现代旅游业的标志。"家外之家"是传统社会家店不分的客栈（inn）的本体存在，其本质是"客随主便"；而"社会之上的社会"则是现代商业饭店（hotel）的本体存在，其本质是"顾客是上帝"。从客栈到商业饭店，其社会价值的意味已远远高过使用价值。考察欧美、中国、日本和一些第三世界国家的饭店发展史，商业饭店总是与大众旅游同期涌现，而对商业饭店品牌建设、星级评定等的强调又总是与大众旅游的大发展同期。

旅游手册与旅游商品。旅游手册与旅游商品是现代旅游业的精神工具。旅游手册与旅游商品是现代旅游"文化地图"（cultural map）最重要的组成部分。旅游文化地图是由主客双方围绕接待地而进行的相互表述（representation）积淀而成的一种现象。它对后继的旅游文化叙事（cultural narrative）具有引导性，因而被旅游人类学理论视为一种规范化的媒介活动。它为接待地建立起符合秩序性与逻辑性要求的情境，本质上是一种标明主客双方权力与利益的物质化话语（discourse materialized），可以"作为旅游者与其所游览的景观或访问的社会之间的中介物或过滤器"。

旅游景区。旅游景区并非单一的实体（a single entity），而是一个类型（pattern），它包括为旅游文化地图指定的一系列特定的地点及与地点相关的范式化的消费活动。跨文化的景区消费天然涉及不同社会阶层、文化区域和民族国家之间复杂的社会历史关系，必然掺入大量政治、经济与文化生态因素，明显带有语言特征和文化特质。传统社会遵循着某种有序而缓慢的、由传统所奠定的、少量而艺术化的形式，其普遍性、公共性甚至其边界都常处于暧昧不明的状态。而现代旅游业则通过权威认证和提供旅游服务等方式，划分出清晰的边界，快速生产景区。对大众旅游者来说，旅游业生产出来的景区，更能提供清晰的认知辅助和行为指导,形成有效的保护。

2. 旅行社与大众旅游

(1) 通过旅行社组织旅游活动,可以实现规模效益,所谓的规模效益是指在一定时期内,当企业绝对产量增加时,其单位产品的成本趋于下降的经济现象。与个别旅游者的旅游行为相比,旅行社能以组团旅行的方式充分利用规模效应,从而降低单位游客的支付成本。旅行社和上游供应商(如接待企业、运输企业等)交易规模大,因而具有更强的讨价还价能力。这是因为:卖方为了获得大规模的购买愿意在价格上做出让步,另外,旅行社的购买是重复的,上游企业愿意为了和这样的购买者建立稳固的业务往来而降低价格。旅行社通过团队旅游的方式,可以提高劳动生产效率,降低单位游客旅游活动过程中的变动成本。

(2) 作为专门的旅游产品的生产者和销售者,旅行社可以凭借其专业化优势,降低大众旅游活动的成本。旅行社将主要的资源和精力集中在旅游活动的组织上,成为该领域的专家,可以有效地提高效率。非专业的零散旅游者在这些方面和旅行社相比,并没有比较优势,旅游者还将面临较高的机会成本,得不偿失。旅行社因其专业生产而充分享受到学习(经验)效应。旅行社是专门性的旅游活动组织机构,在线路的选择和景点的串联、行程的安排、通关手续的办理、交通工具的选择和使用等诸多方面有着丰富的经验和专门的工作人员,能有效地降低旅游者的成本。由于旅行社长期组织旅游活动和专业化等原因,掌握的信息远较零散游客充分和完全,从而能够给游客相应的技术性建议,降低游客收集信息的成本,促进旅游活动的开展。旅行社还能减少游客在旅游过程中的风险和一些额外成本。

(3) 旅行社通过标准化,削减了旅游活动的成本。现代大众旅游中旅行社对旅游活动的组织,大到行程安排,小到导游的讲解,格式化的交易条件等无处不充盈着标准化。虽然目前对团体旅游的标准化行程诟病颇多,但标准化生产所带来的旅游活动的低成本却是大众旅游产生与繁荣的重要基石。旅游产品的不可移动性和无形性等特点也要求旅行社以标准化的生产方式来明确和稳定旅行者的预期,减少游客的心理成本。

(4) 旅行社能降低其他旅游企业的经营成本,间接地减少了旅游者的支出。众多的旅游企业为了获得尽可能多的交易机会,不得不支付相当的费用于营销。作为旅游者和这些旅游企业之间的中介机构,旅行社可以将在一次完整的旅游经历当中把旅游者可能面对的众多企业联结起来,一次性地整体介绍给旅游者。这样,旅行社就可以凭借较少的营销费用,取得由各个旅游企业直接面向旅游者分别进行营销的效果,降低其他旅游企业的营销成本,获得营销经济性。旅行社将零散的旅游者组织起来,以集团购买的方式和其他旅游企业进行交易,这样的交易形式能为这些旅游企业节约交易成本。因为供给者售给单一顾客比之零散的出售给多个顾客更能够降低其成本,比如寻找交易对象的成本、签约的成本、运输的成本、仓储的成本等。

【小思考】

1. 你是怎样理解代大众旅游对目的地造成的"麦当劳化"现象?谈谈你的个人感受?

参考阅读:

现代大众旅游对旅游目的地将会带来一系列显著的影响。这些影响主要表现在以下几个方面:

(1) 旅游目的地的全球化特征与地方化特征都在加强。全球化包括广大地域内的大量社会组织、社会关系等现象在形式上和功能上的日益近似和统一。如金融服务、餐饮住宿的形式和功能也越来越近似和统一,成为全球化的一个重要表现。这种全球化现象使旅游者得以安全、放心地进行旅游。另一方面,全球化的日益加深尽管使世界的广大地区都出现许多近似的现象,但与此同时地方性也在逐渐加强,至少对大多数旅游目的地来说是如此。旅游目的地为了给游客提供便利条件,不可避免地要采取一些全球化措施;但另一方面,为了吸引更多的游客前来观光旅游,这些地区又不得不加强其地方性特征,增强其"卖点",以避免失去特色从而失去游客。

(2) 旅游目的地日益出现一种"麦当劳化"现象,即对旅游产品的生产日益注重可控制性、可预测性、可计算性和提高效率。越来越多的旅游景点提供规范化、标准化的产品和服务以增强旅游产品的可控制性;游览的景点通过媒体或他人的事先介绍实现可预测性;其费用也由旅行社预先安排好,具有可计算性;也有越来越多的景点采取迪斯尼乐园安排交通的做法,目的在于让游客快看快走,在单位时间内游更多的景点,通过最大限度的人流,即具有效率。

(3) 对旅游目的地的居民来说,现代旅游所带来的与外来游客的暂时性接触使其产生了一系列变化,其中最主要的变化包括两个方面:① 旅游目的地居民的功利主义倾向增强。比如河北省涞水县的国家重点风景区野三坡曾经是一个民风淳朴、不重视金钱甚至以收游客的钱为耻的地方,随着当地旅游的逐渐升温,人们的经济意识增强了,唯利是图现象时有发生。这表明现代社会的功利主义倾向开始渗透进这一地区。② 旅游目的地居民在与游客的暂时性接触中多元主义意识有所增强,逐渐学会理解和尊重他人的想法,这显示了社会的日益开放和文明程度的日益提高。

2. 你怎样看待大众旅游的商品化过程?你认为目的地文化商品化是否可取?

参考阅读:

目的地文化的商品化,也就是为了满足旅游市场的需求将文化转换成商品出售是旅游带来的一个主要的负面影响。乍一看,这似乎是一种积极的发展,因为旅游将一种无形的价值加到了已经存在的旅游产品之上,这种产品在以前没有产生任何经济效应。但是问题在于人们开始忽视这些文化手工艺品和表演的原本特质和含义,把获得经济利益作为主要目标。随着大众旅游的发展,为了获得更多的经济利益,地方文化的商品化成为越来越普遍的现象。当文化商品大规模地被复制的时候,为了迎合大众旅游市场的需求,文化可能会被改变,而其原本的重要意义将在这个过程中丧失。

这里给出一个大众旅游发展过程中文化商品化的过程:

1. 在一个原住民社区当中,旅游者非常罕见,当他们出现的时候,被当地居民作为特邀嘉宾参加他们的仪式,并且不收取任何的费用。当地居民还会赠送他们当地特有的手工艺品以表达对游客的尊重。

2. 来参观的游客越来越多,参观次数也越来越频繁,当地居民也不再觉得这是一件稀奇的事,观看当地的仪式和得到手工艺品都要收取一点费用。

3. 原住民社区长期接待大量的游客,人们改变原有的仪式使它更吸引游客,为了满足旅游市场的需求,仪式变成了按时进行的表演。原真性让位于更具吸引力的虚拟表演。观看演出的费用也变成了能有多高就多高,大批量生产的廉价纪念品大量出售。

4. 商品化和现代化使当地文化被完全破坏,尽管人们采取措施保护文化,但是商品化还是延伸到了文化最神圣和最深刻的部分。

Part VI Further Readings
第六部分 课外阅读

如果您想进一步学习本章的内容,探讨大众旅游兴起的原因和意义,建议您阅读以下学者的著作和论文。

一、中文部分

[1] 曹国新.大众旅游对接待地社会文化空间的影响[J].商业研究,2005,(24).
[2] 李泽才.现代性条件下的大众旅游[J].苏州大学学报(哲学社会科学版),2006,(01).
[3] 张凌云.大众的"新旅游"还是新的"大众旅游"[J].旅游学刊,2002,(06).
[4] 何兰萍.大众旅游的社会学批判[J].社会,2002,(10).
[5] 吴波等.非大众型旅游:起源、概念及特征[J].旅游学刊,2000,(03).
[6] 郭伟峰.现代性焦虑下的大众化旅游[J].长春理工大学学报(社会科学版),2011,(11).
[7] 任宁,廖月兰,叶茜倩.大众旅游与选择性旅游概念辨析及运用[J].经济地理,2006,(12).
[8] 于洪贤等.大众旅游与生态旅游的比较研究[J].东北农业大学学报(社会科学版),2005,(08).
[9] 戴斌,夏少颜.论我国大众旅游发展阶段的运行特征与政策取向[J].旅游学刊,2009,(12).
[10] 蔡君.中国西部发展非大众旅游的探讨——以郎木寺为例[J].北京林业大学学报,2001,(11).

二、英文部分

[1] Timothy J. Macnaught. Mass tourism and the dilemmas of modernization in Pacific Island communities[J]. *Annals of Tourism Research*,1982,9(3):359—381.
[2] Graham D. Busby. From explorers to mass tourism[J]. *Tourism Management*,1998,19(5):479—481.
[3] Lynne Taylor. Strength through joy: Consumerism and mass tourism in the third reich[J]. *Annals of Tourism Research*,2005,32(3):816—818.
[4] Jan T. Mosedale. Coastal mass tourism: Diversification and sustainable development in South Europe[J]. *Annals of Tourism Research*,2005,32(1):282—284.
[5] Eugeni Aguilo Perez, Sampol Catalina Juaneda. Tourist expenditure for mass tourism markets[J]. *Annals of Tourism Research*,2000,27(3):624—637.
[6] Enrique Claver-Cortés, Jorge Pereira-Moliner. Competitiveness in mass tourism[J]. *Annals of Tourism Research*,2007,34(3):727—745.
[7] Janet Phillips. Commentary on Macnaught's "Mass tourism and the dilemmas of modernization"[J]. *Annals of Tourism Research*,1984,11(2):299—302.
[8] Eugeni Aguilo Perez, Sampol Catalina Juaneda. Tourist Expenditure for mass tourism markets[J]. *Annals of Tourism Research*,2000,27(3):624—637.
[9] Margam M. Khan. Tourism development and dependency theory: Mass tourism vs. ecotourism[J]. *Annals of Tourism Research*,1997,24(4):988—991.
[10] David B. Weaver. Alternative to mass tourism in Dominica[J]. *Annals of Tourism Research*,1991,18(3):414—432.

Chapter 3 Demand for Tourism and Consumer Behavior
第三章 旅游需求与消费者行为

Learning objects：学习目标

- Study the demand for tourism within N-S pair based on tourism system (Leiper's model)以旅游系统(Leiper 模型)为框架，研究 N-S Pair(需求与供给关系)中的旅游需求
- Appreciate the lifestyle determinants of tourism and their relations 了解哪些是旅游的生活方式的决定因素以及它们之间的关系
- Describe the frame of family life cycle and the travel propensity that an individual has in each stage of FLC 阐述家庭生命周期框架以及个人在家庭生命周期每一阶段中的旅游倾向性
- Understand the interrelationship between the lifestyle and family life cycle 了解生活方式与家庭生命周期之间的相互关系
- Discuss the application of family life cycle for the market segmentation and marketing 讨论家庭生命周期理论在市场细分和营销中的运用
- Use the life-cycle framework and lifestyle variables to jointly analyze the tourism demand 运用家庭生命周期框架和生活方式变量共同分析旅游需求
- Understand the relationship between the travel distance and the attraction of a destination 理解旅行距离与旅游目的地吸引力之间的关系

Ability goals：能力目标

- Case Study 案例分析：旅游需求的增长与变化——以佛罗里达中心地区为例
- Reading Box 阅读分析：Resistance of the Travel Distance 旅游距离抗阻

38

Part I Text
第一部分 课文

Demand for Tourism and Consumer Behavior

【教学要点】

知识要点	掌握程度	相关章节
tourist motivation and consumer behavior 旅游动机与消费者行为	重点掌握	本课文与第 1 单元、第 4 单元、第 5 单元、第 9 单元、第 10 单元、第 15 单元相关内容有联系。
lifestyle determinants 生活方式决定性因素	重点掌握	
family life cycle 家庭生命周期	一般了解	
interrelationship between the lifestyle and family life cycle 生活方式与家庭生命周期的相互关系	重点掌握	
buying decision process in tourism 旅游产品购买决策过程	重点掌握	
energizers of demand and effectors of demand 需求驱动力与需求影响力	一般了解	

We take it for granted that to understand the tourist buying decision process is essential if we are to understand and predict demand for tourism. Demand for tourism at the individual level can be treated as a consumption process that is influenced by a number of factors: needs and desires, availability of time and money, or images, perceptions and attitude. There is a diversity of **consumer behavior** with decision being made for a range of reasons. Many variables will influence the consumption pattern of a tourist. In the chapter, we shall mainly focus on the concepts relating to motivation, and determinants of demand that have a great influence on the decision-making process of a tourist.

Tourist motivation

The classic dictionary definition of motivation is derived from the word "motivation" which is to cause a person to act in a certain way, or to stimulate interest. We can also refer to the word "motive" which is concerned with initiating movement or inducing a person to act. As would be expected, many texts associated with tourism utilize the concept of motivation as a major influence upon consumer behavior. McIntosh, Goeldner and Ritchie (1995) outline four categories of motivation:

1. **physical motivators**: those related to refreshment of body and mind, health purpose, sport and pleasure. This group of motivators is seen to be linked to those activities which will reduce tension.

2. **culture motivation**: those identified by the desire to see and know more about other cultures, to find out about the natives of a country, their lifestyle, music, art, folklore, dance, etc.

3. **interpersonal motivation**: this group includes a desire to meet new people, visit friends or relative, and to seek new and different experience. Travel is an escape from

routine relationships with friends or neighbors or the home environment or it is used for spiritual reasons.

4. **status and prestige motivation**: these include a desire for continuation of education. Such motivators are seen to be concerned with the desire for recognition and attention from others, in order to boost the personal ego. This category also includes personal development in relation to the pursuit of hobbies and education.

Determinants of demand for tourism

Even if an individual has the motivation to travel, he cannot do so at will. There are a lot of factors which can influence the possible decision and choice of his. These factors are connected with the individual factors, the distance between origin region and destination region, as well as the supply environment. Many factors influence the demand of tourism, such as the disposal income, the disposal time, the motivation, the demographics, the political situation, the media, the transportation and the technological renovation, just to mention a few. We refer these factors to the determinants of demand for tourism.

From a perspective of N-S pair within the tourism system, the determinants of tourism demand which influence one's travel propensity fall into two categories: the individual factors and the supply environment. Prom a perspective of the distance within O-D pair, the factors can be classified into three types: the geographical distance, the cultural distance, and the psychological distance. Controlling for all other factors, an inverse relationship is likely to exist between the volume of traffic flowing from an origin region to a destination region. This is what we call the distance decay.

The determinants of demand are mutually affected. For example, a person must have enough disposable income so as to travel. This income and his choice of the type of tourism will, in turn, be affected by many factors such as job type, life-cycle stage, mobility, level of educational attainment and personality.[1]

When making a plan to travel, an individual must take many interrelated factors into account to decide the type of tourism he will participate in. These factors can be broadly divided into two groups. The lifestyle factors and family life-cycle factors always interact and mutually influence each other.

1. The first group of factors has something to do with lifestyle. It is made up of such factors as income, employment, holiday entitlement, educational attainment and mobility.

2. The second group has something to do with life cycle. It mainly refers to the age and family circumstances of an individual, which are crucial to the amount and type of tourism demanded.[2] Naturally, these factors do not function separately. They work together to help the individual to make a decision.

Lifestyle determinants of demand for tourism

Income and employment

Income and employment are two important factors which can influence an individual's decision on such matters as the level and the nature of tourism. It is necessary for the individual to earn a certain amount of income to realize his travel desire. After all, tourism is an expensive activity. This income does not refer to the **gross income** but the **discretionary income**, i.e. the income left over after the expenditures of tax, housing and the basics of life are paid. The nature of employment can determine how much a person can earn and whether he can enjoy a paid holiday or not. These, in turn, affect both **travel propensity** and the type of holiday demanded, just as the mechanism of peer pressure and reference group do.[3]

Paid holiday entitlement

As documents show, most individuals in the developed world have witnessed the increase in leisure time since 1950. However, It is hard to understand the relationship between an individual's total time budget, leisure time and **paid holiday entitlement.** Different nations have different holiday arrangements, of which one-day national holiday takes up a large part. According to the law or collective agreements, people in most nations are also entitled to enjoy annual paid holiday, which obviously influences their travel propensity. But in fact the relationship between paid holiday entitlement and travel propensity is not so simple. And just like the income variable, it is easier to comprehend the relationship when it is at the extremes.[4] For example, if an individual has less chance to enjoy annual paid holiday, he can hardly realize his travel desire. On the contrary, if he has more chances, he is more likely to be motivated to travel. This is partly determined by the interrelationship between entitlement and factors such as job status, income and mobility. However, if an individual enjoys more paid holiday entitlement, he may prefer to spend it at home rather than go traveling.

Education and mobility

Level of **education attainment** plays an important role in an individual's travel propensity. Those who have received a higher level of education have a stronger desire to travel owing to the stimulation of education. And travel can in turn broaden their horizons and enrich their knowledge. Therefore, they are more active to grasp travel opportunities and more likely to be attracted by various information, media, advertising and sales promotion.

Another factor which exerts a great impact on travel propensity is **personal mobility,** especially with regard to holidays spent in one's own country.[5] The car is the main tool a tourist can use to entertain himself during the trip. An individual who owns a car can have more opportunity to enjoy the pleasure of travel than those who don't.

Life-cycle determinants of demand for tourism

An individual's age is an important determinant of travel propensity and the type of tourism. Generally we use **chronological age** to measure them, but "**domestic age**" is more accurate. Domestic age refers to the stage in the life cycle an individual reached. People in different stages have different holiday demand and levels of travel propensity. The specific situations and different life stages that an individual is involved in can influence his consuming behavior. And the concept of family life cycle is helpful for us to understand this. What's more, from this cycle we also know that with the progression of age, an individual is likely to experience ups and downs in disposable income and changes in social responsibilities.[6] The following table shows us the concepts of the life cycle of families in the USA (see Table 3.1). They are provided by Wells and Gubar.

Table 3.1 A traditional family life cycle

Stage in life cycle	Characteristics; Bachelor stage
1. Bachelor stoge:	young single people not living at home
2. Newly married couples:	young, no children
3. Full nest I:	young married couples with dependent children
4. Full nest II:	married couples with dependent children over 6 years old
5. Full nest III:	married couples with dependent children
6. Empty nest I:	older couples, no children living with them, head in labor force
7. Empty nest II:	older married couples, no children living at home, head retired
8. Solitary survivor:	older single people in the labor force

Source: William D. Wells and George Gubar, "Life Cycle Concept in Marketing Research," *Journal of Marketing Research*, November 1986, pp. 355—363 J. Paul Peter and Jerry C. Olson, *Consumer Behavior: Marketing Strategy Perspective* (Homewood, Illinois, Richard D. Irwin). p.459

There are many different distinctive patterns of demand at each stage in the life cycle. Individuals at each stage in the life cycle also show something in common:
- Preoccupations—which are the mental concern out of motivations;
- Interests—which are feeling of what an individual would like to do or represent the awareness of an idea or opportunity;[7]
- Activities—which are the actions of an individual.

At each stage in the life cycle the three factors can be combined together in different ways so that there are different characteristics. For example, in adolescent individuals tend to put more emphasis on joining in social activities and finding independence while in married adulthood they are more preoccupied with business and career. At different stages in the life cycle, the combinations of the factors and the nature of the factors are different. And at certain important moments the whole combination will be completely changed. For example, having children is a big event which can bring about great changes to an individual's life. At this stage, his habit of holiday taking can be totally different from the previous days as holidays have become better organized and less influenced by space limit.[8]

The explanatory framework provided by the domestic life-cycle approach presents the information concerning the supply of facilities and the needs of particular population groups[9] (for example, the large numbers of elderly people which will appear in some Western countries by the end of the century). This framework is very powerful, so the marketers often make use of it to segment the market. However, the life cycle does not take into account such groups as one-parent families, divorcees or other ethnic groups, so it is just a generalization.

We can combine the **life-cycle framework** and **lifestyle variables** to analyze the tourism demand from many different angles. For example, as the level of holiday taking shows, in married middle age, paid holiday entitlement, income and mobility are at the highest level. Equally, companies such as Disney and McDonald's make use of the concept to attract young children so as to keep their attraction for them into later life. As birthrates in the developed world have decreased, it is important to create the hotel, activity and restaurant products which can make children fit for the social life and arouse their interests in certain types of holidays.[10] In this way demand can still be encouraged even when they are old.

The buying decision process in tourism

After we learn the concepts of motivation and determinants of demand for tourism it is important for us to know how a tourist makes the decision for travel. Tourist behavior is quite different from other types of comsumer behavior, for tourism is not a necessity, but a luxurious product which has characteristics of intangibility, inseparability, variability, perishability, and no transfer of the ownership. The buying decision process is influenced by **energizers of demand** such as motivation, **effectors of demand** such as a process of learning, attitudes and associations from promotional messages and information as well as **determinants of demand** such as lifestyle determinants and family life cycle variables. It is normally conceived as a process of 7 stages. The stages can be thought of as: 1. need arousal; 2. information search; 3. identification of alternatives; 4. evaluation of alternatives; 5. choice made; 6. purchase action; and 7. post-purchase behavior.

We can take the tourist behaviour as the research of the ways in which people choose to engage in, negotiate and experience travel away from their normal place of residence in pursuit of particular goals and satisfactions. The **feedback** exerts an important influence on subsequent behavior of each stage. To illustrate the process, we can imagine a potential tourist who is motivated to visit Singapore. After he searches for information and has a comparative study of other destination countries, such as Malaysia, Vietnam, Thailand and Japan, he chooses Thailand as his primary destination. As a result of this trip, he is impressed by the friendliness and hospitality of the people, and the low cost of food and accommodation, but the flood of Bangkok, and the theft of his purse during a break-in also disturbes him. Based on these experiences, his image of Thailand is refined. One year later, he decides to visit China, after considering a variety of alternatives.

New Words

determinant	n.	决定因素
mobility	n.	移动性,机动性
interrelated	adj.	相关的
participate	v.	参与,参加,分享
entitlement	n.	权利
crucial	adj.	至关重要的
discretionary	adj.	任意的,自由决定的
mechanism	n.	机械装置;机构;机制
propensity	n.	倾向
horizon	n.	(知识、思想等)范围,视野
comprehend	v.	理解;包括
domestic	adj.	家庭的,国内的
chronological	adj.	按年代顺序排列的
distinctive	adj.	与众不同的,有特色的
arouse	v.	唤醒,唤起,鼓励,引起
adolescent	adj.	青春期的,青春的

Key Terms

family life-cycle	家庭生命周期	discretionary income	可支配收入
paid holiday	带薪假期	tour operator	旅游经营商

Notes

1. This income and his choice of the type of tourism will, in turn, be affected by many factors such as job type, life-cycle stage, mobility, level of educational attainment and personality.
   反过来说,人们收入水平和旅游类型的选择受到许多因素的影响,如不同职业、生命周期、移动性、受教育程度和个性等。

2. It mainly refers to the age and family circumstances of an individual, which are crucial to the amount and type of tourism demanded.
   这主要指个人的年龄和家庭境况,这些因素对于旅游需求的数量和类型有重要影响。

3. These, in turn, affect both travel propensity and the type of holiday demanded, just as the mechanism of peer pressure and reference group do.
   这些反过来影响旅游倾向和度假需求的类型,正如同类群体和参照群体的影响机制一样。

4. And just like the income variable, it is easier to comprehend the relationship when it is at the extremes.
   正如收入变量一样,只有当带薪休假矛盾突出时,带薪休假同旅游倾向之间的关系才更容易理解。

5. Another factor which exerts a great impact on travel propensity is personal mobility, especially with regard to holidays spent in one's own country.
   对旅游倾向产生重大影响的另一个因素是个人的机动性,特别是国内度假,更是如此。

6. What's more, from this cycle we also know that with the progression of age, an individual is likely to experience ups and downs in disposable income and changes in social responsibilities.
   而且,从这个周期中我们也可以看出,随着年龄的增长,个人的可支配收入会增加或减少,社会责任也会变化。

7. Interests—which are feeling of what an individual would like to do or represent the awareness of an idea or opportunity;
   兴趣就是个人喜好的情绪,或者指知晓一种观念或机会。

8. At this stage, his habit of holiday taking can be totally different from the previous days as holidays have become better organized and less influenced by space limit.
   这个阶段,他的度假习惯与先前完全不同,变得更加有序,很少受空间的限制。

9. The explanatory framework provided by the domestic life-cycle approach presents the information concerning the supply of facilities and the needs of particular population groups.
   运用家庭生命周期研究方法的解释框架提供了关于设施供给和特殊人群需要的信息。

10. As birthrate in the developed world have decreased, it is important to create the hotel, activity and restaurant products which can make children fit for the social life and arouse their interests in certain types of holidays.
    由于发达国家出生率下降,因此,重要的是为孩子们提供适应社会生活的酒店、活动、餐饮等产品,使他们对某些类型的度假产生兴趣。

Exercise

1. Decide whether the statements are true or false. If it is true, put "T" in the space provided and "F" if it is false.

   (1) _____ Determinants of demand are connected with both the individual and the supply environment.

   (2) _____ The discretionary income refers to the gross income an individual earns.

   (3) _____ Those who have received a higher level of education are less willing to travel because they prefer to have leisure at home.

   (4) _____ To measure an individual's travel propensity, chronological age is more accurate than domestic age.

   (5) _____ People in different life stages have different holiday demand and levels of travel propensity.

   (6) _____ The lifecycle outlined in this chapter can be applied to both Chinese families and those families in the western countries.

   (7) _____ Companies such as Disney and McDonald's make use of the lifecycle concept to attract young children.

2. Questions for discussion

   1. What are the main determinants of demand for travel?

   2. In what way is paid-holiday entitlement connected with an individual's travel decision?

   3. What is domestic age? And how is it connected with an individual's holiday demand?

   4. What are the common factors shown by individuals at each stage of the life cycle?

   5. What is the significance of studying lifestyle and life-cycle determinants of demand for tourism?

Part II Guided Reading
第二部分 课文导读

尽管很多人都有旅游需求,但不是每个人都能实现这种需求,旅游需求到旅游实现,这之间存在着障碍。影响旅游需求的因素有很多,包括个人因素和各种社会经济变量。本文把影响旅游需求的因素分为两大类:生活方式(lifestyle)和家庭生命周期(family life-cycle)。生活方式因素包括性别、年龄、个性、收入水平、受教育程度、职业和闲暇时间等,这其中个人的收入水平和闲暇时间是影响旅游需求的最重要的两个因素。

一、旅游需求与个人收入

收入水平中对旅游需求具有直接影响的是旅游支付能力。旅游支付能力是指在人们的全部收入中扣除必须缴纳的税金和必需的生活及社会消费支出后的余额中,可用于旅游消费的货币量,即我们一般所说的可任意支配收入中用于旅游消费的部分。可自由支配收入越高,旅游支付能力就越强。

人们对旅游的支付能力直接关系着旅游需求的实现程度,影响着旅游者的消费水平及其消费结构,并且还会影响到旅游者对旅游目的地及旅行方式的选择。所以,旅游支付能力是决定旅游需求的重要经济因素。

二、旅游需求与闲暇时间

闲暇时间是除旅游支付能力外,形成现实旅游需求的又一重要的客观条件。所谓闲暇时间就是人们在日常工作、学习、生活之余以及必需的社会活动之外,可以自由支配的时间。闲暇时间是个人拥有的不受其他条件限制、完全可以根据自己的意愿去利用和消磨的人生时间,它是以时间形态存在的社会资源。

人们的闲暇时间可以分为四种基本类型:每日工作之余的闲暇时间、每周末的闲暇时间、法定假日的闲暇时间和带薪假期。每日闲暇对现实旅游需求的形成基本没有什么实际意义。周末闲暇可促进短时近距离的旅游需求。法定假日的闲暇可促进时间更长、距离更远的旅游需求。带薪假期是旅游真正走向大众的必需的配套制度。国外的国内旅游之所以能够达到较高的水平,除了旅游支付能力较高外,与带薪假期不无关系。

闲暇时间的长短,除了影响到人们旅游的地域选择,还对人们旅游方式的选择产生重要影响。闲暇时间的空间分布将影响到人们旅游需求的集中程度,如果闲暇时间过于集中,则会造成旅游需求的爆炸性增长。旅游消费行为实际上是对可自由支配时间的消费。时间,特别是连续性的可自由支配时间是旅游需求得以实现的条件。只有当闲暇时间较均匀地分布在全年中时,才可以有效地利用旅游这种休闲方式,同时减轻旅游对旅游目的地社区的压力。

影响旅游需求的另一个重要因素是家庭生命周期,家庭生命周期又与生活方式紧密相关,相互作用,相互影响。本文将家庭生命周期分为八个不同的阶段。人们在家庭生命周期的不同阶段的可支配收入和闲暇时间是不同的,因此,家庭生命周期与旅游需求有着密切的关系。一般来说,单身青年和无小孩的年轻夫妇的收入较低,因此可支配收入也较少,但他们没有小孩需要照顾,家庭事务很少,所以闲暇时间较多,总的来说他们的旅游需求强,但消费能力有限;有小孩的年轻夫妇随工作年限的增加,收入也随之增加,但养育小孩的消费支出也多,因此可支配收入增加的并不明显,同时照顾小孩和处理家庭事务会花去他们很多时间,所以闲暇时间很少,这一阶段他们的旅游需求主要是以小孩的需求为主;有已自立小孩的中年夫妇和还在工作的老年夫妇经过多年的工作积累,收入处于最高水平,且不需要再为小孩支出消费,因此可支配收入也是最多的,虽然他们不需要再花时间照顾小孩,但还是有很多工作和家庭事务需要处理,所以闲暇时间也不会增加很多,总之他们旅游需求水平一般,但消费能力强;退休的老年夫妇靠退休金维持生活,收入有所下降,而且医疗方面的开支也会增加,因此可支配收入也较少,但这一阶段他们已基本没有工作事务,家庭事务也少了,所以闲暇时间也会大大增加,他们的旅游需求较强,但消费能力也有所下降。

旅游需求还对政治环境和经济环境的变化特别敏感,当旅游目的地发生社会动荡或与客源国关系紧张时,旅游者会出于安全的考虑,放弃旅游计划或转向其他旅游目的地。影响旅游需求的政治环境主要是指旅游目的地国,影响旅游需求的经济环境则是指向客源地的经济发展状况和客源地与目的地之间的汇率变动情况。旅游者的需求与所在国的经济发展状况基本呈现正相关关系,经济发展良好则旅游需求旺盛,反之则旅游需求萎缩。另外,当旅游者的本地货币相对于旅游目的地所在国的货币坚挺时,旅游支付能力相对提高,旅游需求旺盛,反之旅游需求萎缩。

文化传播与渗透对旅游需求也有着深远的影响。这主要体现在两个方面:一是旅游者的文化。旅游者的文化水平决定旅游者的习性和行为,尤其是依此而形成的社会阶层、语言、民族、宗教等是影响旅游需求的重要因素。二是文化距离,即旅游客源地与旅游目的地之间的文化差距。

总之,旅游需求受多种因素的共同影响,比一般商品需求更加复杂,更加难以预测。因此,研究旅游需求应当结合个人的生活方式和家庭生命周期,综合考虑各种因素,这样才能正确细分市场、开发产销对路的旅游产品,满足旅游者的需求,提高他们的旅游体验和满意度。

旅游知识测试

正误判断:请在正确的选题上划√,错误的选题上划×。

1. 旅游者的需求受驱动力,如动机的影响,也受到需求影响力,如学习过程、态度、促销、信息等因素的影响。影响旅游者出行的决定性因素是生活方式,并受家庭生命周期的影响。

2. 旅游研究需要借助一些指标测量旅游活动和旅游需求状况,以及借助这些指标对不同国家或不同地区的发展情况进行比较。这类指标有很多,最常用的三个基本指标是旅游人数、旅游收入和旅游支出、旅游者停留天数。

3. 可随意支配收入水平是决定个人旅游需求的最重要的物质基础。所以说凡可随意支配收入达到一定水平的人都会外出旅游。

4. 心理类型为近多中心型的旅游者往往是新旅游地的发现者和首访者,是旅游者大军的先头部队。

5. 旅游需求是人类最基本的需求之一,是"刚需",因此对政治环境和经济环境的变化并不敏感。

Part III　Case Study
第三部分　案例研究

旅游需求的增长与变化——以佛罗里达中心地区为例

分析要点

1. 海湾战争从哪几个方面影响佛罗里达州的旅游需求?
2. 影响银发市场旅游需求的最主要因素是什么?
3. 根据本案例,你认为家庭市场对于主题公园这类旅游产品的价格弹性如何?
4. 会展、会议旅游者的旅游需求与其他旅游者的需求相比有何异同?
5. 为何佛罗里达州人口结构特征会对奥兰多中心地区的旅游总需求产生很大的影响?
6. 从需求的角度出发,对比分析美国佛罗里达州和我国海南岛的旅游现状和市场前景。

> **相关理论和问题**
>
> 1. 家庭生命周期和生活方式(Family life cycle and life style)
> 2. 消费者行为(Consumer behavior)
> 3. 旅游需求弹性(Elasticity of tourism demand)
> 4. 旅游需求价格曲线(Price curve of tourism demand)

佛罗里达州每年接待游客人数位居美国第二,仅次于加利福尼亚州。它每年吸引4000多万的游客,其中大约有700万国际游客。旅游业已成为佛罗里达州最大的产业。1991年,佛罗里达州的国内旅游收入估计为490亿美元左右,创造了150万个工作岗位,大约雇用了本州24%的劳动力。

20世纪50—60年代,佛罗里达因其阳光地带的吸引物在银发市场名声大振,尤其以迈阿密和东南部的其他地区最为出名。许多游客甚至在那里定居下来,结果使佛罗里达州成为美国退休居民比例最高的州。

20世纪70—80年代,旅游发展的重心转移到佛罗里达州的中心地区奥兰多一带。一个主要的催化剂是20多个主题公园的建设,特别是沃尔特·迪斯尼世界的开业。这些旅游产品主要不是吸引银发市场,而是迎合大部分有孩子的家庭。佛罗里达州吸引国际游客的众多旅游资源促进了旅游交通业的增长和当地机场等相关设施的建设,同时也大大促进了当地房地产业的发展。

20世纪80—90年代,会展旅游呈现快速增长的势头。究其原因主要有两个:第一,旅游淡季时存在大量的住宿设施和会议设施可以利用;第二,许多代表(大约占70%)希望把商务旅游与娱乐活动结合在一起,同时带上他们的伴侣,乃至整个家庭。奥兰多地区的公司会议、协会会议、交易会和展览会蓬勃发展。

佛罗里达中心地区的旅游统计

年份	佛罗里达州接待旅游者人数(单位:百万)	佛罗里达中心地区接待旅游者人数(单位:百万)	佛罗里达中心地区客房数(间)	入住率(%)
1988	36.7	10.8	64500	76.5
1989	38.6	12.0	69500	82.0
1990	40.9	13.6	76300	77.6
1991	40.3	13.1	82500	71.6
1992	41.0	14.0	88000	73.0

其中,1992年的数据为估计值。1991年接待旅游者人数和酒店入住率的下滑主要是由于海湾战争所引起的。1992年佛罗里达中心地区大约有13500间酒店客房主要是服务于会展、会议旅游市场,并提供大约150万平方英尺的会议和展览场地。会展、会议旅游者人数大约有250万。

大型主题公园的接待情况(1991)

主题公园	所有者	接待旅游者人数(单位:百万)
沃尔特·迪斯尼世界/EPCOT	迪斯尼公司	28
环球影城主题公园	美国环球影业公司	6
海洋世界	安海斯—布希公司	3.4

佛罗里达各细分市场旅游需求的特征如下:

银发市场停留时间最长,但是由于收入固定,他们的需求常常具有较高的价格弹性。他们对佛罗里达东南部旅游产品的需求高于其他地区的旅游产品。但是,总需求相对稳定,长期增长的主要动力来自美国人口的老龄化趋势。主要竞争对手是那些气候相近并提供类似旅游产品的目的地。

家庭市场更愿意到佛罗里达中心地区去旅游,大部分热衷于主题公园这类旅游产品,平均停留时间为6天。其中有一半住在酒店或者汽车旅馆,超过70%的游客选择私人驾车来佛罗里达。度假旅游产品的销售主要受到自由预算的约束。需求的季节性波动与学校和大专院校的假期相吻合。主题公园的门票费是旅游者主要花费的项目。这项预算对旅游者非常重要,以至于在出发之前都会事先了解主题公园的门票价格。但是几乎没有竞争对手与大型主题公园争夺这个细分市场。

国际游客通常购买包价旅游产品,并享受旅游产品经营者的折扣价格,因此从每位游客所获得的收入有所降低。但是,他们为航空服务、公共交通和汽车出租等创造需求,并且在购买旅游纪念品上的花费比国内游客要多。各个客源国平均每位旅游者的需求量有所不同,因此,某些市场需求的下降可能通过另一些市场需求的增加得到弥补。

会展、会议代表停留时间较短,平均停留4.2天,但是需求的价格弹性较低,特别是那些可扣除税款的开支更是如此。会议、会展旅游需求主要是随着美国商务活动的变化而变化,与人均收入关系不大。据奥兰多旅游局的数据,1989年奥兰多的商务游客人均花费为623美元。目前,奥兰多是美国最主要的会议、会展城市之一,但是存在很多潜在竞争对手。

总的来说,奥兰多中心地区的旅游者大约有60%—65%是来自美国东北部。因此,美国东北部经济状况的变化对佛罗里达中心地区的旅游总需求具有很大的影响。佛罗里达州人口结构特征对奥兰多中心地区的旅游总需求的影响是显而易见的。由于佛罗里达州人口结构的特征,造成奥兰多中心地区的许多旅游部门缺乏劳动力,因此只要增加生产所需的劳动力的投入,佛罗里达旅游业的进一步扩张并非难事。

资料来源:旅游需求的增长与变化——以佛罗里达中心地区为例.亚德里恩.布尔.旅游经济学(第2版)[M].东北财经大学出版社,2004。

Part IV Reading Box
第四部分 阅读与分析

Resistance of the Travel Distance

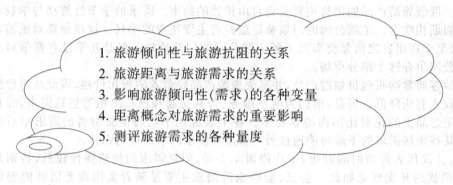

阅读分析要点

1. 旅游倾向性与旅游抗阻的关系
2. 旅游距离与旅游需求的关系
3. 影响旅游倾向性(需求)的各种变量
4. 距离概念对旅游需求的重要影响
5. 测评旅游需求的各种量度

Specifically speaking, the demand for travel to a particular destination is closely connected with the person's propensity to travel and the resistance of the link between origin and destination areas.[1] The stronger the propensity, the higher the demand will be. The higher the resistance, the lower the demand will be. We can use a function to show this relationship.

D=f (propensity, resistance)

where D is demand.

Propensity is a person's tendency to travel—in other words, how strong his desire to travel is, what types of travel he chooses to experience, and where he wishes to visit. There are several personal factors which have a great effect on travel propensity. They include a person's psychological factors, travel motivation and socioeconomic status. Therefore, to understand both **psychographic and demographic variables** is crucial to the estimate of a person's propensity to travel.[2] Propensity is directly related to demand. The stronger the propensity, the higher the demand will be.

Resistance, on the other hand, is concerned with the attraction of various destinations. This factor is closely related to variables such as **economic distance**, **cultural distance**, the cost of tourist services at destination, the quality of service at destination, effectiveness of advertising and promotion, and seasonality. The higher the resistance, the lower the demand will be.

The following illustrates the relationship between propensity, resistance, and demand, in terms of these variables as just described:

Demand=f (propensity, resistance)

PROPENSITY DEPENDS ON: RESISTANCE DEPENDS ON:
Motivation   Geographical distance
Psychographics   Psychological distance
Demographics (socioeconomic status) Cultural distance

Marketing effectiveness Economical distance
Others Cost of service
 Quality of service
 Seasonality
 Others

Economic Distance

Economic distance is connected with the time and money spent in traveling. It is obvious that if the economic distance is high, the resistance for that destination will also be high.[3] That is to say, the individuals will be less willing to visit that destination. As a result, demand will decrease. On the contrary, if the economic distance is low, demand will increase. We can find many good examples of this, such as the introduction of the jet plane in 1959 and the wide-bodied jets in the late 1960s.

Cultural Distance

The origin region a tourist comes from may own a culture different from the culture at the destination area. This difference is called cultural distance. Generally speaking, people like to visit those places with similar cultures. So if there is a big gap between the culture in origin region and in host region, people are more likely to resist this destination. In other words, the greater the cultural distance, the greater the resistance will be. Sometimes, however, the relationship might be different. For example, an allocentric person may prefer to travel to a destination with higher cultural distance to experience this extreme difference rather than to visit a place with similar cultures.[4]

Cost of Service

If the cost of services at a destination is high, the tourist will be reluctant to go traveling there, so the demand will be low. This relationship is similar to that between the price of a good or service and demand for it.

Quality of Service

It is obvious that if the quality of service at a destination is high, it will help to attract more tourists. Therefore, the resistance will be low and the demand will be high. However, It is hard to evaluate the matter of quality. For one thing, different people hold different standard to judge whether the quality is good or not. For another, without previous travel experience at a destination, a tourist cannot accurately judge the quality of services there.[5] They can only make a selection according to the supposed quality of service. So a destination must be very careful to present a true image to tourists.

Seasonality

It is easy to understand the effect of seasonality on demand. Whether the demand for a given destination is high or not will depend on the time of the year. Take the Jiuzhaigou Valley as an example. The demand will be at the highest level in July, August and October. At other times, the resistance will be high.

Demand and supply are closely related to each other. Supply can affect demand and vice versa. So the tourism planners should take both elements into consideration in order to decide whether the supply at a particular destination should be increased to meet the demand or not.[6] We can judge actual demand according to the following measures: 1. Visitor arrivals; 2. Visitor-days or visitor-nights; 3. Amounts spent. However, the demand can change easily at any time while the supply is rather inflexible.[7] Therefore, it is always a hot potato for the tourism marketers to keep the balance between them.

New Words

resistance	n.	阻力
reluctant	adj.	勉强的,不情愿的
demographic	adj.	人口统计的
seasonality	n.	季节性
variable	n.	变量
vice versa		反过来也是一样的
psychographic	adj.	心理的
inflexible	adj.	强硬的,刚性的

Key Terms

travel propensity	旅游倾向
quality of service	服务质量
visitor arrival	游客抵达人数
marketing effectiveness	市场营销的有效性
economic distance	经济距离
cultural distance	文化距离

Notes

1. Specifically speaking, the demand for travel to a particular destination is closely connected with the person's propensity to travel and the resistance of the link between origin and destination areas.
   具体来说,到某一个旅游目的地的需求与其旅游倾向性以及旅游客源地和旅游目的地之间的抗阻大小有密切的关系。

2. Therefore, to understand both psychographic and demographic variables is crucial to the estimate of a person's propensity to travel.
   因此,对心理和人口统计变量的了解对评价一个人的旅游倾向非常重要。

3. It is obvious that if the economic distance is high, the resistance for that destination will also be high.
   很显然,经济距离越长,去往目的地旅游的阻碍就越大。

4. For example, an allocentric person may prefer to travel to a destination with higher cultural distance to experience this extreme difference rather than to visit a place with similar cultures.
   例如,一个多中心型的人可能更喜欢到文化距离更远的目的地旅游,去经历这种完全不同的文化,而不太愿去和自己国家拥有相似文化的地方旅游。

5. For another, without previous travel experience at a destination, a tourist cannot accurately judge the quality of services there.
   另一方面,没有事先在目的地旅游的经验,一个旅游者不能准确地判断那里的旅游服务质量怎么样。

6. So the tourism planners should take both elements into consideration in order to decide whether the supply at a particular destination should be increased to meet the demand or not.
   因此,为了决定是否应该提高某个旅游目的地的供给来满足旅游者的需求,旅游规划者应该将这两个因素都予以考虑。

7. We can judge actual demand according to the following measures: 1. Visitor

arrivals; 2. Visitor-days or visitor-nights; 3. Amounts spent. However, the demand can change easily at any time while the supply is rather inflexible.

我们可以根据以下的衡量标准来判断实际的旅游需求：1. 旅游者抵达人数；2. 旅游者旅游天数或者旅游者过夜人数；3. 旅游者总的花费。但是，需求在任何的时间都可能改变，但旅游供给却是刚性的，不能轻易改变。

Topic discussion

1. The demand for travel to a destination is closely connected with the person's propensity to travel and the resistance. Can you tell the details of the relationship between travel propensity and resistance?
   _____

2. Can you illustrate the factors that influence the travel propensity of people? Give some examples.
   _____

3. Resistance is concerned with the attraction of various destinations. What are the variables that are closely related to resistance of travel?
   _____

4. How does the economic distance influence the People's decision making?
   _____

5. How does the cultural distance influence the People's decision making?
   _____

6. How do cost of services and quality of service influence the demand for tourism?
   _____

7. Demand and supply are closely related to each other. Supply can affect demand and vice versa. Can you give some suggestions about how to keep the balance between demand and supply for tourism?
   _____

【即学即用】

With reference to the theory, information or approach applied in the Reading Box, have a case study of the resistance of travel distance. You may take a trip from Chengdu to Jiuzhaigou or any trip you have taken for an example. Make presentation of your study in Chinese or in English using PPT.

【学习资源库】

为了掌握本章更多的相关专业知识，请您登录 http://sicnu.edu.cn/，点击国家双语教学示范课程《旅游学概论》，进入网络学堂查询相关资料。

Chapter Review 本章小结

This chapter has described the tourist motivation, determinants of demand and the buying decision process of a tourist; discussed the interrelationship between the lifestyle and the family life cycle. Demand for tourism at the individual level can be treated as a consumption process that is influenced by a number of factors. Motivation and determinants of demand are some of important factors that exert an influence on the decision-making process of a tourist. The demand for tourism is connected with both the person's travel propensity and the resistance of the link between the origin and the destination. Generally, travel propensity is associated with psychographic and demographic variables while resistance is always connected with economic distance, cultural distance, quality of service, promotion, and seasonality. The stronger the propensity is, the higher the demand will be. The higher the resistance is, the lower the demand will be.

Part V Additional Know-how of Tourism
第五部分 旅游知识扩展

【关键术语】

Tourism demand: the total number of persons who travel, or wish to travel, to use tourist facilities and services at places away from their places of work and residence

旅游需求：离开自己工作和居住的地方外出旅游或具有旅游的愿望，并使用旅游设施的人数总和。

Effective or actual demand: the actual number of participants in tourism who are travelling

有效需求或现实需求：指参加旅游的实际人数，或指那些正在旅游的现实旅游者。

Suppressed demand: It is made up of that section of the population who do not travel for some reason. (1) potential demand: those who will travel at some future date if they experience a change in their circumstance. (2) deferred demand: a demand postponed because of a problem in the supply environment. (3) no demand those who simply do not wish to travel or are unable to travel, constituting a category of no demand.

受抑制的需求：由人口中因各种原因不能参加旅游的部分构成：(1) 潜在需求：指如果某些条件发生变化，在未来时间将参加旅游的人们；(2) 延缓需求：指由于供给条件出问题而推迟的需求；(3) 无需求：指那些不愿意或不能参加旅游的人，这类人构成无需求。

Travel propensity: indicators of effective demand in any particular population considers the penetration of tourism trips in a population. (1) Net travel propensity refers to the percentage of the population that takes at least one trip in a given period of time. (2) Gross travel propensity gives the total number of tourism trips taken as a percentage of the population.

旅游倾向：测定人口中有效需求的指标，直接考察旅游在人口中的渗透程度。分两类：(1) 净旅游倾向：指在一定的时间内至少参加一次旅游的人数占人口总数的比例。(2) 总旅游倾向：指参加旅游的总人数占人口总数的比例。

LPS models (limited problem-solving models): LPS models are applicable to repeat or mundane purchases with a low level of consumer involvement.

有限解决问题模型：有限解决问题模型适用于购买重复性和日常性的产品,消费者对购买的关注程度很低。

EPS models（extended problem-solving models）：EPS models apply to purchases associated with high levels of perceived risk and involvement，and where the information search and evaluation of alternatives plays an important part in the purchasing decision.

深化解决问题模型：深化解决问题模型适用于高风险意识和高关注程度的购买决策,收集信息和评估备选方案在购买决策中起重要的作用。

Distance-decay：in tourism，the tendency of inbound flows to decline as origin regions become more distant from the destination

距离衰减：在旅游中,客源地距目的地越远,抵达旅游目的地的流量就呈下降趋势。

【知识链接】

1. 旅游需求和旅游者需求

由于旅游产品划分为核心旅游产品和组合旅游产品两种类型,因此,有关旅游需求的定义就自然要发生某种分化。核心旅游产品可以满足的主要是旅游者对愉悦的追求,而组合旅游产品常常可以满足旅游者的全部需要,从这一点看,可以建立两个有关需求的概念:旅游需求和旅游者需求。

旅游需求是指在一定时期内,核心旅游产品的各种可能的价格与在这些价格水平上,潜在旅游者愿意并能够购买的数量之间的关系。而旅游需求量是指人们在一定时间内愿意按照一定价格而购买某一种核心旅游产品的数量。

旅游者需求是指在一定时期内,组合旅游产品的各种可能的价格与这些价格水平上,潜在旅游者愿意并能够购买的数量之间的关系。而旅游者需求量是指人们一定时间内愿意按照一定价格而购买某一种组合旅游产品的数量。

2. 旅游需求的特点

首先,旅游需求是属于一种弹性比较大的需求。旅游需求主要是一种精神性需求,以追求愉悦为目的,以获得愉悦为满足。相对于人的一般消费品需求,旅游需求基本上属于奢侈性需求,因此,总体上来说,具有较大的弹性。

其次,旅游需求存在明显的季节性波动。季节性波动是指现象的发生在时间规律性上的强弱反差。旅游需求之所以会呈现这样的模式,是由旅游吸引物和旅游者双方面的原因造成的。

另外,旅游需求是一种关联性很强的需求。尽管旅游需求在狭义是指对可供旅游者作审美欣赏和愉悦体验的旅游产品的需求,但通过对旅游产品的结构分析就已经看出,当旅游产品利益成分被大量地、频繁地追加其他利益时,旅游需求的内涵和外延都在扩展。旅游需求是一种具有内在扩张性的需求,它的实现总是以各种连带性需求的满足为前提或结果,因此连带性很强。

【小思考】

1. 当旅游产品价格和闲暇时间同时发生变化时,旅游需求量是如何发生的变化的?

参考阅读：

闲暇时间是旅游需求产生的必要条件,同时,它也是旅游消费活动的重要组成部分,因此,闲暇时间尽管不属于经济的范畴,但它同旅游需求也具有密切的联系,会直接影响到旅游需求量的变化。当人们的闲暇时间增多时,人们对旅游产品的需求量会相应的增加;当人们的闲暇时间减少时,人们对旅游产品的需求量则相应减少;当人们完全没有闲暇时间时,人们对旅游产品的实际需求就等于零。旅游需求与人们的闲暇时间基本上呈同方向变化的关系。

上述讨论是在假定其他相关因素不变的情况下,分析旅游需求与某一影响因素之间的对应变动关系。如果这些相关因素发生改变,需求曲线 D-D 在坐标图上的位置就要发生移动,但需求曲线 D-D 本身不会发生变化,这种移动变化如下图所示。

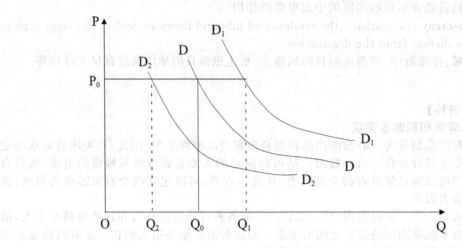

如上图所示,在旅游产品价格 P_0 不变的情况下,当人们的闲暇时间增加时,人们就会增加对旅游产品的需求量,引起需求曲线 D-D 向右移动到 D_1-D_1,并使旅游产品的需求量从 Q_0 增加到 Q_1;反之,在旅游产品价格 P_0 不变的情况下,当人们的闲暇时间减少时,人们则会减少对旅游产品的需求量,引起需求量曲线 D-D 向左移动到 D_2-D_2,并使旅游产品的需求量从 Q_0 下降到 Q_2。

2. 旅游者一般是在哪些时间阶段做出以上决策?旅游企业如何开展市场营销?

参考阅读:
在考虑简单商品的需求时,经济学家通常假定个体消费者必须(而且只需)做出两个决策:是否需要购买某一类产品;在各种替代品之间选择购买某一种产品。然而旅游产品的个体需求通常涉及更为复杂的决策过程。旅游者购买产品时需要做出几个层次的选择,这些选择并不一定就要按照顺序来做。只有当已知个人需求决策的结果时,才可能去测算出旅游产品的总需求。以下是旅游者决策的几个方面:

- 活动类型选择。如观光度假、冬季滑雪、信徒朝圣等等旅游类型。
- 目的地选择。游客必须在目的地之间做出选择。目的地可能是单一地点,也可能是几个地点的组合,甚至是一个"移动"的目的地,如乘坐游轮观光。
- 出行交通工具的选择。旅游类型和选择的目的地经常决定了特定的交通工具,或者只有一种交通工具可供选择。但是,在旅行时游客会考虑旅行的速度、便利、舒适和安全等,其中,价格和时间是两个主要制约条件。
- 住宿和景区的选择。正如交通工具选择那样,其他方面的旅游决策可能已经限制了住宿的选择。由于住宿费用可能是目的地消费支出中最大的一项,因此,住宿的相对价格经常影响旅游者对目的地的看法,从而影响目的地的需求。在大多数情况下,游客在选择目的地时已经做出景区的选择。
- 购买方式的选择。游客最终面临的重要决策就是选择购买方式。这不仅仅是一个选择哪个旅游零售商的简单问题,而且还涉及如下选择:购买包价旅游产品,还是购买零散的服务? 直接向旅游供给商购买旅游产品,还是通过代理商购买? 向旅游批发商或者旅游经营商购买,还是向零售商购买?

Part VI　Further Readings
第六部分　课外阅读

如果您想进一步学习本章的内容,探讨旅游需求的特点,怎样有效地开拓旅游市场,建议您阅读以下学者的著作和论文。

一、中文部分

［1］亚德里恩·布尔著;龙江智译. 旅游经济学[M]. 大连:东北财经大学出版社,2004.
［2］田里,牟红. 旅游经济学[M]. 北京:清华大学出版社,2007.
［3］滕丽,王铮,蔡砥. 中国城市居民旅游需求差异分析[J]. 旅游学刊,2004,(04).
［4］王艳平. 对"旅游需求"概念及其影响因子分析的深度认识[J]. 桂林旅游高等专科学校学报,2005,(03).
［5］朱华. 世界旅游客源地对四川省入境旅游的影响[J]. 乐山师范学院学报,2008,(03).
［6］卢昆. 知觉距离对消费者旅游决策的影响[J]. 桂林旅游高等专科学校学报,2003,(04).
［7］张宏梅,陆林,章锦河. 感知距离对旅游目的地之形象影响的分析—以五大旅游客源城市对苏州周庄旅游形象的感知为例[J]. 人文地理,2005,(06).
［8］王一兵. 基于随机效用模型的黄金周旅游需求分析[J]. 统计与决策,2006,(12).
［9］李坚作. 消费者评价的旅游需求与旅游市场对应关系实证[J]. 求索,2006,(06).
［10］孙睿君,钟笑寒. 运用旅行费用模型估计典型消费者的旅游需求及其收益:对中国的实证研究[J]. 统计研究,2005,(12).

二、英文部分

[1] Haiyan Song, Gang Li. Tourism demand modelling and forecasting-A review of recent research[J]. *Tourism Management*,2008,29(2):203—220.
[2] Chokri Ouerfelli. Co-integration analysis of quarterly European tourism demand in Tunisia[J]. *Tourism Management*,2008,29(1):127—137.
[3] Kevin K. F. Wong, Haiyan Song, Kaye S. Chon. Bayesian models for tourism demand forecasting[J]. *Tourism Management*,2006,27(5):773—780.
[4] Zhongwei Han, Ramesh Durbarry, M. Thea Sinclair. Modelling US tourism demand for European destinations[J]. *Tourism Management*,2006,27(1):1—10.
[5] Fong-Lin Chu. Forecasting tourism demand: a cubic polynomial approach[J]. *Tourism Management*,2004,25(2):209—218.
[6] Adee Athiyaman. Knowledge development in tourism: tourism demand research[J]. *Tourism Management*,1997,18(4):221—228.
[7] Sue Beeton. Recreational tourism: demands and impacts[J]. *Annals of Tourism Research*,2005,32(1):286—288.
[8] Ramesh Durbarry, M. Thea Sinclair. Market shares analysis: The case of French tourism demand[J]. *Annals of Tourism Research*,2003,30(4):927—941.

[9] Sarath Divisekera. A model of demand for international tourism[J]. *Annals of Tourism Research*, 2003, 30(1):31—49.

[10] Fong-Lin Chu. Forecasting tourism demand in Asian-Pacific countries[J]. *Annals of Tourism Research*, 1998, 25(3):597—615.

Chapter 4　Tourist Attractions
第四章　旅游吸引物

Learning objects：学习目标
- Study the authenticity of attractions within the O-D pair based on the tourism system (Leiper's model) 根据旅游系统（Leiper 模型），研究 O-D 对中旅游吸引物的真实性
- Appreciate different interpretations of authenticity and its application in hospitality industry 阐述真实性的不同解释以及真实性理论在接待业中的运用
- Understand the consequence because of the different perception of attractions and performance between tourists and performers 了解旅游者和表演者对旅游吸引物和表演不同的感知所产生的后果
- Describe the process of commercialization of tourist products and its presentation 陈述旅游产品商品化的演进过程以及不同表现
- Have a break-down of the commercialization of cultures and its serious consequence 分析文化商品化及其严重的后果
- Appreciate the application of frontstage and backstage for protection of the tourist resorts 了解"前台"和"后台"理论在保护旅游景区中的运用
- Understand the application of virtual reality in tourism and its benefits and defects in the application 了解"虚拟的真实"在旅游中的运用，其运用中的利与弊

Ability goals：能力目标
- Case Study 案例分析云南民族村主题公园如何走出困境
- Reading Box 阅读分析 Virtual Reality 虚拟的真实

Part I Text
第一部分 课文

Tourist Attractions

【教学要点】

知识要点	掌握程度	相关章节
authenticity of the attraction 吸引物的真实性	重点掌握	本课文与第 1 单元、第 3 单元、第 6 单元、第 10 单元、第 12 单元、第 15 单元相关内容有联系。
different perception of attractions 对吸引物不同的感知	重点掌握	
objective authenticity, constructive authenticity and existential authenticity 客观主义真实性、构建主义真实性、存在主义真实性	一般了解	
cultural commercialization 文化商品化	重点掌握	
frontstage and backstage 前台与后台	一般了解	

Tourist attraction is the most important pull factor in attracting tourists to travel to destination. Social researchers are concerned about whether tourists can appreciate real attractions in a destination. It seems that destinations often provide tourists with some invented attractions or stage some events that are seldom connected with the culture of the local community. Tourists are often misled and go through a journey without enjoying the real things in the destination. This, for tourists, is a **loss of authenticity**.¹

Authenticity of the attraction

In Britain many historic sites put on lifelike representations of different historical periods. Thus tourists can have an idea of the life at those times. The tourists know that they are not real, but the host community still tries every means, even using smells, to make these representations as real as possible.² For example, in the Jorvik Centre in York tourists are offered to visit a recreated Viking village in a "time" car to relive the life of the Vikings.

Of course **genuine experience** is not the choice of all tourists; some of them take part in tourism activities just for entertainment and excitement. The best situation is that both the local community and the visitor think that what they have experienced is real. However, taking into account the large number of mass tourists, the destinations can hardly satisfy tourists if they do not stage big events and provide them with certain aspects of historic attractions.³ **Tourist-resident** tensions may occur when they have a different understanding of the authenticity about the performance at the destination (see Figure 4.1).

Residents' presentation of attraction	Tourists' perception of attraction	
	Genuine	Contrived

Genuine	Positive impact (both parties recognize authentic nature)	Negative impact (tourists believe that a genuine production is contrived)
Contrived	Negative impact (tourist misled or confused into mistaking the contrived for the genuine)	Positive impact (both parties recognize inauthentic nature)

Figure 4.1 Resident tourist cross perception of attractions

The destination should try to offer tourists events which truly reflect the current life of the local community; otherwise, tourists may doubt whether the events or attractions are authentic or not. Performances on the stage which aim to show the history and culture of the local community help tourists understand the conspicuous features of the **community's heritage** without intruding upon the private space of local residents and disturbing their lives. These performances can also make local people recognize the value of their own history and culture and fill them with a sense of pride.[4] However, if tourists think that what the destination offers does not accord with what they expect to see, we can easily imagine their responses and the consequences. A case in point is the disappearance of many ethnic villages in China. Thus, we can see the authenticity issue is of great importance to the sustainable development of the tourism.

Commercialization

With the rapid development of the mass tourism, the tourist market also develops very quickly. As a result, the destination has become highly commercialized. It seems a positive advance at first glance because it brings profits to a product that was originally no monetary value at all, such as culture.[5] However, if too much emphasis is put on the economic effects, the intrinsic qualities and meanings of cultural artifacts and performances would be somewhat ignored. Then, the culture may be changed at the expense of its original importance to meet the demand of the tourist market.[6] The development of tourism can result in **cultural commercialization** in several ways, and we outline the process of the cultural commercialization in the following:

1. If tourists happen to go to a place which is rarely visited, the local community will receive them warmly and invite them to take part in genuine local ceremonies free of charge. Sometimes in order to show their respect they will give tourists some real artifacts made by the local residents as gifts.

2. Tourists visit a place more frequently and the local people have less interest or curiosity about them. Tourists are allowed to pay money to watch local ceremonies and buy some genuine artifacts at a low price.

3. The community has become a regular destination for a large number of tourists. In order to meet the demand of the tourist market, ceremonies are changed and performances are put on regularly. Thus, more attention is paid to the man-made elements of the attractions while authenticity is neglected. If the market allows, prices will be set as high as possible. And there are a large amount of cheaply produced souvenirs available in the market. At the same time, measures may be taken to protect authentic elements and displays of the culture.

4. Commercialization and modernization have led to the total loss of the wholeness of the original culture. Even the most sacred and profound aspects of the culture have been greatly influenced by commercialization.

Even though the residents of a destination may make a big profit from tourism by the fourth stage, it is argued that serious social problems may appear because of the loss of **cultural identity** and the subsequent **breakdown of traditional standards** and structures that helped to maintain social stability. According to Greenwood, "Commercialization of culture in effect robs people of the very meanings by which they organize their lives." Besides, there are many problems appearing in the community. For example, how to distribute income? How much the performers and producers (who may have formerly provided their services voluntarily) should be paid? How to deal with other issues related to the market when the society does not have the ability to handle them. These may lead to the explosion of conflicts. The issue becomes worse because the explosion may happen in a relatively short period of time as tourism spreads in an area so that the community cannot make a timely response and adopt effective and appropriate measures.[7]

Frontstage and backstage

As mentioned above, the commercialization process may have some negative effects on the destination. There are various measures that can be adopted to reduce these effects. One of them is the introduction of the concept of frontstage and backstage. As MacCannell points out, distinctions should be made between frontstage and backstage within the destination, whether they are implied or clearly expressed. The **frontstage** is an area where the large number of tourists can enjoy themselves by watching commercial and possibly changed shows and displays, while the **backstage** is an area where local people live and maintain their traditions, beliefs, and lifestyle.[8] Within the backstage tourists can appreciate the "real life" of the community and "authentic" culture. If both tourists and local residents are aware of the distinctions and try to maintain them, the community can, on one hand, gain economic benefits and, on the other hand, preserve the local way of life.

Although the **distinction between frontstage and backstage** may not be very clear, we can distinguish them with some kinds of barriers. These barriers include the crude canvas screens set up to prevent their lives from being disturbed by tourists, walls, ditches and "do not enter" signs that attempt to keep tourists out of the backstage.[9] Moreover, time can also be used to distinguish them. For example, tourists are allowed to some areas during certain hours while only local people are permitted at other times. In order to adjust contact between local residents and tourists, a comprehensive plan has been adopted all over the country, in which the frontstage/backstage principle plays a very important role.

The distinction, however, may lead to some results out of our expectations. In some native Indian communities in North America, we can find that the frontstage space are filled with some traditional cultural artifacts which are no longer of use for local people but still very attractive for tourists. Contrary to it, we may see some cultural landscape in the backstage space which has some features in common with that found in other communities of a similar size and location. Of course, the frontstage/backstage distinction can be applied not only in traditional communities but also in more developed countries. Some governments in these countries divide their cities into different zones so that the residential areas will not be disturbed by tourism activities and businesses, thus backstage territories are clearly marked out.[10]

New Words

tension	n.	紧张,紧张状态
canvas	n.	帆布,网形粗布

conspicuous	*adj.*	显著的,显眼的
comprehensive	*adj.*	全面的,广泛的
intrinsic	*adj.*	固有的,本身的
expectation	*n.*	期待,预期,期望
backpacker	*n.*	背包族,徒步旅行者
residential	*adj.*	住宅的,居住的
crude	*adj.*	天然的,未加工的
ceremony	*n.*	典礼,仪式

Key Terms

host community	东道主社区	original culture	本源文化
historic attraction	历史吸引物	cultural identity	文化认同
tourist market	旅游市场	frontstage space	前台空间

Notes

1. Tourists are often misled and go through a journey without enjoying the real things in the destination. This, for tourists, is a loss of authenticity.
   旅游者常常被误导,在目的地不能获得真实的体验,对旅游者来说,就失去了旅游的真实性。

2. The tourists know that they are not real, but the host community still tries every means, even using smells, to make these representations as real as possible.
   旅游者知道这些东西不是真实的,但是当地社区仍然千方百计,甚至利用气味,使这些事物尽量显得真实。

3. However, taking into account the large number of mass tourists, the destinations can hardly satisfy tourists if they do not stage big events and provide them with certain aspects of historic attractions.
   然而,考虑到大量的大众旅游者要到目的地旅游,如果目的地不搞重大的节事活动表演,不提供某种有历史意味的吸引物,那么游客的需求就很难得到满足。

4. These performances can also make local people recognize the value of their own history and culture and fill them with a sense of pride.
   那些表演也能使当地居民认识到自身的历史和文化价值,并为之感到骄傲。

5. It seems a positive advance at first glance because it brings profits to a product that was originally no monetary value at all, such as culture.
   起初看来它似乎是积极进步的,因为它为原本毫无商业价值的产品,例如文化带来了利益。

6. Then, the culture may be changed at the expense of its original importance to meet the demand of the tourist market.
   于是,文化可能被改变,以失去其原真性的重要价值为代价来满足旅游市场的需求。

7. The issue becomes worse because the explosion may happen in a relatively short period of time as tourism spreads in an area so that the community cannot make a timely response and adopt effective and appropriate measures.
   随着旅游在一个区域的发展,在一个相对较短的时期内,可能会发生游客人数过多的情况,以至于当地社区不能对此做出及时反应,也不能采取有效、恰当的措施,使问题变得更加糟糕。

8. The frontstage is an area where the large number of tourists can enjoy themselves

by watching commercial and possibly changed shows and displays, while the backstage is an area where local people live and maintain their traditions, beliefs and lifestyle.

前台是指广大游客观赏商业化、经过改编的表演的地方；而后台指的是当地人居住生活，保持其传统、信仰和生活方式的地方。

9. These barriers include the crude canvas screens set up to prevent their lives from being disturbed by tourists, walls, ditches and "do not enter" signs that attempt to keep tourists out of the backstage.

这些障碍物包括为了不让居民的生活被旅游者打扰而设置的粗帆布帷幕以及不让游客进入后台区域的墙、沟渠和"禁止入内"的标语。

10. Some governments in these countries divide their cities into different zones so that the residential areas will not be disturbed by tourism activities and businesses, thus backstage territories are clearly marked out.

这些国家的政府将城市分为不同的区域，防止居民区被旅游和商业活动打扰，因而将后台区域清楚地标示出来。

Exercise

1. Fill in the blanks with proper words to complete the following statements.

| authenticity | about | real |
| with | tourists | backstage |

(1) Social researchers are concerned _____ whether tourists can appreciate real attractions in a destination.

(2) Of course genuine experience is not the choice of all _____; some of them take part in tourism activities just for entertainment and excitement.

(3) However, if tourists think that what the destination offers does not accord _____ what they expect to see, we can easily imagine their responses and the consequences.

(4) Sometimes in order to show their respect they will give tourists some _____ artifacts made by the local residents as gifts.

(5) We may see some cultural landscape in the _____ space which has some features in common with that found in other communities of a similar size and location.

(6) Tourist-resident tensions may occur when they have a different understanding of the _____ about the performance at the destination.

2. Questions for discussion

1. What does the loss of authenticity mean for tourists?

2. Why is the authenticity issue important for the sustainable development of the tourism?

3. How does the culture in the destination gradually become commercialized?

4. What effects does the cultural commercialization have on the destination?

5. What are the frontstage and the backstage? How can we distinguish frontstage and backstage?

Part II Guided Reading
第二部分 课文导读

旅游吸引物是吸引旅游者前往旅游目的地的重要因素,然而,旅游者能否在目的地感受到目的地吸引物的"真实性"呢?这一直是社会学家所关心的问题。"真实性"(Authenticity)一词源于希腊语,意思是"自己做的"、"最初的"。真实性概念最初用于描述博物馆的艺术展品,用来说明博物馆的一切展品是否真实,其价值是否与某个价格相符合,之后被借用到哲学领域的人类存在主义的研究。19 世纪 70 年代,旅游者开始重视"真实性"的旅游体验,期望获得更真、更深入的旅游体验,"真实性"概念延伸到旅游领域。1973 年,迈肯尼尔在《舞台的真实性》(*Staged Authenticity*)一文中首次将真实性的概念引入到旅游动机、旅游经历的研究中。由于"真实性"这个术语未加清晰界定就被引入旅游研究领域,造成了许多混淆,研究者很多时候是靠直觉来揣摩该术语的含义(谢彦君,2006)。在国内 authenticity 也被翻译成"原真性、原生性、可靠性、准确性、本真性"。

关于旅游研究中的真实性理论,学界主要存在三种观点:客观主义真实性——关注旅游客体的真实性;建构主义真实性——在注重客体真实的基础上强调主体的差异性;存在主义真实性——关注主体体验的真实性。

一、旅游研究中的客观主义真实性

旅游者评判旅游产品是否真实的标准是"它们是否在本地由本地居民根据习俗与传统制造或表演",因此,客观主义真实性和"传统文化"、"原先的"、"原创的"、"独特的"等概念相联系,强调旅游客体的真实性。社会学家迈肯尼尔是客观主义真实性的杰出代表,他的理论基础是:现代生活是不真实的。旅游者寻找纯朴的、原始的、自然的、没有被现代化侵染的东西,而且他们认为只能在别的地方和别的时间发现它们,因为自己所处的社会中没有这些东西,他们总是失望而归。

迈肯尼尔认为"前台"(Frontstage)是旅游者与服务人员接触交往的开放性空间。在现代旅游开发中,东道主将他们的文化当作商品展示给旅游者,并导致东道主社会生活真实性的舞台化。舞台化的前台使旅游者很难体验目的地社会的真实文化。因此"前台"成为追求真实性的旅游者竭力回避的社会空间。"后台"(Backstage)是为前台的表现做准备的封闭性场所,常与事实、亲密、真实相连,是旅游者所追求的。迈肯尼尔认为为了保证前台表演的"真实性"和"可信度",就必须保证后台的"封闭性"和"神秘性"。因此,他为旅游业发展了第三个区——"旅游场合中的舞台真实",并认为现代大多数的旅游经历都是体验舞台事实,即当旅游企业意识到旅游者寻找后台真实性时,就凭借旅游行为的组织化、社会化和机构化,给旅游者提供了一个"装饰过了的后台",误导旅游者,而旅游者却信以为真,其实旅游者所看见的都不是真实的,因为并不是"原先的"、"最初的"、"自然的"。

二、旅游研究中的建构主义真实性

建构主义者注重旅游客体真实性基础上的主观评价,认为世界是多彩的、多元的、弹性的,旅游场景并不是一种不动产,其真实性是观者赋予其上的一种价值评价。旅游客体被旅游者体验为真实时,并不是因为事实就是如此,而是被当作真实性的符号和象征(Culler,1981)。明确提出建构主义真实性概念的是布伦尔,他认为传统的旅游体验真实性很难解释现代旅游体验的现象,旅游经营者可根据旅游者的期望、想象、偏好、信仰等设计景区与组织活动,以达到真实性效果。科恩(Cohen,1988)认为真实性是一个相对的、商榷的概念,并将成为旅游社会学、旅游人类学研究的核心。科恩以迪斯尼为例,解释了即使有些事物最初是不真实的或人工的,但随着时间的流逝慢慢会变成"自然而然的真实"。谢彦君(2006)也比较赞同科恩等人的观点,认为不同的旅游者具有不同的体验追求,对自我体验质量的评价取决于旅游者个人的心理标准。从个体评价标准来看,在一定程度上会满足于眼见为"实"。而只要他满足于此,这种"真实"就是他所要的"真实"。

三、旅游研究中的存在主义真实性

与客观主义真实性、建构主义真实性相比,存在主义真实性关注的是旅游主体,完全否定了旅游客体真实性的重要性和必要性。当客观主义者、建构主义者在争论旅游客体是否真实时,存在主义者认为,即使旅游客体完全是假的,旅游者还可以追求一种真实性,即一种替换了的、自由活动激发的存在本真性。

存在主义者不关心旅游客体真实性,强调旅游者的主观体验,强调旅游主体本真的存在状态,即将真实作为一种感觉,与对本真的自我体验结合起来,借助旅游活动或旅游客体寻找本真的自我。比如在古巴伦巴舞表演中,表演者全身心投入,旅游者积极放松地参与,在跳舞中他们发掘身体潜能,适应舞步节奏,在近乎狂欢的状态下,与整个舞蹈融为一体,并感觉到一个不同的自我,一个完整的、真实的自我。在那一刻舞蹈已成为许多旅游者的整个世界,时间和紧张已被延缓。但事实上,伦巴舞已不是原汁原味的伦巴舞了,它已经融入新的元素,但由于它的创造性和舒畅性,旅游者找到了自我本真。

本文着重阐述了旅游者和当地居民对旅游吸引物真实性感知的差异,指出二者对吸引物真实性感知的差异会对旅游者和当地居民产生不同的影响;本文还介绍了旅游商品化的过程以及前台与后台理论,并利用这一理论保护旅游的真实性。真实性理论的重要意义在于从旅游者旅游动机和旅游者认知角度解释旅游资源,并指导旅游资源开发和游客对旅游产品的体验,提高游客的满意度。如何兼顾旅游客体的真实性和旅游主体的差异性,把握旅游真实性和商品化之间的度,以更好地指导旅游资源开发,满足目标游客的体验需求,将是旅游可持续发展的重要课题。

旅游知识测试

正误判断:请在正确的选题上划√,错误的选题上划×。

1. 任何一个旅游吸引物都有吸引力定向的特点,只能吸引某些市场的一部分,而不可能对全部旅游市场都具有同样大的吸引力。

2. 目的地居民对外来访问者的友善和好客态度也可构成当地的一项旅游吸引物,旅游企业可以利用这种友善和好客态度开发旅游产品。

3. 旅游企业凭借旅游行为的组织化、社会化和机构化,给旅游者提供了一个舞台化的真实表演,而旅游者却信以为真。

4. 游客观看民俗表演,表演者在"做秀",游客也认为是在"做秀",在这种情形下,表演者不会感到不快,但游客会感到不快,游客的旅游体验受到极大损害。

5. 存在主义完全抹杀了旅游真实性的界限,强调此时此刻的自我体验,游客自己认为旅游吸引物是真实的就是真实的。

Part III　Case Study

第三部分　案例研究

云南民族村主题公园如何走出困境

分析要点

1. 云南民族村的旅游资源有什么特点？你是如何看待其真实性的？
2. 从游客体验的角度来说，云南民族村与美国迪斯尼乐园等有什么不同？
3. 从主客关系感知的角度，如何将云南民族村以资源导向转变为市场导向？
4. 哪一种真实性的理论更适合云南民族村的节庆旅游和民俗表演？为什么？
5. 从三种不同的真实性理论，谈谈云南民族村如何陷入困境？

相关理论和问题

1. 旅游的真实性（Authenticity of tourism）
2. 旅游商品化（Commercialization of tourism）
3. 虚拟的真实（Virtual reality）
4. 旅游感知和旅游体验（Perception and experience of tourism）

一、云南民族村的概况

云南民族村位于昆明市南部 6000 米滇池之畔，占地面积 2000 亩；南临滇池、北望昆明、西靠西山，湖光山色秀美无比。民族村拟建 25 个少数民俗村寨，现已建成开放的有傣族、白族、彝族、纳西族、佤族、藏族、壮族、拉祜族、布朗族、哈尼族、德昂族、景颇族等 13 个村寨和一个"摩梭之家"。同时还建有民族团结广场、民族歌舞演出厅、民族蜡像馆、民族博物馆以及风味食品城、宿营娱乐区和游艇码头、循环游览车等一批集观赏、游乐、度假、水上娱乐和服务为一体的综合配套设施。

云南民族村寨采用复原陈列的手法展示云南的民族风情，不同风格的民俗村寨分布其间，错落有致。各民俗村寨多以其在当地的典型形态聚集而成，有充满傣乡浓郁风情的缅寺和巍峨壮观的白塔、大理苍山脚下的"崇圣寺三塔"和"大理街"、纳西族的保护神"三朵神"坐骑塑像和充满强烈鲜明的东巴文化大型浮雕墙以及极富特色的丽江"四方街"、太阳历广场中央高耸的彝家图腾柱、彰显拉祜族祖先的葫芦广场、奇特的摩梭人母系社会形态和德昂族的德龙阳塔等，还可欣赏粗犷豪放的佤族"木鼓舞"、基诺族欢快热烈的基诺族"太阳鼓舞"、婀娜柔美的傣族"孔雀舞"、阿昌族的"象脚舞"、景颇族木脑纵歌、悠扬的壮族山歌以及布朗族的婚俗，品尝藏族同胞的糌粑、酥油茶和青稞酒等，各少数民族丰富多彩的村舍建筑和生产、生活、宗教习俗向游客展示出来。

象征各民族团结向上精神的民族团结广场，汇集了云南各民族优秀的体育、民俗活动精华。在广场上最吸引人的是高耸入云的刀杆，这座刀杆高 30 米，杆上傈僳族青年赤足进行"爬刀杆"表演。结合各少数民族节日，在村里还常常举行白族的"三月街"、傣族的"泼水节"、彝族的"火把节"、傈僳族的"刀杆节"、景颇族的"目脑纵歌"、纳西族的"三朵节"等独具民族特色的民族节日活动，村内的服务和表演全部都由土生土长的少数民族青年来表演。

二、云南民族村的发展特色

1991年,云南省政府和昆明市政府在昆明市海埂农场召开现场会,决定在国营昆明市海埂建设文化风景旅游区(取名云南民族村)以集中展示民俗风情和灿烂文化。

云南民族村的特色主要表现在以下几个方面:

第一,民族村向游客展示了云南十多个少数民族所特有的建筑风格、科技生产工艺、生活习俗、婚姻、信仰、服饰、歌舞等绚丽多彩的民族文化。

第二,再现了傣族泼水节、彝族火把节、白族三月街、纳西族三朵节、哈尼族库扎节、景颇族目脑纵歌节、傈僳族刀杆节、佤族新米节、德昂族浇花节、拉祜族的葫芦节、壮族老人节、摩梭人的朝山节、藏族的藏历年等云南少数民族的节庆活动。

第三,云南民族村挖掘保护了一些因失去载体而在消亡的民族文化,包括历史上曾经存在但现在基本上见不到的民族特有的建筑。

第四,云南民族文化村承办了一系列重大国际国内大型活动。如:"95"世界旅游日中国主会场的庆典活动、"97"中国旅游年云南启动仪式、第六届亚洲民间艺术节大联欢、"99"世界园艺博览会大联欢等。

第五,云南民族村以其旖旎的村寨风光、浓郁的民族风情,吸引了大批海内外游客。

三、云南民族村面临问题

云南民族村由于激烈的市场竞争,与其他民族文化村一样,也面临许多问题和困难。自民族文化村在我国出现以来,在全国各地迅速流行发展,如同中华微缩景观、世界微缩景观、"水族馆"、"仿古街"风靡全国一样,大同小异的各种民俗、民族文化村,文化风情园在全国如雨后春笋,市场竞争十分激烈,产品同质化严重,失去了民俗村的原真性。云南民俗村在开发的过程中,保护了一些民族文化传统,但同时一些人文资源也受到不同程度的破坏,出现一些"伪民俗",传统民族文化并没有得到很好的传承。云南民族村产品开发和市场营销单一,没有根据产品特色进行市场细分,针对不同的游客进行产品设计和市场营销。另外,民族文化商品化现象严重。在云南人文旅游资源开发过程中,许多民族歌舞、仪式、礼俗和手工艺品等文化形式已失去原有的意义,而作为纯商品兜售给旅游者。这些原本只有在特定时间、场合,并按传统内容和方式才能举行的仪式,经过舞台化、程式化的包装,打破了传统的规定,被随时出售给旅游者,内容上也被压缩,在一定程度上失去了原有的文化内涵。

总之,云南民俗村这个在全国颇具名气的民族文化主题公园,一方面是巨额投资建设,另一方面是品牌老化,吸引力减弱,处于一种矛盾交织的困惑之中。

资料来源:云南民族村主题公园如何走出困境肖克中国旅游资源概论[M],清华大学出版社,2006。

Part IV Reading Box
第四部分 阅读与分析

Virtual Reality

阅读分析要点

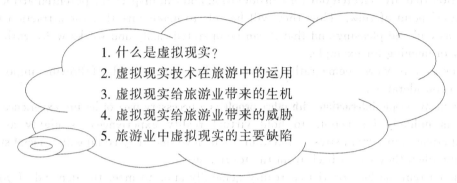

1. 什么是虚拟现实?
2. 虚拟现实技术在旅游中的运用
3. 虚拟现实给旅游业带来的生机
4. 虚拟现实给旅游业带来的威胁
5. 旅游业中虚拟现实的主要缺陷

Virtual reality is one of the hot topics in our time but we did not realize its impact on the attraction until recently. Some believe that virtual reality can bring the opportunity while others believe it will result in the threat.[1]

What is the virtual reality? Instead of using words or pictures virtual reality technology makes use of computers to give one the sense that they are present on the scene although the real "scene" may be far away or may happen long ago.[2] It works directly on the senses and brings to some people the feeling that there is nothing we cannot do. However, at present the technology is just starting to develop. It still has a long way to go to get more advanced, but we can provide a few examples to show how the virtual reality has an influence on the attractions in the world:

- Many entertainment centers in high streets around the UK are opened owing to the development of virtual reality technology, such as the Laser Quest complexes. These attractions make use of computer games, interactive video and virtual reality to attract visitors.
- **Flight simulators**, which are a typical example of virtual reality, are enjoying great popularity, particularly with corporate clients who often hire them for a day as part of training or entertainments offered for its staff and guests.[3]
- In some destinations, especially in the more developed countries, more and more tourists are interested in taking a simulator to undergo an exciting experience.
- Virtual reality has been widely used in some museums to enable visitors to experience **living history** and to offer explanation which can arouse their imagination.[4]

The growth of virtual reality can bring opportunities to attractions in a number of ways. The following are just a few:

- It can help develop various kinds of new attractions. These attractions can be built anywhere as they do not need any physical resource. Therefore, they can be located in some poor areas to help them speed up the development of economy and society.
- The attractions that have difficulty in attracting younger visitors can use virtual

reality technology to draw their attention.⁵
- Virtual reality means opportunities for those attractions that intend to educate visitors, because this technology can help to bring the heritage sites to life. Similarly, with this technology the concept of living history at heritage centers can be illustrated from a new angle.

Furthermore, the development of new attractions will also depend on virtual reality. With it, attraction planners and designers can make realistic **three-dimensional pictures** of the attraction that are selected out for consideration and can inspect the potential attraction from visitors' point of view. Thus they will be able to make sure that the attraction they design is tasteful and pleasing and that it can be operated easily and works well, with less possibility of queuing for example.

However, this view seems rather naïve. It does not take the following important issues into consideration.
- For many people **interaction with other people** is a necessary part of leisure experiences.
- It is unlikely for people to hold virtual reality experiences as highly as the experiences in certain sites. Some tourists believe that they could gain a **social status** only when they travel back from the tourist sites.
- The current market for virtual reality generally aims to meet the demand of young males. Therefore, to develop more rapidly, virtual reality has to try every means to take up more market segments.

Nevertheless, the negative effect of the virtual reality on the tourism industry seems unable to be avoided. The industry may take this as one of the threats which are believed to be brought about by virtual reality to the attractions business.⁶ The threat mainly consists of two parts:

1. If people can enjoy virtual reality in the local place or at home, they would be reluctant to travel for a leisure experience, then the number of visitors to these attractions would go down. This may threaten the development and even the survival of them, especially conventional attractions. Therefore, many attractions incorporate the virtual reality into the product to minimize the threat.

2. To install virtual reality equipments will cost a lot of money. Only those big attractions with a sound financial basis can afford to do so. As for other minor attractions, they may lose their visitors and their existence will be threatened.

The influence of virtual reality will gradually penetrate into the tourism industry. At present, virtual reality cannot substitute other forms of tourism activity, such as **ethnic tourism** because the group the virtual reality attracts is mainly young males. But this may change in the near future as attractions provide more virtual reality experience. Therefore, how to respond to virtual reality is critical to the development and survival of conventional attractions.⁷

New Words

virtual	adj.	虚的，虚拟的
three-dimensional	adj.	三维的，立体的
interactive	adj.	相互作用的，交互性的
naïve	adj.	天真的
simulator	n.	模拟器，模拟设备
conventional	adj.	常规的，传统的

incorporate	v.	合并,并入
penetrate	v.	渗透,穿透,透过

Notes

1. Some believe that virtual reality can bring the opportunity while others believe it will result in the threat.
   有些人认为虚拟现实会为我们带来机遇,而另一些人则认为它将造成威胁。

2. Instead of using words or pictures virtual reality technology makes use of computers to give one the sense that they are present on the scene although the real "scene" may be far away or may happen long ago.
   虚拟现实技术利用计算机替代文字和图片让人们产生身临其境的感觉,尽管真实的场景可能发生在很远的地方或者在很久以前。

3. Flight simulators, which are a typical example of virtual reality, are enjoying great popularity, particularly with corporate clients who often hire them for a day as part of training or entertainments offered for its staff and guests.
   飞行模拟器就是虚拟现实的典型例子,现在这种活动正受到大众的欢迎,特别是企业客户,他们常常租用模拟器一天,为员工和客户提供培训和娱乐。

4. Virtual reality has been widely used in some museums to enable visitors to experience living history and to offer explanation which can arouse their imagination.
   一些博物馆广泛运用虚拟现实技术,使旅游者体验到鲜活的历史,并提供解说以唤起游客的想象力。

5. The attractions that have difficulty in attracting younger visitors can use virtual reality technology to draw their attention.
   对年轻游客缺乏吸引力的旅游景点可以使用虚拟现实技术来引起他们的注意。

6. The industry may take this as one of the threats which are believed to be brought about by virtual reality to attractions business.
   旅游业可能认为这是虚拟现实技术为这一产业所带来的威胁之一。

7. Therefore, how to respond to virtual reality is critical to the development and survival of conventional attractions.
   因此,怎样面对虚拟现实技术对于传统吸引物的发展和生存是至关重要的。

Topic discussion

1. What is the virtual reality? Give an example to illustrate how the technology of virtual realty has been applied in China.

2. What are the benefits brought about by virtual reality to attraction business?

3. What are the threats brought about by virtual reality to attractions business?

4. Do you think that virtual reality can replace the conventional attractions? Why or why not?

5. Which do you think is better? The living attraction or the virtual reality? why?

【即学即用】

With reference to the theory, information or approach applied in the Reading Box, have a case study of the virtual reality. You may take Expo 2010 Shanghai, China as an example. Make presentation of your study in Chinese or in English using PPT.

【学习资源库】

为了掌握本章更多的相关专业知识,请您登陆 http://sicnu.edu.cn/,点击国家双语教学示范课程《旅游学概论》,进入网络学堂查询相关资料。

Chapter Review 本章小结

This chapter has discussed different interpretations of authenticity and its application in hospitality industry. Some people believe that virtual reality can bring the opportunity while others believe it will result in the threat. The influence of virtual reality has exerted a great impact on the industry, but it cannot substitute other forms of tourism activity, such as ethnic tourism. Different perception of attractions and performance between tourists and performers will increase tourist-resident tensions, and commercialization of traditional cultures brings about serious consequences in the destination. To solve the problem, application of frontstage and backstage is one of effective ways to protect the tourist resort and the folk culture in the destination.

Part V Additional Know-how of Tourism
第五部分 旅游知识扩展

【关键术语】

Tourist attractions: specific and generic features of a destination that attract tourists; some, but not all, attractions are parts of the tourism industry

旅游吸引物:指的是旅游目的地中能吸引旅游者的特定的或普遍的事物,其中一些旅游吸引物是旅游业的一部分,但有些不是。

Attraction attributes: characteristics of an attraction that are relevant to the management of an area as a tourist destination and thus should be periodically measured and monitored; includes ownership, orientation, spatial configuration, authenticity, scarcity, status, carrying capacity, accessibility, market and image

吸引物属性:指某一旅游吸引物的若干特点,这些特点与该地区作为目的地的管理是相关的,应从产权、定位、空间配置、原真性、稀缺性、地位、承载力、可进入性、市场以及形象各方面进行定期测量和监测。

Frontstage: explicitly or tacitly recognized spaces within the destination that are mobilized for tourism purposes such as commodified cultural performances. A particular space may be designated as either frontstage or backstage depending on the time of day or year

前台:目的地为开展旅游活动所明确或默许的活动区域,如从事商业化文艺演出的地方。目的地某一特定空间可以在一天或一年内的时间内分为"前台"或"后台"。

Backstage: the opposite of frontstage; areas of the destination where personal or intergroup activities occur, such as non-commercialised cultural performances

后台:与"前台"相反,指目的地个人或社会团体之间开展活动的场所,如非商业性文化演出。

Virtual Reality: Instead of using words or pictures virtual reality technology makes use of computers to give one the sense that they are present on the scene although the real "scene" may be far away or may happen long ago.

虚拟现实:虚拟现实技术利用计算机替代文字和图片让人们产生身临其境的感觉,尽管真实的场景可能发生在很远的地方或者在很久以前。

【知识链接】

1. 影响民族文化真实性的因素

(1) 来自民族文化自身的原因

民族文化旅游产品具有多样性、易被复制和再现等特点,这就决定了旅游者对民族文化真实性感知的难度和不确定性。民族文化的多样性使游客的知识结构和文化素养在感知真实度时受到挑战;民族文化的复制和再现使游客的辨别能力、审美能力受到挑战,导致真伪难辨。

(2) 来自需求方的原因

民族文化旅游不同于传统的自然风光的观光游览,旅游者欣赏自然风光的同时,还会接触到当地奇特的民俗风情、语言、文字、工艺品等,能否体验到这种文化层次的享受,取决于游客的自身素质,旅游者往往由于专业知识或由于个体特征差异,导致他们所感知的民族文化与真实的情形不一致。

(3) 来自供给方的原因

民族文化旅游的供给者不外乎四个主体:旅游地居民、政府、投资商和组织者。这四个主体是作为一个整体为旅游者呈现出民族文化景观,但他们有各自的自主能动性,特别是在呈现民族文化旅游景观过程中发挥不同作用,并在一定程度上影响旅游者的真实性感知度。

2. 舞台的真实性

真实性的概念最初来自希腊语,意思是"自己做的,最初的"。随着现代社会对人们生活的影响,真实性有了新的含义。在旅游研究领域,由社会学家迪·迈肯尼尔于1976年在其著作《旅游者》中首次提出,之后便引起旅游人类学家的广泛关注,成为旅游人类学的热门话题。迪·迈肯尼尔借用高夫曼的"舞台真实"中的"前台"和"后台"理论来阐述这一问题。他认为"前台"是给游客看的,正如宾馆的大厅、招待室、侍者展示给游客,是游客能看到的地方。"后台"是为旅游经营者和出售者所准备的真实现场,是隐藏道具和为表演做准备的地方。

科恩从景观的本质(Nature of Scene)和旅游者对景观的印象(tourist's Impression of Scene)二维角度出发,建立了旅游情形类型框架,为建构主义真实性与客观主义真实性的比较提供了研究基础。

图中横轴表示旅游社区文化或景观的本质,纵轴表示旅游者对社区文化或景观的印象。两轴正方向表示真实,负方向表示舞台化,即不真实。第Ⅰ、第Ⅳ象限反映的是真实的社区文化(后台),是大部分旅游者所要寻求的东西。在第Ⅰ象限中,旅游者对文化的主观印象是真实的,旅游者得到积极的体验。在第Ⅳ象限中,由于各地舞台化特点的普遍和舞台化趋势的加剧,旅游者把真实的文化当作非真实的文化,形成"舞台猜疑",这是经营的失败。在第Ⅱ、第Ⅲ象限中,不同认知水平和知识结构的旅游者,对舞台化的文化有不同的认识,反映了建构主义真实性的观点。在第Ⅱ象限中,不真实的社区文化,通过旅游机构和组织的仿真性包装和舞台演出,旅游者无法分辨文化的舞台化本质,把它视为"真实的情形"加以接受。这种真实性在客观主义眼中,是一种"伪事件",是具有超级谎言性质的"舞台真实",但在建构主义者眼中,却是真实的,是经营的成功,尽管它在保护社区传统文化的同时,对旅游者理解社区文化可能起到了误导作用。

【小思考】
1. 什么是"伪民俗"?怎样根据不同游客类型设计民族旅游产品?

参考阅读:
人类学家科恩把旅游者分成了五种类型:现实性游客、实践性游客、经验性游客、娱乐性游客和转移性游客。他认为前三种类型人类学家、民族志工作者相似,他们到异地旅游,寻求和参与当地人的真实生活,对"真实性"的要求比一般旅游者要高。但是这三类旅游者和学者们又不完全一样,只要他们能够在所游览参与的对象中找到自己所了解的真实就已经很满足了,而不像人类学家或某些学者那样,认为民族文化表演是"伪民俗",为游客生产的旅游工艺品是"假古董"。这是因为两者的旅游目的不同造成的。而后两类旅游者娱乐性游客和转移性游客主要是为了享受、休息或通过旅游来转移自己的注意力,忘却以前的事情,寻求一种平静的心情,对"真实性"的问题并不太关心,因为"不真实"不会给他们的旅游目的带来任何烦扰,甚至"不真实"的虚幻正是要他们追梦的东西。

2. 怎样解决民族文化原真性与商品化这对矛盾?结合自己的旅游经历,谈谈你对民俗表演的看法。

参考阅读：

在民族旅游的开发过程中,真实性和商品化始终是一对矛盾。真实性是民族旅游吸引游客的主要因素,也是民俗最基本的特征。但是,游客数量不断增长,为了满足游客的需求,民族旅游社区不得不提供商品化的民俗以满足市场需求。那么,我们是否只能在追求真实性或商品化二者之中择一呢？其实,民族旅游的真实性与商品化并非截然相对的两个方面。首先,民族旅游中的本真性并非单纯意义上的"本体真实",而是主要侧重于旅游者所经历的"真实",这就为民族旅游的商品化提供了契机。旅游部门通过市场运作,可以为旅游者提供一个体验民族文化的舞台。这样,民族旅游依靠其文化内涵在流通领域中运行,成为一种具有经济外壳和文化内核的产品。其次,旅游地居民、旅游者和旅游企业三方面可以调和本真性和商品化的矛盾。旅游地要尽量提供原汁原味的民俗；旅游者应理解和尊重旅游地的民俗文化；而政府主要是引导和监督开发商协调好民俗文化保护与开发二者之间的关系。

Part VI Further Readings
第六部分 课外阅读

如果您想进一步学习本章的内容,探讨真实性对旅游体验的重要性,建议您阅读以下学者的著作和论文。

一、中文部分

[1] 谢彦君.旅游体验研究———一种现象学的视角[M].天津:南开大学出版社,2006.

[2] 周亚庆等.旅游研究中的"真实性"理论及其比较[J].旅游学刊,2007,(06).

[3] 杨怡,朱华.真实性理论在主题公园管理中的应用——以上海世博园为例[J].宜宾学院学报,2011,(05).

[4] 张军.对民俗旅游文化本真性的多维度思考[J].旅游学刊,2005,(05).

[5] 钟国庆.旅游体验真实性规律和景区经营管理问题[J].桂林旅游高等专科学校学报,2004,(02).

[6] 吴忠才.旅游活动中文化的真实性和表演性研究[J].旅游科学,2002,(02).

[7] 白杨.旅游真实与游客[J].桂林旅游高等专科学校学报,2006,(06).

[8] 任媛媛.民族文化旅游项目的真实性探析[J].桂林旅游高等专科学校学报,2005,(03).

[9] 高燕.旅游者对民族文化真实性感知的差异性研究[J].广西民族研究,2006,(01).

[10] 蒋文中.老牌主题公园如何走出困境——对云南民族村经营与发展的思考[J].云南社会科学,2005,(03).

二、英文部分

[1] Hughes G. Authenticity in tourism[J]. *Annals of Tourism Research*,1995(22).

[2] Hyounggon Kim, Tazim Jamal. Touristic quest for existential authenticity[J]. *Annals of Tourism Research*,2007(34).

[3] Alison J. McIntosh, Richard C. Prentice. Affirming authenticity: Consuming cultural heritage[J]. *Annals of Tourism Research*.1999(26).

[4] Carol J Steiner, Yvette Reisinger. Understanding existential authenticity[J]. *Annals of Tourism Research*,2006(33).

[5] Cohen E. Authenticity and commoditization in tourism[J]. *Annals of Tourism Research*,1988(15).

[6] Deepak Chhabra, Robert Healy, Erin Sills. Staged authenticity and heritage tourism[J]. *Annals of Tourism Research*, 2003(30).

[7] Harkin M. Modernist anthropology and tourism of authentic[J]. *Annals of Tourism Research*, 1995(22).

[8] Trilling L. Sincerity and Authenticity [M]. London: Oxford University Press, 1972.

[9] Taylor J P. Authenticity and sincerity in tourism[J]. *Annals of Tourism Research*, 2001(28).

[10] Carol J Steiner, Yvette Reisinger. Understanding existential authenticity[J]. *Annals of Tourism Research*, 2006(33).

Chapter 5　Mobility and Tourism Transportation
第五章　移动性与旅游交通

Learning objects：学习目标

- Study the access (transit region) which connects origin and destination within the tourism system (Leiper's model)学习旅游系统(Leiper 模型)中连接客源地和目的地的路径(中转地区)
- Understand the important relationship between tourism transportation and tourism resources 了解旅游交通与旅游资源的重要关系
- Have a break-down of the factors which influence passengers' choice of the transport mode 分析影响乘客选择不同交通工具的因素
- Outline the advantages and disadvantages of different transport modes 提出不同交通工具的优点和缺点
- Appreciate how each mode of transport may foster a competitive rather than a complementary relationship 理解不同的交通工具可能形成相互竞争而不是相互补充的关系
- Understand the key role of government in the development and control of tour transport 了解政府在发展和控制交通中所发挥的关键作用
- Appreciate the role of passenger transport in the tourism industry and the challenge it faces 理解旅客交通在旅游业中的作用，以及面临的挑战

Ability goals：能力目标

- Case study 案例分析：奔跑在瑞士山川的"黄金列车"
- Reading Box 阅读分析：Passenger Transport 旅客交通

Part I Text
第一部分 课文

Mobility and Tourism Transportation

【教学要点】

知识要点	掌握程度	相关章节
mobility and tourism transportation 移动性与旅游交通	重点掌握	
relationship between transportation and tourism resources 交通与旅游资源的关系	重点掌握	
factors which influence passengers' choice of the transport mode 影响乘客选择交通工具的因素	重点掌握	本课文与第 1 单元、第 2 单元、第 3 单元、第 6 单元、第 10 单元、第 13 单元、第 14 单元、第 15 单元相关内容有联系。
advantages and disadvantages of different transport modes 不同交通工具的利弊	一般了解	
frequent flyer programs 常飞旅客计划	一般了解	
key role of government in the development of tour transport 政府发展交通的作用	一般了解	

　　Transportation and tourism development has traditionally been regarded as "chicken and egg". Adequate transportation system and access to generating markets is one of the most important prerequisites for the development of any destination. In most cases tourism has been developed in areas where extensive transportation networks were in place and the potential for further development was available.

　　Mobility is an important concept for tourism research. For modern tourism, people have to resort to the means of transport when they travel from the origin to the destination. Transportation for tourism is an essential element of the tourist product in two ways: it is the means to reach the destination and it is necessary as a means of spatial movement at the destination. For some categories of visitor, the trip is therefore seen as an attraction in its own right and certainly part of the tourist experience.

　　With the development of science and technology, tourism transportation develops very quickly and has become very complex. The progress of transportation system leads to the appearance of new tourist sites and **optimizes the existent tourist sites**. There are various vehicles available in the world and now we can choose different transport modes to travel. In order to attract more passengers, different companies and even different countries compete fiercely with each other. In this chapter, we will analyze the competitiveness of different transport modes on the basis of the factors which may influence passengers' choice. These factors are summarized as follows:

- safety;
- price/cost;
- time/speed;
- flexibility;
- service quality;
- comfort/luxury;

- distance;
- convenience;
- departure and arrival times;
- reliability;
- availability;
- incentives;
- ground services;
- terminal facilities and locations;
- status and prestige;
- enjoyment of trip.

Road transportation

Road transport has many advantages. It attracts tourists mainly due to:
- the control of the route and the stops on the way;
- the control of departure times;
- the ability to carry baggage and equipment easily;
- the ability to use the vehicle for accommodation;
- privacy;
- the freedom to use the automobile once the destination is accessible;
- the low expenses.

The car

Compared with other vehicles, car is more frequently used in some nations than in others as the transportation means for recreation and tourism.[1] Of course, this is in part determined by transportation facilities and climate. In Canada and US, 90% of the pleasure/personal and business trips are carried out by car. In Europe, car covers almost 83% of the **passenger kilometers**. Furthermore, when travelers in the Continent of Europe, such as those from Germany, Italy, Austria, Switzerland and France, spend their holiday in the southern Mediterranean and at home, the vehicle they are most likely to choose is car.

The coach

Traditionally, travel groups often hire coaches to conduct their journeys, especially when the journeys are not too long. This mode is very attractive for the elderly (over 50) or the **lower social group**. At the same time, the mini or microbus is becoming more and more popular in the local towns at the destination. For example, the adapted microbus is frequently used by those travelers who go on safaris in Kenya or other African countries. Of course, compared with other modes, coach is not comfortable and its speed is slower. Therefore, when the distance goes beyond a limit, the price has to be set at a cheaper and more appealing level in order to hold its attraction for tourists.[2]

Railway transportation

Trains are regarded as being able to provide us a "green" form of travel. They are safe, inexpensive and convenient and offer us more freedom within the **carrying unit**. Along the way, we can appreciate many beautiful types of scenery and have a good trip. Trains are superior to planes in that railway terminals are often in the centre of the destination while airports are often located 20 or 30 kilometers away from the centre.[3]

Trains also have some negative sides. Some of them are very slow. And the track on which they run makes it impossible for trains to carry passengers to anywhere freely as a car does. What's more, the cost of them is rather high owing to the building of the track and it is often paid by the public. Even if trains can provide us a relaxed journey, the services they offer cannot always be high. We can enjoy ourselves comfortably only within a distance of 200 to 500 kilometers between major cities. Usually, the reasons why we choose to travel by train are:

- safety;
- the ability to look out of the train on the way;
- the ability to move around the coach;
- arriving at the destination rested and relaxed;
- personal comfort;
- centrally located termini;
- environmentally friendly form of transport;
- decongested routes.

As mentioned above, the current image of trains is not so good, which, in turn, hinders their development. Some people intend to change them into a new form of transport. In their eyes, trains should be environmentally friendly, traditional, fashionable, relaxed, reliable and consumer-orientated.[4] Thus new consumers with entirely different lifestyles, besides the old ones, can be attracted and choose trains as the means of transportation. In Europe for tourism purposes, railway systems would become a powerful competitor for other modes in the future.

Sea transportation

Since they are cheap, reliable and safe, ferries are usually the first choice to transport vehicles and goods across the sea if the distance is short. And as for the remote and small islands which have no airport, **ferry transportation** is the only means. In Europe, the competition between various modes of transport has become more and more fierce owing to the gradual liberalization of air transportation, the decrease of air fares and the construction of the Channel Tunnel.[5] Tourists are offered many choices to travel. In order to survive in the sharp competition, ferry companies have to take measures to enhance their facilities and provide good service for customers. For example, they have to speed up their vessels and install them with luxurious facilities such as swimming pools, sports and shopping.

Ferry companies have introduced many modern vessels on some routes in recent decades, such as catamaran, hydrofoils and hovercraft. These vessels have many advantages compared with the conventional ferry. Their speed is very fast and they can move three times as fast as that of the conventional ferry. They are easy to operate. Moreover, they are very agile and have little requirement for the dock facilities. Therefore, many rich tourists choose to travel by them so as to save time and reach the destination as soon as possible.[6]

Cruising is a leisure product rather than a mode of sea transport. Taking the cruise ship, tourists can appreciate the beautiful scenery on the sea, enjoy themselves with the entertainment and leisure facilities on the ship and take short trips at the ports.[7] They take the ship as the destination and spend their time in a leisurely manner. In the past, the **cruise market** was mainly taken up by the older, wealthy and North American. But now the market has been widened and customers with different needs and of different age and purchasing abilities are also absorbed. Another type of entertainment, fly-cruises are offered as well for tourists to experience both the speed and efficiency of air transportation and the relaxing, romantic features of cruise ships.

Air transportation

Airplane is one of the greatest inventions in the 20th century. It has brought a huge innovation to the means of transportation. By air, passengers can go anywhere within the shortest possible time. Even if the destination is in the other end of the world, the time spent on the way is not more than 24 hours. They can be offered a safe, convenient, reliable, happy and relaxing journey so that their demand for long-distance travels has been greatly boosted. Business travelers choose to travel by air for the sake of its speed and flexibility between the various flights, especially on popular routes, while the leisure passengers take it as a way to save time and money and to arrive at the destination quickly.[8] In addition, airlines are always in the lead in providing good services and installing advanced facilities both on the ground and on board, which the other modes of transport try to imitate and overtake. At the same time, various **"frequent flyer" programs** have been worked out to encourage and stimulate their customers to keep loyal to them.

Flights are widely rented to provide convenience for holidaymakers, package tours and so called seat only arrangements.[9] The load of **chartered flights** (of 90% or more) is usually higher than that of scheduled ones (which can be as low as 20%). This, to a great extent, determines the big difference in the unit cost of production and the price of the product. That is to say, we will spend less money if we take a chartered flight. Sometimes charter airlines are owned and directly managed by tour operators such as Britannia Airways and Thomson Holidays in the UK. In this case, they can offer special transportation services including direct flights to the final destination. They can do this by:

- making it less possible to change flights;
- flying at inconvenient and therefore not busy hours;
- increasing seats within the aircraft;
- reducing some luxuries and services and retaining the elementary ones.

The operation of transport for tourism can be carried out only within a competitive political environment. This is mainly due to the attributes of transport, especially the attributes of the international transport: we have to cross the borders and territories of different countries to reach our destinations.[10] How deeply governments are involved in regulating and controlling transport for tourism can best expound this **competitive environment.**

New Words

incentive	n.	刺激,奖励
prestige	n.	声望,威望,威信
vessel	n.	船,舰
decongest	v.	解除拥塞
hydrofoil	n.	水翼,水翼艇
catamaran	n.	双体船,筏
boost	v.	推进,激励
hovercraft	n.	气垫船
elementary	adj.	初步的,基本的
innovation	n.	改革,创新
expound	v.	详细说明,解释
stimulate	v.	刺激,激励
reliability	n.	可靠性

Key Terms

ground service	地勤服务	luxurious facilities	豪华设施
means of transport	交通方式	chartered flight	包机

Notes

1. Compared with other vehicles, car is more frequently used in some nations than in others as the transportation means for recreation and tourism.
   与其他交通工具相比，一些国家更喜欢用汽车作为休闲娱乐和旅游的交通方式。

2. Therefore, when the distance goes beyond a limit, the price has to be set at a cheaper and more appealing level in order to hold its attraction for tourists.
   因此，当距离超出了一定限度时，定价应当更便宜、更具吸引力，以此吸引游客。

3. Trains are superior to planes in that railway terminals are often in the centre of the destination while airports are often located 20 or 30 kilometers away from the centre.
   相比飞机而言，火车的优点是火车站通常建在目的地的中心区域，而机场一般都在离城中心20或30公里外的地方。

4. In their eyes, trains should be environmentally friendly, traditional, fashionable, relaxed, reliable and consumer-orientated.
   在他们眼中，火车应环保、传统、时尚、轻松、可靠，以消费者为导向。

5. In Europe, the competition between various modes of transport has become more and more fierce owing to the gradual liberalization of air transportation, the decrease of air fares and the construction of the Channel Tunnel.
   在欧洲，由于空运的逐步开放、机票价格的下调以及海底隧道的建设，各种交通方式之间的竞争愈演愈烈。

6. Therefore, many rich tourists choose to travel by them so as to save time and reach the destination as soon as possible.
   因此，为节省时间并尽可能快地到达目的地，许多富有的旅游者选择乘坐飞机。

7. Taking the cruise ship, tourists can appreciate the beautiful scenery on the sea, enjoy themselves with the entertainment and leisure facilities on the ship and take short trips at the ports.
   乘坐游船，旅游者能欣赏海上的美景，能享受船上的娱乐和休闲设施，还能在港口短途旅游。

8. Business travelers choose to travel by air for the sake of its speed and flexibility between the various flights, especially on popular routes, while the leisure passengers take it as a way to save time and money and to arrive at the destination quickly.
   商务游客选择飞机，是因为飞机速度快，特别是在某些热点航线上转机灵活方便。而休闲乘客选择飞机是因为它能省时省钱并能更快地到达目的地。

9. Flights are widely rented to provide convenience for holidaymakers, package tours and so called seat only arrangements.
   飞机被广泛地租赁给度假者、包价旅行团以及所谓的只预定位置的乘客，为他们提供方便。

10. This is mainly due to the attribute of transport, especially the attributes of the international transport: we have to cross the borders and territories of different

countries to reach our destinations.

这主要取决于交通的特性,尤其是国际交通的特性,即我们到达目的地需要通过不同国家的国界和领土。

Exercise

1. Fill in the blanks with proper words to complete the following statements.

| Leisure | coaches | political | superior |
| fly-cruises | chartered | airport | |

(1) Traditionally, travel groups often hire _____ to conduct their journeys, especially when the journeys are not too long.

(2) Trains are _____ to planes in that railway terminals are often in the centre of the destination while airports are often located 20 or 30 kilometers away from the centre.

(3) The load of _____ flights (of 90% or more) is usually higher than that of scheduled ones (which can be as low as 20%).

(4) The operation of transport for tourism can only be carried out within a competitive _____ environment.

(5) Another type of entertainment, _____ are offered as well for tourists to experience both the speed and efficiency of air transportation and the relaxing, romantic features of cruise ships.

(6) Ferry transportation is the only possibility in the case of remote and small islands without _____.

(7) Cruising is a _____ product rather than a mode of sea transportation.

2. Questions for discussion

(1) What are the factors that usually affect passengers' choice of transportation modes?

(2) Why do people frequently use car as the transportation means for recreation and tourism?

(3) What measures can be taken to hold the attraction of coach for tourists when the distance goes beyond a limit?

(4) What are the advantages and disadvantages of railway transportation?

(5) What measures should ferry companies take to survive in the fierce competition?

(6) Why do many people prefer to travel by air for long-distance tourism?

Part II　Guided Reading
第二部分　课文导读

交通是旅游完成的必要条件,旅游过程一般以景点为节点,以交通线路为连线而形成闭合系统,其中包含了食、宿、行、游、购、娱等各种活动。从旅游业的发展里程来看,交通始终起着支配作用,是旅游业产生和发展的先决条件;同时,世界旅游业的发展也促进了交通的发展。不管旅游活动是以什么为目的,达到什么等级水平,若要完成这样的闭合系统运转,交通是充分必要条件。换言之,就是既要有交通路线通达、交通工具运输,又要有交通路线,交通活动将所有旅游内容串联起来,设计出一个较优化的旅游计划。可以说,没有交通就没有旅游。

世界大多数地区的旅游发展都非常依赖于交通设施及其交通系统的改善和发展。随着旅游距离的延伸以及景点的增多,交通所占的时间、精力、费用等也均会增加。虽然因为交通水平提高、休闲性增强等要素的变化,交通在旅游中所占时间、精力可能会减少,但费用仍会增加(因为追求高速、舒适、方便等交通服务指标改善)。由此可见,不管旅游业如何发展变化,交通始终占有重要的地位,是旅游活动的重要组成部分。旅游交通是旅游业产生和发展的前提条件,是沟通旅游目的地与客源地以及旅游目的地内各旅游场所之间联系的大动脉,是旅游外汇收入和货币回笼的重要渠道。因此,它与旅行社、旅游饭店并称为旅游接待业的三大支柱。

本文详细阐述了各种旅游交通的特点,从安全、舒适、便利、速度、成本、景观、服务质量、社会地位等方面对各种交通优劣进行了比较分析。旅游交通在旅游成本中占有很大的比例,其本身也可以视为旅游产品的一部分,关系到旅游者出行的选择和旅游满意度,是旅游研究的重要方面。不同的旅行方式各有其特点,就理想情况而言,旅游者对交通运输的要求涉及安全、便利、快捷、高效、舒适、经济等诸多方面。这些方面当然也难以兼而并得,不同的旅游者对上述各方面强调的重点也有顺序和层次上的区别,所以,人们在外出旅行时对旅行方式往往会有不同的选择,游客可以根据自己出游的时间、距离、价格和服务、安全性和舒适程度等因素来选择不同的出行方式。一般说来,旅游交通采用四种形式——汽车、火车、轮船和飞机,这些旅行方式的相互配合和相互补充为旅游活动的开展提供了便利的交通条件。

一、汽车

乘汽车外出旅游包括乘坐私人小汽车和乘坐公共客运汽车或者长途公共汽车两种。20世纪50年代以来,随着社会经济的发展,很多国家,特别是欧美国家中,私人小汽车拥有率不断上升。据1989年的统计数字,注册的私人小汽车在欧洲为平均4.9人一辆。在美国,平均每1.7人便有一辆私人小汽车。自己驱车外出度假具有很多明显的优点:灵活方便、行动自由、交通费用相对较低,便于携带行李和娱乐器具,便于观赏沿途风光等,因而在欧美国家中,人们普遍喜欢自己驱车在国内旅游,尤其是一日游和短期度假。

在公共汽车客运方面,由于同其他公共运输方式相比,汽车客运的运营成本较低,因而在很多国家中,汽车客运服务的价格较为低廉,特别是汽车旅游公司的客运价格更是如此。更重要的是,在旅游公司利用汽车组织包价旅游的情况下,公司可派车上门接送游客,十分方便,从而克服了不便携带行李转车的问题。

二、火车

铁路至今仍是人们开展国内旅游的主要旅行方式之一。但就世界范围来看,火车作为客运交通工具,其营业量已经大大减少。主要原因是,由于路轨铺设的限制,铁路是很难形成较细的线路网路,而选择与火车站相连接的汽车线路时则会使游客感觉不便,而且耗费时间。此外,航空公司和汽车客运公司的竞争,使铁路在旅游客运交通中的地位不断下降。

实际上,铁路运输具有很多其他交通客运方式所不具备的优点,这些优点主要包括:运载能力大、票价低廉、在乘客心目中安全性最强、途中可沿途观赏风景、乘客能够在车厢里自由走动和放松、途中不会遇到交通堵塞、对环境的污染较小等。因而,铁路运输无论是对于社会还是对于旅游者仍有其吸引力。

三、轮船

水路客运业务主要可划分为四种,即海上远程定期班轮服务、海上短程渡轮服务、游船服务和内河客运服务。远洋客运业务的衰落有客观方面的原因,也有其主观方面的原因。客观方面的原因是,自20世纪50年代以后,航空运输技术的发展以及各航空公司间的市场竞争使得大部分远程航线上的机票价格不断下降,致使乘飞机比乘轮船更划算。与此同时,在远洋客运经营方面,在劳动力成本不断上升的同时,许多客轮已经陈旧过时,更新费用颇高。

此外,远洋客运业务的其他经营成本已不断上升,加之航空公司在远距离客运方面占据着快速、安全和舒适等高标准服务的优势,使轮船公司无力与之竞争。主观方面的原因则是轮船公司没能及早意识到航空运输的发展对海上客运未来的威胁,因而未能使其产品及时适应变化中的需求,致使远洋客运业受到极大影响。在远洋客运交通衰落的同时,作为度假产品的海上巡游开始发展起来。游船作为海上度假的最大特点是悠闲、舒适。在海上巡游的过程中,人们既可在不同的地点登岸旅游,又可随时回船休息。这种游船旅游通常比较豪华,价格昂贵,加之游船航行速度的限制,比较耗费时日,所以收入低和闲暇时间较少的游客难以选择。

四、飞机

航空旅行的主要优点是快速,尤其适用于远程旅行。作为现代大众旅游的主要旅行方式之一,航空客运主要分定期航空服务和包机服务两种。定期航班服务是指在既定的国内或国际的航线上按照既定的航运班时刻表提供客运服务。定期航班服务的最大特点是运营有保证,旅行省时且抵达迅速。然而,由于成本方面的原因,定期航班也是较昂贵的交通方式。包机服务是一种不定期的航空包乘服务业务。随着20世纪60年代以来大众旅游的兴起,旅游包机业务有了很大的发展。同定期航班业务相比,包机业务有一定的经营优势,主要表现在:1. 票价较低廉,因而对市场的吸引力较大;2. 不必按固定的时刻表飞行,一般也没有固定的经营航线。

从旅游业自身的发展规律看,凡是交通运输业发达的国家和地区,其旅游业相对较发达。中国国际旅游业首先发源于北京、上海、广州等交通运输业发达的航空口岸城市,然后向交通运输业较发达的其他大、中城市发展,之后才向交通运输业比较落后的偏远城市和地区发展。旅游业发展的现状和现实证明,旅游业的产生和发展离不开交通运输业。良好的交通运输条件,可以促进旅游业的发展,反之将制约旅游业的正常发展。随着现代旅游业向更高层次和专业化方向的发展,客观上要求有更高层次和专业化特征的交通运输与之相适应,重视发展现代旅游交通运输业,以便更好地满足现代旅游者的需求。

旅游知识测试

正误判断:请在正确的选题上划√,错误的选题上划×。

1. 交通与旅游的关系从某种意义上来讲是"鸡生蛋"与"蛋生鸡"的关系。没有交通就没有旅游。

2. 交通旅游是沟通旅游目的地与客源地以及旅游目的地内各旅游场所之间联系的动脉,可以优化旅游资源。

3. 影响游客选择交通方式的主要因素有安全、舒适、便利、速度、成本、景观、服务质量、社会地位等。经济因素(运输价格和收入水平)是影响人们选择旅行方式的决定性因素。

4. 由于科学技术的发展,旅游费用逐渐降低,现代旅游业中交通费用在个人旅游消费中所占的比例减少,已经不是旅游的主要开支。

5. 航空旅行的主要优点是快速和舒适,途中可沿途观赏风景,不会遇到交通堵塞,对环境的污染较小,尤其适用于远程旅行。

Part III　Case Study
第三部分　案例研究

奔跑在瑞士山川的"黄金列车"

分析要点

1. 轨道交通在瑞士旅游业中有什么作用?瑞士政府为什么高度重视轨道交通?
2. 你是如何理解"旅快游慢"是旅游效益最大化这一重要原则的?
3. 怎样将旅途时间转化为观景时间?有什么益处?请举例说明。
4. 你认为旅游交通能否优化旅游资源?"黄金列车"是如何连接瑞士主要旅游景区的?
5. 结合案例,对比青藏铁路,谈谈你对我国旅游交通建设和火车旅游的看法。

相关理论和问题

1. 旅游交通成本(Transport cost of tourism)
2. 旅游时空和交通优化(Time & space of travel and optimization of transport)
3. 旅游距离抗阻(Resistance of the travel distance)
4. 旅游环境(Travel environment)

　　瑞士人有着浓郁的"火车情结",有一项世界冠军:瑞士人每年人均坐火车的公里数达到2103公里;有一项世界亚军:瑞士人年均坐火车47次。坐火车出行已超越汽车,成为瑞士人的首选。瑞士的高品质生活归功于这个覆盖全国的交通网络:它使人们能方便的抵达市中心,并在商务区、居住区和休闲区之间建立起紧密的连接。瑞士人将可持续性和轨道交通服务质量作为交通规划设计的理念,以市场为导向的列车时刻表作为规划核心,使瑞士铁路交通发展更加便捷、速度更快、更直接和更舒适的同时,也吸引了更多的居民和游客利用公共交通设施出行、旅游。

　　到瑞士旅游不坐火车将是人生的一大憾事。没坐过瑞士的火车,就等于没游玩过瑞士,在瑞士乘火车本身就是一大享受。窗外美景流转,车内环境舒适,上网、歇息、美食皆宜,无接缝钢轨铁路使火车行驶起来非常平稳,噪音小,坐在这样的火车里,游客的心情变得非常愉快。瑞士所有的观景火车上都设有特大的玻璃窗,好让乘客的眼睛不会错过任何窗外美丽动人的风景。

　　瑞士的"黄金列车"驰名天下,是游客出行首选的交通工具之一。它并非一列火车,而是由三种观景火车接力完成,包括琉森—茵特拉肯的布宁观景列车、茵特拉肯—兹怀斯文的蓝色景观列车、兹怀斯文—蒙特勒的水晶观景列车。在瑞士,游客还可以乘坐冰河景观列车,以观赏冰川景观为主。火车时速仅为35公里,有"全世界最慢的观景列车"之称。

布宁观景列车

　　在因特拉肯与琉森之间运行的布宁观景列车由安装有巨大车窗的车厢组成。列车为游客提供各种美味佳肴。车内诱人的美食与车外如画的风景融合在一起,令人回味无穷。因特拉肯是少女峰地区众多短途旅行线路的起点。布宁观景列车沿着五个湖泊边缘运行,蔚蓝的湖水中倒映着雄伟神奇的伯尔尼高地阿尔卑斯山,构成了一幅迷人的图画,而布伦迪山口是前往琉森的最后一个山口。

蓝色景观列车

运行于瑞士兹魏西门与因特拉肯之间的蓝色列车配置一等大堂式车厢,车厢内设有独立旋转座椅,为游客提供最舒适的乘车环境。而沙发车厢配有真皮座椅,同时提供酒吧服务,使游客的旅行成为难忘的欢乐时光。蓝色景观列车驶出兹魏西门后,进入曲折蜿蜒的锡默山谷,那里是著名的瑞士西门塔尔牛的故乡。整个旅程中,游客可以在保护完好的自然环境中细细品味伯尔尼高地传统的农牧风光。

水晶景观列车

世界上第一列全景观列车——水晶景观列车首先在瑞士蒙特勒与兹魏西门之间运行。这列极为先进的现代化列车带给游客全新的体验,使游客仿佛置身于一幅幅壮丽的风景画卷中。离开蒙特勒,列车在日内瓦湖畔的山坡上行驶,日内瓦湖的旖旎风光就会映入游客的眼帘。在蒙特勒与兹魏西门之间运行的水晶景观快车分为两种:一种在列车车头部位设有八个贵宾座位,使游客可享受与司机一样的开阔视野;另一种不设贵宾座位。两种水晶景观列车都配有一等车厢和二等车厢。

除了火车而外,瑞士交通系统还有汽车、轮船和高山缆车,这些旅行工具环环相扣,形成覆盖整个瑞士的交通网络,将一个引人入胜的瑞士带到旅客的面前。为了出行方便,游客还可以购买瑞士通票(Swiss Pass)。拿着这张车票,在有效期内可无限次乘坐瑞士境内的一切公共交通工具,包括国营火车、游船、长途汽车、市内公交,还可免费参观该国400多家博物馆。

交通是影响瑞士旅游业的重要因素。为了促进旅游的发展,瑞士在轨道建设和交通工具两方面都下足了功夫。一方面,瑞士把交通路转变为风景路,一路风景。"旅快游慢"是旅游效益最大化的重要原则。瑞士通过利用或改善交通道路两侧的景观,把旅途时间成功地转化为观景时间,让旅游者在不断出现的景点中完美的完成旅途。乘坐瑞士"黄金列车"的游客在旅途中不断地被优美的小镇和古老的城堡所兴奋,被优美的乡村景色而吸引。这样一来,旅游者的出行完就成了真正意义上的旅游,而不是让游客感觉有一半的时间都是待在密闭的交通工具中。

另一方面,瑞士的交通工具不断创新。旅游交通不仅包括交通基础设施,还包括旅游交通工具。传统的马车、自行车可以是创新的来源,用于旅游景区;现代技术的运用也可创新交通工具。"黄金列车"利用现代技术改进传统火车,不仅让游客更容易观看沿途美景,同时列车本身也是一种享受。尤其是改进过后的水晶景观快车,不仅火车本身精致、美观,而且透过火车所欣赏到的风景又让交通路变成了风景道,实现了二者的有机结合。瑞士的"黄金列车"让游客获得了美的享受,也使得"黄金列车"本身成为瑞士旅游一道的靓丽的风景线。

资料来源:1. 黄金列车. http://baike.baidu.com/view/1428142.htm;2. 广州日报[N].巧乘瑞士火车很着迷. http://gzdaily.dayoo.com/html/2010-08/31/content_1098556.htm

Part IV Reading Box
第四部分 阅读与分析

Passenger Transport

阅读分析要点

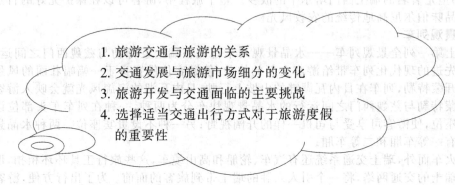

1. 旅游交通与旅游的关系
2. 交通发展与旅游市场细分的变化
3. 旅游开发与交通面临的主要挑战
4. 选择适当交通出行方式对于旅游度假的重要性

People are now traveling very differently from the way they did in the past. They have various modes of transportation to choose, from taking a coach to riding in a supersonic aircraft. In a sense, no transportation means no tourism available. They are closely connected with each other. As the demand for world tourism has increased greatly, the transportation sector will have to shoulder more responsibilities and provide more quick and comfortable services.[1]

However, it is obvious that different modes usually take up different **market segments**. In long-distance or middle-distance tourism, air travel holds the most important position, while shorter trips or domestic trips are mainly controlled by the private automobiles, which are also of great use in regional and international tourism.[2] Although rail travel now plays a minor role, it could also attract more attention and make its market expand greatly.[3] For example, in Europe, rail travel will become more comfortable and appealing owing to the introduction of high-speed trains and the construction of the Channel Tunnel. For those remote areas where services of other public modes are not available, motor-coach is the ideal means of transport, but it just shares a very small part of the market. The fastest-growing segment of tourism is cruise. It has become the focus of public attention and has aroused the interests of many wealthy tourists.[4] However, the part of market it takes is still small due to its high cost and price.

The rapid development of world tourism brings both opportunities and pressure to the growth of transportation.[5] As the demand for traffic increases, the demand for the quality and quantity of transportation facilities will also rise. And this can have **unfavorable effects**. The world is so large that different areas always have different situations and great variations also exist between them, but they may confront the same problems of transportation.[6] The most urgent ones are:

1. Congestion. Congestion is a major problem that has a great impact on most transportation modes, especially road travel and air travel. In big cities serious traffic jams often appear during the rush hours and sometimes the whole traffic may be completely stopped.[7] This problem must be solved as soon as possible; otherwise it will continue to waste our time and energy.

  2. *Safety and security*. Tourism sector should ensure that tourists can enjoy their journeys safe and sound. This is a basic requirement. The air crash and other accidents would hinder tourists from travel. Also the potential tourists may not travel because of the accidents.[8]

  3. *Environment*. Undoubtedly, the growth of traffic can do harm to the environment if an area has no capacity to hold more tourists. Therefore, while planning to expand transportation facilities, such factors as social, cultural, and natural resources should be taken into account.[9]

  4. *Seasonality*. Tourism is a highly seasonal industry. At certain times, an area may be overcrowded with tourists, while at other times, few visitors will come. So during the peak periods, more attention should be paid to the availability of transportation in order to handle the problems of congestion, security, and the environment.

  Transportation planners must try their best to solve these problems even though it is difficult to do so. As is known to us all, transportation problems can, in a certain degree, ruin tourists' vacations and leave them a bad impression on the destination.[10] Consequently, the growth of tourism will be greatly influenced. In fact, there have been so many such examples. And if these problems continue to exist, it is easy for us to predict the results. Therefore, we should make good use of the various transport modes to provide best services for tourists.

New Words

segment	n.	部分,细分
predict	v.	预测,预言
hinder	v.	阻碍,妨碍
crash	n.	碰撞,坠落,失事
availability	n.	有效性,可用性
overcrowd	v.	(使)过度拥挤

Notes

1. As the demand for world tourism has increased greatly, the transportation sector will have to shoulder more responsibilities and provide more quick and comfortable services.
   由于世界旅游需求大幅度增长,交通部门将肩负更多责任并提供更便捷、更舒适的服务。
2. In long-distance or middle-distance tourism, air travel holds the most important position, while shorter trips or domestic trips are mainly controlled by the private automobiles, which are also of great use in regional and international tourism.
   在中、长距离的旅游中,航空旅游占据着最重要的位置,而私家汽车在短途旅游或国内旅游中被普遍使用,航空旅游在地域性和国际性旅游中也发挥着重要作用。
3. Although rail travel now plays a minor role, it could also attract more attention and make its market expand greatly.

目前虽然铁路旅游已退居次要地位,但它仍然可以吸引更多的注意力并不断扩展市场。

4. It has become the focus of public attention and has aroused the interests of many wealthy tourists.
   它(乘坐游轮旅游)已成为公众注意的焦点,并唤起了很多富有的旅游者的兴趣。

5. The rapid development of world tourism brings both opportunities and pressure to the growth of transportation.
   世界旅游的迅猛发展给旅游交通的发展既带来了机遇,也带来了压力。

6. The world is so large that different areas always have different situations and great variations also exist between them, but they may confront the same problems of transportation.
   世界如此之大,不同地区总是有不同的情况和巨大的差异,但它们可能面对同样的交通问题。

7. In big cities serious traffic jams often appear during the rush hours and sometimes the whole traffic may be completely stopped.
   在大城市上下班高峰期通常会出现严重的交通堵塞,有时交通甚至会全部瘫痪。

8. The air crash and other accidents would hinder tourists from travel. Also the potential tourists may not travel because of the accidents.
   空难和其他事故可能会妨碍旅游者出游。潜在的旅游者也可能因为这些事故而不去旅游。

9. Therefore, while planning to expand transportation facilities, such factors as social, cultural, and natural resources should be taken into account.
   因此,当我们计划增加交通设施时,应考虑到诸如社会、文化和自然资源等因素。

10. As is known to us all, transportation problems can, in a certain degree, ruin tourists' vacations and leave them a bad impression on the destination.
    众所周知,交通问题在一定程度上可以破坏旅游者的度假,并使他们对目的地产生不好的印象。

Topic discussion

1. What are the popular modes of transport today? And how do they play their role respectively in the world tourism?

2. How does the development of world tourism affect the growth of transportation?

3. What are the most urgent problems of transportation the people face today?

4. What modes of transport would you like to choose? Why or why not?

5. If you are a transportation planner, what will you do to solve those problems of transportation?

【即学即用】

With reference to the theory, information or approach applied in the Reading Box, have a case study of the passenger tansport in your city. Make presentation of your study in Chinese or in English using PPT.

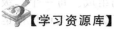
【学习资源库】
为了本章掌握更多的相关专业知识,请您登录 http://sicnu.edu.cn/,点击国家双语教学示范课程《旅游学概论》,进入网络学堂查询相关资料。

Chapter Review 本章小结

This chapter has considered the important relationship between tourism transportation and tourism resources. Passenger transport is one of important income resources for tourism industry. It joins tourist sites and optimizes tourist resources. In a sense, no transportation means no tourism. Different mode of transport usually takes up different market segments, fosters a competitive rather than a complementary relationship. Why a tourist chooses train as a means of transport rather than airplane is a complicated issue; various factors influence his choice of the transport mode. The rapid development of tourism brings both opportunities and pressure to the growth of transportation. Government plays a key role in the development and control of tour transport. There are many transport problems and challenges we have to face.

Part V　Additional Know-how of Tourism
第五部分　旅游知识扩展

【关键术语】

Transportation: the act or process of carrying or moving people or goods, or both, from one location to another

运输:将游客、货物或二者从某处运往另外一处的行为或过程。

Freedoms of the air: eight privileges, put in place through bilateral agreements, that govern the global airline industry

空中自由权(航权):通过管理全球航空业的双边协议实施的八大特权。

Cabotage: the ability of an air carrier to carry passengers exclusively between two points in a foreign country

国内航空运输:航空公司在某国境内的两地间运输旅客的能力。

Frequent flier plan: programs where bonuses are offered by the airlines to passengers who accumulate travel mileage

积点飞行计划:航空公司专门为经常乘坐飞机旅行的乘客所提供的飞行里程积点的奖励性计划。

Infrastructural accessibility: the extent to which a destination is physically accessible to markets by air routes, highways, ferry links, etc, and through entry/exit facilities such as seaports and airports

基础设施可进入性:指旅游者通过航空、高速公路、轮渡等,以及通过港口和机场这样的进出口设施可抵达目的地的程度。

【知识链接】

1. 旅游交通运输市场细分

旅游交通运输一级市场由短距离、中距离、远距离三个二级细分市场组成。每一个二级市场又可根据运输速度细分为低速、中速、高速三个三级市场。每一个三级市场又可根据运输价格细分为低档、中档、高档三个四级市场。在二级市场,公路和特种交通方式占据短距离细分市场的主导地位,铁路和水运占据远距离细分市场的主导地位。在三级市场,公路、水运、特种传统交通方式主导低速细分市场,铁路主导中速细分市场,航空、特种高科技交通方式主导高速细分市场。在四级市场,公路、水运、特种传统交通方式主导低档细分市场,航空、旅游和特种高科技交通方式主导高档细分市场。旅游交通运输市场的细分使旅游交通产业内部分工出现以下特点:

(1) 产业内部工具具有逐级细化的特点。随着旅游交通市场细分程度的加深,旅游需求的条件越来越多,能够满足特定需求条件的交通方式在类型上呈逐级减少的趋势,甚至会出现断档现象。

(2) 随着市场细分的深入以及市场供给断档趋势的出现,交通方式开始进行近似供给,即近似满足特定需求的交通方式成为断档子市场的主导交通方式。

(3) 舒适性、游览性和灵活性也是影响旅游者选择交通方式的主要因素,因而也是旅游交通产业内部分工的重要特征。旅游者对舒适性、游览性和灵活性的追求往往不是单一的,而是综合统一的,比如铁路运输的单项优势并不十分突出,但是其溶舒适性、游览性、灵活性于一炉的综合优势却十分明显,因而可以兼顾多种运输细分市场,具备了较强的市场适应能力和渗透能力。

2. 旅游交通优化战略

交通质量与效果的好坏,直接影响到旅游的成败,并随时间积累可影响一个地区、一条线路的旅游业的兴衰。因此,旅游优化是不可忽视的旅游业发展要点之一。旅游交通优化战略可以从以下三方面考虑:

(1) 交通供给能力的保障,满足旅游最起码的要求;交通基础设施和服务设施的短缺会造成影响游客出行,是困扰旅游业发展多年的难题,是要改善交通供给能力,解决结构性短缺的问题,为旅游业的发展提供保障;

(2) 交通供给的安全可靠性,即交通设施建设质量过关,交通组织管理优良,交通从业人员素质较高,社会与交通环境有保障等;

(3) 交通服务优化,在交通上投入较高的成本,不能急于在游客身上收回,而应着眼于交通优化后产生的吸引力、增加的客源、附加消费产出等方面长远的收益。旅游交通优化旅游交通发展具体实施应"因地而宜,因人而宜,因景而宜,因线而宜"。

【小思考】

1. 交通瓶颈对旅游有什么影响?如何打破旅游交通瓶颈?

参考阅读:

加强交通业管理,是推进旅游交通基础设施建设的重要举措。在我国很多地区,旅游交通已经成为我国旅游业发展的瓶颈,区域内的海陆空三维立体交通网络没有形成,区域内甚至旅游市内的精品景点处于彼此隔离状态,旅客集散功能薄弱,与日益壮大的旅游业不相匹配。为解决旅游交通的供需矛盾,旅游主、交通行业管理的主要内容之一就是创造良好的投资环境。大力吸引社会投资,建成合理的旅游交通网络,消除旅游交通对旅游业的瓶颈作用。我国加入WTO和中国旅游业的成熟要求交通运输市场的健康发展,加强交通行业管理,培育和发展统一开放、竞争有序的旅游交通运输市场,对于我国旅游业的可持续发展具有重要意义。目前我国交通市场处于改革阶段,新旧体制交叉并存,企业经营主体、经营设施、经营方式都将发生重大变化,这对旅游交通运输市场管理提出了严峻挑战,交通行业管理部门必须坚持交通建设和行业管理并重,为旅游业的发展提供良好的交通条件。

2. 国际旅游交通发展趋势对我国开发旅游交通市场有什么启示?

参考阅读：
（1）国内市场自由化与国际市场一体化

世界各国长期以来对国内交通运输采取严格的政府管制,对国际交通运输采取政府间国际协议管理。随着军事运输专业化程度的加深和国内经济对交通运输依赖程度的提高,二战以后公路、水运、铁路和航空逐步由政府管制转向市场调节。许多国家也逐步放松了对本国国内航空运输的管制,使得航空公司在开业、停业,开辟国际、国内航线和制定航空运价等方面获得较多自由,标志着国内交通运输市场全面走向自由化。

（2）企业私营化与国际合作多元化

国家对交通运输的严格管制是通过国有企业独家经营的方式来实现的,随着军事运输与公共交通的分离,国家开始强化民用交通业的经济功能,要求交通运输通过市场化运行形成合理的投入产出比。为适应市场经济规律的要求,政府对交通运输实行产权和经营权的分离,私有化或国有民营的经营管理模式应运而生。

（3）国内集团巨型化与国际同盟超级化

旅游交通运输以低成本、高效为基本运营特征。优势企业兼并劣势企业,优势企业之间强强联合,从而实现最低的资源成本和最佳的经济效益。高效率则取决于规模经营和网络沟通,这要求采用现代化集团管理模式和高科技计算机网络技术以有效地满足不断变化的市场需求。

（4）旅客运输高速化与舒适化

速度是旅客运输永恒的主题,在不断提高运输速度的同时,旅游交通为适应旅游者高层次享受的需要还在不断提高舒适性、高速化和舒适化已成为世界旅游交通发展的显著特点和主流趋势。

Part VI Further Readings
第六部分 课外阅读

如果您想进一步学习本章的内容,探讨不同类型的旅游交通模式的优缺点,深入分析旅游交通在旅游活动中的意义与作用,建议您阅读以下学者的著作和论文。

一、中文部分

［1］崔利.旅游交通管理.［M］.北京:清华大学出版社,2007.
［2］杜学.旅游交通概论.［M］.北京:旅游教育出版社,1995.
［3］孙有望,李云清.论旅游交通与交通旅游.上海铁道大学学报,1999,10.
［4］陈晓,李悦铮.城市交通与旅游协调发展定量评价——以大连市为例［J］.旅游学刊,2008(02).
［5］张兴平,杨建军,毛必林.杭州市区旅游交通网络空间分析及其对策［J］.浙江大学学报(理学版),2000,(04).
［6］来逢波.区域交通与旅游的关联性探析［J］.交通企业管理,2007,(11).
［7］缪婧晶,王劲松.交通成本、消费者选择与旅游目的地发展［J］.思想战线,2003,

(02).

[8] 黄柯,祝建军,蒲素. 我国旅游交通发展现状及研究述评[J]. 人文地理,2007,(01).

[9] 赵中华,贾志宏,张蕾. 国内旅游交通研究十年综述[J]. 桂林旅游高等专科学校学报,2005,(02).

[10] 谭颖青. 从罗定市旅游交通规划看区域旅游交通网络的规划原则[J]. 社会科学家,2004,(01).

二、英文部分

[1] Paul Peeters, Eckhard Szimba, Marco Duijnisveld, Major environmental impacts of European tourist transport[J]. *Journal of Transport Geography*, 2007, 15(2):83-93.

[2] Byung-Wook Wie, Dexter J. L. Choy, Traffic impact analysis of tourism development[J]. *Annals of Tourism Research*, 1993, 20(3):505-518.

[3] Hall D R, Hall D, Kowalski J. *Transport and Economic Development in the New Central and Eastern Europe*[M]. United Kingdom: Belhaven press, 1993.

[4] Ross Nelson, Geoffrey Wall. Transportation and accommodation changing interrelationships on Vancouver Island[J]. *Annals of Tourism Research*, 1986, 13(2):239-260.

[5] Yingzhi Guo, Samuel Seongseop Kim, Dallen J. Timothy, Kuo-Ching Wang. Tourism and reconciliation between mainland China and Taiwan[J]. *Tourism Management*, 2006, 27(5):997-1005.

[6] Robert A. Goehlich, Udo Rucker. Low-cost management aspects for developing, producing and operating future space transportation systems, *Acta Astronautica*, 2005, 56(1-2):337-346.

[7] Bruce Prideaux. The role of the transport system in destination development[J]. *Tourism Management*, 2000, 21(1):53-63.

[8] D. C. Frechtling. Transport for tourism: Stephen Page[J]. *Annals of Tourism Research*, 1996, 23(3):727-729.

[9] Antonio Elias. Affordable space transportation: impossible dream or near-term reality[J]. *Air & Space Europe*, 2001, 3(1-2):121-124.

[10] I. B. F. Kormoss. Future development in North-West European tourism: Impact of transport trends[J]. *Tourism Management*, 1989, 10(4):301-309.

[11] Byung-wook Wie, Dexter J. L. Choy. Traffic impact analysis of tourism development[J]. *Annals of Tourism Research*, 1993, 20(3):505-518.

Chapter 6　Information Technology and Travel Industry
第六章　信息技术与旅游业

Learning objects：学习目标

- Based on tourism system (Leiper's model), study the information technology within the external system which exerts impacts on tourists and industry 运用旅游系统(Leiper 模型)，学习旅游外系统中的信息技术是如何影响旅游者和旅游产业的
- Appreciate the important role of information technology in tourism product development, marketing and training of tourism sector personnel 理解信息技术在旅游产品开发、市场营销以及人员培训中的重要作用
- Understand the benefits that the tour operator gains from information technology 了解旅游经营商从信息技术中获得的益处
- Identify and account for the circumstances under which the small-size travel agencies are unlikely use the information technology 指出并说明在什么情况下小旅行社不愿意使用信息技术
- Discuss how a hotel can use the information technology to upgrade its management 讨论饭店是如何运用信息技术提高饭店管理水平的
- Explain the reasons why the airlines use the information technology and the significance of its application 解释航空公司为什么要运用信息技术及其意义
- Understand the principles of Destination Management System and its application in the destinations 了解目的地管理系统的基本原理以及在旅游目的地中的运用

Ability goals：能力目标

- Case study 案例分析：Amadeus：全球旅游分销
- Reading Box 阅读分析：Management of Tourist Destinations 旅游目的地管理

Part I Text
第一部分 课文

Information Technology and Travel Industry

【教学要点】

知识要点	掌握程度	相关章节
information technologies and tourism sectors 信息技术与旅游业	重点掌握	本课文与第 1 单元、第 4 单元、第 5 单元、第 7 单元、第 8 单元、第 9 单元、第 11 单元相关内容有联系。
database management 数据库管理	一般了解	
CRS and GDS 中央预订系统与全球预订系统	重点掌握	
capacity management and yield management 容量管理与收益管理	重点掌握	
inventory control 库存控制	一般了解	
property management systems (PMSs) 物业管理系统	一般了解	

The development of information technologies (ITs) is one of the most important innovations of the 20th century. It has brought great changes to the industrg and has been regarded as the root cause of the third industrial revolution. In the case of tourism, information technology has been mainly used for tourism product development, marketing, distribution and training of tourism sector personnel; and it has played a vital role in the competitiveness of tourism enterprises and destinations around the world.[1] Tourism industry, to some extent, depends on both the efficient spread of information and effective product distribution.[2] Here, we shall briefly analyze the main developments of information technology (IT) and their impacts on sectors of tourism industry.

Information technologies and tour operators

ITs contribute to a great extent in organizing, promoting, distributing and coordinating package tours. The introduction of **Thomson's Open-line Programme (TOP)** in 1976 is a case in point. It was the first central reservation office making use of computers to deal with information immediately. Moreover, it took two measures separately in 1982 and 1986 which stood for a critical turning point concerning the communication processes between tour operators and travel agencies. These measures were the direct communication with travel agencies and the acceptance of reservations for Thomson Holidays only trough TOP. After that, all major tour operators gradually realized the significance of ITs and began to use **databases** and set up direct communication with travel agencies by computer.[3] This of course led to the reduction of the cost of information handling and the increase of the speed of information transfer and retrieval which were correspondingly helpful to the improvement of productivity and **capacity management** and the providing of better service to agencies and consumers.[4] Nowadays, tour operators continue to make use of recent developments of IT to ensure the smooth growth of their business, such as distributing electronic brochures and booking forms directly to consumers through the **WWW**. The benefits of this approach to tour operators are as follows:

- They can focus on suitable market by organizing proper package tours according to the requirements of customers.
- They can update brochures regularly.
- They can save the 10-20% commission paid to other intermediaries in the distribution chain (e. g. travel agencies).
- They can significantly reduce the costs of incentives, bonuses and educational trips for travel agencies.
- They can save the cost for developing, priming, storing and distributing conventional brochures, which is estimated to be approximately £20 per booking.

Information technologies and travel agencies

ITs are of special significance for travel agencies. They are helpful in several aspects: providing the latest information as soon as it happens; completing reservation facilities (including making the complicated plans of journey) and helping to coordinate the relationship between consumers and principals.

In addition, with the help of ITs, travel agencies have closely combined the two functions together—"**back office**" **functions** (e. g. accounting and personnel) and "**front office**" **functions** (e. g. customer records, itinerary construction, ticketing and communication with suppliers) so that the organizational efficiency has been greatly improved.[5] Even though ITs have been widely used by all travel agencies in the aspect of **financial and operational control** as well as market research and strategic planning, only multiple travel agencies have achieved better coordination and control between their remote branches and headquarters, thus ensuring more benefits.

Making use of Videotext networks and/or GDSs, most travel agencies run reservation systems of various types, which make it convenient for agencies to get information as soon as possible and make reservations on scheduled airlines, hotel chains, car rentals and a variety of additional services. Different agencies and clients will choose different types of ITs. Generally, business travel agencies tend to use GDS, while Videotext systems are the likeliest choice of leisure agencies and holiday shops.

Although ITs have developed very rapidly in recent years and many new technologies have been invented, they have not been fully utilized by most travel agencies.[6] The following factors may be helpful for us to understand this:
- Travel agencies do not fully understand ITs.
- Their profit margin is low so that they cannot invest much in new technology.
- They pay more attention to human interaction with consumers than to ITs.

Combined, these factors result in low level of IT integration, implying that agencies lack access to new ITs and are provided with inadequate information to support strategic marketing.

Information technologies and hotels

Although it was as early as 1970s that central reservation systems began to be used in central reservation offices (CROs), hotels did not fully combine them with other systems until airline CRSs had been expanded and IT had developed further.[7] There are several reasons in the following which can explain why hotels make use of information technologies:
- to connect with external GDSs;

- to make **yield management and inventory control** easier;
- to reduce labour and training costs;
- to respond to customer and management requests quickly;
- to provide cheap and reliable ways for customers to make and confirm reservations easily and efficiently.

In addition, hotels also adopt internal management systems such as **property management systems** (**PMSs**) for the following purposes:
- to make the front office, sales, planning and operational functions cooperate with each other by managing reservations and the hotel inventory so as to improve efficiency of the business;
- to combine the back and front of house management;
- to improve general administration functions such as accounting, budgeting and finance, marketing research and planning, forecasting and yield management, payroll personnel and purchasing.

However, many hotels are run by families independently. They are small and medium-sized and highly seasonal. Many of them do not have the skill and/or money to bring ITs into full use. This is caused by:
- lack of money to buy hardware and software;
- insufficient marketing skill;
- inadequate technological training and understanding;
- small size with no economies of scale;
- the unwillingness of owners to lose control over their property.

Information technologies and airlines

Airlines are the first to take advantage of the development of ITs and create a cheap and accurate way of handling vast quantities of data and inventory.[8] More recently CRSs have developed and expanded into GDSs because air traffic grows very rapidly and air transportation enjoys more freedom granted by the government. Emerging information technologies have brought a lot of benefits to airlines such as the remote printing of travel documents, sale settlements between airlines and travel agencies, and the partnership marketing through frequent flyer programmers.[9] The main benefits of CRSs are as follows:
- having more chance to interact with customers and partners so as to enhance their relationships;
- offering convenient on-line reservations and **electronic ticketing**;
- making **yield management** easier;
- using **last-minute electronic auctions**;
- encouraging direct investment in financial market and reconsidering agency commission schemes;
- improving substantially the productivity of the new electronic distribution media.

As for new mega-CRS distribution networks, we should pay attention to some important issues. The first is about the cost of distribution. Even though efforts have been made to reduce it, it is still very expensive. Therefore, many airlines have difficulty in financing and controlling it. This has a particularly big effect on those small, newly established, developing world airlines and regional carriers because they are usually lacking capital and technology facilities and skills. In addition, compared with other competitors, vendor airlines with CRS influence tend to have a prior claim on CRS screens to display their flights. Obviously, the airlines which are most seriously affected by this strategy are again those new and weaker ones.

Great changes have taken place and considerable improvement has been made in the operation, structure and strategy of tourism organizations all over the world.[10] The invention of new technology leads to the reduction of communication and operational costs and enables tourism organizations to operate flexibly and increase their interaction with customers and partners. Thus, their efficiency, productivity and competitiveness are much enhanced. The competitiveness of both enterprises and destinations can be viewed from a new angle because they put these technologies into use to the maximum extent and boost and speed up their development.

New Words

retrieval	n.	检索
property	n.	财产,资产
update	v.	更新,使现代化
inadequate	adj.	不充分的;不适当的
utilize	v.	利用
partnership	n.	合伙关系,合伙公司
inventory	n.	财产清单,存货单
operational	adj.	操作的,经营的
payroll	n.	工资册

Key Terms

tour operator	旅游经营商	reservation system	预定系统
travel agency	旅行社	hotel chain	连锁酒店
package tour	包价旅游	property management system	物业管理系统

Notes

1. In the case of tourism, information techology has been mainly used for tourism product development, marketing, distribution and training of tourism sector personnel; and it has played a vital role in the competitiveness of tourism enterprises and destinations around the world.
   就旅游业来说,信息技术主要用于旅游产品的开发、市场营销、产品分销和旅游从业人员培训,同时,它在全球旅游企业和旅游目的地的竞争中也起着重要作用。

2. Tourism industry, to some extent, depends on both the efficient spread of information and effective product distribution.
   在一定程度上,旅游业是一个既依赖信息高效传递,又依赖产品有效分销的行业。

3. After that, all major tour operators gradually realized the significance of ITs and began to use databases and set up direct communication with travel agencies by computer.
   此后,主要的旅游经营商逐渐认识到信息技术的重要性,开始使用数据库并且通过计算机和各旅行社建立直接联系。

4. This of course led to the reduction of the cost of information handling and the increase of the speed of information transfer and retrieval which were correspondingly helpful to the improvement of productivity and capacity

management and the providing of better service to agencies and consumers.
这肯定会降低信息处理成本、加快信息传递和检索的速度,这会有利于提高生产效率、改善管理能力,为代理商和消费者提供更好的服务。

5. In addition, with the help of ITs, travel agencies have closely combined the two functions together-"back office" functions (e. g. accounting and personnel) and "front office" functions (e. g. customer records, itinerary construction, ticketing and communication with suppliers) so that the organizational efficiency has been greatly improved.
另外,旅行社利用信息技术将"后台办公"功能(如会计和人事)以及"前台办公"功能(如客户记录、线路设计、票务、与供应商业务往来)紧密地联系在一起,使组织效率大大提高。

6. Although ITs have developed very rapidly in recent years and many new technologies have been invented, they have not been fully utilized by most travel agencies.
最近几年,虽然信息产业发展迅速,新技术不断被开发出来,但并没有得到旅行社的广泛运用。

7. Although it was as early as 1970s that central reservation systems began to be used in central reservation offices (CROs), hotels did not fully combine them with other systems until airline CRSs had been expanded and IT had developed further.
早在20世纪70年代,中央预订办公室就已经开始使用中央预定系统(CRS),但是直到航空公司广泛运用CRS以及信息技术更加成熟后,酒店才将它和其他系统联系起来。

8. Airlines are the first to take advantage of the development of ITs and create a cheap and accurate way of handling vast quantities of data and inventory.
航空公司最早运用信息技术,以低廉的成本准确地处理了大量数据和库存清单。

9. Emerging information technologies have brought a lot of benefits to airlines such as the remote printing of travel documents, sale settlements between airlines and travel agencies, and the partnership marketing through frequent flyer programmers.
新兴的信息技术给航空公司带来了许多好处,如旅行文件的远程打印、航空公司和旅行社之间的销售结账,以及通过飞行常客计划进行关系营销。

10. Great changes have taken place and considerable improvement has been made in the operation, structure and strategy of tourism organizations all over the world.
世界上所有旅游组织的经营管理、结构和战略都发生了很大变化,同时也取得了巨大进步。

Exercise

1. **Fill in the blanks with proper words to complete the following statements.**

   | reduction | revolution | latest | case | independently |

   (1) The development of information technologies (ITs) is one of the most important innovations of the 20th century. They have brought great changes to other industries and therefore have been regarded as the root cause of a second industrial _____.

   (2) The introduction of Thomson's Open-line Programme (TOP) in 1976 is a _____ in point. It was the first central reservation office making use of computers to deal with information immediately.

   (3) ITs are of special significance for travel agencies. They are helpful in several aspects: providing the _____ information as soon as it happens;

completing reservation facilities and helping to coordinate the relationship between consumers and principals.

(4) However, most hotels are run by families _____. They are small and medium-sized and highly seasonal. Many of them do not have the skill and/or money to bring ITs into full use.

(5) The invention of new technology leads to the _____ of communication and operational costs and enables tourism organizations to operate flexibly and increase their interaction with customers and partners.

2. Questions for discussion

(1) What are the benefits brought by ITs to tour operators?
_____

(2) In what way are ITs helpful to travel agencies?
_____

(3) Do you think that ITs have been fully utilized by most travel agencies? Why or why not?
_____

(4) For what purposes do many hotels adopt internal management systems?
_____

(5) Do you think ITs are brought into full use in many hotels? Why or why not?
_____

(6) What issues should we pay attention to as far as new mega-CRS distribution networks are concerned?
_____

Part II Guided Reading
第二部分 课文导读

信息技术的革新被称为"第三次工业革命",它能为旅游系统建立起一个信息空间,使每个旅游企业及其信息基础设施在其中运行。在信息空间中,行业成员能找到超细分市场,与供应商、中介和虚拟企业发展合作伙伴关系以共同开发和生产旅游产品。因此信息空间能给相关利益团体带来潜在的利益和挑战,因为技术革命为行业在全球范围内的有效合作提供了有力工具。信息技术推动了旅游需求和供给的全球化,它给消费者提供了寻找和购买合适产品的工具,同时为供应商提供了在全球范围内开发、管理和分销产品的工具。

信息技术在旅游行业,主要是被用于信息交换和辅助经营。这些技术大部分集中于旅游分销渠道,帮助分销商与消费者进行信息、合同、预定和支付的交换。可以说,信息技术是旅游发展和竞争的助推器,是研究现代旅游不可忽视的重要一面。本文重点分析了信息技术对旅游经营商、旅行社、旅游饭店、航空公司等产生的影响,以及信息技术给旅游产业带来的深刻变化。

一、信息技术对旅游经营商的影响

不同类型的旅游经营商有不同的 IT 要求,商务旅游经营商要求快速有效地了解信息并进行预订,因为他们针对的市场是动态的,而且需求是不断变化的。商务旅游者通常在临行前很短的时间内预订,而且经常变化行程,因此了解信息、制定行程和进行预定的效率决定着经营商的竞争能力。休闲旅游经营商需要了解大量的信息,以满足那些还没确定目的地、度假时间和预算的顾客需要获得度假灵感,经营商需要进行多种商品的预订以满足顾客的要求。无论上述哪种情况,整个旅游企业的关联互动都决定了企业的利润率,包括有效地管理现金流确保佣金的按时支付,节省员工的时间和精力,让他们能更好地为顾客服务,这些都能提高旅游经营商的生产率和利润水平。更多地利用IT支持企业内部功能和预订渠道能使旅游经营商获得更强大的竞争能力。

二、信息技术对旅行社的影响

鉴于旅行社行业在市场中的作用,旅行社必须不断地与所有合作伙伴之间互动,包括住宿和交通主体供应商、旅游代理商和消费者。同时协调大量的旅游顾客在世界各国的活动给旅行社管理带来了极大的挑战,在管理过程中IT能起到重要的作用。

IT对于旅行社包价产品的分销能起到重要作用。传统上旅行社的产品分销方式是把印刷好的介绍旅游产品的小册子放在旅游代理商的货架上,旅行社一般会事先印好一些预订表放在旅游代理商处,由代理商根据销售情况填写,并反馈给旅行社完成预订。而如今,新的网络工具使旅行社能在网上分发电子小册子和电子预订表给旅游代理商和消费者,而且可以实现多媒体展示目的地和旅游包价情况。

IT技术给旅行社带来了机会的同时,也对其提出了挑战。旅行社设计、推销旅游产品和旅游者被动购买旅游产品的关系,将受到旅游者利用旅游信息在电脑网络上自主设计旅游线路的威胁,旅行社组织者的地位受到削弱。传统的旅行社让旅游者无法通过旅行社以外的其他途径获取各种旅游产品要素的综合信息(或者说,旅游者不会有精力和时间去获取和综合这些信息)。基于对这种综合信息的垄断,旅行社业确立了其"旅游产品生产者"的行业地位,而管理信息技术的应用则将打破这种生产者和旅游者之间的传统关系。

三、信息技术对饭店的影响

现代饭店是旅游行业中使用IT较成熟的企业类型。IT技术协调饭店各部门工作,做到高效、准确,同时又能减少员工的工作量,节省人力、物力,使组织机构扁平化,反应更灵活、迅速,在现代饭店活动中起着举足轻重的作用。网络信息咨询提供各种实时、详尽的参考资料,帮助决策者及时了解市场,准确把握形式,迅速做出准确判断,做到知己知彼。

饭店网络预订系统(CRS)是IT技术在饭店业广泛运用的典型,它有效地解决传统预订方式的种种弊端。首先,CRS是饭店集团为控制客源而采用的集团内部计算机客房预定网络。最早的CRS由假日集团于1965年建立,称为假日电讯网。随后,喜来登、福特、希尔顿、雅高等国际饭店集团都建立了自己的中央预定系统,并凭借这个系统实现了集团内部客源的相互介绍和集团整体在控制客源市场上的领先地位。目前,CRS系统运用的范围在不断扩大,包括订票、行程安排、预订饭店、租用汽车、设计线路、飞机保险、为客人订花、提供汇率变动信息、旅游目的地的包价旅游等。

四、信息技术对航空公司的影响

IT技术在航空公司的应用很广泛,从战略角度看,航空公司可以利用技术管理其商业模型,进行收入分析和预测,实施产出管理,监测竞争情况,保存历史数据,预测需求,设计产品和线路。从经营层面看,IT在容量管理、预订管理和票务方面的作用都非常关键。电子票务促进了无纸化交易,节省了航空公司的成本。策略定价、产出管理和特别促销都要以对供需关系的不断评估所做出的预见性和反应性措施决策为依据。IT能帮助航空公司实现很多经营管理方面的功能,包括登机手续、座位安排以及生成各种报表和订单。IT还能支持电子采购和供应商及合作伙伴定期管理以实现运行效率的最大化。另外,航空公司一般在全球各地都有办事机构、分销商,因此有效地与运营站点、分支机构、分销商和顾客的联系和沟通也是非常重要的。

随着IT技术的飞速发展,全球目的地系统(GDS)应运而生。GDS是一个开放的系统,加入这个系统,意味着饭店与大部分潜在市场联为一体。散客或旅行社代理商可以在家中、办公室或附近的服务点利用互联网了解任何地区一家饭店的设施水平、客房价格、房务状态以及其他相关信息,并可完成对饭店客房的预订。因此,GDS已成为饭店盈利的重要方式。大型饭店集团在拥有自己的CRS的基础上与GDS联网,可以保证其在控制客源上的优势;

独立的中小型饭店通过与 GDS 联网,在理论上说和大型饭店集团站在了同一起跑线上。

因此,我们可以毫不夸张地说,信息技术为旅游业的发展、旅游市场的开发和销售、旅游各部门人员培训等带来了巨大的变化,如何利用好信息技术为旅游服务,已经成为影响旅游业发展的关键因素之一。

旅游知识测试

正误判断,请在正确的选题上划√,错误的选题上划×。

1. 在雷柏尔的旅游系统中,旅游者是主体,在客源地和目的地的推拉作用下,旅游者在二者之间进行移动,信息技术对旅游流会产生重要的促进作用。
2. 在一定程度上,旅游业是一个既依赖信息高效传递,又依赖产品有效分销的行业。没有信息技术,旅游者就无法实现从客源地到旅游目的地的双向移动。
3. 电子商务在旅游产业成功运用的典范是携程网,它为旅游企业和旅游者提供了重要的平台,从某种意义上讲,其运作方式颠覆了传统的旅游模式。
4. 信息技术在旅游业中运用的范围不断扩大,包括订票、行程安排、数据库管理、容量管理、收益管理、智能化登机、目的地包价旅游等服务。
5. 目的地管理系统为旅游企业提供的服务,帮助分销商与消费者进行信息、合同、预定和支付的交换,但不能为游客提供服务。

Part III Case Study
第三部分 案例研究

Amadeus:全球旅游分销

分析要点

1. 有些学者认为 GDS 会随着互联网的出现而消失,讨论这个观点并说出你支持或反对这一个观点的理由。
2. Amadeus 的主要功能是什么?它与航空公司预订系统有什么关系?
3. e-Travel 对商务旅游有何影响?Amadeus 如何经营世界最大的 e-Travel 市场?
4. 为什么说 Amadeus 已经不是传统意义上的预定和分销工具?
5. 假如你在北京某旅游公司工作,公司今年计划开辟北京—马尔代夫六日游新线路,请你利用 Amadeus 平台做一项包价旅游的报价。

相关理论和问题

1. 旅游系统（Tourism system)
2. 旅游信息化(Tourism informatization)
3. 旅游电子商务(E-commerce of tourism)
4. 目的地管理系统(Destination management system)

这个案例分析了全球四大 GDS 之一,旅游行业的一个主要技术供应商 Amadeus 系统的发展和经营状况。Amadeus 是一个中立的全球分销系统,提供一系列的解决方案,帮助旅游业实现虚拟化。系统建立于1987年,由法航、伊比利亚、汉莎、北欧航空公司和大陆航空公司共同投资兴建,系统于1992年1月正式开始运作。Amadeus及其竞争对手Galileo在欧洲的出现是为了应对美国CRS在20世纪80年代的发展和扩张。当时大部分欧洲国家的航空公司都开发了自己的预订系统,并分别服务于各自国内市场,但随着欧洲空中交通的开放和与美国的航空公司之间的竞争日益激烈,迫切需要建立一个跨欧洲的机票分销系统直接与各旅行代理商连接。Amadeus的宗旨是取代现有航空公司的预订系统,以先进的技术提供中立的分销系统。Amadeus的经营目标还包括提高航空公司的预订效率,同时提供租车和预订饭店的综合性服务,建立一个全球系统,使各类旅游主体供应商和中介都在这个系统中互动。

目前,Amadeus经营着世界上最大的电子市场之一,它支持旅游代理商和旅游服务供应商的营销和销售合作,以及世界上200多市场上的终极消费者用户。现在超过100家航空公司和旅游服务供应商已使该公司提供的技术实现企业内部管理电子化的要求。Amadeus的核心业务已经得到了拓展,它现在可以为各类旅游企业提供技术服务,包括航空公司、旅行代理商、饭店或租车公司(见图6.1)。

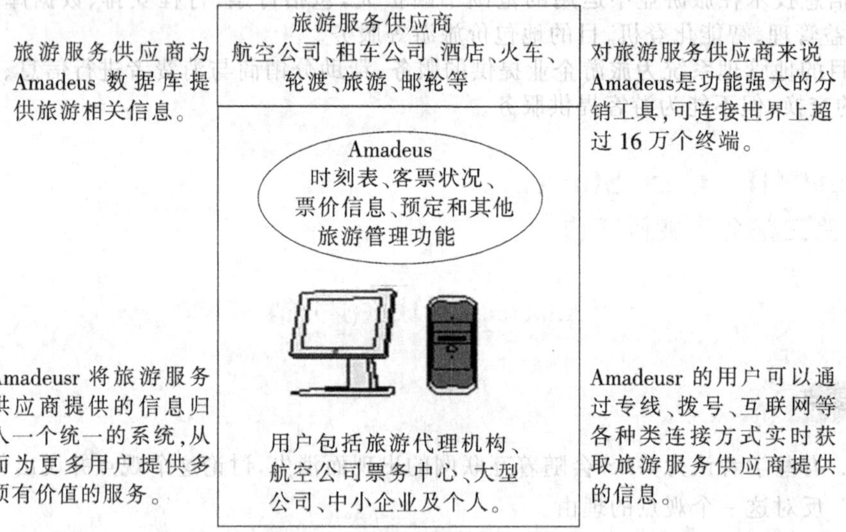

旅游服务供应商为Amadeus数据库提供旅游相关信息。	旅游服务供应商 航空公司、租车公司、酒店、火车、轮渡、旅游、邮轮等 Amadeus 时刻表、客票状况、票价信息、预定和其他旅游管理功能 用户包括旅游代理机构、航空公司票务中心、大型公司、中小企业及个人。	对旅游服务供应商来说Amadeus是功能强大的分销工具,可连接世界上超过16万个终端。
Amadeusr将旅游服务供应商提供的信息归入一个统一的系统,从而为更多用户提供多项有价值的服务。		Amadeusr的用户可以通过专线、拨号、互联网等各种类连接方式实时获取旅游服务供应商提供的信息。

图6.1 Amadeus的主要业务

[Amadeus]系统现拥有18.2万个旅行代理商终端,分布于全世界59 200个旅行代理网点和8 500个机票销售点内,这些终端可以预订500家航空公司的机票,占到世界上定期航班航空业务的95%,此外还可预订58 500家饭店的客房和50余家租车公司的租车业务,这些服务遍及24 900个不同的地方。通过系统还可了解更多其他旅游服务供应商的信息并进行预订,如轮渡、火车、游船、保险公司和旅行社(见图6.2)。Amadeus还拥有美国最大的休闲旅游营销网络之一vacation.com。该公司于1999年上市,当时其三家创始的航空公司占有公司的59.92%的股份:法航23.36%,伊比利亚18.28%,汉莎18.28%,其他股份公开上市发行。

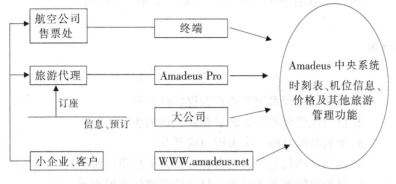

图 6.2 Amadeus 中央系统

Amadeus 总部设在西班牙马德里,其数据中心设在德国的埃尔丁(慕尼黑附近),其发展办公室设在法国的索菲亚安蒂波利斯(尼斯附近)。公司在全世界共有 3950 名员工,在曼谷、布宜诺斯艾利斯和迈阿密设有地区办事处。公司在全球拥有国家市场营销(NMC)网络。e-Travel 是公司的电子商务商业单位,其主要经营活动在美国、欧洲和亚太地区。

旅行代理商仍是系统的主要用户,但系统除了为旅游代理商服务外还为市场上的各供应商提供技术解决方案。e-Travel 就是一个全球在线旅游技术供应商,它为航空公司、企业、旅行代理商及其他在线旅游企业提供电子商务解决方案。e-Travel 的客户遍布 90 多个国家,其中包括空中客车、达美乐·克莱斯勒、捷威、英格索兰、甲骨文和菲利普斯·莫利斯,以及法航、伊比利亚航空公司和快达航空公司等旅游供应商和 Opoodo 之类在线旅行代理商。

e-Travel 已成为一个重要的信息技术供应商和全球旅游行业电子商务支持者。Amadeus 不仅能帮助航空公司分销,而且可以便于机场售票处(ATO)和城市售票处(CTO)进行预订。Amadeus 不再满足于扮演传统的销售和预定应用服务供应商角色,而正在开发新的、更复杂的工具,如开发更多的航空公司其他战略系统的外包业务,特别是容量控制和离港管理业务。已有超过 100 家航空公司在应用这套系统,共安装了 80206 个 Amadeus 终端。系统还为超过 2100 家旅游代理商、173 家公司站点、18 家饭店站点和 39 家航空公司的 128 个网站提供了强大的预订引擎。此外,该公司还为很多合作伙伴提供了电子商务解决方案,包括 Terre Lycos(西班牙、葡萄牙和拉美国家)。Amadeus 的商务旅行管理解决方案使商务旅游者能在自己的台式终端机上直接进行旅行安排和预订。

资料来源:Amadeus:全球旅游分销. Dimitrios Buhalis 著,马晓秋、张凌云译. 旅游电子商务[M],旅游教育出版社,2006.

Part IV Reading Box
第四部分 阅读与分析

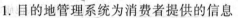

阅读要点分析

1. 目的地管理系统为消费者提供的信息
2. 目的地管理系统为旅游企业提供的服务
3. 加利略项目的三个关键组成部分
4. 加利略项目为个人费者和旅游企业提供的服务
5. 目的地管理系统对提高目的的管理效率的贡献

The Destination Management Systems (DMSs) are very important to tourism industry. They can provide technology which is necessary to coordinate business activities of all partners involved in the management of the destination such as the production and delivery of the tourism product.[1] With more advanced DMSs, consumers can have an idea of amenities and facilities of the destination, and make their own travel schedules according to their own likes and dislikes and conditions.[2] Besides, DMSs are also indispensable for the management of DMOs and the coordination of local suppliers at the destination level as well.

DMSs play a particularly vital role in the management of small and medium-sized tourism enterprises. Being short of money and skill, these enterprises can hardly adopt a comprehensive marketing strategy. Moreover, they have to promote and coordinate their products with the help of destination authorities. Thus, the **functions of DMSs** can be concluded as follows: providing information, accepting reservations for local enterprises, coordinating facilities, promoting tourism policy, controlling operational functions, increasing the expenditure of tourists and boosting the development of the local economy.

It is convenient for destinations to promote and distribute products by means of a centralized facility provided by DMSs. This facility is often coordinated by the public sector. In 1990, the Irish Tourist Braid, working together with the Northern Irish Tourist Board, began to draw up and carry out the **Gulliver project**, which was designed to facilitate the management of Ireland's inexperienced tourism industry and help to distribute tourism products through the provision of on-line information and reservation facilities. With it, Ireland's tourism industry developed very quickly. In 1995, 4.2 million tourists came to Ireland and brought a big profit-IR 1.5 billion in foreign earnings or 6.4% of the gross domestic product (GDP).

Significantly, there are more small and medium-sized enterprises than big ones in the tourism industry in Ireland. Gulliver project is carried out mainly to satisfy their needs and give them access and opportunities similar to those offered to larger enterprises which have already held a firm position in the emerging **electronic market-place**.³

The following organizations were the main financial supporters of Gulliver:
- European Union Development Grants (IR£ 2.9m);
- Bord Failte (IR£ 2.6m);
- International Fund for Ireland Development Grants (IR£ 1.6m);
- The Northern Ireland Tourism Board (IRJsl.5m).

The Gulliver system is made up of three critical elements:
- Gulliver central system. This system deals with and supplies data. It provides a lot of accurate information so that tourism products can be distributed to the customer easily and smoothly.
- Gulliver's supply side. This element of the system is used for the integration of the detailed information of all principals at the destination.
- Gulliver's demand side. This element of Gulliver gives support to such distribution channels as TICs and national, regional and local tourism boards to spread information.

At the same time, it also controls the interconnection between **Gulliver and CRSs** and Videotext networks. Originally the system was planned to facilitate tourists in obtaining information and making reservations. However, it turned out that the gain would not make up for the loss because it cost too much to install many computers and program them to deal with a large quantity of demand during the peak period. As a result, Gulliver project was revised. It put more emphasis on the use of the emerging multimedia technologies and divided **information technologies data** into two categories-**static** (e.g. descriptions, photos, history) and **dynamic** (e.g. availability, rates, schedules). Users can easily search for "static" data on local PCs and "dynamic" data from the central system. It takes only eight seconds or so to make sure whether the products are available or not and principals can receive reservations either on line or by means of fax machines.⁴ In this way, both the requirements on central procession and the cost of communication can be reduced to the minimum extent.

In December 1996 Gulliver began to utilize the **WWW** (http://www.ireland.travel.ie) to distribute the most comprehensive, interactive, multimedia brochure about Irish tourism. It has also drawn up some future plans, one of which is to enlarge the **distribution network** with the support of all Bord Failte offices overseas and through news stands at the destination areas. However, the Bord Failte, a public sector body, has experienced budget cuts. It may make some needed reforms further such as restructuring and downsizing. This may seriously influence the expansion of the project. In that case, the project can continue only on one condition: that a new private sector partner is willing and able to fund it.

Although it was as early as 1968 that destination-orientated CRSs began to be studied, the Destination Management System (DMS) concept appeared almost 22 years later-in the early 1990s. Moreover, at the beginning, most DMSs were just used to help tourist boards to carry out some conventional activities such as the spread of information or local bookings.⁵ In their most advanced form, **DICIRMSs** (or destination integrated computer information reservation management systems) turn out to be more effective. On one hand, they are used to do marketing in a more efficient, systematic and modern way by supporting promotion, distribution and operation in the destination. On the other hand, they better balance the needs and expectations of tourists and locals so as to provide creative tools for tourist boards that can adopt strategic management, differentiate products and improve tourism impacts.

New Words

delivery	n.	交货,交付
integration	n.	成为整体,整合
amenity	n.	令人愉快之物
procession	n.	处理
facilitate	v.	帮助,促进,推动
interactive	adj.	交互作用的

Notes

1. They can provide technology which is necessary to coordinate business activities of all partners involved in the management of the destination such as the production and delivery of the tourism product.
   目的地管理系统能提供必要的技术,以协调目的地管理中各方的商业活动,例如旅游产品的生产与交付。

2. With more advanced DMSs, consumers can have an idea of amenities and facilities of the destination, and make their own travel schedules according to their own likes and dislikes and conditions.
   通过更加先进的 DMS 技术,旅行者能了解到目的地的设施和服务,并按照自己的喜好和条件设计旅行计划。

3. Gulliver project is carried out mainly to satisfy their needs and give them access and opportunities similar to those offered to larger enterprises which have already held a firm position in the emerging electronic market-place.
   Gulliver 项目主要是为满足中小企业的需要,为它们提供在新兴的电子市场中已经占有牢固地位的大公司一样的权利和机会。

4. It takes only eight seconds or so to make sure whether the products are available or not and principals can receive reservations either on line or by means of fax machines.
   旅游者只需八秒钟左右就能判断产品有没有;顾主能在互联网上或通过传真接收预订。

5. Moreover, at the beginning, most DMSs were just used to help tourist boards to carry out some conventional activities such as the spread of information or local bookings.
   而在初期,大多数 DMS 系统仅仅用来帮助旅游机构开展传统的旅游业务,如发布信息或实现本地预订。

Topic discussion

1. What benefits can tourism sectors gain from the DMSs?
2. How can DMSs upgrade the tourist satisfaction in the destination?

3. What are the three critical elements of the Gulliver system?
_____
4. What are the advantages of DICIRMSs?
_____

【即学即用】

With reference to the theory, information or approach applied in the Reading Box, have a case study of the DMS of resorts in your city. Make presentation of your study in Chinese or in English using PPT.

【学习资源库】

为了掌握本章更多的相关专业知识,请您登陆 http://sicnu.edu.cn/,点击国家双语教学示范课程《旅游学概论》,进入网络学堂查询相关资料。

Chapter Review 本章小结

This chapter has described the application of information technology in tourism sectors, such as tour operator, travel agency, hotel, and airline; and it has played a vital role in the competitiveness of tourism enterprises and destinations. Information technology has been widely used for product development, marketing, capacity management, yield management, property management, inventory control and training of personnel. The Destination Management Systems (DMSs) provide information technology which is necessary to coordinate business activities of all partners involved in the destination. In their most advanced form, DICIRMSs are used to do marketing in a more efficient, systematic and modern way. In addition, they better balance the needs and expectations of tourists and locals so as to provide creative tools for tourist boards that can adopt strategic management, differentiate products and improve tourism impacts.

Part V Additional Know-how of Tourism
第五部分 旅游知识扩展

【关键术语】

Yield Management: the use of pricing and inventory controls, based upon historical data, to maximize profits by offering varying fares over time for the same product

收益管理:以历史数据为基准,利用定价和存货的原则,对同一产品在不同时间段的价格进行规定,目的是使利润最大化。

E-commerce: the transaction of commercial dealings (advertising and promotion, sales, billing, payment, and customer servicing) by electronic means rather than through traditional "paper" channels.

电子商务：通过电子手段而不是通过传统的纸上交易所进行的商业交易（比如广告宣传和促销、销售、结算、售后服务等）。

Hub and spoke system：a system that feeds connecting passengers into major gateway airports from short-haul or point-to-point downline routes.

中心轮辐式系统：一种将转乘的游客从短途线路或点对点的路线送到主要门户机场的系统。

Destination Management Systems：systems that consolidate and distribute a comprehensive range of tourism products through a variety of channels and platforms, generally catering for a specific region, and supporting the activities of a destination management organization within that region. DMS attempt to utilize a customer centric approach in order to manage and market the destination as a holistic entity, typically providing destination related information, real-time reservations.

目的地管理系统：该系统通过各种渠道和平台整合并分销各类旅游产品，它通常为一个特定的地区服务，支持该地区内的目的地管理组织的各种活动。目的地管理系统以顾客为中心，把目的地作为一个整体进行管理和市场营销，典型的做法是向旅游者提供他们需要的目的地相关信息，提供实时的预订服务。

Internet service providers：companies that provide domain space for others on computer servers they own, companies that provide travel information that they develop, and companies that provide a combination of the two.

因特网服务供应商：为使用服务器的机构提供空间服务的公司，或是指那些提供旅行信息的公司，也可能是提供以上两种服务的公司。

【知识链接】

1. 旅游目的地信息系统

旅游目的地信息（TDIS）是以计算机软硬件为基础，实现目的地各种旅游资源数据的分析、处理和应用的管理信息系统。按照服务对象的不同，可分为两种：一种是面向游客的信息模式，主要是为旅游者展示各种旅游目的地信息；另一种是面向旅游目的地各管理部门及旅游供应商的管理模式，用以实现各行业之间的信息更新及信息传递。

旅游目的地信息系统 TDIS 基本结构模块：TDIS.jsp 以及内嵌的 Java Applet—Tourism Map，提供旅游地图显示、放大、缩小、距离量算，旅游地理信息查询，添加专题地图等功能。旅游目的地信息系统能查询、统计和进行空间结构分析，空间分析功能是旅游目的地信息系统的一个标志性功能，主要包括通视分析、路径分析以及断面分析三个方面。(1)通过通视分析可以确定某一观察点的最大可观察范围，帮助旅游者选定理想的观察点。(2)路径分析是在给定的限制条件下，在路网中寻找最佳路径。将通视分析和路径分析相结合，可以帮助旅游目的地管理部门规划景区观光路线等。(3)通过断面分析可以了解地形断面的起伏信息、最高点和最低点的位置和高程、两点间的距离等信息，对爱好越野、另辟蹊径的游客很有帮助。

2. 信息通讯技术与旅游目的地营销

当传统的旅游目的地营销系统已不能适应旅游者对旅游信息的需求时，信息通讯技术的发展必然为旅游目的地营销系统的建设和发展带来创新和突破，主要表现在几个方面：

(1) 综合化 信息通讯技术使得旅游目的地营销系统的内容将更加丰富，营销的区域范围将不断扩大。旅游目的地营销系统将提供多层次、全方位的旅游信息和服务：从旅游产品预定、目的地信息指南到网上交流、商务旅行、休闲度假和主题旅游等个性化服务。内容包括出境旅游报名须知及程序、线路推荐、气温状况及当地的吃、住、行、游、购、娱等方面的实用资讯,所提供的信息来自权威部门,最大限度地保证旅游信息最新、最全、最实用。

(2) 细分化 目的地利用分析旅游目的地营销系统的旅游者数据库,可以找到创造利润的超细分市场,为旅游者提供符合旅游市场需求的产品,实现对旅游者的"一对一"营销,满足旅游者的个性化需求。

(3) 服务对象多元化 基于信息通讯技术的旅游目的地营销系统不仅服务于旅游者,满足他们对旅游信息、旅游产品的需求,也服务于旅游目的地,满足目的地树立形象、提升竞争力的要求。

【小思考】
1. 电子商务对旅游者和旅游经营商带来什么便利?请问如何保障网上支付方式的安全?

参考阅读:
(1) 网上促销 旅游电子商务正在改变传统的旅游商务活动方式,WEB 网的广泛应用为旅游业提供了一个全新的信息传播媒体和市场分销渠道。利用网上促销渠道,将特色旅游线路、旅游饭店、旅行社、旅游汽车公司、旅游景点、旅游纪念品等,并配备景点风光照片或音频、视频图像,生动地表现各旅游目的地自然风光和人文风情,发布在旅游专用网站或世界范围内有影响力的网站上,吸引潜在游客,以达到旅游产品促销的目的。

(2) 网上订购 网上订购是旅游电子商务的主要功能。旅游企业和旅游消费者个人的网上订购通常都是由订购网页提供十分友好的订购提示信息和订购交互格式框。当客户填完订购单后,系统会以电子邮件等形式回复订购信息确认单。

(3) 咨询洽谈 旅游电子商务可以使旅游消费者通过非实时的电子邮件、新闻组和实时讨论组来了解旅游市场信息和旅游产品信息,洽谈交易事务。

(4) 网上支付 如果已经在旅游网上进行了订购,可以在网上直接通过信用卡、电子钱包、电子支票和电子现金等多种电子支付方式进行支付。

(5) 传递服务 对于旅游商品等实物的传递,可以通过分销系统及其他方式进行。而对于旅游产品、旅游信息服务等无形商品最适合于网上直接传递,可以从电子仓库中提取货物,用最快的速度发送到用户端。

(6) 交易管理 交易管理涉及旅游商务活动的全过程,牵涉到整个交易中的人、财、物,旅游企业和旅游企业、旅游企业和旅游消费者及旅游企业内部等诸方面的协调和管理。

2. 网上代理和直销对旅游企业有何益处?我国网上代理发展情况如何?

参考阅读:
网上代理,指旅游信息公司(或旅行代理人)抓住某个市场机会,建立网上"虚拟企业",聚集旅游相关的众多商家,形成网上业务联合,为游客提供诸如预订航线机位、饭店房间、租赁汽车等一条龙服务;同时形成网上集团营销,提供多方位销售渠道,为网上企业提供广阔的发展空间。目前 Internet 网上最为出色的旅游"虚拟企业"之一是美国的伽利略国际(Galileo International)公司。伽利略国际公司是全球最早运用信息技术的 CRS(计算机预订系统)进行旅游销售服务的公司之一,业务遍及全球 90 多个国家和地区。世界 525 家航空公司、37 800 家饭店、45 家汽车租赁公司和 47 家邮轮公司及其他旅游经营者通过它的网络系统销售其产品,形成了一整套旅游信息服务网,为企业和游客提供双重便利。同时,网上直销为旅游供应商和游客利用信息平台完成交易。企业可省去大笔原需支付的佣金,游客也省去应支付的服务费,符合双方的利益。

Part VI Further Readings
第六部分 课外阅读

如果您想进一步学习本章的内容,探讨信息技术对旅游者和旅游业的影响和作用,建议您阅读以下学者的著作和论文。

一、中文部分

[1] 查良松,陆均良,罗仕伟.旅游管理信息系统[M].北京:高等教育出版社,2004.

[2] 巫宁.旅游信息化与电子商务经典案例[M].旅游教育出版社,2006.

[3] 孔云峰,论旅游信息系统的概念、内涵与功能[J].桂林旅游高等专科学校学报,2005,(05).

[4] 吴思.信息通信技术(ICT)与旅游产业的潜力和竞争力研究现状[J].旅游学刊,2007,(06).

[5] 汤书昆.Internet环境下中国旅游产业走向全息模块化管理方式初探[J].旅游学刊,1997,(04).

[6] 陈卫民.国内旅游的崛起及其对旅游信息的影响[J].旅游学刊,1996,(03).

[7] 刘锋.中国旅游业信息化:趋势与对策[J].桂林旅游高等专科学校学报,1999,(04).

[8] 汪峰,网络技术:散客旅游市场发展的推进器[J].旅游学刊,2007,(05).

[9] 杨路明,巫宁.旅游产业与电子商务的天然适应性讨论[J].重庆工商大学学报(社会科学版),2003,(06).

[10] 田磊.基于信息通讯技术的旅游目的地营销系统研究[D].山东大学,2005.

二、英文部分

[1] Yeoryios Stamboulis, Pantoleon Skayannis. Innovation strategies and technology for experience-based tourism[J]. *Tourism Management*. 2003(24).

[2] Dimitrios Buhalis. Strategic use of information technologies in the tourism industry[J]. *Tourism Management*. 1998(19).

[3] James Shillinglaw. It was the Week that was in Online Travel[J]. *Travel Agent*, 1999(11).

[4] W. Schertler. Information and Communication Technologies in Tourism[J]. *Annals of Tourism Research*. 2006(24).

[5] Auliana Poon. Tourism Technology and Competitive Strategies. *C. A. B International*, 1993.

[6] Dimitrios Buhalis. Information Technology and Reengineering of Tourism[J]. *Annals of Tourism Research*. 1996(4).

[7] Marianna Sigala. Information & communication technologies in tourism 2002 [J]. *Tourism Management*. 2004(25).

[8] Karl W. Wöber. Information supply in tourism management by marketing decision support systems[J]. *Tourism Management*. 2003(24).

[9] Meral Korzay, Jinhyung Chon. Impact of Information Technology on Cultural Tourism[J]. *Annals of Tourism Research*. 2002(29).

[10] Pauline J. Sheldon. *Tourism Information Technology*[M]. London: Cab International, UK, 1997.

[11] Lawrence J. Trutt, Victor B. Teye, Martin T. Farris. The role of computer reservation systems: International implication for the travel industry[J]. Tourism Management, 1991, 12(1):2—36.

Chapter 7　Tour Operator
第七章　旅游经营商

Learning objects：学习目标

- Study the characteristics of the tour operator who operates within the tourism system (Leiper's model) 学习旅游经营商在旅游系统(Leiper 模型)中经营活动的特点
- Interpret the definition of a tour operator and differentiate a tour operator and a travel agent 解析旅游经营商的定义,区分旅游经营商与旅游代理有何不同
- Have an idea of the operation of a tour operator in the basic structure of the travel industry 了解旅游经营商在旅游产业基本结构中的运作方式
- Appreciate the approaches of the capacity planning in the reservation of a hotel or for an airline, etc. 学习旅游经营商在饭店或航班预订等方面容量计划的制定方法
- Understand the importance of financial evaluation and the measures that can be taken to reduce financial risks 了解财务评估的重要性,以及减少财务风险的措施
- Describe the marketing approaches of a tour operator and its tour management 陈述旅游经营商的营销方法以及旅游管理方法
- Understand who can operate as the tour wholesalers and their distribution channels 了解谁可以做旅游批发商以及旅游批发商分销产品的渠道

Ability goals：能力目标

- Case study 案例分析：中国旅游市场出现 旅游批发商
- Reading Box 阅读分析：Tour Wholesalers in North America 北美的旅游批发商

Part I　Text
第一部分　课文

Tour Operator

【教学要点】

知识要点	掌握程度	相关章节
independent tour operator 独立经营商	重点掌握	本课文与第 1 单元、第 3 单元、第 5 单元、第 6 单元、第 8 单元、第 9 单元、第 15 单元相关内容有联系。
qualifications and categories of tour operator 旅游经营商的资格和类型	重点掌握	
distribution channels of tour operator 旅游经营商的分销渠道	重点掌握	
process of tour operating 旅游经营商运营流程	重点掌握	
capacity planning and financial evaluation 容量计划与财务评估	一般了解	
booking pattern and tour management 预定形式与旅行管理布	一般了解	

　　The tour operator, also called **wholesaler** in some countries, mainly functions as an organizer who combines all the components of a tour to make up a holiday and sells it to the public through his own company, through retail outlets, or through approved retail travel agencies.¹ Tour operators can spend less money buying services of various types in large quantities such as transportation, hotel rooms, sightseeing services, airport transfers, and meals. Therefore, the price of the tour he offers to the public is usually lower than that arranged by an individual traveler.

　　Tour operators can help transportation and ground service suppliers make a big profit every year. They can also organize a variety of tours to a large number of destinations and sell them to the travel agent and the public at different prices according to their durations and seasons.² At the same time, they can inform suppliers of the organized tours in advance and assure them of the number of future passengers.

　　There are usually four kinds of **entities**. They are: (1) the independent tour operator, (2) the airline cooperating closely with a tour wholesaling business, (3) the hotel who provides package tours for its clients, and (4) the operator of motor coach tours.

　　From Figure 7.1, we can easily get an idea of the position of the tour operator in the basic structure of the travel industry. The public or the consumer is the "push" factor which promotes the development of the industry. They can buy travel services from two sources: a retail travel agent or the suppliers of travel services like the airlines, hotels, and other providers of destination services. The tour operator's role is that of consolidating services of airlines and other carriers with the ground services needed into one package, which can be sold through travel agents to consuming public.

◀ 114 ▶

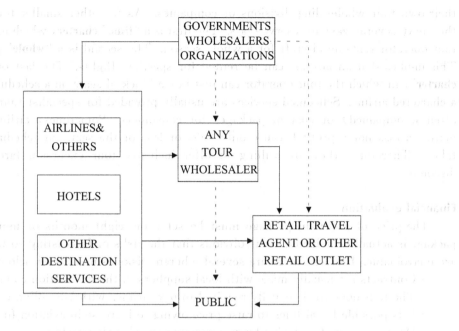

Figure 7.1　Tour operator in the basic structure of the travel industry

Essentially **tour operating** is a process of attempting to provide the possible tourists with aircraft seats and hotel beds (or other forms of accommodation) at an attractive price. It is easy to follow the principles of tour operating-combining transports and accommodation together to create a package and printing it in a brochure for consulting. However, the whole process of tour operating is characterized by practical utility, which requires careful planning, preparation and coordination. For example, in order to promote the packages printed in the brochure, the tour operator has to book the mass media, particularly television, well in advance to advertise them. There are a great number of tasks for the tour company to perform. The following are some main stages of tour operating:

Capacity planning

The tour operator can make use of market forecasts to plan total capacity and combine them with the market strategy to set the type, destination and volume of the tour.[3] Once the tour plan has been made, reservations of beds and aircraft or coach seat must be taken into consideration. There are two forms of bed contracts: **an allocation or a guarantee.** An allocation must be released in time, and the tour operator should return the beds to the hotel on an appropriate day. This type of contract is usually made with the medium-grade hotels and above because it would be easier for them to resell the vacant beds. By doing so, the tour operator can hand over the risk to the hotelier. In turn the hotelier has to make contracts with several operators and offer negotiable prices so as to reduce this risk. Different from an allocation, with a guarantee, hotels get paid for the beds they provide for the tour operator. And this form is mainly used in holidays in which tourists prepare their own meals so that the tour operator can get exclusive contracts.

There are many different ways to book aircraft seats. It is possible for the largest tour operators to run their own airlines while some airlines, particularly in the USA, also have their own tour wholesaling divisions or companies.[4] As for other smaller tour operators, they have several ways to reserve seats. The first is **a "time" charter**, which means that the tour operator rents an aircraft for a whole season. The second is a **"whole" plan charter**. This implies that an aircraft can be rented for specified flights. The last one is a **"part charter"**, in which the tour operator can just buy a block of seats on a scheduled service or a chartered airline. Scheduled services are usually provided for specialist tours (which are often accompanied) or custom packages for consumers. Sometimes, airlines can make neither a loss nor a profit because only 60% or less of the seats on scheduled flights is taken. Therefore, they are willing to offer inclusive tour excursion fares at a good discount.

Financial evaluation

The price of a certain package must be set some eight months or more before the package is actually conducted. It is obvious that the risks of forecasting so far in advance are unavoidable. Besides, there are several inherent risks as mentioned below:
- Contracts are usually made with local suppliers in the destination country;
- The tour operator is usually required to pay airlines with US dollars;
- It is possible for airlines to raise price owing to increase in aviation fuel costs
- Dues, taxes or fees levied by governments are also changeable.

Tour operators have two ways to cope with these risks (called hedging). First, they can set an acceptable range of changes in **exchange rates** so as to determine tour prices and then buy the foreign exchange required at an agreed rate beforehand.[5] Thus, they can be able to meet the obligations required by the contract. Second, they may make an **additional charge** when the customers pay for the cost. However, the second way has brought about some negative impacts and has turned out to be unpopular. In order to avoid these negative impact tour operators should take some measures such as making guarantees that no additional money will be charged, limiting the tendency to ask for more charges, or offering customers the freedom to cancel the tour.[6]

Booking Patterns

Tour operators provide the brochure for tourists to consult the information about specific tours so as to make a decision. The brochure must be launched well before the summer seasons start because a section of the market prefers early bookings so that it can make sure of the destination and make use of any possible promotional prices offered by other sections.[7] **Booking patterns** play a vital role in controlling the progress of advertising and sales campaigns. Typically operators are trying to make their capacity utilization up to 85%—90% in order to balance their income and expenses. The booking patterns concluded from past experience can be used as a reference for tour operators to compare actual with predicted booking. At the time when there are not enough tourists, tour operators have the right to cancel holidays or **consolidate** them into other packages, such as merging flights or combining journey plans and changing accommodation.[8]

As far as customers are concerned, they are often annoyed by the unexpected changes or **consolidation of the journey plans** and it is a hard task for the travel agent to persuade his or her clients into accepting these changes. Tour operators maintain this practice because if they had no right to cancel or consolidate holidays, they would have to raise the average price of a holiday when demand is much less than supply. By contrast, it is easier to solve the problem of underestimating demand because the system enables tour operators to get extra flights or accommodation. On the other hand, tour operators should be cautious about **cancellations** made by their clients and take measures to protect themselves. How much customers can get back is normally arranged on a sliding scale. They may lose part of their deposit if they cancel a holiday six or seven weeks before departure. However, if the cancellation happens only a day or so before departure, they may be refused to get any deposit back.

Tour management

The tours offered by specialist tour operators are often the **escorted tours.** That is to say, tourists conduct the whole journey under the guidance of a tour manager because he intends to supervise arrangements and the process of travel. For the big package tour market, tour operators may send **a representative** to the destination to guide the tour. He must go there in advance and check facilities on behalf of the company. If there are any differences from the brochure, he will request these differences to be put right. When tourists arrive, he should meet them and help them go to the places of accommodation smoothly. Then during the holiday, the representative is required to provide guests such services as giving advice and dealing with the possible problems, as well as supervising, and sometimes organizing social activities and excursions.[9]

After the holiday some customers will write to tour operators to express their compliments, suggestions or complaints. A standard letter can be used as a pattern to deal with most correspondence and tour operators will pay back a little money to those customers who make reasonable complaints. Serious complaints may be settled through arbitration by national associations before legal action is taken.

When we discuss the benefits of direct investment in financial market and the way in which a tour program is organized, we have already taken into consideration many economic aspects of tour operation. The economies of scale resulted from purchases in large quantities is crucial to tour operation. It enables the mass tour operator to set a competitive price for individual packages on the basis of a high rate at which consumers buy the products offered.

Once the tour operator is carrying out a program, he has to take a lot of financial risks, apart from those brought about by such tactical risk avoidance strategies as **a late release clauses,** additional charges and consolidation. This is because there are many unavoidable and fixed costs the tour operator has to pay to run the program. Selling an extra holiday will just need small marginal or variable costs. Therefore, the tour operator can offer large discounts for the trips provided for customers late, sometimes only a few days before departure.

Integration of tour operator The frequent corporate changes and re-alignments that are taking place within the tourism industry are examples of a process known as integration. **Horizontal integration** occurs when firms attain a higher level of consolidation or control with their own sector. This can be achieved in many ways — for example, mergers and alliances with competitors, outright take-overs or the acquisition of shares in other companies within the sector. In contrast, **vertical integration** occurs when a firm obtains greater control over elements of the product chain outside its own sector, e.g. a large tour operator gains control over a company that manufactures small tour buses or the tour operator acquires a chain of travel agents.

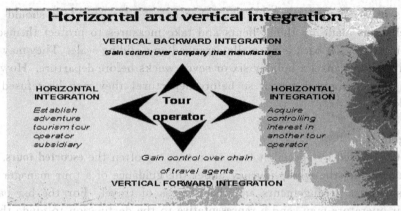

Figure 7.2 Horizontal and vertical integration of the tour operator

New Words

duration	n.	持续时间
discount	n.	折扣
assure	v.t.	担保,保证
launch	v.	创办,开办
coordination	n.	调和,协调
escort	v.	护送
utility	n.	效用,实用性
compliment	n.	称赞,恭维
exclusive	adj.	专有的,独占的

Key Terms

retail outlet　　零售店　　market forecast　　市场预测

Notes

1. The tour operator, also called wholesaler in some countries, mainly functions as an organizer who combines all the components of a tour to make up a holiday and sells it to the public through his own company, through retail outlets, or through approved retail travel agencies.
   旅游经营商,在一些国家也被称为旅游批发商。它是一个组织者,将旅游的所有要素结合起来,组合成一个度假产品,通过自己的公司、零售店或经过批准的零售旅行社销售给公众。

2. They can also organize a variety of tours to a large number of destinations and sell them to the travel agent and the public at different prices according to their durations and seasons.
   他们也可以为许多目的地组织不同的旅行团,并根据旅行团的时间长短和季节情况,以不同的价格将它们出售给旅游代理商和公众。

3. The tour operator can make use of market forecasts to plan total capacity and combine them with the market strategy to set the type, destination and volume of the tour.
   旅游经营商可利用市场预测来规划旅游总容量,并将它们与市场策略结合起来以拟定旅游的类型、目的地和游客量。

4. It is possible for the largest tour operators to run their own airlines while some airlines, particularly in the USA, also have their own tour wholesaling divisions or companies.
最大的旅游经营商可能拥有航空公司,而某些航空公司,尤其是在美国,也有自己的旅游批发部门或批发公司。

5. First, they can set an acceptable range of changes in exchange rates so as to determine tour prices and then buy the foreign exchange required at an agreed rate beforehand.
首先,他们将设定一个可接受的汇率变化范围,以便制定旅游价格,然后以事先商定的利率购买所需外汇。

6. In order to avoid these negative impact tour operators should take some measures such as making guarantees that no additional money will be charged, limiting the tendency to ask for more charges, or offering customers the freedom to cancel the tour.
为了避免这些负面影响,旅游经营商应当采取这样的措施:承诺不增加额外费用、不向游客索取额外费用、游客有权取消旅游。

7. The brochure must be launched well before the summer seasons start because a section of the market prefers early bookings so that it can make sure of the destination and make use of any possible promotional prices offered by other sections.
这本小册子必须在夏季之前推出,因为部分企业倾向尽早预订,以确保安排目的地,尽可能利用其他企业的促销价格。

8. At the time when there are not enough tourists, tour operators have the right to cancel holidays or consolidate them into other packages, such as merging flights or combining journey plans and changing accommodation.
游客数量不够时,旅游经营商有权取消旅行团或并团,如合并航班和旅游计划,改变住宿条件。

9. Then during the holiday, the representative is required to provide guests such services as giving advice and dealing with the possible problems, as well as supervising, and sometimes organizing social activities and excursions.
然后,在旅游度假期间,旅游经营商的代表须向游客提供一些服务,如咨询建议、处理可能发生的问题、监督执行旅游合同、组织社交活动和短程旅行。

Exercise

1. Fill in the blanks with proper words to complete the following statements.

| specialist | escorted | exclusive | once | financial | advance |

(1) At the same time, they can inform suppliers of the organized tours in _____ and assure them of the number of future passengers.

(2) _____ the tour plan has been made, reservations of beds and aircraft or coach seat must be taken into consideration.

(3) And this form is mainly used in holidays in which tourists prepare their own meals so that the tour operator can get _____ contracts.

(4) Scheduled services are usually provided for _____ tours (which are often accompanied) or custom packages for consumers.

(5) Once the tour operator is carrying out a program, he has to take a lot of _____

risks, apart from those brought about by such tactical risk avoidance strategies as a late release clauses, additional charges and consolidation.

(6) The tours offered by specialist tour operators are often the _____ tours.

2. Questions for discussion

(1) How does the tour operator distribute the tourism products?
_____

(2) What is the main process of tour operating?
_____

(3) How does the tour operator carry out the capacity planning?
_____

(4) What should tour operators do at the stage of marketing?
_____

(5) What are the inherent risks that tour operators face and how do they cope with them?
_____

(6) In the escorted tours, what should the tour operator's representative do?
_____

Part II　Guided Reading
第二部分　课文导读

　　旅游经营商又称旅游批发商，即主要经营批发业务的旅行社或其他旅游企业。所谓批发业务，是指旅游批发商根据自己对市场需求的了解和预测，大批量地订购交通运输公司、饭店、目的地经营接待业务的旅行社、旅游景点等有关旅游企业的产品和服务，然后将这些单项产品组合成不同的包价旅游线路产品或包价度假集合产品，最后通过自己的公司或者通过零售代理商用单一价格将包价产品向旅游消费者出售。

　　本文阐述了旅游经营商的类型，旅游经营商在旅游生产活动中的地位和作用，以及旅游经营商的经营流程，包括产品计划、产品分销、成本控制、旅行管理等业务，对我们研究旅游企业如何开发、分销旅游产品，提高旅游服务质量和经济效益都具有重要的借鉴意义。

　　在我国，旅游经营商通常被称为"旅游批发商"，这是为什么呢？因为旅游经营商需要大批量购买三大旅游要素产品，构成了传统意义上的包价旅游，即购买交通（航班、渡轮等）、住宿（饭店客房、自助式公寓等）、接送（通过旅游巴士、出租车）。因此，在旅游产品分销链上，旅游经营商可以被视作旅游业中的"批发商"，他们买进旅游产品，然后通过旅游代理商售出这些产品。

　　那么，旅游经营商是如何将旅游产品销售给旅游者的呢？它与其上下游企业是什么关系呢？旅游经营商是包价旅游产品的组织者，从多家上游服务供应企业批量购入旅游产品，然后将各项服务组合成包价旅游产品一次性销售给旅游者。旅游经营商从上游企业批量购入产品可以获得价格折扣，使包价旅游产品的价格低于各单项旅游产品价格之和，能够帮助旅游者节约费用支出。旅游经营商组织的包价旅游产品还简化了旅游者的购买活动，为其提供了方便，降低了购买风险。旅游经营商的上游企业如航空公司、饭店等一般固定资产比例较高、市场应变性差，旅游经营商与这些企业签有长期的合作契约，在旅游淡季时为之补充大量的客源，使企业的供求状况得以改善。旅游经营商还可以帮助住宿业在异地开辟新的市场、帮助交通运输业创造出新的需求。旅游经营商的专业化经营有助于上下游企业平衡供求关系，有助于提高旅游市场的销售效率。

　　旅游经营商的特点主要包括：第一，包价旅游的低廉花费与个人自助旅游所花费相比更具竞争力。因为经营商可以大批量购买,这样就可以从各个服务提供商那里获得折扣价。第二,旅游经营商可以针对市场的不同需求,设计多样旅游产品,供旅游代理商和旅游者选择。第三,因为旅游经营商可以提前给地接供应商提供未来的有关信息,减小了旅游目的地的经营风险。第四,绝大多数旅游经营商都拥有自己的零售网络,但因投入人力、物力过多,以及希望有更广阔的销售渠道,旅游代理商仍然是旅游产品的主要销售渠道。

旅游经营商有两种主要的类型:独立经营商和生产商拥有的公司。独立旅游经营商是指那些属于完全独立的实体并且可以随意与任何生产商洽谈业务的旅游经营商;生产商拥有自己的旅游公司是指那些为某一生产商所拥有的旅游经营商。由于生产商拥有其包价产品中的某一要素,因此这类旅游经营商自主权相对较少,其包价产品主要是为了销售母公司剩余产品。

当一家旅游代理商同意出售某一旅游经营商的产品时,他们通常会拟定一份代理协议,并借以正式明确双方的关系。那么,这家旅游代理商就成了旅游经营商的指定代理机构,旅游经营商将根据其服务付给旅游代理商一定数额的佣金。为了便于旅游代理商销售其旅游产品,旅游经营商必须定期向旅游代理商提供旅游产品宣传资料以及高效的预订系统。旅游经营商的传统做法是雇佣实地销售代表,把他们派到销售其产品的各个旅游代理商。销售代表的职责就是检查各旅游代理商是否收到旅游产品宣传册并提供产品介绍材料的场地等。此外,销售代表还要解答旅游代理商关于销售方面的疑问,有时还要对旅游代理商进行培训。

尽管大多数的旅游经营商都是通过旅游代理商来销售自己的产品,但仍然有一部分旅游经营商,尤其是专项旅游经营商更愿意直接面对市场。直接面对市场就无法通过代理商来展示自己的产品,于是他们不得不将更多的钱花费在做广告和其他宣传方式上来向公众传递其产品信息。

旅游经营商与国家旅游管理部门之间的关系通常非常密切,因为国家旅游管理部门举办的促销活动对旅游经营商的营销活动来说是一种有益的补充。例如,如果某一国家的旅游管理部门大张旗鼓地举办一次全国性的电视或报刊宣传活动,那么经营前往该国旅游的旅游经营商就可能获得额外的旅游预订。相反,如果没有国家旅游管理部门的推广活动,旅游经营商很难向消费者传递这个国家值得一游的信息。例如,在1993年以前,印度尼西亚一直都没有在英国设立旅游办事处,所以旅游经营商要想说服游客到巴厘岛以外的印尼景点旅游是一件非常困难的事。对于希望开发新项目的旅游经营商来说,各国的旅游管理部门是相关信息的来源和进行联系的对象。若没有旅游管理部门的支持,旅游经营商在旅游市场上的发展是相当艰难的。

旅游知识测试

正误判断:请在正确的选题上划√,错误的选题上划×。

1. 旅游经营商在我国也称作"旅游批发商",购买交通(航班、渡轮等)、住宿(饭店客房、自助式公寓等)、接送(通过旅游巴士、出租车)产品,组成单一价格,并通过旅游代理商将包价旅游产品出售给旅游者。

2. 旅游经营商从上游企业批量购入产品可以获得价格折扣,使包价旅游产品的价格低于各单项旅游产品价格之和,能够帮组旅游者节约费用支出。

3. 旅游经营商与其上游企业如航空公司、饭店等签有长期的合作契约,在旅游淡季时不能为上游企业补充客源,与这些企业有时会发生利益冲突。

4. 为了便于旅游代理商销售其旅游产品,旅游经营商定期向旅游代理商提供旅游产品宣传资料,但是旅游代理商要自备预定系统。

5. 旅游经营商可以派出自己的销售代表,为旅游代理商解答关于销售方面的疑问,指导、监察销售情况,对旅游代理商进行培训。

Part III　Case Study
第三部分　案例研究

中国旅游市场出现旅游批发商

分析要点

1. 为什么较具实力的旅行社纷纷争做上游批发商？
2. 青旅控股在争做旅游批发商上采取了什么措施？
3. 广东国旅假期是如何建立旅游批零网络体系的？
4. 青旅控股与广东"国旅假期"批发体系有何不同？横向一体化与纵向一体化各有何利弊？
5. 假如你上任一家旅游企业的总经理，你如何开展旅游产品的批发业务？

相关理论和问题

1. 旅行社分类和组结构（Categories and structures of travel agencies）
2. 旅游上游企业与下游企业（Upstream and downstream enterprises in tourism industry）
3. 旅游产业链（Tourism industrial chain）
4. 旅游产品销售渠道（Sales channels of tourism products）

我国旅游业发展趋势正处于从观光旅游向休闲度假旅游转型的阶段，消费者对旅行社的依赖正在降低，旅行社在价值链上需要重新定位。旅行社的核心竞争力在于对旅游价值链关键要素的控制，渠道分销网络和对客源目标市场的影响力，产品优化设计能否成为同类的标准，是否能提供优质和差异化的服务。旅游批发商大多是专线批发，涵盖省内、国内、出境旅游市场，有较好的分销渠道和市场规模，获取利润的能力较强。目前，我国中小旅行社面临着短期内规模无法扩张、客源市场竞争激烈等各种问题，国外旅行社正在进入国内市场，中小旅行社面临着为生存而战的困境。近几年，旅游批发商是旅游界出现频率较高的一个词。旅游业内人士普遍认为，中国入世后旅行社市场会逐步分流，形成上层批发商、中层代理商、下层零售商的金字塔型结构。由此，争做上游批发商成为较具实力旅行社的共同想法。

一、青旅控股：锁定国际化旅游批发商

2001年6月，青旅控股首席执行官蒋建宁在接受记者采访时指出："加入WTO之后，国内旅行社将遇到国外旅行社的直接竞争。为此，中青旅将把成为国际化的旅游批发商作为自己发展的明确定位。公司采取的相应策略包括：扩大市场份额，树立规模优势，为今后参与国际竞争与合作打下基础；大幅度增加对新产品开发的投入，设计新的旅游模式和旅游产品，以跳出单纯价格战的恶性循环。已经推出的产品包括商务旅游、休闲旅游、散客自助旅游等一系列新业务；建立先进的企业制度，重视用灵活的机制吸引人才。"蒋建宁介绍公司对于旅游产业未来发展的模式时说："公司以中青旅的母体作为青旅控股旅游产业的核心和后台，以青旅在线和中青旅连锁作为电子网络和实体网络两大销售平台。在业务上，母体更多地侧重于批发业务和后台服务，中青旅连锁侧重于零售和直销业务，而青旅在线则偏重于创新业务,三者通过管理系统有机地联系在一起,形成规模优势。青旅在线网站主要是提供个性化服务,以顺应市场需求。青旅在线的推出,对于母体业务的整合是一个很大的促进,母体作为批发商,在产品研发、服务监控、投诉接待及酒店、票务中心的整合方面都已取得了相当大的进展。"

二、广东"国旅假期":打造华南最大旅游批发商

近年来,一些旅行社也先后提出"成立连锁企业"、"互为代理"等近似旅游批发商的概念,但是广东"国旅假期"却直接提出"打造华南地区最大旅游批发商"的口号并公开展示实力,在旅游业内引起巨大反响。广东"国旅假期"采取了以下几次大的举措:

(1) 广东"国旅假期"买断神农架旅游景区专营权。2002年4月8日,广东"国旅假期"买断神农架旅游景区专营权,这种"景区专营权"的方式,在中国旅游市场尚属首次。"国旅假期"与神农架的协议为期两年。据"国旅假期"与湖北神农架林区政府的协议,该旅行社两年内将要投入二百万元人民币用于景区的宣传推广,"国旅假期"2002年要为神农架输送一万人次的客源,2003年则达到二万人次,以帮助神农架稳定客源。神农架林区政府则承诺,通过门票、饭店的打折优惠政策,使旅行社获得绝对的价格优势。广东其他旅行社如果组团游览神农架,须经"国旅假期"批准。

(2) 2003年广州国际旅游展销会上推出"国旅假期连锁企业展厅"。广东"国旅假期"旅行社在2003年广州国际旅游展销会上,一举包下近30个展位,成为此次交易会上最大的企业展馆——"国旅假期连锁企业展厅"。"国旅假期连锁企业展厅"集了广东旅游集团公司麾下全体成员,包括:国旅假期、白云宾馆、国旅旅游汽车公司等,另外还有日本豪斯登堡、HELLO KITTY株式会社、日本长崎观光、东南旅游(泰国)公司、香港越海旅游、神农架旅游集团公司等100多家中外景点、景区、旅行社及旅游相关企业。这是自2002年8月13日挂牌和连锁企业网络正式投入运转后"国旅假期"的首次集体公开亮相,是专业实力群体的展示。业内人士指出,"国旅假期"此举,昭示华南地区最大的旅游批发商网络已具雏形。

中国旅行社协会副会长、广东"国旅假期"总经理李进茂表示:旅游线路专营权是市场化的一种尝试,"国旅假期"很想改变中国旅行社的产业结构,由目前的水平经营状况,向垂直方向发展,逐步构筑旅游批零网络体系。"华南地区最大旅游批发商"这一概念,是强调"华南地区"指的是国旅假期网络的规模和实力已达到华南最大,而不是指其网络只是面向华南地区。

"国旅假期"多年来,一直致力于建设一个以代理商为中坚,以旅游营销网络为基础,完全自由开放、互利互惠的金字塔形批发营销网络,而不是某一封闭市场、封闭地区或封闭系统内的。"国旅假期"各连锁企业及广东国旅旅游汽车公司、国旅股份旅游服务公司、旅游房地产牧业管理公司的资源经过全面整合后,利用大家共建的批发与零售实体网络入"国旅假期互联网报名系统"、国旅假期网站等虚拟网络,打造出华南地区最大旅游批发、零售系统。其旅游资源包括其"国旅假期连锁企业"品牌全部共享,其连锁企业保留完整的个性品牌,以"国旅假期"长期打造的品牌和质量凝聚连锁企业,希望各连锁企业能借助这一批发网络做大做强,从而透过旅游批发商为其他网络成员提供更多利益,达到利益共享,最终将整个网络做大做强。

资料来源:中国新闻网. 市场观察:中国旅游市场首次出现"旅游批发商". http://www.chinanews.com.cn/2002-05-28/26/189433.html.

Part IV Reading Box
第四部分　阅读与分析

Tour Wholesalers in North America

阅读要点分析

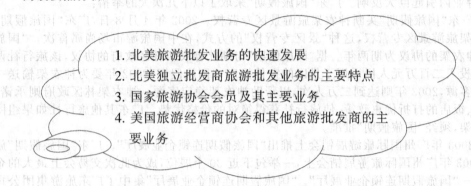

1. 北美旅游批发业务的快速发展
2. 北美独立批发商旅游批发业务的主要特点
3. 国家旅游协会会员及其主要业务
4. 美国旅游经营商协会和其他旅游批发商的主要业务

Tour wholesaling in the U.S. began to expand in the 1960s due to air carriers' efforts to increase the increasing numbers of aircraft seats. Now, it has developed into one of the most important parts of the U.S. travel industry. Its business is mainly made up of planning, preparing, and selling a vacation tour. The wholesaler usually combines transportation, food, accommodation, sightseeing and other services to make a package tour. Travel agents will sell these **package tours** to the public on behalf of the wholesalers.

In the past ten years, the number of the independent tour wholesalers has grown dramatically and now there are more than 2000 wholesalers. However, it is only a small number of large operators who control the large part of the business. There are many typical characteristics in the independent tour wholesaler's business.

- It is relatively easier to start the business.
- The speed of cash flow is fast.
- Their products on sale are seldom returned.
- It is possible for them to make a big profit from equity because they need less money to start such a business.

It was estimated that in 1996, the tourism industry in North America created approximately $11.6 billion in U.S. dollars, which is mainly composed of all the estimated expenditures tour operators spent for the tours they operate and for other transportation expenses, as well as expenditures made by tour travelers while traveling.[1]

Impact happened mainly in the United States, which was estimated $9.6 billion in 1996, while Canada just took $2.0 billion in U.S. dollars. It usually costs a typical group tour of 40 passengers $6270 or so to spend one night in a medium-sized North American city.

According to the **United Motor Coach Association**, the number of tours operated by tour companies in the United States and Canada in 1996 increased 6.6% over 1995. Specifically it added up to more than 600,000 (accurately 624,626). There were averagely 36,400 passengers on one-day tours and totally 13.3 million passenger days in 1996, while the passengers on multi-day tours averaged 32,900 and amounted to 12.0 million in the whole year.[2] In total the tour passenger days in 1996 were 74.1 million. And the full-time jobs created by the group tour business are 194,149.

The primary tour wholesaler organization in North America is the **National Tour Association (NTA)**, which was set up in 1951. It mainly consists of (a) group tour operators, who organize and sell package tours in the United States, Canada, and Mexico, and (b) suppliers, who provide the package components for tour operators and can be regarded as anyone of the following: hotels, attractions, restaurants, bus companies, airlines, passenger vessels, sightseeing companies, destination marketing organizations, and other travel and tourism entities.

The services the association offers aim to provide its members business opportunities and professional education so that they can be able to develop their business. These services include marketing assistance, educational programs, government mental representation, and communications for its **membership**. What's more, the association produces two big events every year. One is the NTA Convention and Tour and Travel Exchange, which is one of the largest travel industry gatherings held in North America and in which its members can hold business meetings frequently and take part in educational programs such as seminars to enhance their knowledge and professionalism in this field.[3] The other is the Spring Tour and Travel Exchange, which again provides them a chance to do business and improve themselves.

NTA has established a strict **code of ethics**, which its members are required to observe. This code is very helpful for the members to conduct their business activities smoothly, which benefits the traveling public a lot.[4] The association is the primary supporter of the group tour product in North America. It makes an effort to promote group tours and help consumers realize that there are substitutes for the vacation. At the same time, it has made Consumer Protection Plan for the purpose of providing the traveling public protection. Their web site is http://www.nta.online.com.

Another organization representing tour wholesalers is the **U.S. Tour Operators Association (USTOA)**. It aims to provide protection of the consumers; to educate the travel industry, government agencies, and the public about tours, vacation packages, and tour operators; to maintain a high level of professional standards within the industry; and to develop travel worldwide. The organization also carries out a strict code of ethics and requires its members to abide by it. In addition, USTOA's members must represent all facts, conditions and requirements concerning tours and vacation packages truthfully and accurately so as to maintain a high level of professionalism.[5]

There are many other organizations which offer helps for tour operators or wholesalers such as the American Society of Travel Agents, PATA (Pacific Asia Travel Association), ACTO (Association of Caribbean Tour Operators), and TIAA (Travel Industry Association of America).

The business of sightseeing companies is to operate local or short tours. They also take part in various organizations, such as American Sightseeing International and Grayline and those mentioned above so that they can get help in the aspect of local sightseeing services and personnel.

New Words

dramatically	adv.	引人注目地
seminar	n.	研讨会
approximately	adv.	大约，大致
professionalism	n.	专业精神；专业技巧
representation	n.	代表；表征
abide	v.	遵守，信守

Notes

1. It was estimated that in 1996, the tourism industry in North America created approximately $11.6 billion in U.S. dollars, which is mainly composed of all the estimated expenditures tour operators spent for the tours they operate and for other transportation expenses, as well as expenditures made by tour travelers while traveling.
   据估计,1996年北美地区的旅游业创造了约116亿美元,这些利润主要包括旅游经营商经营旅行团的费用和其他交通费用以及游客在旅游中的支出。

2. There were averagely 36,400 passengers on one-day tours and totally 13.3 million passenger days in 1996, while the passengers on multi-day tours averaged 32,900 and amounted to 12.0 million in the whole year.
   1996年,一日游旅客全年共计1330万人次,平均每天36,400人次;多次游旅客全年共计1200万人次,平均每天32,900人次。

3. One is the NTA Convention and Tour and Travel Exchange, which is one of the largest travel industry gatherings held in North America and in which its members can hold business meetings frequently and take part in educational programs such as seminars to enhance their knowledge and professionalism in this field.
   一个是国家旅游协会大会和观光旅行交流会,这是在北美举行的最大的旅游业界聚会之一,其成员可以在此频繁举行商务会议,并且参加如研讨会之类的教育项目以加强他们在此领域的知识及专业技巧。

4. This code is very helpful for the members to conduct their business activities smoothly, which benefits the traveling public a lot.
   此行为规范有助于引导成员们顺利进行商业活动,这对公众也是非常有利的。

5. In addition, USTOA's members must represent all facts, conditions and requirements concerning tours and vacation packages truthfully and accurately so as to maintain a high level of professionalism.
   此外,USTOA的成员必须如实、准确地描绘有关旅游和度假线路的所有事实、条件和要求,从而保持高水平的专业技巧。

Topic discussion

1. What are the main businesses of tour wholesalers?

2. What are the typical characteristics of the independent tour wholesaler's business?

3. What is the National Tour Association (NTA) and what are the main services it offers?

4. What does the U.S. Tour Operators Association (USTOA) aim at?

5. What do the tour wholesaler organizations in the United States contribute to the development of tourism?

【即学即用】

With reference to the theory, information or approach applied in the Reading Box, have a case study of the tour operator you know. Make presentation of your study in Chinese or in English using PPT.

【学习资源库】

为了掌握本章更多的相关专业知识,请您登录 http://sicnu.edu.cn/,点击国家双语教学示范课程《旅游学概论》,进入网络学堂查询相关资料。

Chapter Review 本章小结

This chapter has differentiated a tour operator and a travel agent, and described the operation of a tour operator in the basic structure of the travel industry. The business of tour operator is mainly made up of planning, preparing, and selling a vacation tour. It also provides such services as making reservations and combining transportation and ground services to create a package tour. National Tour Association is a successful example of tour operating. Not all entities can operate as tour wholesalers; each of them has its own distribution channel. Retail outlets such as travels agents and airline ticket offices are the main entities that operate on behalf of the tour operator. Marketing approaches of a tour operator and tour management are essential for the tour operating. Measures such as proper financial evaluation and reasonable booking patterns can be taken to reduce financial risks.

Part V Additional Know-how of Tourism
第五部分 旅游知识扩展

【关键术语】

Tour operators: a company that specializes in the planning and operation of prepaid, preplanned vacations and makes these available to the public, usually through travel agents, a business providing a package of tourism-related services for the customer, including some combination of accommodation, transportation, restaurants and attraction visits.

旅游经营商:对已经预先计划和预先付费的度假方式进行规划和操作,通常是通过旅行代理商把它销售给公众的公司。旅游经营商是为顾客提供包括食宿、交通、景区参观等一揽子包价旅游相关服务的企业。

Tour wholesaler: A company that plans, markets, and operates tours. Marketing is always done through intermediaries such as retail travel agents, association, a club, or a tour organizer-never directly to the public as is sometimes done by tour operators. In industry, tour operator and tour wholesaler are synonymous.

旅游批发商: 是指计划、销售和经营旅游的公司。它的销售过程往往通过中间商,比如零售旅游代理、协会、俱乐部或旅游组织者来进行。同旅游经营商一样,从不直接向公众销售。在行业的术语中,旅游经营商与旅游批发商在概念上的相同的。

Travel agencies: a business providing retail travel services to customers for commission on behalf of other tourism industry sectors

旅行社: 代表旅游产业其他部门,向顾客提供零售服务获取佣金的企业。

Tour package: A prepaid tour that includes transportation, lodging, and other ingredients, usually meals, transfers, sightseeing or car rentals. Maybe varied, but typically includes at least three ingredients sold at a fixed price.

包价旅游: 一种预付费用的旅行,包含运输、住宿和其他方面,通常是餐饮、中转、观光或汽车租赁。服务内容繁多,但一般至少包括三个方面的产品组合,且价格是固定的。

Horizontal integration: occurs when firms attain a higher level of consolidation or control within their own sector

横向整合: 横向整合时,公司通过整合自身所在产业领域内的企业达到较高程度的整合或控制。

Vertical integration: occurs when a corporation obtains greater control over elements of the product chain outside its own sector

纵向整合: 纵向整合时,公司能更好地控制自身产业领域以外的产业链要素。

【知识链接】

1. 批发旅游经营商

批发旅游经营商是指主要从事批发业务的旅行社和旅游公司,是连接生产者与零售商、消费者的桥梁。它是通过大批量地购买其他部门产品,将这些产品按日程编排为报价旅游产品,然后通过各种零售渠道出售给旅游者。因此,旅游批发经营商通过大量旅游交通运输企业、饭店、旅游景点等企业的单项产品,将这些产品编排成多种时间、价格的包价旅游项目,然后再批发给旅游零售商,最终出售给旅游消费者。旅游批发经营商的经营范围有宽有窄,可在外地设置办事处或建合资企业开展销售,也可在特定目标市场经营某一块旅游产品,如探险旅游等。批发旅游经营商又可分为旅游经营商和旅游批发商,两者概念相近,但是又有一定区别:旅游批发商是通过中间人出售自己的包价旅游产品,一般不会零售;旅游经营商则通过其零售机构从事零售、批发和零售兼有。旅游批发商通过购买并组合现成的服务,形成新的包价;而旅游经营商通常设计新产品。旅游批发商一般不从事地方接待业务,而旅游经营商则从事接待业务。虽然旅游经营商和旅游批发商的概念在意义上并不完全相同,但随着国外旅游业的发展和变化,国外旅游研究权威者认为其概念现在已经没有明显区别,一般情况下可以通用。

2. 专业媒介者

在国外,存在着许多被称为专业媒介者的中间商,主要包括旅游经纪人、奖励旅游公司、会议计划者、协会执行人、公司旅游办公室等。它们不同于经营商和代理商,通常不收取佣金,除奖励旅游公司以外,他们都是典型的工薪职员代表本组织以较低成本承办旅游业务。在专业媒介者的构成中,旅游经纪人是一个特殊的旅游中间商,它不拥有旅游产品的"所有权",不控制旅游产品价格及销售条件,不卷入交易实力,只为旅游企业与旅游消费者牵线搭桥,促成双方交易,成交后,旅游企业付给他佣金,因此,旅游经纪人不承担任何风险。一般情况下,旅游经纪人主要销售汽车旅游。如美国南加州汽车俱乐部有500万成员,有40多个旅行代理人,这些人属于专业媒介者。

【小思考】
1. 旅游经营商的存在对游客来说有何利益?旅游经营商如何为上游企业规避风险?

参考阅读:
从旅游者的角度来说,旅游经营商从上游企业批量购入产品并获得折扣,使得包价旅游产品价格低于各单项旅游产品之和,能够帮助旅游者节约支出。旅游经营商的包价旅游产品简化了旅游者的购买活动,为其提供了便利。旅游是一次经历,旅游者不能事先检验其产品质量,旅游服务的供应企业大部分远离旅游者的居住地,使得旅游产品的购买风险较大,旅游经营商的存在减少了产品的不确定性,降低了旅游者的购买风险。从供应企业的角度来看,旅游经营商的上游企业如航空公司、饭店等固定资产比例高、市场应变差,旅游经营商与这些企业签有长期合作协议,在需求淡季时为他们补充大量客源,使企业的供求关系得以改善。旅游经营商的专业化经营有助于上游企业平衡供求关系,有助于提高市场的销售效率,因而得以存在。

2. 如何理解小型旅游经营商?小型旅游经营商的目标市场是什么?

参考阅读:
小型旅游经营可以提供大型竞争对手无法提供的好处:第一,小型旅游经营商往往专门经营需要专业技能的细分市场,对具体某一项旅游的特点更了解,可以树立优质和独一无二的形象。例如其所设计的特种旅游项目,可以给旅游者提供尽可能完善的服务,又留有许多让旅游者自主参与的余地,通过形式各异的自然环境的探险,满足旅游者求异和征服的欲望需求,从而树立了在这一旅游项目上的专业性。第二,小型旅游经营商可能经营那些大型旅游经营商看来难度大而不值得开发的世界某些地区(如非洲、南美等地)。他们利用自身的优势,集中主要的财力、物力和人力,大力开发某一目标市场,确立自己在这一市场上的有利地位。例如集中优势开发非洲某一地区的野生动物体验旅游,让旅游者在非洲草原上感受到原始地球的同时感受到旅行社在这一旅游项目上的绝对优势。第三,小型旅游经营商只面对相对较少的客人,所以能够为客人提供更加个性化的服务,有时甚至还为以前的客人提供业务通讯期刊。

Part VI Further Readings
第六部分 课外阅读

如果您想进一步学习本章的内容,探讨饭店的在旅游业中的作用,如何经营管理旅游饭店,建议您阅读以下学者的著作和论文。

一、中文部分
[1] Pat Yale. 程尽能等译. 旅行社经营业务[M]. 北京:旅游教育出版社,2004.
[2] 杜江等. 旅行社经营与管理[M]. 南京:南京大学出版社,2001.
[3] 佟伟,燕兴. 中美旅游产品销售渠道管理比较研究[J]. 桂林旅游高等专科学校学

报，1998(03).
[4] 何云霞. 旅行社的流程再造及其组织变革[J]. 旅游学刊，1998(05).
[5] 杜江，戴斌. 中外旅行社制度环境比较研究[J]. 旅游学刊，2000(01).
[6] 姚延波. 我国旅行社分类制度及其效率研究[J]. 旅游学刊，2000(02).
[7] 刘赵平. 美国旅行社业最新发展态势研究——兼议对中国旅行社业的启迪[J]. 旅游学刊，1999(03).
[8] 张建梅，韦广平. 我国旅行社经营资格对旅游业的影响——兼与日本旅行社经营资格比较[J]. 桂林旅游高等专科学校学报，1999(01).
[9] 代葆屏. 旅行社供应链管理模式初探[J]. 北京第二外国语学院学报，2002(01).
[10] 陈永昶. 从旅游业发展模式看我国旅行社的跨国经营[J]. 桂林旅游高等专科学校学报，2005(04).

二、英文部分

[1] Marianna Sigala. A supply chain management approach for investigating the role of tour operators on sustainable tourism: the case of TUI[J]. *Journal of Cleaner Production*，2008，(10)：1589—1599.
[2] Sofronis Clerides, Paris Nearchou, Panos Pashardes. Intermediaries as quality assessors: Tour operators in the travel industry[J]. *International Journal of Industrial Organization*，2008，(26)：372—392.
[3] Jeroen Van Wijk, Winifred Persoon. A Long-haul Destination: Sustainability Reporting Among Tour Operators[J]. *European Management Journal*，2006，(24)：381—395.
[4] Michael Grosspietsch. Perceived and projected images of Rwanda: visitor and international tour operator perspectives[J]. *Tourism Management*，2006，(27)：225—234.
[5] Constantinos Bastakis, Dimitrios Buhalis, Richard Butler. The perception of small and medium sized tourism accommodation providers on the impacts of the tour operators' power in Eastern Mediterranean[J]. *Tourism Management*，2004，(25)：151—170.
[6] Rita D. Medina-Muñoz, Diego R. Medina-Muñoz, Juan M. García-Falcón. Understanding European tour operators' control on accommodation companies: an empirical evidence[J]. *Tourism Management*，2003，(24)：135—147.
[7] Nevenka Cavlek. Tour operators and destination safety[J]. *Annals of Tourism Research*，2002，(29)：478—496.
[8] Seyhmus Baloglu, Mehmet Mangaloglu. Tourism destination images of Turkey, Egypt, Greece, and Italy as perceived by US-based tour operators and travel agents[J]. *Tourism Management*，2001，(22)：1—9.
[9] Michael Bottomley Renshaw. Consequences of integration in UK tour operating[J]. *Tourism Management*，1994，(15)：243—245.
[10] Pauline J. Sheldon. The tour operator industry: An analysis[J]. *Annals of Tourism Research*，1986，(13)：349—365.

Chapter 8 Accommodation and Hotel Chain
第八章 住宿与饭店连锁

Learning objects：学习目标

- Study the important role of the hotel which provides services for tourists in the destination as well as in the transit region within the tourism system (Leiper's model) 在旅游系统(Leiper's model)中的框架中，学习饭店在旅游目的地和中转地为游客提供各种服务所发挥的重要作用
- Understand the star classification of a hotel and the service facilities it provides 了解饭店星级分类以及饭店提供的服务设施
- Describe the functions of the "front house" and "back house" of a hotel 陈述饭店"前房"和"后房"的作用
- Appreciate the guest cycle and its working procedures of each stage in the cycle 理解什么是顾客活动周期以及顾客活动周期中每一阶段的工作程序
- Explain the reasons why the front office is called the "hub", "the nerve centre" or the "brain" of the hotel 解释为什么前厅被称为饭店的"中心"、"中枢神经"或"大脑"的原因
- Describe the measures that can be taken to secure the properties of a hotel and prevent the fraud 陈述饭店采取什么措施确保饭店的财产安全，防范欺诈
- Understand the ways which are used to expand a hotel chain and the benefits that the franchising offers 了解扩大饭店联销经营的方法以及特许经营的益处

Ability goals：能力目标

- Case study 案例分析：盖特威饭店的经营管理
- Reading Box 阅读分析：Hotel Chains 饭店连锁

Part I Text
第一部分 课文

Hotel Management

【教学要点】

知识要点	掌握程度	相关章节
star classification of a hotel 饭店星级分类	重点掌握	本课文与第 1 单元、第 3 单元、第 5 单元、第 6 单元、第 8 单元、第 9 单元、第 15 单元相关内容有联系。
organizational structure of a hotel 饭店的组织结构	重点掌握	
"front house" and "back house" of a hotel 饭店"前房"与"后房"	一般了解	
guest cycle 顾客活动周期	重点掌握	
prevention from fraud 防范欺诈	一般了解	

Accommodation is a major sector of the hospitality industry which is both national and international in nature. It includes hotels of different grades, city centre business properties, tourism resorts, motels and health spas. Apart from these, timeshare, caravanning and camping can also be regarded as a part of it. Nowadays, the modern society is characterized by rapid changes, and so are hotels. We should, therefore, change or upgrade the techniques of management of modern hotels so as to adapt to the changing society. Of course, just as they have played a strong influence on other businesses, computers and other labor-saving mechanical equipment will also greatly affect the management and operation of hotels.[1]

As mentioned above, there are many kinds of accommodations, in which hotel is the most important one. In order to regulate the management of hotels and protect the interests of the users, the United Nations Conference on International Travel and Tourism held in Rome in 1963 introduced the **star classification**. According to it, hotels can be classified into five categories and stars are used as a sign to differentiate them. The number of stars indicates the quality of the accommodation and service the hotel can provide and those with five stars are in the highest grade.[2]

Different hotels provide different package of facilities. Apart from the basic ones as accommodation, food and drink, a hotel should also offer many other **auxiliary facilities**, which mainly include a telephone, a radio and TV in the room, a place where a guest can telex or fax urgent messages, laundry service, a place in which newspapers and magazines can be bought. Besides, many hotels also provide hairdressing service, a gift shop where the guest can buy presents and souvenirs. They will also help guests reserve tickets for the theatre or make travel arrangements. Such sports facilities as tennis court or swimming pool can also be found in many hotels. And conference facilities are available too in the hotels. Aside from the guests, non-residents can make use of all or some of these auxiliary facilities and enjoy themselves in the restaurants and bars.

There are usually six major departments constituting the **organizational structures** of most hotels, such as administration, front office, housekeeping, food and beverage, engineering and security.³ These departments can be roughly divided into two parts-the **"front of the house"** and the **"back of the house"**. The former includes the lobby and front desk which are easily noticed. And the latter, though equally important, is often ignored by the guest. It includes the kitchen, storage areas, administration, engineering, and security.

The transactions the guests make during their stay in a hotel is a determining factor of the flow of business which is composed of four stages and we can refer it to as **a guest cycle**.⁴

1. The first is the **contact or pre-arrival stage** during which the guests will make a choice among many hotels. Which hotel they choose to stay is dependent on a variety of factors including previous experiences with the hotel, advertisements, recommendation, etc. If the guests call to inquire more information about the hotel, the attitude, efficiency and knowledge of the front office staff may also have a strong influence on their decision.

2. The second stage is called **check in or arrival stage** which involves such steps as arriving at the hotel, filling in registration information and having their rooms assigned. It is the front office staff who receives the guests when they arrive at the hotel. So, they are also responsible for making an explanation of the guest-hotel relationship and the expectation from the guest.

3. The third stage is the **occupancy stage** at which the front office will, on behalf of the hotel, keep in contact with the guests and help them handle any problem they may meet during their stay.⁵ The front office has the obligation to provide satisfactory service for the guests so that they will choose to stay at the hotel again and again.

4. The last stage of the guest cycle is **departure or check-out stage**. At this stage, the hotel will settle the accounts with the guests and stop providing services. At the same time, the room will be cleaned out and put in order for service again and the housekeeping department will receive some advice to enhance the quality of their service further.

Among the four stages of a guest cycle the front office is called the "hub," "the nerve centre" or the "brain" of the hotel. The front office and reception departments are obviously one of the most important sections of the modern hotel industry. It is the most visible area and it is in this department that the public makes their first contact with the hotel and gets the first impression of it.⁶ Whether the impression is favorable or not depends on the attitude and efficiency of the front office staff. Therefore, the work of the department plays a vital role in the development of the hotel. The following are some of the most important works the front office staff does:

1. Welcoming arriving guests

When the guests arrive at the hotel, the receptionist should give them a warm welcome and make them feel at home. Otherwise, they would think that they were neglected and would cause many problems on purpose during their stay.

2. Completing the hotel register

The receptionist must make sure that all guests go through the legal formality of registration. The information filled in will be inspected by the police at times. Meanwhile, the hotel can also collect some useful marketing information in this way.

3. Recording reservations

The selling of rooms tends to make the highest profit within the hotel, and therefore, is crucial to hotel profitability and effective development.

4. Compiling guest's bills

During their stay, the guests may make various expenses at different departments of the hotel. All of these expenditures should be recorded and added on to one bill accurately lest the guests be overcharged or undercharged. When the guests check out, the bill should be prepared and presented to them at once.

5. *Providing information*

The reception desk provides service directly for the guests. It is the place that the guests may solve their problems and get information about the hotel, the surrounding areas and activities.

6. *Dealing with complaints*

Another task of the reception desk is to deal with the complaints from the guests. If any guest has a complaint to make, he will go and ask for a solution from it. In a large hotel, the reception desk undertakes just a small portion of the work of a front office while in a small hotel it shoulders all the duties of it.[7]

As a public place, a hotel receives different types of customers. Some of them may cheat the hotel in many different ways or bring some security problems. It is the responsibility of the receptionist to try their best to prevent the happening of these problems with the help of various measures.[8] One of the measures they have taken is the practice of **deposit**. According to it, upon arrival all guests have to pay a certain amount of money which will be returned to them when they check out. In case some guests, particularly the chance guest, should leave the hotel without paying, the deposit can partly cover the loss. Generally speaking, a hotel should accept every one who arrives unless it is full. However, by law, some unfit customers such as a drunken man or a known prostitute can be refused. If so, the better excuse is that the hotel is full.

New Words

labor-saving	*adj.*	省力的
occupancy	*n.*	占有，入住
hairdressing	*n.*	理发，美发
departure	*n.*	出发，启程
receptionist	*n.*	接待员
profitability	*n.*	盈利，收益性
registration	*n.*	登记，注册
complaint	*n.*	投诉，埋怨

Key Terms

auxiliary facility	辅助设施
chance guest	散客
front/back of the house	前/后台
organizational structure	组织结构

Notes

1. Of course, just as they have played a strong influence on other businesses, computers and other labor-saving mechanical equipment will also greatly affect the management and operation of hotels.

当然,正如它们对其他商业产生巨大作用一样,计算机和其他节约劳动力的机器设备也会对酒店的管理和运作产生很大影响。

2. The number of stars indicates the quality of the accommodation and service the hotel can provide and those with five stars are in the highest grade.
   星的个数代表酒店提供住宿和服务的质量,最高级别是五星。

3. There are usually six major departments constituting the organizational structures of most hotels, such as administration, front office, housekeeping, food and beverage, engineering and security.
   大多数酒店通常都由六个主要部门组成,构成酒店管理的组织结构:它们是行政部门、前厅、客房部、餐饮部、工程部和保安部。

4. The transactions the guests make during their stay in a hotel is a determining factor of the flow of business which is composed of four stages and we can refer it to as a guest cycle.
   客人在酒店住宿期间进行的交易活动是酒店业务流程的决定性因素,这一流程由四个阶段构成,我们称之为顾客活动周期。

5. The third stage is the occupancy stage at which the front office will, on behalf of the hotel, keep in contact with the guests and help them handle any problem they may meet during their stay.
   第三阶段是住宿阶段,此时前台将代表酒店与顾客保持联系,并协助他们处理在住宿期间遇到的任何问题。

6. It is the most visible area and it is in this department that the public makes their first contact with the hotel and gets the first impression of it.
   它是最显眼的部门,公众通过它首次与酒店接触并产生第一印象。

7. In a large hotel, the reception desk undertakes just a small portion of the work of a front office while in a small hotel it shoulders all the duties of it.
   在大酒店里,接待处只承担了前厅部的小部分工作;而在小酒店里,它承担了前厅所有的工作。

8. It is the responsibility of the receptionist to try their best to prevent the happening of these problems with the help of various measures.
   接待员的职责就是采取各种手段全力阻止这些问题的发生。

Exercise

1. Fill in the blanks with proper words to complete the following statements.

| differentiate | techniques | check in | previous | the front office |
| on behalf of | deposit | obligation | registration | complaints |

(1) Nowadays, the modern society is characterized by rapid changes, and so are hotels. We should, therefore, change or upgrade the _____ of management of modern hotels so as to adapt to the changing society.

(2) According to the star classification, hotels can be classified into five categories and stars are used as a sign to _____ them.

(3) Which hotel they choose to stay is dependent on a variety of factors including _____ experiences with the hotel, advertisements, recommendation, etc.

(4) The second stage is called _____ or arrival stage which involves such steps as arriving at the hotel, filling in registration information and having their rooms

assigned.

(5) The third stage is the occupancy stage at which the front office will _____ the hotel, keep in contact with the guests and help them handle any problem they may meet during their stay.

(6) Called the "hub," "the nerve centre" or the "brain," _____ and reception departments are obviously one of the most important sections of the modern hotel industry.

(7) The receptionist must make sure that all guests go through the legal formality of _____.

(8) Another task of the reception desk is to deal with the _____ from the guests.

(9) In case some guests, particularly the chance guest, should leave the hotel without paying, the _____ can partly cover the loss.

(10) The front office has the _____ to provide satisfactory service for the guests so that they will choose to stay at the hotel again and again.

2. **Questions for discussion**

(1) How can a guest determine the quality and service a hotel offers?
_____

(2) What are the major departments in most hotels? And which part belongs to the "back of the house"?
_____

(3) What are the facilities that a hotel usually provides?
_____

(4) How many stages are there in a guest cycle? And what are they?
_____

(5) What factors would possibly determine the choice of the guests?
_____

Part II Guided Reading
第二部分 课文导读

当今社会正进入一个知识经济时代、经济全球化时代和信息化时代。社会的高速发展和科技的日新月异,使得住宿业中最重要的类型——饭店也面临着激烈的竞争,唯有不断提高现代饭店的管理技术和水平,才能适应日益变化的社会和满足顾客多样化的需求。饭店管理是饭店管理者选择目标市场,确定服务内容、经营方针、营销策略,对饭店所拥有的资源进行有效的计划、组织、指挥、控制和协调,形成高效率的服务生产系统,以达到饭店经营目标的一系列活动的总和。

本文介绍了饭店的类型、星级标准、组成部分和服务设施,重点介绍了饭店前厅的作用以及顾客活动周期,强调饭店经营管理要以顾客为中心,"以人为本"是饭店管理的核心理念,在旅游饭店管理中占据中心地位。不同的饭店为顾客提供了不同的设施,除了基本的住宿和餐饮设施外,饭店还提供不同的辅助设施,如美容美发中心、旅游纪念品商店、运动场地、会议设施等。

大多数酒店通常都由6个主要部门组成,构成酒店管理的组织结构,它们是行政部门、前厅部、客房部、餐饮部、工程部和保安部。各部门要在时序上和空间上进行业务的组织和协作,把各生产要素结合起来使得宾客在使用饭店产品的过程中得到满足。在饭店管理过程中,前厅部是整个饭店业务活动的中心,因其主要服务部门总服务台(Front Desk)通常位于饭店最前部的大堂,因而称为前厅部(Front Office)。

饭店的业务繁杂,宾客的需求也呈现出多样化,饭店的业务运行也不得不面临层出不穷的变化和突发事件,但是,饭店业务始终是以为宾客服务为中心,是随着宾客在饭店的活动而进行的,客人在饭店住宿期间进行的交易活动是饭店业务流程的决定性因素,这一流程由四个阶段构成,我们称之为顾客活动周期。

第一阶段是联系或顾客尚未到达阶段。顾客在众多饭店中基于以往的经验、广告信息、推荐信息等,通过对各种因素的比较,从而选择入住的饭店。有效的饭店营销策略和手段以及畅通的信息沟通有助于潜在的顾客最终选择本饭店。

第二阶段是入住登记或抵达酒店阶段。顾客到达饭店,填写登记信息,办理入住手续和安排客房。在此阶段中,饭店要提供直接的面对面的对客服务,服务效率的高低和质量好坏直接影响客人对饭店的评价,影响客人对饭店产品和服务的认可度和满意度。

第三阶段是住宿酒店阶段。前台代表酒店与顾客保持联系,并协助他们处理在住宿期间遇到的任何问题。在这一阶段不仅需要提供面对面的对客服务,还需要提供间接的服务,如工程部要负责检查饭店各种设施设备是否安全,性能是否完好。

第四阶段是离店结账阶段。饭店应该核算并收取客人各项费用,同时整理客房准备迎接下一位住店客人。前台也可以通过沟通,了解客人的住店感受,其反馈信息为提高饭店服务质量尤为重要。

前厅部犹如饭店的网络中心、神经中枢和大脑,对饭店的整体形象、服务质量乃至管理水平和经济效益有至关重要的影响,它是饭店销售产品、组织接待工作、调度业务以及为宾客提供一系列前厅服务的综合性服务机构,因为它在业务运行中接触面广、政策性强、业务复杂而在饭店中占据举足轻重的地位。前厅的作用主要体现在以下几个方面:

1. 前厅是饭店的窗口,集中体现了饭店的整体形象和服务水平。前厅是硬件设施及其豪华程度以及员工的工作态度和精神面貌,直接体现了饭店的标准和服务水平。

2. 前厅是给客人留下第一印象和最后印象的地方。客人抵店的第一站和离店的最后一站都是前厅,第一印象有助于客人树立对饭店的整体认知,最后印象又会在客人脑海中停留很长时间,前厅的工作效率和服务质量直接影响了客人的心理活动,从而影响了客人对饭店产品的满意程度。

3. 前厅的销售业绩直接影响饭店的收入和效益。前厅除了销售饭店产品,还可以提供电讯、订票等服务,销售和各项服务工作的好坏直接影响了饭店的经济收入。

4. 前厅是信息传递的枢纽和业务协调的中心。前厅部能直面客人提供各种"面对面"的服务,它是收集信息、处理信息、传递信息和反馈信息的中心,也因此对饭店不同部门进行组织协调,为顾客提供更好的服务。

当前饭店竞争的新形势已将创新进取战略推向了企业管理的中心地位,以创新求发展已成为各国政府和企业界的共同呼声。饭店业缺乏个性化建设也就是缺乏创新。饭店要实行可持续发展就需要在饭店管理的各方面进行创新策划,包括产品创新、饭店硬件创新、人力资源管理创新、财务管理和采购管理创新、饭店营销创新、服务创新等。做好各方面的创新策划是饭店走上可持续发展的关键,更是饭店获取最大效益的切实途径。

旅游知识测试

正误判断:请在正确的选题上划√,错误的选题上划×。

1. 饭店集团是指以经营饭店为主的联合经营的经济实体,在本国或世界各地以直接或间接形式控制多个饭店,是以相同的店名和店标、统一的经营程序、同样的服务标准、管理风格和水准进行联合经营的企业集团。饭店企业的集中化程度越高,则意味着竞争者数目越大。

2. 饭店业务始终是以为宾客服务为中心,是随着宾客在饭店的活动而进行的,客人在饭店住宿期间进行的交易活动是饭店业务流程的决定性因素,这一流程一般由四个阶段构成,称之为"顾客活动周期"。

3. 饭店设施设备质量的好坏在很大程度上影响到旅游服务产品的质量,但这并不是说提供服务所凭借的设施设备等物质条件需要如何高级豪华,而主要是说提供服务所凭借的设施设备等物质条件必须保持良好的使用状态。

4. 连锁饭店集团成员主要有从房地产开发商或者从其他饭店业主手中租来经营的饭店;饭店连锁公司代管经营的饭店;饭店连锁公司特许经营的饭店;饭店连锁公司自己拥有产权,并且自己经营的饭店。

5. 在饭店竞争中,饭店连锁集团比独立经营的单体饭店有着较大的优势,表现在数量优势、技术经济优势、市场营销优势、物资采购优势、管理方面的优势、风险扩散优势,但是资本优势不明显。

Part III Case Study
第三部分 案例研究

盖特威饭店的经营管理

分析要点

1. 请分析盖特威饭店的市场环境。盖特威饭店有何竞争优势?原因是什么?
2. 盖特威饭店的目标客源市场是什么?其目标客源群体有哪些基本特征?
3. 试分析盖特威饭店营业收入的主要来源。其经营状况如何?
4. 结合盖特威饭店预算表,分析饭店如何编制预算表以及预算表在饭店管理中的作用。
5. 请你评价盖特威饭店的年度计划,你认为该年度计划是否能够帮助饭店提高管理效能?
6. 如果你是盖特威饭店经理,为了实现饭店计划的目标,你认为盖特威饭店今后需要在哪些方面做出努力?

相关理论和问题

1. 营销信息和营销环境(Marketing information and marketing environment)
2. 目标市场选择和定位(Choice and positioning of the target market)
3. 营销计划和控制(Marketing plan and control)
4. 企业竞争战略(Corporate competitive strategy)

一、基本情况

盖特威饭店是一家三星级饭店,位于英国盖特威飞机场以南4公里处,饭店每半小时就有班车来往于机场。饭店有226间客房,包括10个商务套房,5个女子客房,44个无烟客房,1个带温泉的客房。

盖特威饭店于1960年由Enterprise Hotels建造,当时只有91间客房。1972年增加了

140 间客房,但公共区域未增加。1951 年被 Crest 饭店集团收购。1986 年盖特威饭店安装了一个新的电话总机系统和工资系统,1987 年将第六层改为商务楼层,1988 年对餐厅、商务中心、宴会设施、啤酒园、酒吧等公共区域进行了大规模装修,并开始兴建一个娱乐中心,扩建了前台与餐厅计算机信息系统,共花费 450 万英镑。休闲酒吧于 1989 年 11 月开业,现有 450 个会员,会员主要是家庭和新婚夫妇。当地居民通常在下午 5:30—8:30 和早餐前使用该设施,娱乐设施受到会议和商务客人的欢迎。当地另外五家饭店也有娱乐设施。盖特威饭店进行装修的主要原因是盖特威地区饭店业的激烈竞争。

盖特威饭店有四个主要竞争对手:Penta、the Copthorne、Post-house、Hilton 饭店和另外九家饭店。1990 年将有三家新建饭店开业,新增约 1000 间客房。在第一个新建饭店开业之前,盖特威饭店仍有六个月的时间在市场上建立和巩固自己的地位。由于新近的装修和扩建,盖特威饭店处于一个比一些现存竞争者更有利的地位。盖特威饭店每年有 400 万英镑的收入,表 5—2 和表 5—3 分别为该饭店 1989 年营业收入构成表和 1990 年的预算。

表 5—2　盖特威饭店 1989 年营业收入构成表　　　　　　　　　　　　　　单位:百万英镑

项目	营业收入	营业收入比率
客房	2.4	60
食品	0.8	20
饮料	0.5	12
电话、传真	0.1	3
娱乐	0.04	1
其他	0.16	4

表 5—3　盖特威饭店 1990 年预算表

项目	1989 年实际	1990 年预算	说明
全年客房出租间数	66,034	66,241	1989 年客房出租率为 80%,由于将改变客房构成,预计 1990 年客房出租率将有小幅增长
平均房价	£41.04	£51.12	由于新增设施,希望吸引更多的商务和会议客人,从而平均房价提高。
全年营业收入(万英镑)	400	569	增加近 170 万英镑。
工资(万英镑)	128.94	150.08	反映出每年提高的工资和工资水平。另有一些相关的员工费用,如员工住房。
营业费用(万英镑)	100.57	126.94	由于棉织品和水电费用的上涨,营业费用增加。
利润(万英镑)	118.96	222.81	

二、饭店的组织结构

盖特威饭店有 10 个主要部门,总经理的任务是评估饭店的运行,制定饭店的中长期计划,做出有关销售和成本的主要决策。5000 英镑以上的采购额,他需要请示本饭店集团的地区负责人,但 20000 英镑以下的维修工程他可以自己决定。副总经理处理日常业务,其他重要的部门经理和管理人员有:房务主管、前厅经理、大厅行李主管、餐厅经理、总厨、维修工程师和商务中心联络员。饭店现有192名员工,仍缺15—16名员工,目前主要的人事问题是缺员。由于本地区失业率低,又有15家饭店,盖特威饭店很难雇到合适的员工。他们部分是通过英格兰北部城市寻找员工来解决这个问题的,现在饭店有一半员工来自北部,许多还来自爱尔兰。在盖特威地区,机场的工资收入要比饭店多得多。许多员工不仅是离开饭店,而是离开这个行业。以下为1990年部门工作计划。

前厅计划:
1. 有效地促进各种客房的销售,以取得预计收入;
2. 显著增加商务、会议和流动性人口用房;
3. 增加周末的商务客房的销售;
4. 把开发新婚市场作为一个重要的任务。

餐厅部计划:
1. 接待超过预计的餐厅和啤酒园客人数,增加人均消费特别是非住店客人的消费;
2. 餐厅、啤酒园、宴会达到与新硬件设施水平相一致的热情好客的服务水平,预测早、午、晚餐的客流量,在圣诞节期间推出新的菜单,提高餐饮销售量;
3. 制定商务客人名单。

会议部计划:
1. 将饭店建成英国伦敦南部接待中等规模会议的最好饭店;
2. 有效地销售客房和会议设施,确保客房销售率不低;
3. 有效地把新设施销售给会议代理人和本地商务客人。

人事培训部计划:
1. 促进本饭店所有部门的人事和培训工作,目标是进一步提高本饭店的服务水平;
2. 提高员工的在岗培训量;
3. 显著地降低员工流失率;
4. 将员工的工资水平控制在预算范围内。

三、销售和市场营销

1989年盖特威饭店各类客源住房情况是:临时流动性客人占10%,商务客人占6%,会议客人为4%,旅游团队为2%,有较多折扣的客人占45%,周末度假客人占13%,全年客房出租率为80%。

盖特威饭店希望减少有较多折扣的客源市场,增加会议、商务和流动性客人的用房,销售部经理尽力预测每个市场的需求,在营业旺季尽可能为会议、商务客多留房间,特别是临时住店客人,因为他们可能给饭店带来更多的收入。但对于临时住店客人和商务客人,很难预测其住房的需求量。会议客人由集团公司来整体促销,制作特殊的会议宣传册,同时邀请本地会议市场上的有关公司以提高回头客生意。会议和较大折扣市场的决策者往往不是使用者,如果饭店拥有较新的娱乐、会议设施,他们可能更容易做出决定。

盖特威饭店的较大折扣市场主要由两部分组成:本地公司和航空公司。本地公司客人是盖特威饭店营业的基础。饭店也与航空公司签约接待机组人员,一类是定期航班的机组人员,他们的住宿较有规律;另一类是季节性的包机机组人员。如果从饭店收入角度出发,接待两个机组人员相当于接待一个临时性住客所带来的收入。商务市场可以通过品牌形象和便捷的预订来吸引客人,但对临时流动性住客市场很难施加影响,应预测一些重要的外部影响因素。例如1990年,Feinborogh的航空展览会,人们会提前几个月预订房间。盖特威饭店每年5—9月为旺季,1—2月营业最为清淡。周一和周四是商务客人最为集中的时间,而周四和周日临时住店客人较多。

资料来源:盖特威饭店的年度计划. 肖忠东,黎洁. 饭店管理概论[M]. 南开大学出版社,2005.

Part IV　Reading Box
第四部分　阅读与分析

Hotel Chains

阅读分析要点

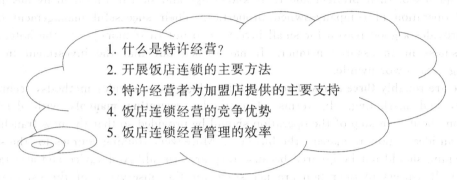

1. 什么是特许经营？
2. 开展饭店连锁的主要方法
3. 特许经营者为加盟店提供的主要支持
4. 饭店连锁经营的竞争优势
5. 饭店连锁经营管理的效率

With the increased leisure time and income, people are becoming more interested in traveling. This has led to the rapid growth of the hotel industry which, in fact, has begun to develop quickly since the 1920s. In the last twenty years, **franchise** has been widely used to expand business in many fields such as fast-food restaurants, income tax preparation services and the hotel/motel industry. Franchise is a leasing arrangement made by a company which gives or sells a special right to a person or a business who can then sell its services or goods.[1] This way has been very popular with the hotel industry and has led to the establishment of a lot of hotel chains.

There are a number of ways which are very helpful for the expansion of hotel chains:

- Direct investment. The head office has two approaches to invest directly. One is to build and run a new hotel. The other is to buy an old one and bring its facilities and management up-to-date.
- Contract management. In this way, management contracts will be signed between the head office and the actual owner of the hotel so that the chain will have the right to run the hotel according to its own particular ways.[2] The condition is that the chain will get a certain amount of money or a certain percentage of the profits every year.
- Joint venture. The chain will pay part of the capital necessary for the building of a new hotel or the purchase of an old one. The other part of the capital will be supplied by local investors.
- Franchising. In fact, it is a leasing arrangement. According to the leasing arrangement, if the hotel operator pays the parent corporation a fee, he will be granted the right to use its plans, manuals of procedures, advertising materials, and to run his business in the name of the parent corporation.[3]

Of the four ways mentioned above, franchising is the most popular one to set up hotel chains at present. The franchise operator invests in a product which fits a certain standard and which is possible to bring a big profit.[4] Then if he has any difficulty or meet any problem in the process of operation, he may ask for help from the corporation that grants the right to him to operate the business. Some franchise operations are also joint ventures, with both the corporation and individual owner supplying part of the initial capital.

As a matter of fact, franchising also means that the **franchisor** sells a special right to one person or group of people (called **franchisee**) that allows them to sell the product which quality and sales potential have been proved.[5] Thus, in order to attract more people to buy their franchises, the major franchisees in the hotel and motel industry have to, first of all, prove the quality of their product and their knowledge and skill in this field by means of successful operation of company-owned properties. Their successful management of a product provides a good reason for small investors to put their money into the hotel and motel business in an assured manner. It has turned out that the investment in the franchising area is worthwhile.

There are roughly **three kinds of services** a franchiser can provide: methods, technical assistance, and marketing. In terms of methods, **operating manuals** with detailed information about each step of the operation should be provided so that the new franchisee may have an idea of how to manage the business. Moreover, training courses for the staff before opening should not be ignored because they are crucial. And advice and assistance concerning all aspects of operation are necessary for the observance of the established standards. Another type of service is technical assistance which is often offered to help the new franchisee to build a new hotel or to buy an old one. The last type of service is marketing which is the most important and indispensable term in any franchise agreement. The franchisee must take advantage of the successful marketing techniques of the franchiser, which have been proved and tested by the market, to run his hotel.

The standard course of hotel marketing which has been adopted by many hotels and motels and which has been helpful for the rapid expansion of the hotel chain involves three main elements: advertising, sales and reservations.[6] On one hand, the hotel chain often utilizes the mass media such as newspapers, magazines, radio, and particularly television to make joint advertisements. On the other hand, it also sets up a sales network to spread its product. For example, regional sales offices of the chain are established in almost all important areas throughout the country. They sell both the regional properties and member properties of the chain. And a large portion of the properties is sold to the group and convention market while a small part is sold to the corporate and travel-agent areas.

Compared with those hotels operated by individual owners, hotel chains have many **advantages**. One of the most important advantages that enable the chain to win in the competition is that the hotel chain can gather enough resources and money from all members to pay for the high cost of advertising, especially television advertising while most individual operators can hardly afford it.[7] Meanwhile, there are more professionals who have specialized knowledge in advertising and public relations at the chain's head office. They can help to promote the image of the chain as a whole with various publicity campaigns.

Another advantage comes from the observance of the standards set by the head office to equip and operate the hotel. In order to make its members follow the same operating steps, the head office prepares and publishes operating manuals offering detailed information about the specific steps in operation, even including such tasks as making beds and setting tables.[8] It is obvious that the facilities and service all members of the chain provide are almost the same. Although some people dont think it is good to make everything alike, customers can easily have a clear idea of the quality of the accommodations at the mention of any member unit of the chain.

Hotel chains can provide more convenience for customers to make reservations quickly while it is easier for them to control bookings. For example, it usually takes a guest only a few minutes to make certain about the room he has booked. And it is also very easy to book a room in the chain by telephone, whether it is a nationwide telephone number or a local one in an important market city. This is obviously the most important advantage of hotel chains.

The establishment of the hotel chain has also increased the sales in the **conference market**. This is another advantage compared with individually-operated hotels. In the head office, there are some conference salesmen who are responsible specially for this market and who try hard to promote the sales not only for the parent corporation but also for the whole chain. Now, more people have accepted the idea that a conference should not only provide opportunities to do business but also offer them a chance to enjoy themselves. Therefore, the hotel chain which can easily provide different locations for conferences is more attractive to many sponsoring groups.

There are many other examples which can prove the increased efficiency resulted from **chain management**. It is possible for customers to make very large purchases for many kinds of equipment and supplies. The chain brings the accounting and auditing systems under its control so as to improve its efficiency. What's more, a centralized personnel office is set up to attract competent people for managerial and technical positions throughout the chain.

New Words

franchise	n.	特许经营权
observance	n.	遵守,奉行
franchisee	n.	特许经营人
professional	n.	专业人员,内行
franchisor	n.	特许权拥有人,授权方
procedure	n.	程序,手续

Key Terms

joint venture	合资企业	parent corporation	母公司
initial capital	启动资金	franchise operator	加盟经营者,特许经营者
public relation	公共关系	auditing system	审计系统

Notes

1. Franchise is a leasing arrangement made by a company which gives or sells a special right to a person or a business who can then sell its services or goods.
   特许经营是一种租赁关系,它是指某公司授予或出售特殊权利给个人或公司,使其有权出售其产品或服务。

2. In this way, management contracts will be signed between the head office and the actual owner of the hotel so that the chain will have the right to run the hotel according to its own particular ways.
   通过这种方式,总公司和饭店的实际拥有者签订管理合同,以便连锁饭店有权按照自己特有的方式经营。

3. If the hotel operator pays the parent corporation a fee, he will be granted the right to use its plans, manuals of procedures, advertising materials, and to run his business in the name of the parent corporation.
   饭店经营者给母公司支付一定费用后,它将获得授权使用母公司的计划、操作手册、广告材料,并以母公司的名义来经营。

4. The franchise operator invests in a product which fits a certain standard and which is possible to bring a big profit.
   特许经营者对符合一定标准并可能为其带来巨大利润的产品进行投资。

5. As a matter of fact, franchising also means that the franchisor sells a special right to one person or group of people (called franchisee) that allows them to sell the product which quality and sales potential have been proved.
   事实上,特许经营也是指特许授权人出售某种特殊权利给个人或者团体(称为特许经营者),允许他们出售质量和销售潜力都被证实为合格的产品。

6. The standard course of hotel marketing which has been adopted by many hotels and motels and which has been helpful for the rapid expansion of the hotel chain involves three main elements: advertising, sales and reservations.
   许多饭店和汽车旅馆采用的营销标准流程,包括广告、销售和预订三个主要方面,这对饭店连锁迅速扩张非常有利。

7. One of the most important advantages that enable the chain to win in the competition is that the hotel chain can gather enough resources and money from all members to pay for the high cost of advertising, especially television advertising while most individual operators can hardly afford it.
   连锁饭店在竞争中取胜,其中最重要的优势是连锁饭店可以从所属成员饭店中聚集足够的资源和财力,以支付高额的广告费,特别是电视广告费,而大部分个体经营者几乎无力承担这些费用。

8. In order to make its members follow the same operating steps, the head office prepares and publishes operating manuals offering detailed information about the specific steps in operation, even including such tasks as making beds and setting tables.
   为了所属成员遵循相同的经营流程,总公司准备、印刷酒店经营指南,提供详细、具体的运作步骤,甚至包括怎样整理床铺和布置餐桌。

Topic discussion

1. What are the ways which are helpful for the expansion of hotel chains? And which one is most popular at present?

2. What are the services a franchisor can provide?

3. What marketing advantages does a hotel chain have to compete with other hotels?

4. What are the advantages of hotel chains over those individually-operated ones?

5. Some people think it is not good to make everything alike. What do you think of the same facilities and services provided by a hotel chain?
_____

【即学即用】

With reference to the theory, information or approach applied in the Reading Box, have a case study of the hotel chains. You may take 7 Days Inn or Home Inn as an example. Make presentation of your study in Chinese or in English using PPT.

【学习资源库】

为了掌握本章更多的相关专业知识,请您登陆 http://sicnu.edu.cn/,点击国家双语教学示范课程《旅游学概论》,进入网络学堂查询相关资料。

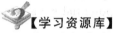
Chapter Review 本章小结

This chapter has described the star classification of a hotel and the service facilities it provides. It describes the functions of the "front house" and "back house" of a hotel, the guest cycle and its working procedures of each stage in the cycle. The front office is the "hub", "the nerve centre" or the "brain" of the hotel. For the safety of a hotel, measures can be taken to secure the properties of a hotel and prevent the fraud. Compared with those hotels operated by individual owners, hotel chains have many advantages. Franchising is the most popular one to set up hotel chains, and has been widely used to expand its business in the hospitality industry. There are three kinds of services a franchisor provides: methods, technical assistance, and marketing.

Part V Additional Know-how of Tourism
第五部分 旅游知识扩展

【关键术语】

Accommodation: within the context of the tourism industry, commercial facilities intended to host stayover tourists for overnight stays. The most common forms are hotels, motels, campgrounds, bed & breakfasts (B & Bs), dormitories, hostels, and the homes of friends and relatives.

住宿业:就旅游业来讲,住宿业是为过夜游客提供住宿的商业设施。最常见的形式有酒店、汽车旅馆、露营地、含早餐服务的旅馆、宿舍、招待所及亲朋好友的家。

Timesharing: an accommodation option in which a user purchases one or more intervals (or weeks) per year in a resort, usually over a long period of time

分时度假:用户每年在某景区可购买一个或几个时间段(或几周),通常是一种长期住宿的选择。

Concierge: This is a European invention. Depending on the hotel, the concierge is a superintendent of service, source of information, and link between the guest and city or area.

礼宾部经理：欧洲人的发明，指在不同的酒店里负责监督礼宾部服务的最高主管，为顾客提供信息，或者担当客人与城市或地区的联系人。

Guest cycle: The transactions the guests make during their stay in a hotel is a determining factor of the flow of business which is composed of four stages: contact or pre-arrival stage, check in or arrival stage, occupancy stage and departure or check out stage. We refer it to as the guest cycle.

顾客活动周期：客人在酒店住宿期间进行的交易活动是酒店业务流程的决定性因素，这一流程由四个阶段构成：接触或顾客尚未到达阶段、入住登记或抵达酒店阶段、住宿阶段、离开或离店结账阶段，我们称之为"顾客活动周期"。

Franchise: The franchisor sells a special right to one person or group of people (called franchisee) that allows them to sell the product which quality and sales potential have been proved.

特许经营：指特许授权人出售某种特殊权利给个人或者团体（称为特许经营者），允许他们出售质量和销售潜力都被证实为合格的产品。

【知识链接】

1. "金钥匙服务"

金钥匙既是一种专业化的饭店服务，又指一个国际化的民间专业服务组织，此外还是对具有国际金钥匙组织会员资格的饭店礼宾部职员的特殊称谓。饭店金钥匙的本质，是指饭店中通过掌握丰富信息并使用以共同的价值观和信息高速公路组成的服务网络，为宾客提供专业个性化服务的委托代办个人或协作群体的总称。

金钥匙服务是饭店内由礼宾部职员（如具有国际金钥匙组织会员资格则可称为"金钥匙"）为其所在饭店创造更大的经营效益的目的，按照国际金钥匙组织特有的金钥匙服务理念和由此派生出的服务方式为宾客提供的"一条龙"个性化服务，这种服务通常以"委托代办"的形式出现，即宾客委托，职员代表饭店为宾客代办。因为它的高附加值区别于一般的饭店服务，具有鲜明的个性化特点，被饭店业的专家认为是饭店服务的极致，因此被称为金钥匙服务。

2. 饭店管理职能

（1）计划职能。饭店计划职能是指饭店通过周密、科学的调查研究，分析预测，并进行决策，以此为基础确定未来每一时期内饭店发展的目标，并规定实现目标的途径、方法的管理活动。

（2）组织职能。饭店的组织职能是管理者对企业组织机构的确定，对企业的各要素和各资源的调配，对企业部门、部门权力分配与协调业务活动的管理过程。简言之，就是旅游饭店管理者对组织的管理。

（3）控制职能。控制职能是为了使旅游饭店计划与实际结果尽量保持一致，通过控制过程的各环节达到企业制定的目标。

（4）领导职能。领导职能是旅游饭店管理者通过塑造形象，影响员工价值观的过程。它的基本内容包括：科学决策、合理用人、统筹协调和统一指挥。

（5）创新职能。企业管理需要创新来适应环境的变化，谋求较好的企业发展，创新也是取得市场竞争的有力手段，旅游饭店创新需要遵循以下基本原则：顾客导向原则、特色性原则、文化性原则、参与性原则及经济可行性原则。

【小思考】
1. 主题饭店是采取的是什么样的定位？举例说明饭店市场定位的重要性。

参考阅读：
饭店的市场定位主要是两个方面：一是客源定位；二是饭店产品定位。

客源定位的内容大致有：(1) 客源类别定位，主要指客源是境外的还是境内的，境外的要确定主要国家和地区，境内的要确定主要地区。(2) 市场群体定位，即是团体、散客，还是会议、会展等。(3) 消费层次定位，即确定消费层次的高、中、低档。(4) 饭店类型的定位，即确定饭店的类别是商务、度假、旅游、综合还是内部接待等。客源定位是前提，有了客源定位，才有饭店产品的定位。

饭店产品的定位是根据客源定位，确定饭店的档次、规模、产品结构、优势产品、设施水平及配套、价格等。确定了饭店的市场定位，饭店就可以以主题饭店的形式轻装上阵，参与竞争，形成饭店产品特色、风格特色、经营特色，从而使饭店品牌带有明显的市场特征和品牌联想。

2、现代旅游饭店管理的本质是什么？

参考阅读：
(1) "以人为本"的理念在旅游饭店业管理中占据中心地位

随着社会的发展和旅游饭店业劳动者素质的提高，理解人、尊重人的价值观将会在旅游饭店业管理中得到广泛认同。通过具体管理理论和实践的创新，"以人为本"管理的内容将会在各类旅游饭店管理中得到进一步的丰富和发展。

(2) 无形资产管理将成为饭店业管理的重要内容

随着旅游饭店业之间竞争的日益激烈，竞争制胜的关键已不再仅仅取决于完善的硬件设施等有形资产，更多的是依靠知识、技能、信息等无形资产。围绕无形资产管理进行的管理创新也将成为现代旅游饭店业管理创新的一个重要组成部分。

(3) 信息技术的发展将给饭店业管理带来全方位的影响

为了成功地运用信息技术，旅游饭店业必须进行组织机构和管理的变革；旅游信息管理，即建立在旅游业信息化、网络化基础之上的以信息为中心的管理模式将是旅游饭店业管理创新的一种途径；信息社会的到来将带来新的旅游竞争方式，给旅游饭店业带来新的、战略性的机遇；信息技术的运用将提高旅游饭店业管理的科学性和效率。

(4) 旅游饭店管理组织将网络化和柔性化

在旅游饭店业发展趋于全球化、市场化和信息化的时代背景下，发达的技术支持使得旅游饭店管理组织创新呈现出网络化，减少固定和正式的组织机构，而进行一些临时性的、以任务为导向的团队式组织，体现组织结构的柔性化，借助组织结构的柔性化，可以实现旅游饭店企业集权化和分权化的统一，稳定性和变革性的统一，使之更适应现代旅游饭店业灵活性的要求。

Part VI Further Readings
第六部分　课外阅读

如果您想进一步学习本章的内容，探讨饭店在旅游业中的作用，如何经营旅游饭店，建议您阅读以下学者的著作和论文。

一、中文部分

[1] 蒋丁新.饭店管理[M].北京:高等教育出版社,2004(8).
[2] 翁刚民.现代饭店管理——理论、方法与案例[M].天津:南开大学出版社,2004.
[3] 谢彦君.旅游与接待业研究:中国与国外的比较——兼论中国旅游学科的成熟度[J].旅游学刊,2003,(05).
[4] 王大悟."宾至如归"析——关于酒店服务产品与时俱进的认识[J].桂林旅游高等专科学校学报,2004,(01).
[5] 黄燕玲.现代饭店中的ES与EL[J].桂林旅游高等专科学校学报,2000,(04).
[6] 魏小安.重新审视饭店职业经理人[J].饭店现代化,2003,(04).
[7] 蔡丽伟.饭店员工职位变动管理[J].饭店现代化,2004,(06).
[8] 张志全,马伟新,王宇倩.核心竞争力比较研究——我国旅游饭店企业核心竞争力与世界著名饭店集团的差距[J].经济理论研究 2006,(03).
[9] 邹益民,黄浏英.论旅游饭店品牌建设的基本模式[J].旅游学刊,2000,(05).
[10] 宁泽群.旅游饭店业的企业集团化发展与体制障碍[J].旅游学刊,2002,(01).

二、英文部分

[1] Sedat Yüksel. An integrated forecasting approach to hotel demand [J]. *Mathematical and Computer Modelling*,2007,(46):1063-1070
[2] Hong-bumm Kim, Woo Gon Kim. The relationship between brand equity and firm's performance in luxury hotels and chain restaurants [J]. *Tourism Management*,2005,(26):549-560
[3] Morten Heide, Kirsti Lardal, Kjell Gronhaug. The design and management of ambience-implications for hotel architecture and service [J]. *Tourism Management*,2007,(28):1315-1325
[4] Hanny N. Nasution, Felix T. Mavondo. Customer value in the hotel industry [J]. *International Journal of Hospitality Management*,2008,(27):204-213
[5] Choon-Chiang Leong. Service performance measurement: Developing customer perspective calculators for the hotel industry[J]. *Advances in Hospitality and Leisure*,2008,(04):101-120
[6] Paul Whitla, Peter G. P. Walters, Howard Davies. Global strategies in the international hotel industry [J]. *International Journal of Hospitality Management*,2007,(26):777-792
[7] Darlene McNaughton. Hospitality, Violence and Tourism [J]. *Annals of Tourism Research*,2006,(33):645-665
[8] Ray Pine, Paul Phillips. Performance comparisons of hotels in China [J]. *International Journal of Hospitality Management*,2005,(24):57-73
[9] Vincent C. S. Heung, Hanqin Zhang, Chen Jiang. International franchising: Opportunities for China's state-owned hotels [J]. *International Journal of Hospitality Management*,2008,(27):368-380
[10] Carina Antonia Hallin, Einar Marnburg. Knowledge management in the hospitality industry: A review of empirical research[J]. *Tourism Management*,2008,(29):366-381

Chapter 9 Distribution of the Tourist Product
第九章 旅游产品的分销

Learning objects：学习目标

- Study how tourism marketing can influence the tourist flow and distribution of tourist products within the origin and destination of the tourism system (Leiper's model) 学习旅游营销如何影响旅游者在旅游系统（Leiper 模型）中客源地和目的地之间的流动以及对旅游产品分销产生的影响
- Understand the essence of tourism marketing and the distinctiveness of service distribution 了解旅游营销的本质以及服务产品分销的独特性
- Appreciate the direct channel and indirect channel; the wide channel and narrow channel 理解什么是直接渠道和间接渠道；什么是宽渠道和窄渠道
- Differentiate distribution channels for manufactured products and those for tourism and travel 区分一般生产商品和旅游产品分销渠道的异同
- Discuss the benefits and risks of intensive distribution, selective distribution and exclusive distribution 讨论密集分销、选择分销和独家分销的益处和风险
- Outline the factors which influence the choices of distribution channels 指出影响选择分销渠道的各种因素
- Study the marketing approaches for tourism products, including marketing mix of 4Ps and 7Ps 学习旅游产品的营销方法，包括 4Ps 和 7Ps 营销组合

Ability goals：能力目标

- Case study 案例分析：时运假日旅行社的市场营销
- Reading Box 阅读分析：The Marketing Approach for Tourism Products 旅游产品的营销方法

Part I Text
第一部分 课文

Distribution of the Tourist Product

【教学要点】

知识要点	掌握程度	相关章节
physical distribution and service distribution 商品营销和服务营销	一般了解	本课文与第 1 单元、第 3 单元、第 5 单元、第 6 单元、第 7 单元、第 8 单元相关内容有联系。
direct channel and indirect channel 直接渠道和间接渠道	一般了解	
intensive distribution, selective distribution and exclusive distribution 密集分销、选择分销和独家分销	重点掌握	
chain of tourism distribution 旅游分销链	重点掌握	
factors that affect the choice of distribution channels 影响选择分销渠道的因素	重点掌握	

Tourism has undergone a rapid growth in recent years. However, now it is facing significant and radical changes in business methods in response to the enormous changes taking place in the elements of the product and conditions of the market in the last few decades.[1] A case in point is the adoption of tourism marketing which greatly depends on distribution to achieve success. The change of distribution can alter the price of a product or service. For example, the product or service provided for certain consumers in particular can be very expensive. Different distribution methods require different costs. The ability to supply the product also has a great influence on the choice of the right promotional strategy because it is a kind of information about the product in itself and can help to attract consumers.

Physical distribution and service distribution

The focus of the study of distribution management has long been put on physical distribution while service distribution has been neglected, although they are two different areas.[2] However, more and more people have gradually realized that services distribution is also a very important area for both academic study and management practice. Compared with physical products, tourist products have their unique characteristics. They are **intangible, inseparable** from the point where they are consumed as both consumers and providers are involved, and **perishable** in that once the person who performs service stops doing so, they cannot exist. Therefore, it is hard for people to understand that there should be a choice of the right distribution channels for tourist products. We should take into consideration some of their characteristics when we study the distinctiveness of service distribution.[3]

Direct versus indirect distribution methods

It is necessary to establish marketing or distribution channels to allow consumers to obtain products and services easily and conveniently. And usually there is more than one channel available for organizations. In many industries, organizations deliver products from their own hands to the hands of consumers through **intermediaries** or middlemen who generally purchase ownership of products with the intention of selling to others and therefore hold stock and share financial risks.[4] To distribute services, a series of firms will work together to constitute a distribution channel to move them which are in the form of physical products from the producer to the consumer.

Tourism marketers may use either direct sale or indirect sale or even the combination of both to sell services. As mentioned above, tourist products are intangible and cannot be stored. Tourism intermediaries therefore cannot hold stock and of course will not carry any risk. Different distribution channels need different costs and bring different benefits. Like selling physical goods, tourism marketers should take these aspects into consideration and carry out some evaluation work so that they can determine the most suitable distribution channels. Usually several intermediaries cooperate with each other to help sell products and thus form a channel network. There are generally three main distribution methods as far as channel network is concerned.

Intensive distribution

This form allows a product to be distributed in the given market through as many intermediaries as possible. A case in point is the strategy used by a tour operator of all ABTA travel agents in the UK. It is suitable for the selling of those products which share a large market and have a big sales volume.

Selective distribution

Compared with intensive distribution, the number of intermediaries used in this form is smaller. It focuses on certain selected markets and assists the producer to achieve its economic goals with the help of those intermediaries who create best selling results.[5] In recent years, UK principals are inclined to choose more selective distribution strategies to improve efficiency.

Exclusive distribution

Exclusive distribution refers to the practice of selling products or services within a certain area through a single intermediary or agent. Thus, it is not easy for customers to search for such products. This form is often adopted by those organizations whose product is highly specialized and confronts little competition.

It is easy to distinguish direct and indirect distribution. As the word implies, direct distribution methods refer to the selling of products or services to the consumer directly without the use of intermediaries.[6] These methods include the use of direct mail, retail at an orgallizati on-owned outlet, catalogs, and even the Internet. Indirect methods include the use of one or more intermediaries. As far as tourism is concerned, travel agents work as intermediaries to distribute tourism products. They have faced little competition so far except that from direct distribution.

Which method, direct or indirect distribution, will be chosen to sell products and services is determined by many factors such as size of **selling organization**, **characteristics of the product** and current **marketing environment**. The organization should constantly review and evaluate the method they choose in terms of speed, efficiency, control, flexibility and cost so that they can decide which one is more beneficial.[7] Both the costs and benefits of using intermediaries should also be evaluated when selecting suitable distribution channels. To determine which of the important distribution methods is appropriate is a long process of application in which every method should be tried and constant reviews and evaluations should be made.

The chain of tourism distribution

Figure 9.1 is a comparative study of the traditional distribution channels for manufactured products and those for tourism and travel. Here we can easily recognize the differences between the distribution channels for physical products and those for tourism products. The first difference is the distinctive channels between manufacturers in the traditional model and principals in the model for travel industry. A second difference is that what the tour operator sells is not the element of a package to the agent, but information about the created package.

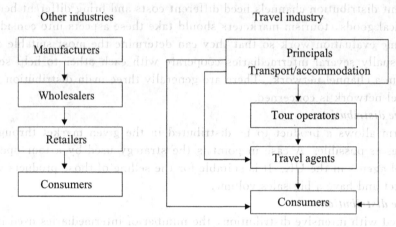

Figure 9.1 Distribution channels in the travel industry compared with other industries

In the hospitality, travel intermediaries, which mainly consist of **tour operators** and **travel agents**, play an important role in the whole distribution system. The usual practice is that tour operators organize packages by combining the components of tourist trip together and then travel agents help to sell the package to the public.[8] In general, the work of the retail travel agent is to actually sell tours, tickets and travel services, such as insurance or foreign exchange. However, there are also other distribution channels to move tourist products to the consumer. As figure 9.2 shows, some of the main suppliers, such as airlines also choose to sell the tourist products to the customers. Thus the structure of intermediation becomes more complicated with the increasing number of intermediaries.

Figure 9.2 Tourism distribution channels.

After determining the quantities of the product which will be supplied, the organization will put their concentration on the choice of marketing channels. First, they have to decide which distribution channel is suitable to move a product or service to final consumer. Their choice is often affected by **four factors**: the tourism product itself (its type, nature, level, etc.); the customer (the population, purchasing ability, geographical distribution, etc.); the travel intermediaries (their quality, their ability to promote and make sales, etc.); and the marketing environment (competitive situation, the distribution system of the main competitors, etc). A careful analysis of these factors can be helpful to enhance their competitiveness and avoid direct confrontation.

New Words

confrontation	n.	对立,对抗
principal	n.	主体,业主
intermediary	n.	中间人,中介
flexibility	n.	灵活性,弹性
specialty	n.	特产,特制品
retail	n./adj.	零售(的)
intensive	adj.	密集的,集中的

Key Terms

tourism marketing	旅游营销
intensive distribution	集中分销

physical distribution	有形分销
exclusive distribution	独家分销
selective distribution	选择性分销
direct distribution channel	直接销售渠道
distribution management	分销管理
indirect distribution channel	间接销售渠道

Notes

1. However, now it is facing significant and radical changes in business methods in response to the enormous changes taking place in the elements of the product and conditions of the market in the last few decades.
   然而,在过去几十年中,产品要素和市场环境发生了巨大变化,由此也使旅游业面临着经营方式的重大变革。

2. The focus of the study of distribution management has long been put on physical distribution while service distribution has been neglected, although they are two different areas.
   尽管有形商品分销和服务分销是两个不同的领域,但分销管理研究一直着重于有形分销,而服务分销却被忽略了。

3. We should take into consideration some of their characteristics when we study the distinctiveness of service distribution.
   在研究服务分销的特点时,我们应该考虑旅游产品的特性。

4. In many industries, organizations deliver products from their own hands to the hands of consumers through intermediaries or middlemen who generally purchase ownership of products with the intention of selling to others and therefore hold stock and share financial risks.
   在许多产业中,企业通过中间商把他们的产品从自己手中卖到消费者手中;中间商通常则购买产品的所有权,把产品卖给他人,由此拥有存货并承担经济风险。

5. It focuses on certain selected markets and assists the producer to achieve its economic goals with the help of those intermediaries who create best selling results.
   选择性分销着重于选择某些特定的市场,这有助于厂商在最佳销售中间商的帮助下,实现其经济目标。

6. As the word implies, direct distribution methods refer to the selling of products or services to the consumer directly without the use of intermediaries.
   正如这个词所指,直接分销法是不通过中间商把产品或服务直接卖给消费者。

7. The organization should constantly review and evaluate the method they choose in terms of speed, efficiency, control, flexibility and cost so that they can decide which one is more beneficial.
   企业应该不断地从速度、效率、控制、灵活性和成本等方面重新审视和评估他们选择的方法,以便决定哪种方法更为有利。

8. The usual practice is that tour operators organize packages by combining the components of tourist trip together and then travel agents help to sell the package to the public.
   通常旅游经营商把旅游各要素结合起来组成包价旅游团,再由旅游代理把产品卖给公众。

Exercise

1. Decide whether the statements are true or false. If it is true, put "T" in the space provided and "F" if it is false.

   (1) _____ Tourism is facing significant and radical changes in business methods in response to the enormous changes taking place in the elements of the product and conditions of the market.

   (2) _____ Once the organizations choose a distribution channel, they can hardly change it.

   (3) _____ The focus of the study of distribution management has long been put on physical distribution while service distribution has been neglected.

   (4) _____ The usual practice is that tour operators organize packages by combining the components of tourist trip together and then sell the package to the public themselves.

   (5) _____ Intensive distribution is often adopted by those organizations whose product is highly specialized and confronts little competition.

   (6) _____ The ability to supply the product also has a great influence on the choice of the right promotional strategy because it is a kind of information about the product in itself and can help to attract consumers.

   (7) _____ Only the direct distribution channels are suitable to sell tourist products to the consumer because the tour operator often uses such a channel.

2. Questions for discussion

   (1) What approaches can the tourism marketers use to distribute their tourism products?
   _____

   (2) What are the main distribution methods as far as channel network is concerned?
   _____

   (3) How can the organization decide which method is appropriate for distribution channels?
   _____

   (4) What are the differences between the distribution channels for tourism and travel and those for other industries?
   _____

   (5) What factors can affect the organization's choice of marketing channels?
   _____

Part II   Guided Reading
第二部分   课文导读

旅游产品分销渠道是指旅游产品从旅游企业向旅游消费者转移过程中所经过的一切取得使用权或协助使用权转移的中介组织和个人,也就是旅游产品使用权转移过程中所经过的各个环节连接起来而形成的通道。本文主要探讨旅游产品作为一种服务产品的分销与有形产品分销的差异,用图例直观地阐明旅游分销的各种渠道,着重介绍了直接和间接分销渠道的特点以及影响企业选择分销渠道的主要因素。

一般来说,在旅游市场不断发展并逐渐成熟的条件下,大多数旅游产品并不是由旅游企业直接供应给旅游消费者,而是要经过或多或少的中介组织,即旅游中间商。在市场营销中,由于旅游市场、旅游企业、旅游中间商及旅游消费者等多种因素的影响,旅游产品分销渠道也就形成了多种多样的状态,即便是同一种旅游产品,也有可能通过不同的分销渠道销售。旅游产品的分销渠道有直接和间接、长和短、宽和窄等多种类型。

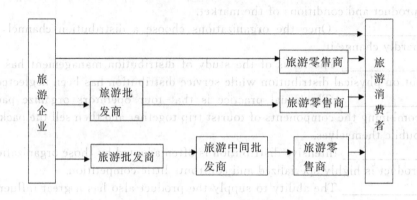

图1 旅游产品分销渠道结构

由图1可以看出,旅游产品分销渠道按照中间商的数量可分为两种,即直接分销渠道和间接分销渠道。

直接分销渠道指旅游企业在其市场营销活动中不通过任何一个旅游中间商,而直接把旅游产品销售给消费者的分销渠道。通过这种分销渠道,旅游企业直接和顾客交往,有利于直接获得旅游消费者的信息,有利于提高旅游产品的质量,控制旅游产品的成熟过程和程度,强化旅游企业的形象。在旅游产品直接销售量大和旅游消费者购买力较为稳定的情况下,旅游企业可以省去中间商的营销费用,以较小的成本获取较大的利润。

间接分销渠道指旅游企业通过两个或两个以上的旅游中间商向旅游消费者推销旅游产品的分销渠道。间接营销渠道是目前主要的旅游产品的分销渠道。渠道越长,旅游产品市场扩展的可能性越大,但旅游企业对旅游产品销售的控制能力和信息反馈的清晰度就越差。在间接分销渠道中,按照渠道的宽度可以将其分为:密集分销、选择分销、独家分销。

密集分销是指在渠道层次中选择尽可能多的中间商,充分与旅游产品的营销市场相接触。在旅游消费者集中的地方,或者企业的主要目标市场,就应采取这种渠道形式。这种渠道的优点是可以扩大旅游产品生产者或提供者的销售面和销售量,但是使用这种宽渠道形式,旅游企业可能会碰到一系列不利的结果:如销售费用较大,易对产品营销失去控制,因竞争激烈而跌价,渠道成员服务质量滑坡以致旅游企业形象受到损害,因而旅游企业采用此种渠道时要充分考虑到其负面影响。

选择性分销是指只选择那些有支付能力、有推销经验以及服务上乘的旅游中间商在特定区域与层次推销本企业的产品。这种渠道形式适用于价格较高的产品。这是因为消费者购买这些产品要通过慎重考虑与选择,因而要求中间商具有一定的专业知识、服务水平以及较高的信誉。这种分销渠道的优点是:第一,旅游企业只与少数中间商合作,可把精力集中于这些精选的中间商,增强对渠道的控制。第二,旅游企业与旅游中间商联系紧密,有利于建立良好的关系,从而使中间商更好地完成旅游企业赋予的营销职能,扩大产品的销售。第三,经过认真挑选,旅游中间商都有着较强的经营能力与良好的声誉,有利于提高绩效,降低成本,建立产品声誉。但在激烈的市场竞争中,旅游企业与中间商的选择是双向的,如果旅游企业的规模不大,知名度不高,挑选满意的中间商就会受到限制。

独家分销是指在一定的市场区域内仅选用一家经验丰富、信誉卓著的中间商来推销旅游企业产品,这是最窄的渠道形式。产销双方一般都签订合同,规定双方的销售权限、利润分配比例、销售费用和广告宣传费用的分担比例等。旅游企业开拓新市场时,这种营销渠道可以密切与中间商的协作关系,提高中间商的积极性,从而有利于旅游产品市场的开拓和信誉的提高。另外,一些特殊的高价旅游产品也常采用这种分销渠道。这种分销方式的优点是双方关系紧密,利益互动,有利于双方真诚合作,共同开拓有利的市场机会,提高销售能力和企业盈利能力。另外,可以提高对销售渠道的控制。不足之处在于只与一家中间商合作,风险较大,如果选择不当,即将失去这一地区的市场。再者,销售面窄,灵活性小,不利于旅游消费者的选择购买。

旅游产品是旅游企业进行营销渠道类型决策时首先考虑的因素。其影响和制约作用主要从旅游产品的性质、种类以及档次、等级等方面表现出来。一般来说,餐厅、旅游景点、商务性饭店、汽车旅馆、旅游汽车公司等旅游企业主要是采取直接分销渠道销售自己的产品或服务;而游船、度假饭店、机场旅馆、包机公司等尤其经营跨国旅游业务的旅游企业,由于市场销售面广,则往往采用间接分销渠道开展市场营销活动。对于高档的旅游产品,购买者较少,并且许多人为回头客,因而这类产品的营销工作,往往采用直接分销渠道进行,如探险旅行社等旅游企业经营的特种旅游产品就是如此;而大众化的较低档次的旅游产品,由于市场面较广,消费者较多,采用间接分销渠道的优点就很突出,易于在较大的空间内吸引、争取广大的客源。

旅游知识测试

正误判断:请在正确的选题上划√,错误的选题上划×。

1. 旅游中间产品一般是通过旅行社将它们组合起来,形成能够满足旅游者在旅游过程中各种需要的旅游最终产品。旅游者购买旅游产品以后,可以同时拥有旅游产品的使用权和所有权。

2. 如果要控制销售成本,旅游企业应该采用直接分销的形式,通过这种分销渠道,有利于获得旅游消费者的信息,提高旅游产品的质量,强化旅游企业的形象。

3. 如果旅游产品销售量大、消费者购买力较为稳定,旅游企业可以采用选择性分销的方法,以便省去营销费用,以较小的成本获取较大的利润。

4. 密集分销如销售费用较大,易对产品营销失去控制,因竞争激烈而跌价,渠道成员服务质量滑坡以致旅游企业形象受到损害。

5. 一些高价旅游产品常采用独家分销渠道。销售费用和广告宣传费用一般由销售代理承担,这种销售方式风险较小,有利于旅游批发商规避风险。

Part III Case Study
第三部分 案例研究

时运假日旅行社的市场营销

分析要点

1. 时运假日旅行社为何要开辟远程度假旅游市场？
2. 时运假日旅行社为何要对旅游目的地进行市场调查？对其促销有何意义？
3. 时运假日旅行社是如何细分市场的？针对目标市场设计了哪些旅游新产品？
4. 时运假日旅行社是如何建设分销渠道的？如何设计旅游宣传品的？
5. 结合实践教学，制定一份你所在城市的旅行社开辟度假旅游的市场调查报告。

相关理论和问题

1. 旅游市场调查(Investigation of tourism market)
2. 分销渠道(Distribution channels)
3. 市场细分(Segmentation of the markets)
4. 营销组合——4Ps(Marketing mix—4Ps)

历史背景

时运假日旅行社的前身是麦昂旅行社，办事处设在英国中部的汉普郡，专营欧洲乡村别墅短程旅游业务。当时，欧洲短程旅游市场竞争激烈，各旅行社可得的经营利润极低、交通费用昂贵、货币兑换率低以及国内居民存款利率高等因素严重冲击着短程旅游市场。从1983年以来，世界远程度假旅游市场看好，英国经营这方面旅游业务的旅行社逐渐增多。1984—1985年间，英国去西欧和地中海国家旅游人数的增长率为7.8%，而同期世界其他国家进行远程度假旅游人数的增长率为12.9%。

当时，经营远程度假旅游价格高、利润大，可以专门满足那些高收入、高消费阶层旅游的需求。远程度假包价旅游的日程安排复杂，活动范围较广，机动性强。旅游经营者可以比较灵活地调整线路价格内包含的各项费用。即使是经营散客的远程包价旅游，也会使旅行社获得较好的利润。经营远程度假包价旅游的优势和对这一市场需求的不断增长对当时麦昂旅行社改变经营方向和项目产品的类型有着极大的影响。1984年1月，麦昂旅行社做出决定，与英国一家较大的时运烟草公司签订联营合同，以时运烟草公司作为后盾，开辟远程度假包价旅游新市场，开始经营去世界各地的远程度假旅游，并将原来麦昂旅行社的名字改为时运假日旅行社。

新旅行社成立后采取的第一个措施就是聘任一位工作经验丰富的总经理格雷厄姆·菲力普。在这之前，他正受雇于世界有名的托马斯·库克旅行社。1984年1月3日，菲力普先生走马上任，并决定在1984—1985年的旅游旺季到来之时，首次推出远程度假旅游线路。

市场调研与分析

时运假日旅行社成立后，首先对远程度假市场进行调查分析，调研的主要内容是：哪些远程度假线路有较大的潜在市场？

哪些类型的客人愿意参加远程度假旅游？

3个月后，调研结果表明：

一、客人对各类远程度假旅游的偏好比重不同：

喜欢海边度假的客人	17%
喜欢海边度假＋购物的客人	33%
喜欢文化旅游的客人	19%
喜欢参加各种兴趣度假的客人	16%
喜欢在度假中"体验新的经历"的客人	15%

根据开辟新的客源市场、"不与其他旅行社争夺原有的客源市场"的指导思想，时运旅行社在分析调查结果后认为：喜欢在度假中"体验新的经历"的客人是一个潜力很大的新市场，时运旅行社决定重点开发并占领这个新市场。

二、市场调研的结果还表明，喜欢参加远程度假的客人大多数是地位和收入较高的客人，年龄并不受限制。远程度假既适合度蜜月的年轻人，也适合直到退休老人的各年龄段的客人。

三、主要竞争对手在远程度假旅游市场中所占的份额是：

库尼旅行社：占有20%，并且一直具有很好的信誉，已经牢固地确立了在这一市场的领先地位；

信诚旅行社：占有20%；

速鸟旅行社：占有10%（该社归英国航空公司所有）；

康肯·库恩旅行社：占有5%，它是托马斯·库克旅行社专门经营远程旅游业务的分社；

飞翼旅行社：占有5%。

通过市场调研，时运旅行社的目标十分明确。他们认为，要取代库尼旅行社的市场领先地位是十分困难的，但可以全力去争夺这一市场的第二领先地位。时运旅行社计划用5年时间达到这个目标，力争占有15%的远程度假客源市场份额，成为这一市场的第二霸主。

对旅游目的地的调查

当目标市场和产品类型确定后，时运旅行社紧接着对旅游目的地的设施和旅游资源进行调研，以弄清哪些目的地能满足客人的需求。1984年1—5月间，菲力普先生8.3万英里，走访了20多个国家的100多家饭店，寻找和确定适应不同客人需求的不同类型的旅游目的地。同时，他与有关目的地的部门重点协商了度假价格、住宿和交通三方面的问题。

一、住宿情况

对时运旅行社来说，一个非常重要的问题是如何在度假目的地以合理的价格，向远程旅游度假的客人提供能满足他们要求的食宿设施。菲力普亲自进行调研，一边旅行，一边住饭店，仔细考察了各饭店的服务标准、设备设施和到度假活动区的距离等。考察的结果令他非常满意。其后，他与各饭店的销售经理协商房价问题。最终达成的协议是：时运旅行社将这些饭店编印在旅行社出版的旅游宣传品上，散发给顾客。这既为旅行社本身宣传促销，也为各饭店做了广告。这种形式的宣传广告发放面广、数量多、针对性强、影响大，时运旅行社还可以从这些饭店获得30%的房价折扣。

二、交通情况

远程度假费用中。有很大比例用于支付从出发地到目的地之间的国际航运费和目的地国内的航运费。为了保证旅行社能获得较好的机票折扣，时运旅行社决定全部使用目的地国家的航空公司。这些航空公司可以保证向时运旅行社长期提供60%以上的机票折扣。

三、目的地旅游资源情况

为了旅行社开辟"求新和体验不同经历"的客源目标市场，菲力普先生考察了竞争对手所提供的线路中从未涉及的目的地。他认为必须以新的目的地、新的旅游资源来满足客人求新和体验不同经历的需要,时运旅行社才能扩大影响,占有足够的市场份额。

旅游宣传品的编制

市场和目的地的调研工作结束之后,时运旅行社开始编制下一个旅游季节的旅游线路,并把这些线路都鲜明地囊括在宣传品中。这里,旅行社碰到的一个很大困难是:旅游线路作为一种无形产品,能否被预订,完全依靠客人的感觉和偏好。因此,宣传品的设计至关重要。首先,宣传册封面的设计要有很强的吸引力,摆在琳琅满目的宣传品陈列架,能够引起客人的注意,使他们产生兴趣。其次,宣传册要针对教授、医生、律师、商人、专业技术人员等高薪阶层各年龄段的需要,准确地描绘各种线路和多种吸引物的特点,度假日程和活动安排也要有鲜明的针对性,切忌面面俱到、贪多求全。此外,宣传用纸要好,印刷质量要高,图片及说明要有新意,整体布局要合理,注意宣传品给客人留下的第一印象。这些都是宣传品制作过程中应当慎重处理的重要环节。如果处置不当,宣传品的效果将会受到影响,甚至前功尽弃。经过研究,旅行社决定宣传品的封面要突出海边度假、文化访问、兴趣活动和探险旅行四个主题,并附有四幅主题照片,以吸引那些喜欢单独探险、求奇活动的旅游者。

为此,时运旅行社特聘了一家专业广告公司承担宣传品的设计工作,设计制作费高达25万英镑。宣传品共84页,总体质量高,编入了能够吸引潜在客人的全部信息资料。

分销渠道的建立

宣传品制成后,另一项重要的工作是选择合适的旅行社作为代理商,确保宣传品能够展放在这些旅行社陈列架最显眼的位置上。由于时运旅行社刚开始经营远程度假业务,在那些为它散发宣传品的旅游代理商中取得信誉是非常重要的。时运旅行社选择了知名度较高、受游客欢迎的霍格·罗宾逊连锁旅行社。经过协调,这家旅行社同意将时运旅行社的宣传品放在其所辖的旅行社中试展一个时期。然后选择并确定合适的分销渠道。

在旅行社中,各种宣传品在展览架上展放位置的竞争十分激烈。由于旅行社要从出售的每一条包价线路中获得一定比例的佣金,出售的线路越多,得到的佣金也就越多,因此,旅行社都愿意将那些知名度高、受顾客欢迎、比较容易出售的线路宣传品摆放在明显位置;对有一定风险的新线路产品则另眼看待。时运旅行社希望自己的宣传品能够摆放在明显的位置以引起客人的注意。但事与愿违,双方为宣传品的摆放发生了争论,协议中止。

为此,时运旅行社采取其他措施,将自己的宣传品大量发给附近的各个独立的小旅行社和一些小型的连锁旅行社。时运旅行社还在办事处内培训了自己的推销人员,规定了推销数量与报酬发放相当的原则。

在发放宣传品的同时,时运旅行社还针对其客源目标市场在一些报纸杂志上刊登广告。到1984年12月,时运旅行社为迎接一年旅游旺季的到来而做的促销工作全部就绪,并期望自己所提供的产品能够吸引和满足那些具有特别需求的远程度假客人。

结论与市场战略

在旅行社最早印制的宣传品上,对所有年龄段的客人提供的海滨、文化、兴趣、探险四种产品,现在已细分为对两个年龄段的客人提供两种类型的度假产品。

一、两个年龄段:

旅行社发现,参加远程度假的客人大多为两个年龄段的人:一是25~34岁之间的客人,占28%;二是35~45岁之间的客人,占22%。年龄较年轻的一组客人均属于年轻的富有阶层。他们大多数是年轻夫妇,两人都有较好的职业和较高的收入,没有子女。年龄较大的一组中,大多数客人的子女已长大成人,离开家庭,夫妇两人有较高的收入和较多的余暇时间,人们把这类客人称为空巢的鸟。

二、两种度假形式:

海边度假和文化旅游是两种主要的度假形式。时运旅行社原来制定的让客人"体验新的经历"的市场策略没有产生很大的效果。因为人们对度假旅游市场的需求仍然是以海边度假活动为主。在经营中,时运旅行社为了适应上述趋势,对原来的经营战略进行了调整,变换了产品类型，使之更加适合市场的需求。具体做法是：

（一）探险求新旅行者对度假目的地的住宿设施，主要着眼于地处偏僻、新奇而小型的饭店、宾馆。旅行社的宣传品中相应增加了这种类型饭店的介绍，而由此增加的部分费用由这些被介绍的饭店分摊。

（二）传统的度假目的地已经不能满足"独立的旅游者"的需求，如埃及、印度等已从原有的线路中删掉，在1989—1990年新线路中增加了南美洲的危地马拉、马来西亚的沙巴和非洲科摩罗群岛等目的地国家或地区。

（三）根据客源市场的变化，在新宣传品的封面上只刊登两幅代表两种最流行度假活动的照片：一幅是海滩，一幅是文化遗址。

时运假日旅行社在进入远程度假旅游市场的第一年，销售了900人次的旅游产品，其平均价格为1200英镑。在1988—1989年旅游季节中，旅行社销售的产品数量上升为3500人次，平均价格为1440英镑，大约占整个远程度假市场10%的份额。5年中，时运旅行社累计销售产品为1.2万人次。数据表明，作为一家名不见经传的小型旅行社，时运假日旅行社的市场定位和营销是非常成功的。

资料来源：叶万春 宋先道.英国时运假日旅行社开辟新市场.市场营销案例荟萃[M].武汉理工大学出版社，2004。

Part Ⅳ　Reading Box
第四部分　阅读与分析

The Marketing Approach for Tourism Products

阅读分析要点

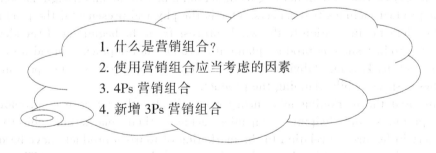

1. 什么是营销组合？
2. 使用营销组合应当考虑的因素
3. 4Ps 营销组合
4. 新增 3Ps 营销组合

　　While making a choice among marketing channels, travel and tourism marketers should pay attention to not only the characteristics of services and their possible influence on marketing but also the unique characteristics of the tourism product. The marketing approach for tourism products should be effective enough to combine a number of elements used to form a workable, complete and strategic plan to satisfy both the consumer and the marketer.¹ To achieve this purpose, it is necessary for the tourism marketer to evaluate and change the elements of the marketing mix constantly. The successful **marketing mix** should take the following factors into account.

　　1. *Timing*. Choosing the right time can help us make a big profit. It includes such elements as holidays, high season, off season, the rising period of economy, and so on.

2. *Brands*. Here brands refer to identification marks such as names, trademarks, labels, logos, etc. which can help the consumer remember and recall information about our product and our company.

3. *Packaging*. Unlike physical goods, tourism services are intangible. But packaging still plays an important role in tourism. Transportation, lodging, amenities, and recreation activities can be sold separately, but more frequently they are combined together to form a package which will be sold to the consumer. Other forms of packaging include family plans or single plans.

4. *Pricing*. Sales volume and the image of the product are closely related to pricing. There exist a large number of choices of pricing such as discount prices, privileged prices, premium prices, and so on.

5. *Channels of distribution*. The ultimate purpose of production is to move the product to the consumer. Various distribution channels including direct selling, retail travel agents, wholesale tour operators, or a combination of these methods are used and developed.

6. *Product*. The features of the product play a vital role in determining its position in the competition and seeking for the best way to compete.

7. *Image*. To a great extent, reputation and quality of the product can leave a deep impression to the consumer.

8. *Advertising*. As is known to all, advertising is a kind of paid promotion and is of great importance to the selling of the product. But the question is how to choose the best timing, place and way to promote.

9. *Selling*. It is obvious that selling is the critical factor of success. While drawing up the marketing plan, we should take various sales techniques into consideration.

Many elements in the marketing mix are generally classified into four categories called **"the four Ps"**. They are product, place, promotion, and price. Although this classification is too simple, it plays a vital role in helping us understand marketing and design marketing program.[2] The product includes two aspects. One is the physical presence of the product. The other is the elements in relation to the whole process from the beginning of the idea to the selling of the product such as product planning, product development, breadth of the line, branding and packaging. Obviously a sensible tour operator should pay much attention to these aspects while planning the product.

Borden invented the marketing mix theory originally for the purpose of promoting manufactured products and helping companies achieve their marketing objectives. However, as certain features in relation to the marketing of tourism products have become recognized as being important, it has been adapted and expanded in recent years.[3] There are additional **"three Ps"** proposed by Booms and Bimer for services.

People

Undoubtedly people are the most important element of any service or experience. Services tend to be produced and consumed at the same moment. Therefore, here people involve not only the providers of services but also consumers who enjoy the services together. These consumers may be selected and organized or may happen to come at the same time. Anyone who takes part in the experience expects to enjoy it happily. But their expectations would be spoiled by the bad behavior of any of these people. For example, a good theatre performance may be spoiled by some disruptive audience. Similarly tourists may have a miserable trip due to the bad attitude of the tour guide. So it is necessary to carry out close management control over the behavior of people.

Physical evidence

A service tends to be an experience that is consumed at the point where it is purchased and cannot be owned since it quickly perishes.[4] Therefore, it is of vital importance to provide physical evidence so that consumers can make a judgment on the possible services the organization offers if they have no other ways to know about them.[5] There are many examples of physical evidence such as photographs in a holiday brochure from which consumers can have an idea of some aspects of an unseen product, the physical setting in which a service is delivered, or even furnishings, light and color which are influential to the whole atmosphere of the setting.

Process

Since it is controlled by people, process is an important element closely related to the importance of people.[6] From the perspective of the consumer, it can be viewed as an element of the service that sees the consumer experiencing an organization's offering or something that the consumer participates in at different points in time.[7] For example, the marketing process of booking a flight on the Internet is made up of such steps: visiting the website of the airliner, entering details of the flight and booking them, getting the tickets by e-mail or post, catching the flight on time and arriving at the destination. With the development and popular use of computer, the delivery of some services has become highly automatic and different services require different level of involvement of people.[8]

Although these additional elements are very important, some people still think that it is not necessary to separate them from the original "four Ps" of the mix as these ideas are embodied in those four categories.

New Words

category	*n.*	部门，种类
expand	*v.*	扩充，使发展
objective	*n.*	目的，目标
critical	*adj.*	重要的，关键的
perish	*v.*	毁坏，消失
disruptive	*adj.*	扰乱性的，破坏性的
automatic	*adj.*	自动的
embody	*v.*	具体表现，体现

Notes

1. The marketing approach for tourism products should be effective enough to combine a number of elements used to form a workable, complete and strategic plan to satisfy both the consumer and the marketer.
   旅游产品的营销方法应该足够有效，它能将许多因素组合起来满足消费者和营销者的需要，这些因素可构成一个可行的、全面的和具有战略性的计划。

2. Although this classification is too simple, it plays a vital role in helping us understand marketing and design marketing program.
   尽管这种分类很简单，但对帮助我们理解市场营销、设计营销计划都起着重要的作用。

3. However, as certain features in relation to the marketing of tourism products have become recognized as being important, it has been adapted and expanded in recent

years.

然而,由于人们认识到旅游产品营销的某些特征是重要的,近年来,营销组合理论得到了修改和补充。

4. A service tends to be an experience that is consumed at the point where it is purchased and cannot be owned since it quickly perishes.

服务往往是一种购买和消费同步的经历。它不能被拥有,因为它(随着消费结束)很快就不存在了。

5. Therefore, it is of vital importance to provide physical evidence so that consumers can make a judgment on the possible services the organization offers if they have no other ways to know about them.

因此,提供有形证据是十分重要的,消费者在没有其他方式了解产品的情况下,有形化便于消费者判断企业可能提供的服务。

6. Since it is controlled by people, process is an important element closely related to the importance of people.

由于过程是由人控制的,因此它与人同等重要。

7. From the perspective of the consumer, it can be viewed as an element of the service that sees the consumer experiencing an organization's offering or something that the consumer participates in at different points in time.

从消费者的角度来看,过程可以被当作服务的一个要素,从中消费者可体验企业提供的产品;过程也可指消费者在不同时间参与的消费活动。

8. With the development and popular use of computer, the delivery of some services has become highly automatic and different services require different level of involvement of people.

随着计算机的发展与普及,一些服务的销售变得高度自动化,不同的服务需要人员参与的程度不同。

Topic discussion

1. Why do you think people are important in tourism marketing?

2. What factors should be taken into account for a successful marketing mix?

3. What is the physical presence of the product? Why is it very important for distributing tourism products?

4. What are the additional "three Ps"? And why are they regarded as being important?

【即学即用】

With reference to the theory, information or approach applied in the Reading Box, have a case study of the marketing approach you use to sell a tourist product. Make presentation of your study in Chinese or in English using PPT.

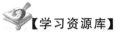【学习资源库】

为了掌握本章更多的相关专业知识,请您登陆 http://sicnu.edu.cn/,点击国家双语教学示范课程《旅游学概论》,进入网络学堂查询相关资料。

Chapter Review 本章小结

> This chapter has discussed the essence of tourism marketing and the distinctiveness of service distribution. Marketers may apply the direct channel or the indirect channel; but many factors will certainly influence the choices of different distribution channels they adopt. The tourism product, the customer, the travel intermediaries, and the marketing environment are the most important factors they have to consider. In addition to distribution channels, the marketing mix is of great importance to tourism sectors. Various elements in the marketing mix are generally classified into four categories: "the four Ps". They are product, place, promotion, and price. There are additional "three Ps" proposed by Booms and Bimer for services: people, physical evidence and process. All of them are basic marketing approaches in the hospitality industry.

Part V Additional Know-how of Tourism
第五部分 旅游知识扩展

【关键术语】

Marketing: the interaction and interrelationships that occur among customers and producers of goods and services, through which ideas, products, services and values are created and exchanged for the mutual benefit of both groups

市场营销:消费者与提供产品和服务的生产者之间的互动和相互关系;在这些互动和相互关系中创造思想、产品、服务和价值,并得到交流,双方都获取利益。

Services marketing: The marketing of services such as those associated with the tourism industry, as opposed to the marketing of the goods industry. The following characteristics distinguish service marketing from goods marketing: intangibility, inseparability, variability and perishability.

服务营销:与旅游业相关的服务营销不同于一般商品的市场营销。服务营销与一般商品的营销相比有以下特点:无形性、不可分离性、差异性和不可储存性。

Market segmentation: The division of the tourist market into more or less homogenous subgroups, or tourist market segments, based on certain common characteristics and/or behavioral patterns; distinctions are made from geographic segmentation, sociodemographic segmentation, psychographic segmentation and behavioral segmentation

市场细分:根据游客的某些共同特征和/或行为模式,把不同的游客划分为若干具有同质性的子群落。市场细分可分为:地理学细分、社会人口统计细分、心理学细分和行为学细分。

Database marketing: a comprehensive marketing strategy that is based on a memory of prior business transactions with customers; the use of accumulated customer data to inform marketing decisions

数据库营销:一种综合的市场营销策略,其基础是此前业务交易所建立的客户资料数据库;使用长期积累的客户数据进行市场营销决策。

Strategic marketing: marketing that takes into consideration an extensive analysis of external and internal environmental factors in identifying strategies that attain specific goals. SWOT analysis: an analysis of a company or destination's strengths, weaknesses, opportunities and threats that emerges from an examination of its internal and external environment.

战略营销:为达到特定目标,对内在和外在环境因素进行综合分析的市场营销手段。SWOT 分析(SWOT:Strength, Weakness, Opportunity, Threat):考察某个公司或目的地的内部和外部环境,分析其优势、劣势、机遇和威胁。

【知识链接】

1. 营销渠道成本

旅游直接分销渠道与间接分销渠道的区别,实际上就是旅游企业在市场营销活动中是否使用旅游中间商的问题。在实际工作中,旅游企业采用直接分销渠道还是间接分销渠道,最终以两项标准来判断,即销出本企业产品的数量或销售额,本企业为维护各种分销渠道所必须支付的营销费用,这一费用标准可用单位产品销售量所耗费用或单位产品销售额所耗费用来表示。若旅游分销渠道销出的产品数量多,且单位产品销售量所耗费用低(或单位产品销售额所耗费用低),则该种类型的营销渠道就为理想的渠道。但是,若在此基础上选择的是旅游间接分销渠道,则还应针对旅游中间商在目标市场、经营规模、营销实力、偿付能力、信誉程度和合作意愿等方面的不同,准确地评估挑选旅游中间商,使纳入营销渠道的中间商具有较高的质量。

旅游营销渠道的选择还与旅游企业的实力和在市场上的地位有紧密的关系,实力雄厚的旅游企业,往往自身可以建立强大的营销网络,对旅游中间商的依赖性相对小些,实力较弱的旅游企业对旅游中间商的依赖性就大一些;若目标市场广阔或欲进入新的市场时,旅游企业就必须建立间接分销渠道才能取得良好的营销效果。另外,旅游企业欲提高产品的销售量或市场竞争加剧时,也必须较多地依赖旅游间接分销渠道。总之,无论选择哪一种营销渠道,都应考虑使用渠道的成本。

2. 旅游中间商

旅游营销在很大程度上依赖于旅游中间商的作用。旅游中间商是指介于旅游生产者和旅游消费者之间,专门从事转售旅游企业的产品、具有法人资格的经济组织或个人。由于旅游中间商在旅游市场营销中的作用不同,旅游生产者与这些组织和个人的责权关系不同,因而旅游中间商也有多种类型。

(1)旅游经销商

旅游经销商又称为旅游经营商,它从各种旅游商品生产者那里大批量地购买单项旅游产品和服务,再把他们组合成包价旅游产品,投放市场。它的利润主要来源于旅游产品购进价与销出价之间的差额,拥有旅游产品的所有权,与旅游生产者共同承担市场风险。旅游经营商主要分为旅游批发商和旅游零售商两种。

旅游批发商是指从事批发业务的旅行社或旅游公司,主要从事组织、宣传和推销团体包价旅游业务。它将航空公司或其他交通运输企业的服务产品与旅游目的地旅游企业(饭店、餐馆、景点经营者等)的地面服务组合成一个整体的旅游产品,然后通过某一销售途径推向广大公众。旅游批发商一般与上述旅游产品和服务的供给者签约,包定大量客房、租用交通工具、购买景点门票等,并享有批量折扣,然后组织成各种报价旅游产品向旅游零售商出售,由零售商最后出售给旅游消费者。

旅游零售商是指直接向旅游消费者销售旅游产品及提供旅游咨询等服务的旅游中间

商。它主要的业务范围是:为旅游者提供各种咨询服务;为旅游者计划、组织、安排旅游线路和日程;为旅游者具体安排食宿、交通、娱乐、观光、购物等活动和服务;负责宣传、促销、招揽旅游者等。它的利润来自于销售所获得的佣金。

目前,有些旅游批发商也直接向团体旅游者出售包价旅游,或者拥有零售机构,也兼营零售商的业务。而旅游零售商为了拓展规模,同时兼营零售与批发。所以,对许多旅游中间商来说,很难区分它是批发商还是零售商。

(2) 旅游代理商

旅游代理商是指接受旅游产品生产者和供给者的委托,在一定的时间、一定区域内进行宣传、促销并代理销售其产品的旅游中间商。它的利润主要来源于为委托人和消费者提供服务而获取的佣金。旅游代理商不拥有产品的所有权,因而其承担的市场风险远小于旅游经营商。旅游企业一般在自己营销能力难以达到的地区,或是新产品投放期,产品销路不好的时候利用代理商寻找机会。它是旅游经营商的一种补充。

【小思考】

1. 旅游产品分销渠道的特性给旅游企业带来哪些启示?如何根据分销渠道的特点开展旅游市场营销?

参考阅读:
旅游产品分销渠道有以下特点:

(1) 稳定性

一个旅游企业的营销渠道系统是企业的一种重要组成部分,它不仅代表着企业产品的一种分销渠道,也代表着构成渠道系统的一系列政策和实践活动,而这些政策和实践将形成一个巨大的长期关系网。旅游企业一旦选择了某种营销渠道,将在一定时期内依赖于该营销渠道,不会发生重大变化,所以营销渠道存在着一种强大的保持现状的惯性,具有相对稳定性。因而,企业在选择分销渠道时,既要考虑企业的现状与市场环境,也要考虑今后企业的发展趋势与动态及市场变化情况。

(2) 协调性

分销渠道系统中,执行不同功能的机构必须"分工不分家",相互配合,协调一致,才能有效完成分销任务。任何一个中间环节的失误都会导致整个营销链条的断裂,营销目的的无法实现。在实践中,营销渠道的运营往往由于渠道组成成员的矛盾冲突或动作的不一致而导致失败。只有各层级步调一致,互相支持,互相配合,才能顺利完成整个营销目的。

(3) 整体性

营销渠道与旅游企业的所有其他营销环节是一个有机的整体。旅游企业的产品决策、价格决策、促销决策都与营销渠道的决策息息相关,分销渠道的选择直接影响到市场上产品的最终价格、产品形式及促销方式等诸多分销环节。为达成共同的分销目标,必须将渠道策略与其他策略相互配合,组成一个有机的整体。因而,要强调以系统的、动态的观点来看待渠道决策与其他营销决策的关系,而不应将渠道系统决策孤立起来。

2. 以一旅游目的地为例,谈谈怎样才能有效地开展旅游目的地营销。

参考阅读:
旅游宣传促销越来越受到政府和旅游部门的重视,建立科学高效的旅游目的地市场营销体系主要有以下六个环节:市场分析、品牌定位、资源整合、过程管理、专业分工、绩效评估。

(1) 市场分析:市场分析是市场定位的基础,科学的市场定位是有效的市场营销的前提。通过对客源市场的调查,分析其客源结构和潜在的客源所在,以指导本地区有针对性地开发客源市场,同时通过了解市场需求变化信息和游客对本地区旅游产品及服务的意见反馈,即时调整产品和服务内涵,适应客源市场的需求。

(2) 品牌定位:市场分析使我们明确了目标市场所在,同时也明确了适应特定市场需求的资源与产品,从而也为确立针对特定目标市场的目的地品牌打下基础。品牌定位,就是要在市场分析的基础上,针对特定目标市场的需求和特点,确立对该市场具有较高好感和吸引力的目的地品牌。

(3) 资源整合:旅游目的地营销部门要根据市场反馈信息对旅游资源进行适度的整合,形成可消费的产品以适应市场的需求,将本地区最具有品质和特色的旅游资源推介给旅游者,同时深化旅游产品,使资源的整合伴随市场的开发逐步深入。

(4) 过程管理:一是通过对旅游市场营销全过程的管理,达到对旅游市场营销成本和绩效的控制;二是通过对旅游目的地产品、服务、环境等的全过程管理,实现旅游市场营销所追求的高好感度、美誉度和高重游率。

(5) 专业分工:旅游市场需求的多样性和旅游资源、旅游传播手段的多样性、复杂性,使得旅游市场营销需要建立严密科学的专业分工,提升旅游营销的专业化水平。

(6) 绩效评估:绩效评估既是对前期实施的旅游营销工作结果的评估,更是对下一步旅游营销工作所需的市场分析的开始。旅游营销的绩效评估需要一套科学可操作的评估方法与手段,需要建立一套反映旅游营销绩效的指标体系。

Part VI Further Readings
第六部分 课外阅读

如果您想进一步学习本章的内容,探讨旅游产品的特点,如何开展旅游市场营销,建议您阅读以下学者的著作和论文。

一、中文部分

[1] Philip Kotler, John Brown, James Markens 著;谢彦君译. 旅游市场营销[M]. 旅游教育出版社 & 培生教育出版集团,2002.

[2] 赵西萍. 旅游市场营销学[M]. 高等教育出版社,2002.

[3] 维克多. 密德尔敦著,向萍等译. 旅游营销学[M]. 中国旅游出版社,2001.

[4] 谢彦君. 对旅游产品及相关问题的探讨[J]. 东北财经大学学报,1999,(03).

[5] 钱祖煜. 旅游企业的体验营销策略[J]. 商场现代化,2007,(01).

[6] 伍延基. 旅游目的地营销中值得深入探讨的两个问题[J]. 旅游学刊,2006,(08).

[7] 廖启安,郭峰,刘虎承,邹超. 体验经济时代的旅游服务营销[J]. 财经界(下半月),2006(10).

[8] 金准. Web2.0 和旅游目的地营销生态系统[J]. 旅游学刊,2006,(07).

[9] 马爱萍,朱蕴波,吕勤,韩玫丽. 北京地区居民旅行社产品消费特征实证研究——兼对旅行社产品设计和营销的建议[J]. 旅游学刊,2004,(01).

[10] 周笑源. 生态旅游市场营销内涵及其产品策略[J]. 旅游学刊,2004,(01).

二、英文部分

[1] Stephen L. J. Smith. The tourism product[J]. *Annals of Tourism Research*,1994(21).

[2] Peter Hodgson. New tourism product development: Market research's role[J]. *Tourism Management*, 1990(11).

[3] Ralf Buckley. Adventure tourism products: Price, duration, size, skill, remoteness[J]. *Tourism Management*, 2007(28).

[4] Ken W. McCleary. A framework for national tourism marketing [J]. *International Journal of Hospitality Management*, 1987(6).

[5] Peter O C, Andrew J F. The future of hotel electronic distribution expert and industry perspectives [J]. *Cornell Hotel and Restaurant Administration Quarterly*, 2002(24).

[6] Francesca d'Angella, Frank M. Go. Tale of two cities' collaborative tourism marketing [J]. *Tourism Management*, 2009(3):429—440.

[7] Asad Mohsin, Tourist attitudes and destination marketing-the case of Australia's Northern Territory and Malaysia [J]. *Tourism Management*, 2005, (26):723—732.

[8] Robyn Stokes, Tourism strategy making: Insights to the events tourism domain [J]. *Tourism Management*, 2008, (29):252—262.

[9] H. Ruhi Yaman, Eda Gurel, Ethical ideologies of tourism marketers [J]. *Annals of Tourism Research*, 2006, (33)2:470—489.

[10] Laurel J. Reid, Stephen L. J. Smith, Rob McCloskey, The effectiveness of regional marketing alliances: A case study of the Atlantic Canada Tourism Partnership 2000—2006 [J]. *Tourism Management*, 2008, (29):581—593.

Chapter 10 Destination Life Cycle
第十章 目的地生命周期

Learning objects：学习目标

- Study the supply-side (destination) which pulls tourists from the origin to the tourist site within the N-S pair of the tourism system (Leiper's model)在旅游系统（Leiper 模型）需求与供给关系中，学习拉动游客从客源地到旅游地的供给方面——旅游目的地
- Understand the evolution of the destination life cycle and the significance of Butler's curve of destination life cycle 了解旅游目的地生命周期的演进过程以及巴特勒目的地生命周期曲线的意义
- Outline the factors which influence the process of the destination life cycle 指出影响目的地生命周期演进过程的因素
- Describe the variables that may determine the stages of the life cycle into which the destination evolves, and its presentation in each stage 陈述目的地生命周期进入某一阶段的变量以及在每个阶段的表现
- Appreciate the basic approaches that are applied to overcome the problems at each stage of destination life cycle 学习解决生命周期各个阶段问题的基本方法
- Understand the two tendencies of tourist markets which have different impact on the destination life cycle 了解旅游市场的两种发展趋势，以及对目的地生命周期的不同影响
- Discuss the difficulty of application for Butler's destination life model 讨论应用巴特勒目的地生命周期模型的困难之处

Ability goals：能力目标

- Case Study 案例分析：周庄古镇生命周期研究
- Reading Box 阅读分析：Destination in Decline 目的地的衰落

Part I Text
第一部分 课文

Destination Life Cycle

【教学要点】

知识要点	掌握程度	相关章节
Butler's curve of destination life cycle 巴特勒目的地生命周期曲线	重点掌握	本课文与第 1 单元、第 2 单元、第 3 单元、第 4 单元、第 5 单元、第 11 单元、第 12 单元、第 13 单元、第 14 单元、第 15 单元相关内容有联系。
factors which influence the process of the destination life cycle 影响目的地生命周期演进过程的因素	重点掌握	
two tendencies of tourist markets 旅游市场发展的两种趋势	一般了解	
authentic travel 真实旅游	一般了解	
enclave resort 旅游飞地	重点掌握	

It is well known that the development of tourism has had strong influence on the evolution of destinations, especially resorts. Meanwhile, transport developments also have played a vital role in the evolution of resorts. Now most resorts are not just destinations. They have, according to their own conditions such as scenic sites and auxiliary facilities, developed into touring centers around which many touring routes and a number of attractions have appeared.[1] At the same time, the resorts have had to make some improvements in their tourist facilities and services so as to adapt to the constant changes and development of markets. We can use a formal term—the **destination life cycle** (**DLC**) to refer to these ideas (see Figure 10.1) The cycle destinations go through is similar to the life cycle of a product (which usually involves four stages—launch, development, maturity, and decline while sales grow in the process). Obviously, each destination has a unique DLC curve, but there are some similar determining factors which can be summarized as follows:

• the speed of development;
• access;
• government policy;
• the tendency of market;
• destinations competing with each other.

The progress of every stage in the cycle is closely related to each of these factors, which can either delay or speed it up.[2] Not every development except those which are expected to bring big profits can go through all stages of the cycle. In fact, at any stage development will be held back by this or that factor. On the other hand, each stage, even the cycle itself can last for a different period of time. Some can exist longer while others shorter. For example, instant resorts such as Cancun (Mexico) or time-share developments grow very rapidly and come into the stage of development soon after the business starts. On the contrary, well-established resorts usually develop very slowly and need more time to move from one stage to another. Take Scarborough (England) as an example. It takes almost three centuries to go from exploration to rejuvenation.

The concept of destination life cycle can help us understand the process of the evolution of destinations and their markets.[3] Such **supply-side factors** as investment and capacity constraints may bring about various shape of the curve. In other words, they may influence the development of destinations.

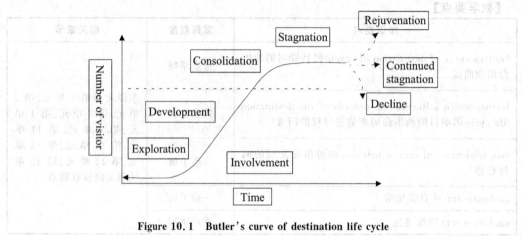

Figure 10.1 Butler's curve of destination life cycle

Exploration
At this stage, only a small number of people who are interested in new sites choose to visit the resort. What mainly attract them are the natural attractions and culture of the resort. However, inconvenient transport and lack of facilities restrict the number of visitors and influence its development. But here visitors are more likely to enjoy authentic attractions and have more chances to get in touch with the local people and learn about their real life.[4] Parts of southwest China are typical resorts of this stage.

Involvement
Involvement here refers to the participation of local communities in making a decision about whether tourism should be encouraged and what type and scale they prefer to choose. They will actively provide services for visitors and take part in planning, developing and advertising the resort to attract an increased and regular number of visitors. Correspondingly, this may lead to the appearance of a tourist season and market area. Meanwhile, the public sector has to be responsible for building and maintaining infrastructure and providing institute controls. So, it is obvious that at this stage the establishment of appropriate organization and decision-making processes for tourism are becoming necessary and urgent. At the same time, local communities should shoulder the responsibility to determine how many people they can accept at one time and make sure that this capacity limits can be observed strictly.[5] They should also introduce sustainable principles for the further development of the resort. We can find examples in the less-developed areas of northwest China.

Development
With the word-of-mouth about its attractions as well as the increase and improvement of the facilities, more and more visitors are attracted to the destination. By then,

companies from outside begin to involve in local tourism industry by providing products and facilities for tourists and gradually replace those local ones to control part of tourism. The enterprises go into the market with different aims. They may aim at making big profits in a short period of time regardless of whether the resort can continue to develop or not.[6] Therefore, serious problems may appear unless local decision-making structures can take effective measures to deal with them. With the change of tourismi and the provision of more facilities, the very nature of the resort can be altered too. In order to help solve problems, regional and national planning structures are involved in the business while the control in the public sector is weakened. This stage is therefore very important for the development of the resort. However, there is an obvious problem. That is, the resort may be exploited too much and the conditions of its facilities may become worsening, which of course will lead to the decline of the resort and its quality. Parts of east and west China exemplify this stage.

Consolidation

At this stage, the resort has become a mature part of the tourism industry. It provides a recreational business district (CRBD) which can be identified easily. However, the growth rate of visitors is slowing down while the number of visitors is still increasing and sometimes even exceeds permanent residents. Many Caribbean and Mediterranean destinations can prove this. The West Street of Yangshuo, Guilin of China is also a typical example of this stage.

Stagnation

Stagnation, as the word implies, here refers to the stop of the development of destinations. At this stage, the number of visitors has reached the highest point and the destination has lost most of its attraction. New visitors are few and those who come to travel are mainly conservative ones who make repeat visits. To avoid leaving the resort's large number of facilities unused, business use is also sought, but great efforts have to be made to develop and promote the product so that the number of visitors will not decrease.[7] Compared with many firmly established and mature resorts, resorts at this stage often meet many problems concerning environment, society and economy. They may also find that it is hard to compete with those resorts for visitors. A number of resorts in China which were developed in early 1980s are examples here.

Decline

Visitors are now drawn away by other newer resorts and a large number of them prefer to take day trips and weekend visits which usually cover a short distance. As a result, resorts in this stage suffer heavy decreases in their share of the market. However, they should get rid of the idea that decline and the end of their business are inevitable. On the contrary, they should try their best to revive their attraction by taking effective measures such as seeking new markets, re-positioning the resort, or finding new uses for facilities.

Rejuvenation

In order to rejuvenate or revive the destination, destination managers will use new attractions and develop new products such as mega events to create new markets.[8] However, it does not mean that traditional markets will be totally replaced. The destination should also protect and develop them, which, combined with the creation of such new markets and products as business, conference or special interest tourism, will help to maintain visitation levels and weaken the influence of seasonality and declining market segments.

At the very beginning, sustainable tourism strategies based on local communities should be adopted. And we can say that the development of a destination is dependent on the understanding of the cycle. At each stage of the cycle, tourists of different numbers and types come to the resort one group after another. They usually have different and **changing preferences**, motivations and desires. In response, tourist destinations will also have to provide different and changing facilities and access, the quality and quantity of which can only be matched by an evolving market.[9] However, these approaches have some significant problems:

- The difficulty of recognizing what stage the resort is in and distinguishing **turning points between stages.**
- The difficulty of obtaining a long series of visitor arrivals data to draw the curve accurately.
- The warning signs which planners respond to may be false. And their response is, to some extent, influenced by management interference.
- The danger of a strategy particularly made for each stage.

There are many interpretations for the level of combination of these approaches. After all, the concept of life cycle can be applied to a hotel, a resort and a region. And different market segments have different curves.

According to Middleton (1992), there are two tendencies contrary to each other in destination development for the future.[10] First, there is the development and provision of new products. They include closely controlled environments or **enclaves** (such as large-scale theme parks) which are surrounded by walls and which are built for special purpose, independent resorts which can provide almost everything for tourists, and cruise ships which can offer tourists service of high quality and give them a chance to escape from the reality for the time being and enjoy themselves in a safe, fantastic world. These products will be further developed and improved with the development of economy.

Second, more and more tourists are inclined to choose **authentic** or **sensitive travel** where the influence of management is slightest so as to avoid being controlled by the travel trade. They want to control the experience themselves and enjoy real and unspoiled landscapes and/or cultures without being affected. However, this tendency may bring more serious problems, even damages to the destination than enclave tourism which controls tourists' contacts with local cultures and environments on a routine basis. In the future, destinations should improve their management and enhance their ability to provide human resources, technology and sustainable principles for the development of the new tourism. Thus, along with their intrinsic attractions, they can maintain their competitive advantage in the market.

New Words

curve	n.	曲线,弧线
stagnation	n.	停滞期

rejuvenation	n.	恢复活力,复原;再生
conservative	adj.	保守的
infrastructure	n.	基础设施
inevitable	adj.	不可避免的,必然的
consolidation	n.	巩固期
revive	v.	恢复,复兴
permanent	adj.	永久性的,常住的
preference	n.	偏好,喜好

Key Terms

| destination life cycle | 目的地生命周期 | public sector | 公共部门 |
| supply-side factor | 供方因素 | market segment | 市场细分 |

Notes

1. Now most resorts are not just destinations. They have, according to their own conditions such as scenic sites and auxiliary facilities, developed into touring centers around which many touring routes and a number of attractions have appeared.
   现在,大多数旅游胜地不仅仅是目的地,根据其自身景点和配套设施等条件,它们已发展成为很多旅游线路和大量景观聚集的旅游中心。

2. The progress of every stage in the cycle is closely related to each of these factors, which can either delay or speed it up.
   生命周期的每个阶段的发展都和这些因素紧密相关,能加快或延迟各阶段的发展进程。

3. The concept of destination life cycle can help us understand the process of the evolution of destinations and their markets.
   目的地生命周期的概念有助于我们理解旅游目的地及其市场的发展演化过程。

4. But here visitors are more likely to enjoy authentic attractions and have more chance to get in touch with the local people and learn about their real life.
   然而,旅游者更有可能享受到真实的旅游吸引物,更有机会接触当地居民并了解他们真实的生活。

5. At the same time, local communities should shoulder the responsibility to determine how many people they can accept at one time and make sure that this capacity limits can be observed strictly.
   同时,当地社区有责任确定旅游目的地一次能容纳多少游客,确保这一容量限度能够得到严格地遵守。

6. They may aim at making big profits in a short period of time regardless of whether the resort can continue to develop or not.
   他们可能不考虑旅游胜地能否持续发展而追求短期利益最大化。

7. To avoid leaving the resort's large number of facilities unused, business use is also sought, but great efforts have to be made to develop and promote the product so that the number of visitors will not decrease.
   我们可以探寻旅游地众多设施的商业用途,以免它们被闲置,但更应努力开发和推销新产品来保证旅游者数量不会减少。

8. In order to rejuvenate or revive the destination, destination managers will use new attractions and develop new products such as mega events to create new markets.
   为了使目的地恢复活力或生机,目的地的管理者应该利用新的旅游吸引物和开发新产品,例如重大节事活动来开拓新的旅游市场。

9. In response, tourist destinations will also have to provide different and changing facilities and access, the quality and quantity of which can only be matched by an evolving market.
因此,旅游目的地必须提供不同的符合市场变化的旅游设施和交通路径。这些设施的数量和质量应当与不断发展的市场相匹配。

10. According to Middleton (1992), there are two tendencies contrary to each other in destination development for the future.
1992年Middleton提出,今后旅游目的地的发展有两种完全相反的趋势。

Exercise

1. Fill in the blanks with proper words to complete the following statements.

   development; evolution; sustainable; authentic; new; permanent

   (1) In fact, at any stage of the destination life cycle, _____ will be held back by this or that factor.

   (2) By the _____ stage, the number of visitors is so large that at peak periods it even equals or exceeds the number of local inhabitants.

   (3) At the consolidation stage, the growth rate of visitors is slowing down while the number of them is still increasing and sometimes even exceeds _____ residents.

   (4) At the involvement stage, _____ tourism strategies based on local communities are adopted.

   (5) In the future, destinations should improve their management and enhance their ability to provide human resources, technology for the development of the _____ tourism.

   (6) More and more tourists are inclined to choose _____ or sensitive traveling where the influence of management is slightest so as to avoid being controlled by the travel trade.

2. Questions for discussion

   (1) How many stages are there in the development of destinations? And what are they?

   (2) What is the attitude of visitors at the exploration stage?

   (3) What should the local communities do at the involvement stage?

   (4) Do you think that destination is likely to decline according to destination life cycle?

   (5) What approaches should the destination take to cope with tourists of different numbers and types at each stage of the cycle?

   (6) According to Middleton, what are the two tendencies in the destination development for the future?

Part II　Guided Reading
第二部分　课文导读

　　旅游目的地的发展必然要与旅游活动的发展相关。旅游目的地为旅游活动提供了空间和载体，同时旅游活动又进一步促进了旅游目的地的发展。本文探讨了影响旅游目的地生命周期的主要因素，它们是目的地发展速度、路径、政府政策、市场变化和与其他目的地的竞争。事实上，旅游目的地的发展也具有与产品的生命周期相似的发展阶段，大致经历出生、发展、成熟、最终衰亡的过程，这个过程被人们通常称为旅游目的地的生命周期。本文详细介绍了巴特勒于1980年提出的描述旅游目的地生命周期的S型模型(图1)，并阐述了不同生命周期内旅游目的地旅游者、东道主和旅游企业活动的特征。

图 1　巴特勒生命周期曲线

　　巴特勒将旅游目的地的发展分为五个阶段：第一阶段称为探索期，以较少的旅游者、简单的旅游设施、未被破坏的自然环境以及未被打扰的地方社区为特征。第二阶段称为参与期，地方社区都参与到旅游地的建设中来，建立了一些基础设施和辅助设施，甚至还设立了旅游协会，明确了旅游地的目标市场，这些因素都加快了旅游地的开发和建设。第三阶段是开发期。在开发期，旅游目的地开发新的吸引物，进行广告活动以影响潜在旅游者的知觉，但地方的新奇性随着旅游者数量的稳定增长而逐渐消失。第四阶段是巩固期。在巩固期，旅游者的数量仍在增长，但增长率是下降的。目的地不断加强市场营销，因为旅游业对于地方经济已相当重要。最后，第五个阶段停滞期。旅游者数量达到最大值，目的地不再是一个时兴的度假胜地了，旅游对环境、社会文化以及经济都产生了一定的影响。经过这个阶段，旅游地就面临两种命运：要么衰退，要么复兴。

　　旅游地生命周期与旅游产品生命周期是同时存在的，旅游地生命周期的产生是具有不同生命周期的多种旅游产品共同作用变化的结果。旅游地生命周期的考察因素要比旅游产品生命周期复杂得多。旅游地发展演化除了受到其中旅游产品的影响外，还受到系统中的各种内在和外在因素制约，使旅游地在发展演化中呈现不同时间尺度的周期特点。在构建旅游地演化模型的过程中，我们将旅游地中各旅游产品对旅游目的地演化的影响作为内在因素，表现为旅游地游客的增长率，将其他要素包括其他旅游地对该旅游地的影响作为外在因素，表现为其他旅游地对该旅游地的争夺率，旅游地游客自身增长率和其他旅游地对该旅游地游客的争夺率是制约旅游目的地演化的主要动力，旅游目的地演化将随着这两者的变化而变化，当旅游地游客增长率大于其他旅游地对该旅游地游客争夺率时，该旅游地将会经过探索阶段、参与阶段、发展阶段、巩固阶段后进入稳定的停滞阶段；反之，如果当旅游地游客增长率小于其他旅游地对该旅游地游客争夺率时,该旅游地则会出现衰落并最终进入消亡阶段。由此可以看出开发新的旅游产品以提高旅游地游客增长率是延长旅游地生命周期的重要手段。

旅游地系统是旅游系统研究的主体,旅游吸引物(旅游产品)是旅游地系统中的重要组成部分,旅游产品的发展变更直接影响到旅游地的发展变化。我国自20世纪80年代以来,旅游研究和旅游地发展都取得很大进步。张朝枝在研究几处旅游地:丹霞山、鼎湖山和七星岩、岳阳楼的演化特点时指出,对于出现衰退迹象的旅游地,可以通过完善产品,在该产品类型中推出新产品,使旅游地走向复苏,如丹霞山的阳元石景区的开发;如果经调查该旅游地所提供的产品已经没有潜在的市场,但该旅游地的现有资源可以开发成其他类型的旅游产品,则可以通过开发其他一些有潜在市场的产品类型来使旅游地走向复苏,如鼎湖山的负离子产品的开发。杨振之在以四川省都江堰风景区和四川省碧峰峡风景区为例探讨延长旅游地生命周期的策略时,提到通过推出新产品,树立新形象以延长旅游地的生命周期。这说明了旅游地的发展离不开旅游产品的发展,在旅游地发展研究中对旅游产品的分析研究是重要的方面,两者是紧密联系的。

旅游目的地种类繁多,形式多样,大多数旅游目的地都具有下列基本特性:(1)综合性。旅游目的地是综合性很强的集合体,集合体中的各个组成部分通过不同的方式组合在一起,为旅游者提供综合性的服务,并通过这种综合性的服务使旅游者获得愉悦的度假体验,得到最大的物质和精神满足。(2)文化性。旅游者之所以要花费时间和金钱去访问某个目的地,是因为那里有令其神往的异域文化。例如,中国的长城和故宫、埃及的金字塔、法国的卢浮宫、希腊的竞技场等。(3)不可分离性和不可储存性。与消费其他产品不同,旅游消费者必须亲身进入旅游目的地后才能消费旅游产品,从消费旅游产品的过程中获得愉悦的体验。另外旅游目的地也具有不可储存性,如果旅游者不访问,旅游目的地的价值就会流失。(4)共享性。旅游目的地具有共享性,因为旅游目的地既要为外来旅游者提供设施和服务,也要满足当地居民和旅游业从业人员的休闲消遣需要。由于旅游目的地的复杂性,环境质量与容量、区位条件、交通条件、基础设施、旅游资源品位、商业化进程、居民的支持度、外部投资、政府与旅游经营者的作用、外部竞争环境的变化、客源市场的改变等因素对目的地的生命周期都会产生重大影响,因此要预测旅游目的地何时进入巴特勒所说的衰退期或复兴期是一个十分复杂的问题。

本文在结尾时阐述了当今旅游者偏好对旅游目的地的影响以及旅游目的地的发展趋势,对我国旅游目的地建设和管理具有启发和借鉴意义。虽然巴特勒的旅游目的地生命周期理论有一定缺陷,其操作性也有一定难度,但至少为我们走旅游可持续发展道路提供了一个分析框架,对旅游资源开发和旅游目的地管理都具有前瞻性的警示作用。国外旅游地案例研究成果表明,如果缺乏良好的规划和管理,那么,旅游地将经历一个比较大的衰退期。因此,运用旅游地生命周期理论,通过对比性研究,以空间尺度代替时间尺度,了解旅游地的发展演化过程,找出旅游发展的限制因子,主动调整,延后衰退期,延长旅游地的生命周期,已成为我国众多旅游目的地的重要任务之一。

旅游知识测试

正误判断:请在正确的选题上划√,错误的选题上划×。

1. 旅游目的地发展的演进过程与一般产品的生命周期不同,因为旅游目的地生命周期要经历出生、发展、成熟、最终衰亡的过程,而一般产品却没有。

2. 旅游目的地演化模型中,旅游地中旅游产品对旅游目的地演化的影响是内在因素,表现为旅游目的地游客的增长率。

3. 当旅游目的地游客增长率小于其他旅游目的地对该旅游地游客争夺率时,该旅游目的地则会出现衰落,但不会进入衰亡阶段。

4. 旅游目的地开发新的吸引物,广告活动影响潜在旅游者,但地方的新奇性随着旅游者数量的稳定增长而逐渐消失。这时,旅游目的地进入停滞期。

5. 如果旅游地所提供的产品已经没有潜在的市场,但该旅游地的现有资源可以开发成其他类型的旅游产品,旅游目的地的生命周期可以延长,走向复苏。

Part III Case Study
第三部分 案例研究

周庄古镇生命周期研究

分析要点

1. 与周边地区的古镇旅游相比,周庄古镇旅游资源有什么特色?
2. 周庄古镇有哪些旅游产品,与其他古镇的竞争状况如何?
3. 你认为有哪些因素会影响周庄旅游目的地的生命周期?
4. 为了延续周庄旅游地的生命周期,你认为还需要采取哪些有效措施?
5. 你认为周庄目前是在目的地生命周期的哪一个阶段?有何证据?请你分析预测周庄旅游发展的趋势。

相关理论和问题

1. 目的地生命周期(Destination life cycle)
2. 目的地承载力(Destination bearing capacity)
3. 旅游商品化(Commercialization of tourism)
4. 旅游的可持续发展(Sustainable development of tourism)

一、周庄古镇概况

周庄古镇位于苏州昆山市,占地 24 平方公里,其间面积约为 4 平方公里的历史文化保护区已有长达 900 多年的历史。镇内 46% 的建筑是属于公元 15—20 年初的传统建筑,现设有 2 个省级文物保护单位,4 个市级文物保护单位和 20 个市级文物控制单位,优美独特的水乡风貌,深厚浓郁的历史文化氛围,淳朴的民风民俗,使其成为江南水乡古镇中旅游发展最早,发展最快的地方。旅游的发展促进了古镇的开发和保护,同时也带来了一系列的问题,因此要探求其旅游生命周期因子,并制定相应的对策、措施,以确保周庄旅游的可持续发展,并为古镇型旅游目的地的开发提供一定的指导。

二、周庄旅游地生命周期

悠久的历史使得周庄旅游地生命周期的探索阶段实际上可追溯到几百年前,但实际意义不大。考虑到对实践的指导意义以及数据来源的可靠程度,现将周庄旅游地生命周期分析的开始时间定在 1989 年,周庄历年的游客数量如表、图所示:

表一　周庄历年游客数量统计表(单位:万人)

年份	人数	年份	人数	年份	人数
1989	5.50	1994	35.00	1999	125.00
1990	12.50	1995	46.00	2000	150.00
1991	20.00	1996	50.00	2001	200.00
1992	25.00	1997	80.00	2002	240.00
1993	30.00	1998	100.00	2003	260.00

数据来源:周庄镇旅游集团公司

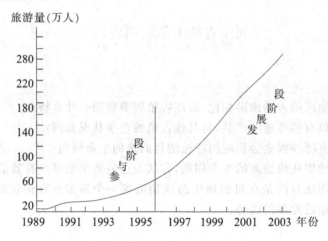

图1　周庄旅游生命周期曲线图

1. 参与阶段(20世纪80年代—1995年)

从20世纪80年代到1995年周庄处于生命周期的广泛参与阶段,在80年代初期苏州市旅游局为周庄古镇旅游资源的开发勾勒出蓝图,出版了包括音、画、建筑等影像资料,在珠海举办的国际旅游展销会上以大幅背景宣传展示水乡美景,并成立了镇办的旅游公司,旅游公司群策群力,采取了一系列有效措施,加大对古镇的宣传力度,使其在起步阶段发展较为迅速,游客数量稳步上升,客源市场基本形成,多为附近的居民和慕名而来的周边地区游客。随着当地政府的重视和各种旅游设施逐渐到位,旅游环境亦呈现出良好发展势头,好多游客在去苏州市旅游时将此处作为一个选择点,周庄旅游业稳定、快速地向前发展。

2. 发展阶段(1996年—2002年)

1996年由国家、省和苏州市旅游部门同周庄联合主办第一届周庄国际旅游摄影节,标志着周庄开始走向国外旅游市场,从表中我们也可以看出从1995年开始,周庄连续6年游客量年增长率保持在20%左右,2002年接待游客高达240万人次,旅游收入达到6亿元,明确的客源市场开始形成,游客主要以外省市和国际游客为主,旅游设施完善,并积极拓展旅游空间,收到了较好的经济和社会效益,周庄亦成为一个具有相当知名度的旅游地。

3. 巩固阶段(2003年至今)

自2002年以来,周庄虽然保持了较高的游客量,但游客增长率已有所下降,进入旅游目的地生命周期的巩固阶段。游客量自2002年已接近容量的临界值。周庄旅游承载力有限,有限到什么程度呢?有一种计算是这样的:周庄镇古镇区地面面积为10000平方米,游客人均占地面积为15平方米,人均停留时间为3小时,每天可游览时间为9小时,每年可游览天数为300天,每天最佳游客容量为2000人次,最大游客容量为6000人次。按这个计算办法,周庄每年最佳旅游人数为60万人,最多也不应超过180万人。可实际情况是,2002年到周庄旅游的人数是206万人次,是最佳容量的3.43倍。这是按年平均数计,如果以游人最高日计算,游客容量面临的问题就更严重了。周庄镇多次采用提高门票价格的办法限制游人数量,但是"越提人越多"。

不少游客近日到过有"中国第一水乡"之称的周庄后,都慨叹当地昔日的水边小筑,很多都已变成一个个鳞次栉比的小商铺,以往纯朴的民风,已逐渐淹没在日益浓厚的商业化气息之中。满街商店林立,特产"万三蹄"肉香飘满整个小镇,一到节假日游人摩肩接踵挤得连桥上也无立锥之地的景象,与原有的小镇风貌已再无和谐可言。当地居民一味追求眼前利益,把周庄作为手中的摇钱机。一些人还向游客追讨肖像费,随口哼几句小曲也索要小费,种种举动都显示出当地原有的淳朴民风已不复存在。

三、周庄旅游地生命走向

经过近30年的旅游开发,周庄所承受的社会和环境压力已经显露出来,主要表现在:游客流量增长过快,超过环境容量限度;日益增多的商铺和小摊,导致建筑用途改变;过度商业化,丧失了街区的历史真实性;土生土长居民的逐步外迁,使当地的人文环境发生变化;以及旅游管理能力与旅游发展不平衡等问题。如果不尽快有效地解决这些问题,一座座充满灵性的古村落最终恐怕会成为名不符实的空壳。

昆山市旅游业当局注意到这些问题。最近修编的昆山市旅游业发展总体规划提出开发周庄之外多种多样的旅游资源,以"二河、二湖、三镇、四园、五场"构建昆山市大旅游格局,摆脱古镇观光旅游形式的单一性。即以水乡古镇旅游而言,正在开发千灯镇和锦溪镇两个水乡古镇的旅游资源。实现这个新规划,将会对去周庄的游客起到分流的作用,缓解大量集中的游客与周庄承载力低的矛盾。

周庄镇当地政府也采取措施进行调整:如利用提高票价作为手段来控制游客量,利用修建周庄舫、民俗一条街来开发新市场、扩大旅游空间,然而过度的商业化又破损了原有的古镇风貌,同时同里等古镇的旅游业开始崛起,周庄的发展步伐开始放缓,已出现Butler模型停滞阶段的一些现象。

根据Butler模型旅游地生命周期模型,旅游地进入巩固阶段后随之而来的有可能就是停滞阶段。如果没有出现新的旅游吸引物和旅游产品,衰落阶段是可以预见的结果,但许多国外学者的研究表明,旅游地生命周期演化可以脱离Butler模型的后续阶段,进入较为理想、持续时间较为长久的成熟阶段,甚至进入复兴和新的发展时期。周庄旅游发展已经进入生命周期的敏感时期,必须采取积极有效措施克服目前出现的游客流量过大,民俗过度商品化,水景美学价值降低、游客满意度下降等诸多问题,防止周庄旅游进入停滞阶段,确保周庄旅游在今后很长的时期保持健康持续发展的势头。

资料来源:庄秀琴.郑海涛.周庄古镇生命周期研究,商场现代化[J],2006,(3).

Part IV　Reading Box
第四部分　阅读与分析

Destination in Decline

阅读分析要点

1. 游客趣味的变化
2. 旅游地生命周期衰退的表象
3. 影响旅游地生命周期的主要因素
4. 防止旅游地生命周期衰退的主要方法

　　Until now, more attention has been paid to the positive aspects of growth and development of tourism while the decline stages of **the tourist area life cycle (TALC)** have been seldom mentioned.[1] However, mass international tourism has reached the mature stage and many mass tourism destinations have gone through a long history and become out of date such as the Spanish Costas which started in the 1960s and many British and northern European resorts which can be traced back to the eighteenth and nineteenth centuries. Therefore, an increasing number of destinations in many countries and regions have to, though reluctant, face the reality that they are coming into the decline stages of the life cycle.[2]

Setting the scene

　　Almost all destinations at the decline stage of the TALC confront a similar problem. With time passing by, the destinations are becoming outdated and can hardly cater for **the ever-changing tastes** and preferences of tourists, which is best expressed by their physical facilities, architectural styles and layout.[3] So loss of market is unavoidable if they do not take any effective actions. Generally, there are two solutions but it is hard for destinations to make a choice between them. One is to withdraw from tourism completely and change the resort into a retirement centre, dormitory town or health center. The other is to adopt new marketing plans and development strategies to renovate and revive the resort.

The problem

　　When they develop into the decline stage, resorts or destinations will come across a number of similar problems as follows:
　　1. a depressed tourism industry;
　　2. staying and day visitors from lower social groups who are unwilling to spend much money;
　　3. a low percentage of new clients;
　　4. environmental problems;

5. high rate of unemployment in the off seasons;
6. a poor competitive position;
7. high dependence on seasons;
8. lack of market research.

Clearly, some of these problems are **internal** while others are **external**. For those internal ones, the resort can try every means to deal with them but they can do nothing to control the external ones. And such a situation is hard to reverse. What's more, at this stage, the difference between the TALC and product life cycle becomes very obvious. According to the concept of the product life cycle, if a product comes into the decline stage, the marketing manager can reduce its production or stop producing it. However, tourism is closely related to and joined together with other sectors of the town, providing jobs, retailing entertainment and other facilities. Therefore, for resorts, they cannot simply withdraw from tourism industry. Otherwise, a lot of problems may appear. As a result, resorts have to try their best to seek new markets and redevelop their product so as to maintain and expand their share of the market in the fierce competition with new destinations.[4]

Approaches

However difficult, it is possible to overcome these problems and revitalize the resort successfully. We can find many examples in the world. Meanwhile, a lot of approaches being used are recorded in documents so that we can easily classify them. The following four possible approaches are introduced by Diamond (1988):

1. **Turnaround.** With this approach, the resort should make great efforts to increase investment, make detailed market plans and promote the product. In addition, they need to raise a lot of resources to support the practice of this approach while the lead of a public sector and backing from both the industry and residential population are also indispensable.

2. **Sustainable growth.** Compared with the turnaround strategy, this approach is not so radical. It requires the resort to seek out new markets to make up for the loss of the original ones.[5] However, this does not mean that they should give up the original markets completely. On the contrary, they will continue to maintain them and provide resources for their development. This approach is more influenced and controlled by the market. It needs less investment and development in physical facilities.

3. **Incremental growth.** Here the resort usually spends a number of years in developing new markets and product by stages. The approaches it often uses are test marketing and development projects. Development of tourism in the hinterland of a resort on the basis of its natural attractions or development of sports tourism with improved existing facilities sets good examples for this.

4. **Selective tourism.** Using this strategy, the resort should, first of all, accurately recognize and choose new markets which are suitable for its development. Then, it should carry out forceful marketing campaigns to sell its products while developing facilities to serve these markets. In other words, the resort should choose appropriate market segments as its targets according to its own strengths or particular character. The redevelopment of spa tourism in parts of Eastern Europe, or in the old spa towns of England and Wales are good examples here.

Which is the most appropriate strategy for each resort is determined by a variety of closely-related factors:

- the competitive position of the resort;
- the existing market;
- the stage in the life cycle;
- available investment and public funds;
- political and community support;
- attitude of the tourism industry.

However, while carrying out these strategies, we learn that what are crucial to the successful re-launch of a resort are the political will and the driving force of examples set by individual winners of these projects.⁶

New Words

decline	n.	下降，衰落
reverse	v.	转换，改变
reluctant	adj.	勉强的，不情愿的
revitalize	v.	使恢复元气，使有新的活力
outdated	adj.	陈旧的，过时的
radical	adj.	彻底的，激进的
renovate	v.	恢复，使呈现新面貌
appropriate	adj.	适当的
depress	v.	使萧条，使沮丧

Notes

1. More attention has been paid to the positive aspects of growth and development of tourism while the decline stages of the tourist area life cycle (TALC) have been seldom mentioned.
   我们过于注意旅游成长和发展的积极方面，而忽略了旅游地生命周期的衰落阶段。

2. Therefore, an increasing number of destinations in many countries and regions have to, though reluctant, face the reality that they are coming into the decline stages of the life cycle.
   因此，在许多国家和地区，尽管越来越多的目的地不愿意看见，但它们仍必须面对进入生命周期衰落阶段的现实。

3. With time passing by, the destinations are becoming outdated and can hardly cater for the ever-changing tastes and preferences of tourists, which is best expressed by their physical facilities, architectural styles and layout.
   随着时间推移，目的地会逐渐失去吸引力，难以迎合游客不断变化的口味和喜好，主要表现在硬件设施、建筑风格和布局方面。

4. As a result, resorts have to try their best to seek new markets and redevelop their product so as to maintain and expand their share of the market in the fierce competition with new destinations.
   最终，旅游地必须努力寻找新的市场并开发新产品，以便在与新目的地的残酷竞争中维持和扩大自己的市场份额。

5. Compared with the turnaround strategy, this approach is not so radical. It requires the resort to seek out new markets to make up for the loss of the original ones.
   与全面改组战略相比，这种方法更为稳妥。它要求旅游地寻找新市场以弥补原有市场的损失。

6. However, while carrying out these strategies, we learn that what are crucial to the successful re-launch of a resort are the political will and the driving force of examples set by individual winners of these projects.

但执行这些战略时,我们知道恢复旅游地活力的关键是政治意愿,以及这些项目的成功典范所带来的市场驱动力。

Topic discussion

1. What are the similar problems confronted by the destination at the decline stage of the tourist area life cycle?

2. Why can't the resorts can not simply withdraw from tourism industry when they reach the decline stage?

3. What approaches do you think destination manager can adopt to revitalize the resorts?

4. What factors should be taken into account when the destination chooses appropriate strategy for its revitalization?

【即学即用】

With reference to the theory, information or approach applied in the Reading Box, have a case study of the destination life cycle of a tourist resort you know. Make presentation of your study in Chinese or in English using PPT.

【学习资源库】

为了掌握本章更多的相关专业知识,请您登陆 http://sicnu. edu. cn/,点击国家双语教学示范课程《旅游学概论》,进入网络学堂查询相关资料。

Chapter Review 本章小结

This chapter has described the evolution of the destination life cycle and the significance of Butler's curve. It outlines the determining factors, such as the speed of development, access, government policy, the tendency of market, destinations competing with each other, and so on, which influence the process of DLC. The difference between the destination life cycle and product life cycle is obvious, so tourism sectors should adopt different methods to control the process of OLC. Some approaches can be applied to overcome the problems at each stage of destination life cycle, but the difficulty of application for Butler's destination life model is obvious, too. At present, there are two tendencies of tourist markets that have a different impact on the destination life cycle. One is the authentic travel; another is the enclave resort.

Part V Additional Know-how of Tourism
第五部分　旅游知识扩展

【关键术语】

Destination life cycle：the theory that tourism-oriented places experience a sequential process of birth, growth, maturation, and then possibly something similar to death, in their evolution as destinations

目的地生命周期：阐释旅游地从出生、成长、成熟到类似有可能死亡的进化过程的理论。

Butler sequence：the most widely cited and applied destination life and model, which proposes five stages of evolution that are described by an S-shaped curve; these might then be followed by three other possible scenarios

巴特勒序列：引用和应用最为普遍的旅游地生命周期模型。该模型认为旅游地生命周期一般经历以下五个进化阶段，这几个阶段可以用 S 型曲线加以描述，随后可能还有三种其他情况。

Matrix model of life cycle trigger factors：a four-cell model that classifies that various actions that induce change in the evolution of tourism in a destination

- **Internal-intentional actions**：deliberate actions that originate from within the destination itself; the best case scenario for destinations in terms of control and management
- **External-unintentional actions**：actions that affect the destination, but originate from outside that destination, and are not intentional; the worst case scenario from a destination perspective
- **Internal-unintentional actions**：actions that originate from within the destination, but are not deliberate
- **External-intentional actions**：deliberate actions that originate from outside the destination

生命周期触发因素矩阵模型：一种四元矩阵模型，它把导致目的地旅游进化进程发生改变的不同行为划分为四类组合，即：**内部——刻意行动**：由目的地自身诱发的有目的行为；这种情况最利于目的地旅游的控制与管理；**外部——随意行动**：这种行动会影响目的地，但它产生于目的地的外部环境，并且不是有目的的行动，从目的地的角度看，这是最糟糕的情况；**内部——随意行动**：由目的地内部诱发的、但并非有目的的行动；**外部——刻意行动**：产生于目的地之外的有目的的行动。

Destination index：the proportion of trip time (exclusive of transit time, but including overnight stays during transit) spent in a particular destination

目的地指数：在某一特定目的地所花费的旅游时间比例（不包括中转时间，但包括中转期间的过夜住宿）。

Destination image：the sum of the beliefs, attitudes and impressions that individuals or groups hold towards tourist destinations or aspects of destinations. It is a critical factor in attracting or repelling visitors

目的地形象：个人或团体对旅游目的地或者目的地某些方面所表现出的信任、态度和印象，是影响游客去留的关键因素。

【知识链接】

1. 旅游目的地形象的形成

Gunn 认为形象包含两个层次：诱导形象和自身形象。诱导形象是目的地通过大众传媒直接向目标客源市场传递目的地信息而形成的形象。自生形象是指受新闻报道、电影、杂志等社会舆论力量影响而形成的形象。两者的差别在于目的地形象推广者是否直接干预信息的传递。应用 Gunn 的分类方法作为起点，根据传播媒介的不同，可以将目的地形象的形成过程分成八个阶段：

（1）大众传媒传播阶段。一个旅游目的地刚刚建立的时候，目的地形象的传播往往首先采用各种传统的传媒手段：电视、报纸杂志、广告牌和各种印刷品。（2）旅行中间商传播阶段。这一阶段是市场营销者向旅行批发商、旅行社以及其他的旅游组织传递目的地信息。（3）形象代言人传播阶段。虽然还使用传统的广告手段，但是与第一阶段所不同的是借用形象代言人来进行营销。目的地可以借助形象代言人的声望来增加其吸引力，还有助于提高广告的可信度。（4）知名人士传播阶段。主要通过知名人士写的论文、报告、故事等来进行目的地营销。（5）社会舆论影响阶段。它的传播手段包括对某一目的地的各种新闻报道、电影、论文和报告等，最有影响的是电视新闻报道。（6）非正式传播阶段。是指人们在游览了某一目的地之后，不经意地在各种非正式场合向其周围的人传递目的地信息。（7）主动索取信息阶段。是指人们主动去搜集有关目的地的信息，这些信息大部分来自他们的亲朋好友和周围的熟人。（8）实地旅游阶段。是旅游者到达目的地旅游之后对目的地的真实形象的感知。

2. 旅游目的地系统的功能分区

旅游目的地系统是旅游目的地内部各种对旅游活动过程产生作用和影响的所有因子共同作用而形成的，具有其独特的结构体系与功能的旅游系统。要素主要包括旅游资源与旅游产品、旅游设施、旅游企业和旅游行政组织等。

旅游目的地系统是一种等级网络系统，各等级系统有其相对应等级的核心旅游资源与旅游产品。所以一个旅游目的系统是由一个核心区和多个配套区（二级核心区）构成，每一配套区同样是由一个核心区和多个配套区（三级核心区）构成，从而形成不同等级的旅游目的地系统。旅游目的地系统根本目标在于满足旅游者在旅游活动过程中的各种需求，即我们通常所称的旅游六要素（行、住、游、购、吃、娱）。目的地系统的不同部分满足旅游者需求的内容是不同的，形成旅游目的地系统内不同功能区，其中住、购、吃往往形成三位一体区，我们可将其称之为集散区。目的地旅游系统通常可分为四大功能区：集散区、观光游览区、娱乐区和游览通道区。

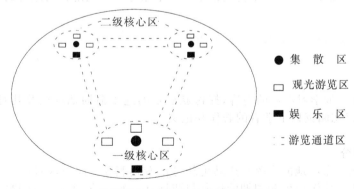

旅游目的地系统结构功能分区图

【小思考】
1. 以你所在城市的旅游景区为例,谈谈影响目的地生命周期的主要因素有哪些。

参考阅读:
我国旅游学者谢彦君在理论上探讨了影响旅游地生命周期的因素,认为直接影响旅游地生命周期的是需求因素、效应因素和环境因素。保继刚在对丹霞山进行研究时指出,影响该旅游地生命周期的主要因素是旅游形象危机和景区开发不足。保继刚研究认为喀斯特洞穴旅游地生命周期的主要影响因素是旅游资源的共性大、独特性小和空间竞争替代性强。

国外学者认为影响旅游目的地生命周期的因素有:
(1)环境质量与容量;(2)过度商业化;(3)区位条件;(4)交通条件;(5)基础设施;(6)旅游资源品位;(7)居民的支持度;(8)旅游形象;(9)旅游地的竞争力;(10)旅游发展速度;(11)外部投资;(12)政府与旅游经营者的作用;(13)外部竞争环境的变化;(14)客源市场的改变;(15)外部政治环境。

2. 为什么说巴特勒的旅游目的地生命周期理论模型是一个"理想的"理论模型?

参考阅读:
巴特勒的旅游目的地生命周期理论模型可以被当作一个"理想的"理论模型,但是现实社会是不断变化的,是多样化的,因此这个"理想"理论模型具有很大局限性,雷柏尔(Leiper)和库珀(Cooper)等人总结出了旅游目的地生命周期理论的一些缺陷:

(1)旅游目的地生命来自于旅游客源地,因此,单纯地针对旅游目的地,用生命周期的理论来解释旅游目的地的旅游发展是不完全的,应该把生命周期的理论应用到整体旅游系统中。而整体旅游系统又是与外部环境密切相关联的。

(2)根据旅游目的地的生命周期理论,一些旅游研究者常把到访旅游者数量的增加当作旅游目的地向成熟期发展的征兆,把到访旅游者数量的减少作为旅游目的地老化的标志。但是,在旅游目的地长期发展的过程中出现短期的到访人数增加或减少,并不一定意味着该目的地就会走向繁荣或衰落。

(3)巴特勒的旅游目的地生命周期理论只关注单一的因素(旅游产品),而旅游经济开发通常都采用多因素的方法。

(4)由于外界因素的影响,旅游目的地生命周期曲线有多种可能形式。曲线有时是加速型的,有时是延迟型的。尽管可以用游客增长率的变化、游客的消费量、游客类型、市场占有率或盈利能力来帮助判断,但是仍然很难清晰地划分一个旅游目的地所处的阶段。

Part VI Further Readings
第六部分 课外阅读

如果您想进一步学习本章的内容,探讨旅游目的地生命周期理论及其对旅游地开发与保护的意义,建议您阅读以下学者的著作和论文。

一、中文部分
[1] 金颖若. 旅游地的衰落与产品更新[J]. 旅游科学,2002,(04).
[2] 谢彦君. 旅游地生命周期的控制与调整[J]. 旅游学刊,1995,(02).
[3] 吴焕加. 我看周庄[J]. 建筑学报,2004,(01).
[4] 阎友兵. 旅游地生命周期理论辨析[J]. 旅游学刊,2001,(06).

[5] 林明水,谢红彬. 旅游地生命周期理论中关于成长的若干思考[J]. 山西师范大学学报(自然科学版),2010,(03).

[6] 邵晓兰,高峻. 旅游地生命周期研究现状和展望[J]. 旅游学刊,2006,(06).

[7] 张惠等. 基于旅游系统的旅游地生命周期问题探讨[J]. 中国软科学,2004,(11).

[8] 李亚. 旅游地发展因子分析与研究[J]. 云南师范大学学报,2004,(03).

[9] 朱华,李峰. 乡村休闲旅游地游客满意度评价研究——以成都市三圣乡幸福梅林为例[J] 桂林旅游高等专科学校学报,2007,(5).

[10] 杨振之. 试论延长旅游地生命周期的模式[J]. 人文地理,2003,(06).

二、英文部分

[1] Butler R W. The Concept of a tourist area cycle of evolution: implications for management of resources [J]. *Canadian Geographer*, 1980(24).

[2] Dibc, Bojanid. Tourism area lifecycle extensions [J]. *Annals of Tourism Research*, 1993(20).

[3] Douglasn. Applying the lifecycle model to melanesia [J]. *Annals of Tourism Research*, 1997(24).

[4] Maria Francesca Cracolici, Peter Nijkamp. The attractiveness and competitiveness of tourist destinations: A study of Southern Italian regions [J]. *Tourism Management*, 2009(3):336—344.

[5] Stansfield C. Atlantic city and the resort cycle [J]. *Annals of Tourism Research*, 1978(05).

[6] Haywood K M. Can the tourist area lifecycle be made operational? [J]. *Tourism Management*, 1986(07).

[7] Tooman L A. Applications of the life cycle model in tourism [J]. *Annals of Tourism Research*, 1997(24).

[8] Di Benedetto C, D Bojanic. Tourism area life cycle extensions [J]. *Annals of Tourism research*, 1993(20).

[9] Winston Moore, Peter Whitehall. The tourism area lifecycle and regime switching models [J]. *Annals of Tourism Research*, 2005(32).

[10] Marcelo Royo-Vela. Rural-cultural excursion conceptualization: A local tourism marketing management model based on tourist destination image measurement [J]. *Tourism Management*, 2009(3):419—428.

Chapter 11　Economic Costs of Tourism
第十一章　旅游的经济成本

Learning objects：学习目标

- Appreciate the economic costs of tourism within both origin and destination of the tourism system (Leiper's model) 从旅游系统(Leiper 模型)中客源地和目的地两个方面考察旅游的经济成本
- Understand the direct economic costs brought about by tourism industry 了解旅游业产生的直接成本
- Explain the reasons why revenue leakage is incurred and its adverse effects on the destination economy 解释收入漏损产生的原因以及对目的地经济产生的负面影响
- Understand the fragile nature of tourism which is likely affected by political and economical uncertainty 理解旅游的脆弱性,政治经济不稳定会影响旅游。
- Discuss the demand-side and supply-side factors which may affect tourists' satisfaction and return of fixed costs 从供需两方面讨论影响游客满意度和固定成本回收的因素。
- Understand the competition of tourism industry with other sectors and opportunity cost incurred by such competition 了解旅游业与其他产业之间的竞争,以及竞争所产生的机会成本
- Appreciate the danger of dependency on tourism industry and importance of the diversified economy 了解过于依赖旅游业的危险以及经济多样化的重要性

Ability goals：能力目标

- Case Study 案例分析：旅游对上海经济的影响——基于投入产出模型的研究和评价
- Reading Box 阅读分析：Dependency on Tourism Industry—A lesson from the Caribbean island of Antigua 对旅游业的依赖——加勒比海安提瓜岛的教训

Part I　Text
第一部分　课文

Economic Costs of Tourism

【教学要点】

知识要点	掌握程度	相关章节
direct costs and indirect costs 直接成本与间接成本	一般了解	本课文与第1单元、第3单元、第5单元、第6单元、第8单元、第15单元相关内容有联系。
revenue leakage 收入漏损	重点掌握	
multiplier effect 乘数效应	重点掌握	
fluctuations in intake and market failure 收入的波动与市场失灵	一般了解	
economic inflation 通货膨胀	一般了解	
opportunity cost 机会成本	重点掌握	

　　As with any economic activity, the tourism industry is associated with an array of potential **benefits and costs**. From a destination perspective, the tourism-derived **direct revenues** such as the tourism receipts and the taxation revenues have long been the most compelling incentive to initiate or maintain the process of tourism development. In addition to the direct revenues, tourist activities will produce more **indirect revenues**. The indirect revenue generation involves the circulation of tourist expenditure within a destination, from which the other sectors will benefit. For example, imagine that an inbound tourist spends $100 on dinner at a hotel. If the hotel uses this $100 to purchase products from a local farmer, then the direct tourism expenditure is displaying indirect circulation effect beneficial to other sectors such as agriculture, fertilizer and machinery in the destination.

　　The indirect circulation of revenue is described as the **income multiplier effect** (IME), which, technically speaking, is a measure of the subsequent income generated in a destination's economy by direct tourist expenditure. In general, the destination's economy is most likely to benefit from tourism, since it can generate the **backward linkages** that foster a strong multiplier effect. According to WTO, in 1955, every $1 of direct expenditure generates an additional $1.73 in secondary impacts in the United Kingdoms. In other words, the total international British receipts of $19 billion generate almost $33 billion in additional revenue, making an overall total of $52 billion if the primary and secondary effects are combined.

　　However, with the rapid development and expansion of the global tourism industry in the late 1960s and 1970s, the negative economic impacts of tourism began to be recognized. Tourism is not necessarily as profitable as we expect. In fact, the losses in economy, society, culture and environment caused by unregulated tourism tend to be bigger than the benefits it brings. Therefore we should be careful to choose a right way to develop tourism. This chapter will focus on the major economic costs brought about by tourist destinations and emphasize the necessity to take steps to overcome these unfavorable impacts.

Direct financial costs

Direct financial costs are direct expenses that the public sector uses to sustain the development of the tourism sector. When we assess the revenue of the tourism industry we should take these costs into consideration. Here the mention of such costs is not to criticize, but to show that in tourism, just as in any other economic activity, **financial inputs** are necessary for the realization of a net profit. [1] In the public sector, the areas which usually require much cost are administration and bureaucracy, marketing, research and incentives. [2]

The situation in Australia may serve as a good example to show the nature and importance of these costs. In 1996/97 budget year, the ATC spent more than $100 million to operate the business. Most of the money was expended on advertisements, promotion and publicity, and salaries and wages. This is by far the highest cost of all federal tourism agencies, but it is worthwhile if we take into account the fact that the area is faced with the problem of **market failure.** [3]

Obviously direct financial costs include those spent on incentives which are paid by non-tourism agencies within government for the development of tourism in the destination. As the purpose of entrepreneurs is to make strong profits, destination governments have to provide some favorable terms such as capital grants, labor and training subsidies and/or infrastructure disbursed by the public to attract entrepreneurs to invest their resources in the area. Generally speaking, incentives are necessary in particular in those destinations which offer almost the same, undifferentiated product, such as a generic 3S experience. On the contrary, even without the offer of incentives, entrepreneurs will still be attracted to those destinations which can provide unique and high profile attractions such as Niagara Falls, the Sydney Opera House or the Eiffel Towel as big financial returns are possible.

Indirect financial costs

The concept of indirect financial costs which are brought about by tourism in a destination is an important issue. The indirect circulation effect is beneficial to other sectors of the destination's economy, but only a portion of the tourist expenditure circulates within the local economy, and the remainder is excluded from the subsequent circulation effect. More indirectly, expenses on some or all of the following items may not circulate in the destination economy, and thus incur the **revenue leakage**, which have an unfavorable impact on the **income multiplier effect (IME)**:

- imported current goods and services that are required by tourists or the tourist industry (e.g. petrol, food)
- imported capital goods and services required by the tourist industry (e.g. furnishings, taxis, architect's fees)
- factor payments abroad. These include returned profits, wages and hotel management fees.
- imports for government expenditure (airport, road and port equipment)
- induced imports for domestic producers who supply the tourist industry (e.g. fertilizer to grow the food consumed by tourists)

There are two situations in which serious revenue leakages are more likely to occur. First, in the **less-developed countries (LDC)**, those countries that cannot provide goods and services up to the standard required by the tourism industry have to import. In addition, in such destinations, it is non-local or foreign businesses instead of local residents who possess sufficient capitals to develop tourist resort up to the desired level. As a result, when these investors take their profits back to their country of origin, revenue leakage arises. Second, **enclave resort** developed in some destinations. Consumers are encouraged to consume everything within the resort, for the resort can provide everything they need. What's more, almost all of the goods offered in the resort are imported or bought from outside the local community.[4] This leaves little opportunity for local residents to profit from tourism. To avoid severe revenue leakage, while designing tourism management strategies, the ways to foster and increase the linkages between tourism and the destination economy should be emphasized.

Fluctuations in intake

Tourism is easy to be heavily influenced by changes in weather, fashion and sociopolitical conditions. This is mainly due to the fact that tourism products can be enjoyed only at the place of "production"—the destination. Visitor intakes are often closely related to the situation in the destination. If some disruptive incidents happen, such as political uncertainty or a disruption of infrastructure, the number of visitors will fall sharply. And the tourism industry there will be greatly affected or beaten, sometimes to the extent that recovery is almost impossible.

Second, as tourism is basically a luxurious product which consumers may buy or may not buy. Demand-side factors such as the disposal income of the consumers and the change of their preference have a great impact on tourism. As tourism product is intangible and cannot be stored, tourism industry has to shoulder all additional fixed costs. For example, although an empty hotel room cannot produce any economic value, fixed costs such as those for maintenance and mortgage repayment are still indispensable.[5]

Seasonality

Tourism is an industry which depends heavily on seasonal variations. A large amount of economic and social disruption would therefore appear unless tourism managers take appropriate steps to deal with the problems caused by the change of seasons. The problem can be explained from two aspects. One is **undercapacity**, the other is **overcapacity**. During the "off-season," the sharp decrease of the number of visitors usually results in the increase of laid-off workers, which may have a serious influence on the economy at the destination because of the income and **employment multiplier effects**. In contrast, during the "high season," the number of visitors is so large that the destination may be overcrowded. And this can bring heavy pressure on infrastructure and lead to shortages of goods and services. At the same time, the destination has to employ labor from outside to meet the demand.

Inflationary Pressure

Tourism can bring a large sum of money into the destination economy and increase the income of the region, but it may also make local residents confront the danger of **economic inflation**. Compared with the residents, tourists are usually able to afford a higher expenditure mainly due to the fact that maybe their incomes are higher or that they are willing to spend lavishly what they have saved on vacation. As a result, the prices of such commodities as food, transportation, and arts and crafts will rise to a certain degree which may lead to the happening of economic inflation and do harm to the economic welfare of residents of the host community.[6] This is most likely to happen when the prices of necessities such as food, clothing, transportation, and housing are affected. As is known to all, land prices have risen rapidly in tourist destination areas. And it is less possible for residents to afford their "first homes" as the prices that foreigners are willing to pay for "vacation homes" in the area, and this will certainly lead to the rise of prices of land and housing.[7]

The development of tourism industry in an area may lead to the sharp rise of its land prices. In an area where tourism is particularly underdeveloped, the amount of money used to buy land only takes 1% of the total investment for a hotel project while in an overdeveloped area, this ratio will increase to 20%. We can safely draw the conclusion from such increases in land prices that local residents with their lower incomes can hardly afford their own houses in a tourism-developing area.

Competition with other sectors

The IME encourages and stimulates various sectors within the destination to cooperate closely with each other to push local economy forward in the direction of diversity.[8] However, instead of cooperation, sometimes tourism and other sectors compete with each other fiercely. For example, food imports required by the development of tourism may reduce or even chase out local production if the foreign tour operator enlarges his business to the extent that he provides a cheaper and better quality product for the wider market.[9] As far as farming is concerned, tourism tends to attract labor away from agriculture, as it can provide higher wages, relatively comfortable working conditions and more opportunities for employee advancement.

Agriculture is further ignored because tourism can bring more profits to the land than agriculture does. For instance, a sugar cane plantation is less profitable than a golf course or resort hotel. If farming cannot bring much profit and thus becomes a dispensable activity, the located land owners will choose tourism as an alternative land use, which may lead to further decline of farming, just like the case happened on the Caribbean Island of Antigua in the 1960s. Finally, when using a resource for tourism instead of some other activity, we should consider the **opportunity cost**. Money or land used for tourism development is money or land not applied for agriculture, which thus represents a forgone opportunity for the agricultural development in the region. In other words, if a resource can be used in two ways—tourism and agriculture and we choose tourism, then the opportunity for tourism is at the cost of agriculture.[10]

For the sake of convenience, we can classify the impacts on the destination as economic, socio-cultural or environmental. However, we should always keep in the mind that all these impacts, in fact, are closely interrelated, and will mutually influenced. For example, negative social reactions to tourism could result from its perceived economic and environmental costs, and vice versa.

New Words

generic	*adj.*	属性的，类别的
undifferentiated	*adj.*	无差别的，一致的
sociopolitical	*adj.*	社会政治的

architect	n.	建筑师
lavishly	adv.	浪费地，奢侈地
undercapacity	n.	非饱和容量

Key Terms

revenue leakage	收入漏损
operating expense	营业费用
capital goods and service	资本货物及服务
current goods and service	流动货物及服务
repatriated profit	遣返利润
factor payment	生产要素费用
capital grant	资本补助金
enclave resort	飞地

Notes

1. Here the mention of such costs is not to criticize, but to show that in tourism, just as in any other economic activity, financial inputs are necessary for the realization of a net profit.
   我们提到这些成本，并不是要批评，而是说明旅游活动也像其他经济活动一样，为了获得净盈利，财政投入是必要的。

2. In the public sector, the areas which usually require much cost are administration and bureaucracy, marketing, research and incentives.
   在公共部门中，管理部门、政府机构、市场营销、调研和奖励往往需要大量费用。

3. This is by far the highest cost of all federal tourism agencies, but it is worthwhile if we take into account the fact that the area is faced with the problem of market failure.
   到目前为止，这是所有联邦旅游机构中最昂贵的支出。但是，如果我们考虑到该地区面临市场失灵的问题，就会觉得这些成本支出是值得的。

4. What's more, almost all of the goods offered in the resort are imported or bought from outside the local community.
   而且，这些旅游地提供的商品大都是进口或从当地社区以外的地方买来的。

5. Fixed costs such as those for maintenance and mortgage repayment are still indispensable.
   固定成本，例如维护费用和偿还抵押贷款的支出，仍然是必不可少的。

6. The prices of such commodities as food, transportation, and arts and crafts will rise to a certain degree which may lead to the happening of economic inflation and do harm to the economic welfare of residents of the host community.
   食品、交通、艺术品以及手工艺品等的价格上涨到一定程度，就可能导致通货膨胀，并会损害当地社区居民的福利。

7. And it is less possible for residents to afford their "first homes" as the prices that foreigners are willing to pay for "vacation homes" in the area, and this will certainly lead to the rise of prices of land and housing.
   外国人愿意在当地高价购买"度假屋"，这必然导致土地价格和房价上涨，而当地人不大可能按照这一价格购买"第一套房"。

8. The IME encourages and stimulates various sectors within the destination to

cooperate closely with each other to push local economy forward in the direction of diversity.

收入乘数效应促进旅游目的地内各个行业紧密合作，促进当地经济多元化发展。

9. For example, food imports required by the development of tourism may reduce or even chase out local production if the foreign tour operator enlarges his business to the extent that he provides a cheaper and better quality product for the wider market.

例如，外来的旅游经营商为了扩大市场规模，在提供更加质优价廉的商品的规模达到一定程度的时候，发展旅游所需的进口食品就会挤压当地商品的生产，甚至使其破产。

10. In other words, if a resource can be used in two ways—tourism and agriculture and we choose tourism, then the opportunity for tourism is at the cost of agriculture.

换句话说，如果一种资源既可以用于旅游也可能用于农业，当我们将它用于旅游时，旅游发展的机会就是以损害农业为代价的。

Exercise

1. Decide whether the statements are true or false. If it is true, put "T" in the space provided and "F" if it is false.

   (1) _____ Financial inputs are necessary for the areas which are faced with the problem of market failure.

   (2) _____ Direct financial costs for tourism are the direct expenses of tourism agencies within government for the development of tourism in the destination.

   (3) _____ Indirect financial costs and direct financial costs can be classified into revenue leakages.

   (4) _____ The more revenue leakages, the more opportunities that people can gain profits from tourism.

   (5) _____ Less-developed countries should establish non-local or foreign businesses to reduce revenue leakages.

   (6) _____ Tourism makes it possible for the destination to confront the danger of economic inflation.

   (7) _____ Most of the local residents with their increasing incomes can hardly afford to buy houses in a tourism-developing area.

   (8) _____ Tourism and other sectors do not have mutual influence because they do not compete with each other.

2. Questions for discussion

   (1) Why should destination managers be careful to choose a right way to develope tourism?

   (2) What are direct financial costs? Are these costs necessary?

   (3) What are the two situations in which serious revenue leakages are more likely to occur?

(4) Why does tourism make it possible for the destination to confront the danger of economic inflation?

(5) What are the problems caused by the change of seasons?

(6) Can you describe the relationship between tourism and other sectors within the destination?

Part II Guided Reading

第二部分　课文导读

旅游不仅给旅游目的地带来可观的直接经济收入，而且会产生乘数效应，带动相关产业的发展，但并不是所有的旅游项目都是有利可图的，旅游开发的成本和负面效应也许会大于旅游收益。本文论述了旅游开发可能造成的经济成本。这些成本分为两类：一种是直接经济成本，另一种是间接经济成本。直接经济成本有：旅游主管部门的行政开支、市场营销、市场调研、旅游奖励等；间接成本主要是旅游收入漏损。有两种情况可能会给旅游目的地造成严重的经济漏损：一种是在发展中国家，由于发展旅游基础设施进口设备和物质，支付高级旅游管理人才工资和特许经营费等产生漏损；一种在"旅游飞地"，旅游地的经营权被外来企业控制，经营旅游项目所有的物质和管理人才都需进口，旅游项目与当地社区隔离，当地企业或居民未能从旅游项目获得收益而产生漏损。

以下是旅游开发的主要间接经济成本和风险。

一、收入漏损

什么是漏损？国际旅游中，外国旅游者在接待国的全部旅游消费（即接待国直接旅游收入）一部分会流出国外，这就是漏损。其中一部分旅游收入在没有进入接待国经济系统前便已经漏损出国外，我们称之为直接漏损。比如旅游企业支付外方人员的工资、支付外国贷款的利息，以及旅游企业中外资输回母国的利润等。另外用于购买进口商品和服务的旅游收入部分，也不会刺激当地经济生产。此外，按照乘数理论中的假设，旅游企业上缴政府的税金和用于储蓄的部分也视为漏损。这里的储蓄是旅游消费所带来的增加收入中节余的部分，在规定期间内（通常一年）不放贷给其他用款人。由于旅游的示范效应，增加了国内消费者对外国商品的需求，生产诱导进口，使接待国的漏损也会增大。

二、季节性变化

季节性指旅游现象的发生在时间规律上存在强弱反差，这种现象由旅游吸引物和游客双方面的原因造成。就旅游吸引物而言，由于气候条件的变化，景观在一年中会发生变化；就游客而言，由于出游目的、可自由支配时间等因素，导致一年中游客来访数量也会发生变化。

旅游目的地较大的季节性波动属于正常的旅游周期，但如果没有适当的管理措施，就会对目的地经济和社会带来负面影响，造成旅游目的地非饱和容量和生产力过剩。在淡季，旅游设施使用率较低，导致大量旅游直接从业人员失业。由于收入和就业乘数的影响，经济将做出连续的消极反应。在旺季的时候，又会出现超额预定，对基础设施造成压力，过度拥挤，食物和服务短缺，不得不依赖进口来满足游客的需求。

三、流行趋势变化

旅游产品消费偏好的改变可能增加或者减少某类旅游产品的消费量。消费偏好的改变一般要经历相对长的时间，因此旅游目的地可以跟随趋势做出必要的调节。一种观点认为，流行趋势会带来短期影响。比如，因为人们好奇心的驱使3S旅游成为较时尚的旅游产品，但是很快人们就会选择到提供类似产品（容易替代的产品）的新地方去旅游，其他的产业也会有类似的经历。

但是旅游面临的一个尴尬境地就是目的地按比例增加接待设施的总量,以满足在接待高峰期的需要。但是由于流行趋势的影响,游客数量减少,而这些旅游设施又很难改为他用,由于固定成本很高,这就成为接待地沉重的经济负担。正因为旅游者消费趣味的变化,所以并非越早发展旅游产业就越能获得更多的利益,也并非旅游规模做得越大越好,而应当视该地区现有旅游资源的存量和特色,合理规划和开发,并注意消费者市场的变化,减少各种不确定因素对旅游目的地的影响。

四、目的地通货膨胀压力

当旅游把资金注入到了目的地经济系统,随着这一地区经济的增长,有可能给旅游目的地带来通货膨胀压力。一般来说,旅游者比当地居民的消费能力更强,因为外来旅游者的收入较高或者因为他们将长期积累用于旅游,在旅游中存在消费高攀的行为。他们愿意以较高的价格购买各种产品和服务,这必然会造成旅游目的地的粮食、蔬菜、副食品等价格上涨,交通、商店、公共娱乐场所拥挤,从而损害目的地居民的生活质量。

此外,旅游目的地的房地产价格会随着旅游业的发展迅速上升。一个地区旅游产业的发展需要建设饭店、餐饮和娱乐设施,占用土地增多,地价必然剧烈上涨。在旅游还不发达的地区修建一个宾馆,土地投资的金额只占了总投资额的1%;而在旅游已经非常发达的地区修建宾馆,对土地的投资会达到总投资额度的20%。由于土地价格的增长,在旅游发达的地区,当地较低收入的居民,实际上已被剥夺了购买住房的权利。

五、与其他部门的竞争

虽然旅游业显著的后向关联能带动目的地经济的多样化发展,然而在某种情况下,旅游与其他部门在当地经济中的关系是竞争关系而不是互补关系。比如,当外来旅游经营商的进口的产品更便宜、质量更高,当其进口形成一定规模以后,那么旅游经营商的进口食物就可能替代当地的农业产品。

旅游与农业的竞争关系最为明显。许多研究者注意到旅游业将劳动力从农业中吸引出来。由于旅游业是劳动密集型产业,劳动力技术含量较低,可以吸引那些从事农业生产的劳动力,给他们提供工资和劳动环境相对较好的工作岗位,这就势必影响农业生产,逐渐引起当地社会经济结构的变化。此外,由于旅游是一个更有竞争力的土地出价者,农业的边际化现象非常严重。旅游业可能给土地提供者更多的赚钱机会,从而使当地政府和居民更愿意将土地用于发展旅游,加速农业的衰退。因此,应该考虑用于旅游的资源的机会成本。用于旅游开发的土地就不可能再用于农业,因此发展旅游业是以发展当地农业为代价的,使得当地农业失去了发展的机会。

六、旅游经济的不确定性

旅游经济比较脆弱,受多种因素影响,给旅游目的地经济带来不确定因素,表现在以下几个方面。首先,由于旅游产品的生产与销售是同步进行的,消费者必须到旅游产品的生产地(旅游目的地)才能消费。其次,旅游属于高层次消费,每当经济状况不理想时,人们必将首先保证基本消费,削减包括旅游消费在内的高层次消费;其三,旅游业具有综合性特点,所涉及的行业、部门和其他各种因素极多,任何行业和部门的变化都会波及旅游业,影响旅游经济收入;其四,旅游产品具有不可储存性,当天没有售出的宾馆房间等就无法再产生经济价值,但是仍然有房间维护费、贷款利息等成本的付出。其五,旅游活动具有高度的不稳定性,容易受天气、时尚、社会思潮、政治因素等情况的影响。从需求方面讲,如可自由支配收入、休假时间改变等都会对旅游者出行造成影响;从供给方面讲,旅游目的地政治不稳定、旅游基础设施遭到破坏等,也将会对旅游者到旅游目的地旅游造成巨大影响,对旅游目的地经济造成许多不确定因素。

随着旅游业在全球范围内的持续增长,种种证据表明旅游业对社会经济的贡献并非完全是积极的。缺乏科学规划和管理的旅游项目对当地的经济、社会、文化、环境带来的损失可能超过它带来的好处。因此,发展旅游不能只看旅游收入,而且还要权衡经济成本,以及发展旅游可能面对的不确定因素,如季节性变化、流行趋势变化、通货膨胀压力、其他部门的机会损失、经济的不确定因素等,以便在开发旅游项目时,当地政府采取有效措施,克服旅游发展带来的各种消极影响,为旅游的可持续发展创造有利的政策环境和经济环境。

旅游知识测试

正误判断:请在正确的选题上划√,错误的选题上划×。

1. 旅游研究中使用的乘数类型有四种:第一、收入乘数;第二、产出乘数;第三、营业额或营业收入乘数;第四、就业乘数。

2. 旅游产品换汇率较高的直接原因是,由于旅游出口是一种有形贸易,并且旅游者必须要到旅游产品的生产地点进行消费。

3. 营业收入乘数和产出乘数的不同点在于,营业收入乘数所测定的只是单位旅游消费对接待国经济的直接效应和继发效应所导致全部有关企业营业收入总额的增长量;而产出乘数既考虑这些企业营业总额的增长情况,同时也考虑与之有关库存的实际变化。

4. 对一个国家来说,其国际收支经常会出现不平衡的情况。当一个国家的国际收入大于国际支出时,其国际账户便会出现逆差或赤字;反之则会出现顺差或剩余。

5. 漏损量越大,乘数的值也就越大。也就是说,在所得收入中的储蓄以及用于进口和其他对外支付的数量越大,乘数效应也就越高。

Part III　Case Study
第三部分　案例研究

旅游对上海经济的影响
——基于投入产出模型的研究和评价

分析要点

1. 从以上案例分析中,你认为旅游与哪些部门的关联度较大?请例举5个部门。
2. 旅游者消费对上海经济有哪些直接影响?你认为哪一种对上海经济影响更大?
3. 旅游者消费对上海经济有哪些间接影响?哪一种乘数高,给上海带来的经济收入多?
4. 通过本案研究,你认为上海的旅游产业链是否完整?对上海旅游发展会有什么影响?
5. 对比上一年度上海旅游收入和你所在地区的旅游收入情况,从投入产出的角度简要分析两地旅游收入差距的原因。

相关理论和问题

1. 旅游乘数效应(Multiplier effect)
2. 收入漏损(Revenue leakage)
3. 旅游产业链(Tourism industrial chain)
4. 投入产出模型(Input-output model)

旅游经济影响研究内容包括旅游业对地区经济的产出、收入和就业的贡献；旅游业内部要素变化如季节性波动对经济收入或劳动力市场的边际影响；旅游业与其他产业间的相互关系等等。该案例采用投入产出模型，分析上海市国内旅游对经济所产生的影响。

投入产出计算公式为：$X=(I-A)^{-1}\times Y$，

其中：X 为产出，Y 为最终需求，$(I-A)^{-1}$ 是列昂惕夫逆矩阵，I 是 $N\times N$ 的单位矩阵，N 是国民经济部门数量。

一、直接影响

旅游者消费直接影响的行业包括旅客运输业、餐饮业、旅馆业、商业、公用和文化娱乐业、旅行社业和邮电业等。旅游者消费对这些行业来说就意味着产出和收入的直接增加。

(1) 直接产出影响

根据 2002 年上海市统计年鉴数据，2001 年国内旅游者在上海的旅游消费是 779.6350 亿元，平均每人消费 1223 元。

表1 国内旅游者在上海消费构成

消费类型	2001年/元	百分比
人均消费支出	1223	100.0
购物费	356	29.1
长途交通费	247	20.2
餐饮费	205	16.8
住宿费	193	15.8
市内交通费	79	6.5
门票费	49	4.0
娱乐费	46	3.8
交付旅行社费	20	1.6
邮电通信费	10	0.8
其他	18	1.5

通过表1可见，旅游者在交通、住宿和餐饮、购物等几个部门花费最多。将旅游者消费构成和国民经济的相应产业对应，就可以得到旅游直接影响产业因旅游消费增加的产出量。

旅游消费对经济部门产出增加的直接贡献是 634.9658 亿元。

(2) 直接收入影响

直接产出增加值将通过劳动者工资、奖金和企业利润的形式转化为收入，形成旅游对收入的直接影响。收入包括劳动者报酬和营业盈余。

表2 旅游对收入和产出的直接影响

旅游消费类型	对应产业部门	直接产出/亿元	百分比/%	单位消费的直接产出	直接收入/亿元	百分比/%	单位消费的直接收入
长途交通费	旅客运输业	159.81	25.17	0.0083	29.04	17.50	0.0478
餐饮费	饮食业	132.64	20.89	0.1182	30.00	18.08	0.0373
住宿费	旅馆业	124.87	19.67	0.1701	33.55	20.22	0.0405

市内交通费	公用和文化娱乐业	112.58	17.73	0.2050	37.28	22.46	0.0039
门票费							
娱乐费							
购物费	商业	92.13	14.51	0.1444	31.56	19.01	0.0385
交付旅行社费	旅行社业	12.94	2.04	0.1602	1.51	0.91	0.0019
邮电通信费	邮电业	6.47	1.02	0.0166	3.02	1.80	0.0430
	总计	634.97	100.00	0.8144	165.96	100.0	0.2129

直接收入影响根据产出增加值乘以各行业收入系数计算得出。收入影响比较表明，城市文化艺术和娱乐服务、住宿、购物等领域的收入系数比较高。总的来说，每1元旅游消费直接产生收入 0.2129 元。

二、间接影响

旅游收入的间接影响是游客在旅游目的地的开支循环使用中产生的。旅游者的部分开支在旅游相关部门循环使用产生收入的乘数效应，对旅游产业链的各部门带来经济收益。乘数效应可由投入产出矩阵模型计算得出。

表3 旅游对各行业产出和收入的乘数效应

	产出乘数效应/亿元	百分比/%	单位旅游消费的产出乘数效应	收入乘数效应/亿元	百分比/%	单位旅游消费的收入乘数效应
农业	95.79	4.25	0.1229*	32.87	6.49	0.0422
采掘业	0.08	0.00	0.0001	0.02	0.00	0.0000
食品制造业	114.12	5.07	0.1464	11.39	2.25	0.0146
纺织业	45.11	2.00	0.0579	7.42	1.47	0.0095
化学工业	212.30	9.43	0.2723	32.79	6.47	0.0421
企业服务业	281.32	12.50	0.3608	90.28	17.82	0.1158
木制品业	11.32	0.50	0.0145	1.42	0.28	0.0018
城市能源供应业	83.24	3.70	0.1068	12.43	2.45	0.0159
纸制品业	66.82	2.97	0.857	13.05	2.58	0.0167
金属非金属制品业	132.37	5.88	0.1698	19.87	3.92	0.0255
机械工业	49.41	2.19	0.634	9.02	1.78	0.0116
电子制造业	74.73	3.32	0.959	12.04	2.38	0.0154
交通设备制造业	32.95	1.46	0.423	5.20	1.03	0.0067
建筑业	12.35	0.55	0.0158	2.02	0.40	0.0026
货运业	61.37	2.73	0.0787	17.66	3.49	0.0226
社会服务业	46.77	2.08	0.0600	18.80	3.71	0.0241

居民服务业	9.61	0.43	0.0123	2.67	0.532	0.0034
商业*	195.84	8.70	0.2512	67.08	13.24	0.0860
饮食业*	148.31	6.59	0.1902	33.55	6.62	0.0430
旅客运输业*	146.52	6.51	0.1879	26.63	5.26	0.0342
旅行社业*	17.78	0.79	0.0228	2.08	0.41	0.0027
公用和文化娱乐业*	116.55	5.18	0.1495	38.60	7.62	0.0495
邮电业*	36.00	1.60	0.0462	16.78	3.31	0.0215
旅馆业	122.41	5.44	0.1570	32.89	6.49	0.0422
合计	2251.27	100.00	2.8876	506.53	100.00	0.6497

(1) 产出乘数效应

结果表明，旅游消费导致部门产出的乘数增加值主要集中在企业服务业、化学工业、商业、餐饮业、旅客运输业 5 个部门。国内旅游消费总共导致上海各经济部门增加产出 2 251.27 亿元。平均每 1 元旅游消费给上海各经济部门的产出乘数效应是增加产值 2.8876 元。

(2) 收入乘数效应

收入的增加值根据产出的增加值乘以各行业收入系数计算得到。根据表 3 收入乘数最大的部门依次是企业服务业、商业、公用和文化娱乐业、餐饮业、农业和旅馆业。平均每 1 元旅游消费增加企业和劳动者的收入 0.6497 元。

三、研究总结

（一）旅游对上海市经济的各层次影响

表 4　旅游对上海经济的各层次影响

	产出影响/亿元	单位消费的产出影响	收入影响/亿元	单位消费的收入影响
直接影响	634.9658	0.8144	165.9587	0.2129
间接影响和诱导效应	1616.3019	2.0732	340.5696	0.4368
乘数效应	2251.2677	2.8876（产出乘数）	506.5283	0.6497（收入乘数）

将前述研究结果进行汇总，可得到旅游消费的各层次影响结果（见表 4）。研究表明，旅游消费的产出乘数效应是增加上海市各行业总产值共计 2251.2677 亿元，是初始旅游消费额 779.6350 亿元的 2.8876 倍，即上海市旅游产出乘数为 2.8876。旅游消费引起的间接产出和引致产出，合计 1 616.3019 亿元，是直接产出 634.9658 亿元的 2.5455 倍，这揭示了旅游消费在上海市国民经济循环中产生的后续影响作用远大于其初始影响。从收入来看，旅游消费产生了 165.9587 亿元的直接收入、340.5696 亿元的间接收入和引致收入，总共产生收入 506.5283 亿元，即平均每 1 元旅游消费转化为 0.6497 元的企业和劳动者收入，表示上海市旅游收入乘数是 0.6497。

（二）旅游对各行业产出增长的乘数效应排名

在旅游对经济的直接影响阶段，旅游消费引起的行业产出增加值前五名依次是旅客运输业、餐饮业、旅馆业、公用和文化娱乐业、商业。

在乘数影响阶段，旅游消费引起的行业产出增加值前五名依次是企业服务业、化学工业、商业、餐饮业和旅客运输业，这些产业中集中了旅游消费引起的近一半的产出增加值。其中商业、餐饮业、旅客运输业是旅游者直接消费的主要行业，而企业服务业和化学工业则是旅游者间接消费的主要行业。

以上分析说明企业服务业和化学工业是上海都市旅游业发展的重要支持产业,其原因在于都市旅游消费的综合性和规模性。应该指出,这些行业如化学工业、企业服务业等不只为旅游者服务,其产出的大部分还是被市民消耗,旅游者消耗掉的只占这些行业总产出的小部分。

(三)旅游对各行业收入增长的乘数效应排名

在旅游对经济的直接影响阶段,旅游消费引起的行业收入增加值前五名依次是公用和文化娱乐业、旅馆业、商业、餐饮业和旅客运输业。

在乘数影响阶段,旅游消费引起的行业收入增加值前五名依次是企业服务业、商业、公用和文化娱乐业、餐饮业、农业和旅馆业(并列),它们占到总收入增加值的一半多。说明上海都市旅游者消费大部分转化为这些行业的收入增长,这些行业更能从上海都市旅游业发展中获得益处。

应当注意的是,投入产出模型分析相对重视 GDP 受益于旅游经济的影响,但是对旅游行业本身受到的影响分析不够深入,同时忽视进口漏损等问题,甚至没有考虑其他行业受到的负面影响,这就可能夸大旅游区域经济影响的正面效应。近来,投入产出分析已经得到扩展,引入了对跨区域产品流、能源消耗、环境污染、生产就业等的核算,出现了社会核算矩阵(SAMs,social accounting matrices)和可计总量平衡(CGE,computable general equilibrium)两种新的评价模型方法。

资料来源:乔玮.用投入产出模型分析旅游对上海经济的影响[J].经济地理,2006(12).

Part IV   Reading Box
第四部分   阅读与分析

Dependency on Tourism Industry
—A lesson from the Caribbean island of Antigua

阅读分析要点

1. 旅游对安提瓜岛 GDP 的贡献
2. 安提瓜岛 3S 旅游资源
3. 安提瓜岛旅游收入的漏损
4. 安提瓜岛对旅游业的依赖

The case of the Caribbean Island of Antigua can serve as the best illustration of the difficult situation small islands face as they develop international tourism. Antigua has only 230 square kilometers with a population of about 65,000 but it was famous for its sugar production. Soon after the first settlers came in the early 1620s, sugar began to be planted almost all over the island with the hard work of slaves of African descendants in big plantations. However, in the 1800s the opening up of large sugar-growing plantations and the emergence of the sugar beet industry led to the decline of the value of sugar.[1] Accordingly, Antigua became a poorer backward island, but it still entirely relied on the weakening **sugar sector** because its resource is not suitable for the development of other industries.

During this pre-tourism era, there had always been a small number of visitors in Antigua. But after World War II tourism began to develop because more and more estate owners, developers and visitors gradually realized the importance of the extraordinary 3S resource. The first resort hotel was opened in 1954, and by 1963, the units of accommodation amounted to 527 which could hold 43,000 visitors or so. The rise of the tourism industry led to the fall of agriculture, especially sugar production. This is mainly because tourism was a feasible substitute for the sugar sector which was filled with problems.[2] It provided a chance for estate owners located on or near the coast to move their investment from sugar so as to make a bigger profit.

By the early 1970s all sugar refineries were closed and tourism became the dominant support of Antigua's economy. In 1978 tourism contributed 22.2% of Antigua's GDP or 36% if we consider indirect incomes. By 1995 this figure came up to more than 70%, while agriculture accounted for 3.5% and industry contributed 17.9%. In the same year, 220,000 visitors checked in those 3,185 hotels on the island. And another 300,000 excursionists arrived by cruise ship.

Indeed, tourism brought huge profits to Antigua. For example, in 1996, tourist receipts amounted to US$257 million. Antigua became one of the wealthiest countries in the entire Caribbean, as calculated according to the average **per capita income**. However, if we examine the distribution of this wealth carefully, we can recognize a pattern of inequality.[3] Antigua society is mainly composed of three groups—a small number of wealthy elite, a somewhat larger middle class and a very large group of extremely poor residents. Among them, the wealthiest are those hotel owners who are mainly light-skinned or foreign and the poorest are those descendants of slaves, which constitute a structure similar to that of the old plantation system.

Such structural similarities between the old plantation system and the tourism industry appear no matter which sector dominates the economy in its respective eras. They also exist in seasonal patterns of activity, which result in frequent failures of the power supply during the high season and a large number of laid-off workers during the off season.[4] In addition, tourism in Antigua suffers from an extremely high rate of **revenue leakage** and incurs much criticism. This is because almost all of the hotel owners are foreigners and almost all inputs for the tourism sector are required to be imported from other countries, which were mainly responsible for the recorded **trade deficit** of US$254 million in 1994. In addition, Antigua has provided too generous incentives to the tourism industry in order to make up for the losses brought about by the failure of the sugar industry by attracting even more foreign investment.[5] For instance, **the incentives** provided for hotels of at least 10 bedrooms include a five-year tax holiday and exemption of all equipment, material and furniture from customs duties and consumption taxes.

Antigua continues to take its classic 3**S resource** as the selling point and launches advertising campaigns to promote its so-called 365 beaches—one for every day of the year. However, in spite of the efforts made to hold its position as a unique 3S tourist destination, it has also taken measures both within and outside of the tourism sector to weaken the dependency of its economy on 3S component.[6] Investigations are made into the possibility of restoring the sugar industry partially and cultivating specialized fruits and vegetables for export. In the late 1980s Antigua also developed its offshore banking, but it has not yet made any progress in this business until now, just like the islands of Bermuda and Cayman. Besides, it also set up a free trade zone in 1993 for the purpose of stimulating the establishment of small factories to produce light manufactured goods for export.

Within tourism sector itself, Antigua makes an attempt to restore its famous plantation as a cultural site attraction instead of emphasizing further development of the coast and 3S tourism. A case in point is the **Betty's Hope Trust** which was established in 1988 with the grants from UNESCO and investments from a variety of foreign and local investors. The purpose of its establishment was to create an outdoor history centre which presented a fully restored and operating sugar mill in front of visitors. Developing such an attraction would bring at least two benefits. On one hand, it would enhance the diversity of its tourism monoculture; on the other hand, it would be helpful for the restoration of the sugar industry.[7] Although it makes great efforts to diversify its economy, the government seems to be concentrating on the rapid development of the tourism sector.[8] In 1997, the government approved the construction of a 2000-room hotel which had a budget of US$300 million. when this project was completed, the number of the hotel room in Antigua would increase by two-thirds.

One problem that is threatening this small island chronically is hurricanes. In 1995, Hurricane Luis brought heavy losses to the island: 75% of all buildings were seriously damaged and vital tourism receipts decreased by 19% as against that of the previous year. This event let us realize that all small island countries are faced with a fundamental problem—the threat of natural disasters which can cause serious damages to the whole country rather than to just a small part of a large country. Similarly, some man-made "disasters" also have a heavy influence on the whole country. For example, the closure of a single large hotel may result in the increase of the unemployment rate by 5% or more. There are indeed many problems in Antigua such as horrific revenue leakages, foreign ownership, **dependency** and other systemic problems and these have incurred much criticism.[9] However, for such a small, resource-poor island, what other realistic choices can they make?

New Words

colony	n.	殖民地;侨民
incur	v.	招致
era	n.	时代,时期
campaign	n.	(政治或商业性)活动
estate	n.	不动产,财产
monoculture	n.	单一经营
refinery	n.	提炼厂,精炼厂

Notes

1. However, in the 1800s the opening up of large sugar-growing plantations and the emergence of the sugar beet industry led to the decline of the value of sugar.
 然而在18世纪,大型甘蔗种植园的开垦以及甜菜制糖业的出现导致了白糖价格的下跌。

2. This is mainly because tourism was a feasible substitute for the sugar sector which was filled with problems.

这主要是因为旅游业可以替代问题成堆的制糖业。

3. However, if we examine the distribution of this wealth carefully, we can recognize a pattern of inequality.
   然而，如果仔细分析这些财富的分配，我们就会发现一种社会不公的现象。

4. They also exist in seasonal patterns of activity, which result in frequent failures of the power supply during the high season and a large number of laid-off workers during the off season.
   它们也同样存在于旅游活动的季节性中。旺季时常常停电，淡季时许多人失业。

5. In addition, Antigua has provided too generous incentives to the tourism industry in order to make up for the losses brought about by the failure of the sugar industry by attracting even more foreign investment.
   此外，安提瓜为旅游业提供了特别优惠的鼓励政策，以吸引更多外资来弥补制糖业损失。

6. However, in spite of the efforts made to hold its position as a unique 3S tourist destination, it has also taken measures both within and outside of the tourism sector to weaken the dependency of its economy on 3S component.
   但是，为保住3S旅游目的地独特地位，安提瓜做出了许多努力，但是安提瓜还是在其旅游部门内外采取了多项措施，以减弱其经济对3S旅游的依赖性。

7. On one hand, it would enhance the diversity of its tourism monoculture; on the other hand, it would be helpful for the restoration of the sugar industry.
   一方面，它可以使旅游业的单一经营多样化；另一方面，也可以帮助恢复制糖业。

8. Although it makes great efforts to diversify its economy, the government seems to be concentrating on the rapid development of the tourism sector.
   尽管极力促使经济多元化，但政府似乎还是把主要精力放在旅游的快速发展上。

9. There are indeed many problems in Antigua such as horrific revenue leakages, foreign ownership, dependency and other systemic problems and these have incurred much criticism.
   安提瓜确实存在很多问题，诸如严重的收入漏损、外资垄断、经济过于依赖旅游业，以及其它系统性问题，这些问题招致许多批评。

Topic discussion

1. What resources did Antigua have? What were the problems Antigua was faced with in 1950s?

2. Why did tourism industry fail to revitalize Antigua's economy? What are the major causes that affect the development of Antigua's tourism?

3. What measures are being adopted in Antigua to solve these problems?

4. Is it wise to encourage the large-scale tourism development on Antigua? Why or why not?

【即学即用】

With reference to the theory, information or approach applied in the Reading Box, have a case study of the economic impact on the destination you know. Make presentation of your study in Chinese or in English using PPT.

【学习资源库】

为了掌握本章更多的相关专业知识,请您登陆 http://sicnu.edu.cn/,点击国家双语教学示范课程《旅游学概论》,进入网络学堂查询相关资料。

Chapter Review 本章小结

This chapter has discussed both direct and indirect costs brought about by tourism industry, and explained the reasons why revenue leakage is incurred and its adverse effects on the destination economy. When we evaluate the revenue of the tourism sectors we should take various economic costs into consideration. Tourism sectors are likely affected by economic uncertainty; both the demand-side and the supply-side factors will affect the return of fixed costs. Tourism industry competes with other sectors, and development of a tourism project, to some extent, is at cost of the other industry. It is dangerous if the national economy mainly depends on tourism industry. Antigua is a case we should learn when we plan or develop tourism projects. For a country or a destination, it is of great importance to diversify its economy while developing tourism industry.

Part V Additional Know-how of Tourism
第五部分 旅游知识扩展

【关键术语】

Income multiplier effect(IME): a measure of the subsequent income generated in a destination's economy by direct tourist expenditure

收入乘数效应(IME):一种衡量尺度,用于衡量在目的地经济由于旅游者直接支出而产生的后续收入。

Backward linkages: sectors of an economy that provide goods and services for the tourism sector; typically includes agriculture, fisheries and construction, etc.

后向链接:为旅游业提供产品和服务的经济部门,主要包括农业、渔业和建筑业等。

Revenue leakages: a major category of indirect financial costs, entailing sources of erosion in the IME that occur indirectly through the importation of goods and services that required by tourists or tourist industry, through factor payments abroad such as repatriated profits, and through imports required for government expenditure on tourism-related infrastructure such as airports, road and port equipment; revenue leakages can also involve direct financial outlays

收入漏损:间接财务成本的主要类别。它包括收入乘数效应的各种损耗,这些损耗是通过以下渠道间接发生的:1. 进口游客所需或旅游业所要求的商品和服务;2. 向国外付款,诸如汇出利润;3. 由于政府在旅游相关基础建设(例如机场、道路和港口设施建设)方面支出而导致的进口。收入漏损也可能包括直接财政支出。

Enclave resort: usually a self-contained resort complex that caters to a tourist clientele; enclave resorts are often associated with high revenue leakages because of their propensity to encourage internal spending and to import goods from outside without any economic contact with the local community.

旅游飞地：通常是指游客服务自成一体的旅游景区；旅游飞地经常会造成很高的收入漏损，因为这类旅游地倾向购买来自当地社区以外的商品，鼓励景区内部消费，不与当地社区产生经济往来。

Growth pole strategy: A strategy that uses tourism to stimulate economic development in some suitably located area, so that this growth will eventually become self-sustaining

增长极战略：利用旅游刺激某些地理位置优越的区域发展经济，逐渐使当地经济实现自给自足的一种战略。

Demonstration effect: in economics, the tendency of a population, or some portion thereof, to imitate the consumption patterns of another group; this can result in increased importation or goods and services to meet these changing consumption patterns.

示范效应：经济活动中一个国家的人或其中一部分人模仿另一人群消费模式的趋势，这种趋势会导致进口商品与服务增加，以满足消费模式的变化。

Opportunity cost: The idea that the use of a resource for tourism precludes its use for some other activity that may yield a strong financial return (e.g. agriculture)

机会成本：某个资源用于旅游业以后，就无法用于可能产生投资回报良好的其他活动（例如农业）。

Displacement effect: where tourism development substitutes one form of expenditure and economic activity for another.

替代效应：旅游业的发展以一种形式的支出和经济活动替代另一种形势的支出和经济活动。

【知识链接】

1. 旅游外汇漏损

旅游外汇漏损一般是指旅游目的国或旅游目的地的有关部门和企业为了满足旅游者旅游活动及相关消费活动而发生的外汇支出，即旅游外汇收入流失到国外的部分。

旅游外汇漏损发生的途径主要有：

（1）购买旅游开发建设与经营运转所需要的各种设备和原材料的外汇支出。

（2）因发展旅游大量筹措外资而产生的海外贷款利息，以及支付合资、独资旅游企业中外国投资者利润的外汇支出。

（3）旅游企业支付给海外员工的工资以及人力资源的海外培训。

（4）为开拓国际旅游市场而进行的海外促销，需要直接用外汇支付海外促销费，以及海外长驻旅游机构的活动费用和人员工资。

（5）本国居民出境旅游而产生的外汇消费。

（6）向旅游业提供各种物资和劳务的企业或其他机构为满足旅游业需要而从国外进口物资而消耗的外汇。

（7）由于旅游示范效应改变了本地人的消费模式造成的本地居民对进口商品的额外消费。

（8）由于外汇管理的漏洞，致使一部分海外旅游者通过非官方渠道进行外汇兑换，造成国家外汇实现量减少，即黑市漏损。

2、旅游卫星账户

卫星账户是用于测量那些现有国家核算体系中尚未或不能作为一个产业的经济部门的规模的一个核算方法。旅游卫星账户（Tourism Satellite Account，缩写为 TSA），就国家报告网络中有关旅游的投入——产出表的框架提供了一个标准。它能够在一个均衡的情况下，检验旅游业的需求和供给双方的关系，说明生产和需求在整个经济系统中的作用。旅游卫星账户能够确定哪个行业将从旅游业的需求获取利润，表明旅游业的增加值，旅游商品的供求关系，旅游业方面的就业率，以及通过卖商品和服务给游客所带来的间接税收。旅游卫星账户的核心内容包括 10 张内容上相互连接的账户和表格，建立旅游卫星账户，也就是完成这 10 张表格的编制工作，从这些内容来看，旅游卫星账户可以在国民经济核算通用概念、体系内，实现对旅游业的生产、消费、就业、投资等领域的核算，提升了传统的以需求方调查为主的旅游统计指标体系。具体来说，TSA 通过编制 10 张表格来综合全面地反映旅游的经济影响。

表 1	按照产品和游客类型编制的以现金方式支付的入境游客最终消费的表格
表 2	按照产品和游客类型编制的以现金方式支付的国内游客最终消费的表格
表 3	按照产品和游客类型编制的出境旅游消费的表格
表 4	按照产品和游客类型编制的境内旅游消费的表格
表 5	旅游业和其他产业的生产账户
表 6	按照产品编制的国内供给和境内旅游消费的表格
表 7	有关旅游业就业的表格
表 8	有关旅游总固定资产形成的表格
表 9	有关旅游集体消费的表格
表 10	有关各类定性指标的表格

【小思考】

1. 旅游目的地旅游经济效益如何衡量？你认为是否旅游收入越多旅游经济效益越好？

参考阅读：

经济效益是指在经济过程中，生产要素的占用、投入、消耗与有效成果产出之间的数量比例关系。一般认为，生产同样数量、质量的产品和服务，要素投入越少，经济效益越高；在一定的要素投入总量和结构下，产出越多，经济效益越好。由此可以得出，旅游经济效益就是在合理开发利用旅游资源和环境保护的前提下，旅游经济活动过程中生产要素的占用、投入、耗费与成果之间的数量对比关系。产出最终体现于营业收入、税金、利润之中，反映了费用与效果的比例关系、投入与产出的比例关系。用公式表示如下：

$$旅游经济效益 = \frac{旅游业的经营成果 - 生产要素的占用与消耗}{生成要素的占用与消耗}$$

2. 旅游市场失灵的时候，政府该不该干预？应该以什么样的方式干预？

参考阅读：

造成市场失灵的一个重要原因是信息不对称。面对巨大的市场需求，旅游经营者不可能全面掌握其所需的信息，做出理性的选择。旅游者也不可能掌握众多的旅游目的地和服务经营者情况,以从中选取能实现自己旅游效用最大化的服务及提供者。即使人们可能搜索到旅游经济所需全部信息,但是其付出的成本是如此之高,人们宁愿保持对信息的一定限度的无知。

旅游企业的垄断是使市场失灵的另一个原因。垄断会掠夺一部分旅游者的消费者剩余,并且造成一部分旅游消费者剩余的无谓损失。

公共物品的存在也会导致市场失灵。旅游目的地环境是一个公共产品,但是维持这个公共产品需要付出成本,需要旅游活动的受益者共同承担。但是无论旅游活动的参与者是否付出了代价,都可以从环境中受益,就形成了"搭便车"现象。于是市场对公共物品进行资源配置的机制失灵。由于市场失灵,市场供需关系失去长期平衡状态。例如个体经营者不愿提供赞助开展旅游目的地营销以增加市场需求,因为这种投资不仅对自身有利,也使其他竞争者获利。

Part VI Further Readings
第六部分 课外阅读

如果您想进一步学习本章的内容,探讨旅游经济成本和经济效益,建议您阅读以下学者的著作和论文。

一、中文部分

[1] 田里.牟红.旅游经济学[M].北京:清华大学出版社,2007.

[2] 余书炜.论旅游者人均支出水平的地区差异——预漏损现象的发现及其分析[J].旅游学刊.1999,(02).

[3] 张骁鸣,保继刚.旅游区域经济影响评价研究综述[J].桂林旅游高等专科学校学报,2004,(04).

[4] 戴学锋,巫宁.中国出境旅游高速增长的负面影响探析[J].旅游学刊,2006,(02).

[5] 陶卓民,华东.假日经济对旅游业的影响及旅游发展因应对策[J].经济地理,2001,(S1).

[6] 吴宗友.黄山市文化旅游资源漏损问题暨开发的动态模式研究[J].经济问题探索,2005,(12).

[7] 朱华.乡村旅游利益主体研究——以成都市三圣乡红砂村观光旅游为例[J].旅游学刊,2006,(05).

[8] 吴殿廷,武聪颖,王欣.旅游开发损益和风险评价的初步探讨——以白潭湖开发为例[J].旅游学刊,2004,(04).

[9] 刘益.旅游开发对社区居民经济影响的时空分异特征研究——以丹霞山、世外桃源景区为例[J].经济地理,2006,(04).

[10] 牛亚菲,宋涛,刘春凤,陈田.基于要素叠加的旅游景区经济影响域空间分异——以八达岭长城景区为例[J].地理科学进展,2010,(02).

二、英文部分

[1] Sugiyarto, Guntur;Blake, Adam;Sinclair, M Thea. Tourism and globalization-economic impact in Indonesia[J]. *Annals of Tourism Research*,2003,30(3):683—701.

[2] Ayele Gelan. Local economic impacts—The British Open[J]. *Annals of Tourism Research*,2003(30):406—425.

[3] L. Valdés, E. Torres, J. S. Domínguez. A model to study the economic impact of

collective accommodation in a region[J]. *Tourism Management*, 2007(28):152—161.

[4] Murillo Viu, Joaquín; Romaní Fernández, Javier; Suriach Caralt, Jordi. The impact of heritage tourism on an urban economy: the case of Granada and the Alhambra[J]. *Tourism Economics*, 2008(14):361—376.

[5] Narayan, Paresh Kumar. Economic impact of tourism on Fiji's economy: empirical evidence from the computable general equilibrium model[J]. *Tourism Economics*, 2004, 10(4): 419—434.

[6] Xiao, H. Tourism and Local Economic Development in China[J]. *Annals of Tourism Research*, 2002, 29(4):1201—1203.

[7] *LeiPer*, Neil. Why "the tourism industry" is misleading as a generic expression: The case for the plural variation, "tourism industries"[J]. *Tourism Management*, 2008, 29(2):237—251.

[8] Miller, G. Corporate responsibility in the UK tourism industry[J]. *Tourism Management*, 2001, 22(6):589—598.

[9] Lafferty, G.; Fossen, A. v. Integrating the tourism industry: problems and strategies[J]. *Tourism Management*, 2001, 22(1): 11—19.

[10] Dong, Rencai;Yu, Lijun; Liu, Guohua. Impact of tourism development on land-cover change in a matriarchal community in the Lugu Lake area[J]. *International Journal of Sustainable Development and World Ecology*, 2008, 15(1):28—35.

Chapter 12 The Socio-cultural Impact of Tourism
第十二章 旅游的社会文化影响

Learning objects：学习目标

- Appreciate the socio-cultural impact of tourism on both origin and destination within the tourism system (Leiper's model) 从旅游系统 (Leiper 模型) 客源地和目的地两方面考察旅游的社会文化影响
- Describe the benefits that tourism can realize for the society and culture of a destination 阐述旅游对目的地社会和文化带来的益处
- Explain the consequences of the lost authenticity of tourism and understand how tourism contributes to the commercialization 解释旅游失去真实性的后果以及旅游导致商品化的原因
- Appreciate the linkages that can exist between tourism and crime, such as sex tourism 理解旅游业可能与犯罪之间存在关联，如性旅游。
- Discuss the demonstration effect in both positive and negative nature 讨论积极的示范效应和消极的示范效应。
- Describe the concept of irridex and proactive responses to the different levels of the irridex 阐述愤怒指数的概念以及针对不同阶段愤怒指数应积极采取的应对措施

Ability goals：能力目标

- Case Study 案例分析：野三坡旅游发展跟踪调查
- Reading Box 阅读分析：Irridex 旅游愤怒指数

Part I Text
第一部分 课文

The Socio-cultural Impact of Tourism

【教学要点】

知识要点	掌握程度	相关章节
cross-cultural understanding 跨文化认识	一般了解	本课文是绪论，与其他章节是"纲"与"目"的关系，与课文所有章节相关联，学习教材其他章节应以本文为"纲"，作为指导整个教学的框架。
heritage preservation 遗产保护	重点掌握	
demonstration effect 示范效应	重点掌握	
commercialization of tourism 旅游商品化	重点掌握	
tourism and crime 旅游与犯罪	一般了解	
foreign control and dependency on tourism 外资控制与对过分依赖旅游业	一般了解	

The socio-cultural impacts of tourism penetrate into almost all aspects of our lives, ranging from the arts and crafts to the fundamental behavior of individuals and collective groups.[1] The impacts are both positive and negative. On one hand, tourism plays a vital role in conserving or even reviving the craft skills of the host and promoting cultural exchanges between two distinct populations. On the other hand, it speeds up the commercialization of arts and crafts, as well as ceremonies and rituals of the host, and spoils them in a certain degree. Furthermore, the impacts can create a limited and distorted impression of the destination and thus influence its cultural exchange with other populations.

Researchers tend to ignore the socio-cultural impact of tourism on the visitor population. For instance, in UK there was an increasing number of people who chose to travel in Spain during the 1960s and 1970s. English visitors' behaviors brought some changes in the Spanish habit of cooking and beverage. And two Spanish products—Paella and Rioja wine benefited a lot from these changes. Similarly, the beach-based lifestyle and the barbecue in Australia would give a deep impression on visitors and would bring about some changes in their lifestyle. In fact, almost everything, such as the clothes we wear, the food we eat and our general lifestyles and attitudes can be affected by places we visit, which best illustrates the existence of socio-cultural impacts.[2]

Socio-cultural benefits
1. Promotion of cross-cultural understanding
Lack of direct contact with a particular culture usually leads to the appearance of conventional, formulaic and oversimplified conceptions of the culture and its members. These conceptions or **stereotypes** often mislead us in our expectations of members of that culture when we encounter them. There are some commonly held stereotypes such as the beliefs that the English are unpleasantly proud and conservative, that the Scottish are gloomy and heap, and that Americans are loud, ambitious and wealthy.

Such stereotypes can, as some researchers suggest, disappear with the increase of direct contacts between tourists and residents, which are helpful to enhance their mutual understanding.[3] Extensive traveling cannot only make a person become more open-minded and tolerant but also widen his horizons. Therefore, tourism can be viewed as a powerful force for promoting **cross-cultural understanding** because of the wide variety of opportunities it offers for people to contact members of other cultures both at home and abroad.

2. *Incentive to preserve culture and heritage*

Some people believe that it is tourism that helps to conserve or restore historical buildings and sites. This can be realized through both direct and indirect ways. For example, the residents can gain benefits from these buildings and sites for they can collect entrance fees, sell souvenir and receive donations. They can also obtain part of tourism revenues for preservation. In fact, the large-scale restoration is at least in part dependent on tourism revenues. All of these can bring two distinct benefits to destination residents:

- the restoration enhances the attraction of the historical sites and therefore brings additional revenues;
- if appropriate restoration has been done, residents can appreciate their **historical heritage** directly.

Similar situation also happens to cultures and traditions. Many ceremonies and traditions have been conserved and revitalized owing to tourist demand. Otherwise, they would disappear because of the harsh attack of modernization. We can find numerous examples to prove this, such as the revival of traditional textile and glass crafts in Malta and the *naghol* ceremony in Vanuatu, in which, similar to bungee jumping, boys and young men jump from tall wooden tower. The expansion of Native American arts and crafts in the American Southwest and the revitalization of traditional dances and ceremonies on the Indonesian Island of Bali are also good examples.

3. *Fostering of social wellbeing and stability*

If all other things are equal, people who have a rich and comfortable life prefer to live in a prosperous and stable society. Tourism contributes to **social wellbeing** and stability in that it can create jobs and produce revenues and thus help to improve the level of economic development. This improvement also happens if a destination tries to offer services and health standards according to the level of the more developed countries so as to enhance its international competitiveness.[4] Meanwhile, for the development of tourism, many practical things have been done, such as the elimination of a local malaria hazard or the introduction of electricity, anti-crime measures or paved roads to the district where an international-class hotel is located. These have also brought an obvious and tangible social benefit to local residents.

Socio-cultural costs

1. *Authenticity lost*

As more and more people have realized cultural and ethnic differences, the demand for tourism products that offer cultural authenticity has been on the rise.[5] Destinations have stressed environmental, climatic and cultural differences of these products so that they can be easily separated from other tourism products in the market. Here their cultural heritage serves as a promotional device to attract more tourists. This can contribute to a growing awareness of cultural differences and greater **empathy** between tourists and local residents. However, it also reveals a deeper layer of the sociological structure and takes the risk of being further affected or changed by the introduction of tourism. The cultural authenticity is likely to be greatly eroded owing to the commercialization of the cultural events on the stage offered to tourists.

2. *Commercialization*

Tourism speeds up the commercialization of culture and art in the destination and has long been criticized for this. Crafts, ceremonies and rituals are often simplified and adapted to be more colorful, more dramatic and spectacular so that they can attract those visitors who do not have enough related knowledge to appreciate the "authentic and original version".[6] We can find countless examples to illustrate this, such as the sale of concrete carvings of Bob Marley in Jamaica, the "Bola Fiji" carved wooden knives and clubs, the Polynesian dances of Western Samoa and the limbo dancers of the Caribbean. Once culture becomes a commodity and holds big financial returns as its purpose, it is difficult to maintain its **objectivity**. Although foreign demands may be different from local demands, the preservation and restoration of decaying and dying skills and performances are to a certain extent dependent on the demands of foreign visitors who can only spend a very short time in the destination according to a fixed schedule.

3. *Prostitution*

The early European tourists chose to travel in some Third World countries partly due to these countries' liberal attitude towards sex. In some regions, sex tourism has grown up in recent years. Although the further development of this tourism has been greatly held back because of the rapid increase of AIDS, it still plays an important role in the tourism industry in some destination.[7] Some people even think that it is the sex trade that has pushed the tourism market forward in such areas, while some others insist that it is tourism that has created the social disruption associated with the sex trade. Which opinion is right is hard to determine.

4. *Demonstration effect*

The demonstration effect can bring about not only economic cost for destinations but also socio-cultural costs. Tourists tend to be wealthier than local residents. The luxurious goods they use or the drugs and liberal sexual modes showed by some "backpacker"-type tourists may attract the attention and imagination of local residents, especially young people, who may think that the outside world is superior to the local world and thus refuse to accept local culture and tradition.[8] As a result, the relationship between the older and the younger generation in local community will be greatly affected. However, **demonstration effect** is not always a one-way influence. Sometimes, tourists may be deeply impressed by destination culture attributes and try to adopt them. Therefore, the demonstration effect may bring good influence to both sides if attention is paid to avoiding negative elements of the tourist culture.

5. *Dependency*

Too much dependency on tourism or foreign control over the sector can cause a lot of problems. Among them, socio-cultural problem may indirectly result from seasonal or cyclical changes in demand which often bring about the sharp growth of unemployment rate during the off season and the pouring-in of a large number of outside workers during the high season.[9] Meanwhile, there are several reasons to explain why the high levels of **foreign control** are the source of many problems. Usually, locals can not restrain their resentment when the foreign owners take the profits back to their own countries and when high positions are occupied by non-locals. In addition, they may also have the feeling that they cannot control those events related to their daily lives. And this feeling is strengthened by the increased power of large transnational corporations, which is accumulated in the process of globalization.

From what we have discussed we come to know the socio-cultural impact is an important issue in the development of tourism. We should also aim to bring the greatest possible economic, socio-cultural and environmental benefits to a destination and lessen the associated costs to the smallest degree.[10] To reach this goal, we should understand what impacts tourism can bring and under what circumstances these impacts are most likely to happen. Considering the socio-cultural impacts does not necessarily mean that the economic and environmental impacts are of less importance. We should also keep in mind that tourism exerts the socio-cultural impacts not only on hosts but also on guests, and these impacts can be either positive or negative.

New Words

encounter	v.	遇到,偶然碰到
empathy	n.	同感;移情
open-minded	adj.	虚心的,无偏见的
stereotype	n.	老套,成规
commercialization	n.	商业化
tolerant	adj.	忍受的,容忍的
ritual	n.	仪式,典礼

Key Terms

socio-cultural impact	社会文化影响
environmental benefit	环境收益
tourism revenue	旅游收入
cross-cultural understanding	跨文化理解
socio-cultural cost	社会文化成本
historical heritage	历史遗产

Notes

1. The socio-cultural impacts of tourism penetrate into almost all aspects of our lives, ranging from the arts and crafts to the fundamental behavior of individuals and collective groups.
   旅游的社会文化影响几乎渗透到我们生活的各个方面,从艺术、手工艺到个人与集体的基本行为都可以看到这种影响。

2. In fact, almost everything, such as the clothes we wear, the food we eat and our general lifestyles and attitudes can be affected by places we visit, which best illustrates the existence of socio-cultural impacts.
   事实上,几乎一切,例如我们穿的衣服、吃的食物以及日常生活方式和态度都受到我们所到地方的影响,这些是社会文化影响存在的最好证明。

3. Such stereotypes can, as some researchers suggest, disappear with the increase of direct contacts between tourists and residents, which are helpful to enhance their mutual understanding.
   正如一些研究者所指出的那样,这样的刻板印象将随着旅游者与居民直接接触的增多而消失,这种接触有助于加强相互了解。

4. This improvement also happens if a destination tries to offer services and health standards according to the level of the more developed countries so as to enhance its international competitiveness.

   倘若目的地为增强其国际竞争力,尽力提供符合发达国家水平的服务和健康标准,那么其社会经济发展水平也会提高。

5. As more and more people have realized cultural and ethnic differences, the demand for tourism products that offer cultural authenticity has been on the rise.

   由于越来越多的人意识到不同文化和种族的差异,人们对保持文化原真性的旅游产品的需求也不断增加。

6. Crafts, ceremonies and rituals are often simplified and adapted to be more colorful, more dramatic and spectacular so that they can attract those visitors who do not have enough related knowledge to appreciate the "authentic and original version."

   工艺品、仪式和礼仪往往被简化和改变,使之更加丰富多彩、引人注目,更加壮观,以便吸引那些没有足够相关知识的游客了解欣赏其"原真性"。

7. Although the further development of this tourism has been greatly held back because of the rapid increase of AIDS, it still plays an important role in the tourism industry in some destination.

   尽管艾滋病的快速蔓延严重阻碍了性旅游的进一步发展,但有些目的地仍将其作为旅游业的重要支柱。

8. The luxurious goods they use or the drugs and liberal sexual modes showed by some "backpacker"-type tourists may attract the attention and imagination of local residents, especially young people, who may think that the outside world is superior to the local world and thus refuse to accept local culture and tradition.

   旅游者使用的奢侈品或毒品以及"背包族"开放的性观念会引起当地居民,尤其是年轻人的注意,激发他们的想象。他们可能会认为外面的世界比当地要好得多,从而拒绝接受自己本地的文化和传统。

9. Among them, socio-cultural problem may indirectly result from seasonal or cyclical changes in demand which often bring about the sharp growth of unemployment rate during the off season and the pouring-in of a large number of outside workers during the high season.

   其中,社会文化问题可能是由于需求的季节性和周期性变化间接造成的,在淡季这种变化往往引起失业率快速增长,在旺季又导致大量的外来劳工流入。

10. We should aim to bring the greatest possible economic, socio-cultural and environmental benefits to a destination and lessen the associated costs to the smallest degree.

    我们的目标应当是给目的地带来最大的经济、社会文化和环境效益,把相关成本降到最低程度。

Exercise

1. Decide whether the statements are true or false. If it is true, put "T" in the space provided and "F" if it is false.

   (1) _____ Tourism is not important in conserving or reviving the craft skills of the host and promoting cultural exchanges between two distinct populations.

   (2) _____ Many researchers tend to focus on the study of the socio-cultural

impact of tourism on the visitor population.

(3) _____ Lack of direct contact with a particular culture usually leads to the appearance of conventional, formulaic and oversimplified conceptions of the culture and its members.

(4) _____ Tourism speeds up the commercialization of culture and art in the destination that is beneficial to the destination.

(5) _____ Some people believe that it is tourism that helps to conserve or restore historical buildings and sites.

(6) _____ Locals cannot restrain their resentment when the foreign owners take the profits back to their own countries and non-locals take high positions.

(7) _____ To consider the socio-cultural impacts means that the economic and environmental impacts are of greater importance.

2. **Questions for discussion**

(1) How can tourism development preserve culture and heritage?
_____

(2) Can you give us some examples to illustrate the impact of tourism on the visitor population?
_____

(3) What are the socio-cultural benefits of tourism and what are its costs?
_____

(4) Why is the loss of authenticity regarded as a socio-cultural cost?
_____

(5) How do you understand the demonstration effect of tourism?
_____

Part II　Guided Reading
第二部分　课文导读

本文从正反两个方面阐述了旅游给目的地带来的社会文化影响。旅游活动是一种以不同地域、不同民族、不同社会以及具有不同文化传统的人群之间的相互接触为特征的活动。接触和了解异域社会和文化是某些旅游者外出旅游的重要动机。旅游者在旅游目的地的活动过程中，由于同当地居民的直接接触，其行为有意或无意地影响了当地居民的生活和行为方式，同时旅游者也会受到异国他乡的社会文化的影响。因此，我们不仅要看到旅游对目的地的社会文化影响，同时要研究旅游对旅游者自身和客源地居民的各种影响。旅游影响是双向的，不仅包含了旅游者对目的地的社会文化的冲击，也包含了旅游对于客源地的社会文化的影响。旅游活动所带来的社会文化影响既有积极的一面，又有消极的一面。

一、旅游对社会文化的积极影响

1. 有助于增进国际间的相互理解，促进双方的相互交流。

由于旅游是不同国度、不同民族、不同信仰以及不同生活方式的人们之间直接交往，而不是通过中间媒介，因而彼此能更好地相互了解。旅游是人类的和平交往，是人类文化最理想的交流方式。以旅游活动开展的对外文化交流虽然离不开政府的参与，但主要是一种民间文化交流活动，这种民间活动常常能发挥正式的外交活动所不能发挥的作用。接待地通过发展旅游，一方面可以了解别人，促进相互理解和包容；另一方面通过游客宣传本地的民族文化，树立良好形象，促进社会和谐发展。

2. 有助于传统文化的保护和发展。

体验和了解不同的文化是旅游者的主要动机之一,所以接待地在旅游开发中就有可能会重视自己历史文化遗产的保护、开发和利用,以便尽可能多地吸引旅游者。随着旅游业的发展和接待外来旅游者的需要,当地一些几乎已经被人们遗忘了的传统习俗和文化活动重又得到开发和恢复,如某些传统工艺受工业化产品和西方消费口味的冲击,正濒临绝迹,旅游业则帮助他们起死回生,传统的音乐、舞蹈、戏剧等受到重视和发掘,几近湮没的文物古迹得到维护和整修。因此,世界旅游组织指出:具有文化价值和旅游价值的东西,旅游有能力保护、拯救和复兴它们。

3. 有助于促进目的地生活环境的改善,增加社会稳定性。

为了适应旅游业发展的需要,旅游接待地区的基础设施会得以改进,生活服务设施和其他方便旅游者的设施也会有所增加。虽然这一切都是因为发展旅游业的需要,但是客观上也改善了当地居民的生活环境,方便了当地人民的生活。此外,旅游业的发展,可以促进目的地产业结构的调整,提供大量直接或间接的就业机会。一个国家或地区的旅游业越发达,带来的经济效益就越明显,从而影响当地居民的生产和生活方式,使当地居民生活水平和文化素质不断提高。这在一定程度上缩小了贫富差距,增加了社会的稳定性。

二、旅游带来的社会文化成本

1. 社会结构变化

随着旅游活动的开展,外地甚至外国众多游客的大量涌入,有意无意地带来了各自不同的价值标准、道德观念和生活方式,势必引起以往相对封闭的接待地居民价值观念上的急剧变化。由于旅游者往往来自经济发达和收入比较高的地区,其自身意识、生活方式以及言谈举止都能够产生示范效应,当地居民会因此产生崇洋媚外的心理,导致当地居民传统的社会心理与行为方式等发生变化,甚至有可能带来家庭和社会结构的变化,如离婚率上升、放弃自己的传统工作到旅游行业工作等。此外,由于旅游目的地利益主体在旅游发展中的利益分配不均,造成部分居民因没有获得应有的旅游收入对游客产生敌意态度,影响社区和谐和社会稳定。

2. 文化商业化

传统的民间习俗和庆典活动都是在传统的特定时间、特定地点,按照传统规定的内容和方式举行的。但是,为了迎合旅游者的需求和经济利益的驱使,许多传统活动都纷纷被搬上舞台,为了迎合旅游者一时的兴趣,压缩、修改传统的表演程式。这些传统和庆典虽然通过表演的形式被保留下来,但已经基本上失去了其原有的意义。而大多数旅游者并不可能真正关注接待地传统文化的真实内涵,仅仅只是从猎奇的角度在旅游过程中去追求美感、新鲜感。旅游企业开发的过程中也经常为了使产品更符合市场的需求,而把原有的传统文化加以改动,使目的地文化不再具有原真性,成为一种固定的商业表演,这就不可避免地造成了接待地传统文化在旅游发展过程中被商业化、程序化,大大降低了传统文化的吸引力。

3. 性旅游兴起

在西方一些国家,一些旅游者为寻求不受禁止的、暂时性的性享受而去国外旅游已经不是什么新鲜的现象。欧洲早期的旅游者去一些第三世界国家旅游,在某种程度上就是抱着对性行为的放纵态度。近年来,一些旅游客源市场"性旅游"的人数有所增长,而一些旅游目的地也在积极推销性内容的旅游产品。艾滋病的蔓延使这种旅游的发展速度有所减慢,但它还占有一定的市场份额。当然,是旅游导致了社会道德沦丧与性交易,还是因为一些卖淫活动刺激了旅游市场,这是一个值得研究的问题。

4. 不良示范效应

随着旅游活动的开展,旅游者不可避免地会将自己的生活方式带到旅游目的地。特别是在国际旅游方面,由于旅游者来自世界各地,具有不同的价值标准、道德观念和生活方式,这些东西无形之中也在传播和渗透,对目的地社会产生"示范效应"。虽然旅游者和当地居民的行为是相互作用和相互影响的,但实际上,旅游者对目的地的社会影响更大一些。旅游者对目的地的社会影响主要表现在:首先,思想和行为变化。目的地居民开始模仿,继而发展到有意识地追求游客的生活方式和行为,从而使如赌博、吸毒等不良社会现象增多,影响社会稳定。其次,受西方性自由思想的影响,传统的道德观念受到冲击,使得离婚率不断上升。最后,崇洋媚外的思想泛滥。由于旅游者在目的地集中消费的原因,目的地居民普遍认为游客来自的地方或国家比自己的居住地好,因此产生一种自卑心理,崇尚外来文化。

5. 过于依赖旅游业

一个国家或地区不宜过分依赖旅游业来发展自己的经济。旅游活动有很大的季节性,如果过于依赖旅游业,在淡季时旅游接待地不可避免地出现劳动力和生产资料闲置或严重的失业问题,从而会给接待地区带来严重的社会和经济问题。此外,旅游会受到很多因素的影响,一旦非旅游业所能控制的因素发生,导致旅游需求大幅度下降,整个国家或地区的旅游业就会受挫,造成严重的社会问题和经济问题。因此,任何一个国家或地区都应控制好旅游业在国民经济中所占的比例。

在我们审视旅游的社会文化影响时,我们应该看到任何文化交流,不论是旅游带来的文化交流还是其他途径产生的文化交流,都不可避免地使交流双方受到相互影响。至于双方在多大程度上接受和吸收对方的影响,则须视这些影响的具体情况而定。但通常来讲,旅游者对旅游目的地社会文化影响是巨大的,在开发旅游地的时候,必须充分评估旅游目的地的社会容量,只有充分认识旅游对目的地可能产生的各种社会文化的影响,才能因地制宜、统筹兼顾,做到旅游目的地社会、文化、经济的和谐发展。

旅游知识测试

正误判断:请在正确的选题上划√,错误的选题上划×。

1. 旅游的社会文化影响是双向影响,既有对目的地的影响,也有对客源地的影响,但总体而言,旅游对客源地的影响超过了对旅游目的地的影响。

2. 由于旅游者来自世界各地,具有不同的价值标准、道德观念和生活方式,这些东西无形之中也在传播和渗透,对目的地社会产生"示范效应"。这种示范效应是负面的。

3. 性旅游的漏损很小,产生的乘数效应却很大,对当地社区的经济发展有较大的支撑作用,在一些国家被视为合法行业,产生了良好的社会经济效应。

4. 文化遗产不能出售,也不能商品化,因为这将不可避免地造成接待地传统文化的商业化、程序化,大大降低传统文化的吸引力,产生负面的社会文化影响。

5. 旅游是对国民经济的拉动作用很大,所以各国都在大力发展旅游业,旅游在国民经济中的比例越大越好。

第十二章 旅游的社会文化影响

Part III　Case Study
第三部分　案例研究

野三坡旅游发展跟踪调查

分析要点

1. 旅游对野三坡居民的经济意识和消费倾向有何影响？请举例说明。
2. 你怎样看待野三坡居民生活中出现的各种变化？这些变化是否影响野三坡社会结构的变迁？
3. 保护当地社区的社会文化与旅游开发是否矛盾？野三坡案例能否说明"旅游能够提高人们的文明素质"？
4. 野三坡并非所有的人都在从事旅游业。你认为野三坡旅游经营者与非旅游经营者的利益应该如何分配？
5. 野三坡东道主与游客的关系如何？你认为应当怎样融洽双方的关系？为什么？

相关理论和问题

1. 旅游商品化（Commercialization of tourism）
2. 企业伦理（Corporate ethics）
3. 示范效应（Demonstration effect）
4. 东道主与客人关系（Relation between host and guest）

　　野三坡位于河北省保定市涞水县境内，北部和北京房山接壤，距北京市中心约100公里。由于交通和历史方面的原因，这里虽然毗邻首都，长期以来却与外界隔绝。在20世纪80年代中期开发旅游之前，当地依然保持着山区农村的传统习俗和朴实的民风。1985年正式开发旅游之后，打破了当地与外界常年隔绝的状况，野三坡在经济、社会、文化等方面都发生了显著的变化。

　　1991年，刘振礼教授在野三坡进行了有关旅游对接待地社会文化影响的问卷调查，并采取了以旅游强度序列来代替旅游的发展阶段序列的变通方法，分别在风景区内选择了交通不便、游人尚未涉足的南禅房，距景点较远、个别农户从事旅游业的上庄，和旅游热点、80%以上农户从事旅游业的下庄进行问卷调查。问卷的内容涉及经济、文化、婚姻、家庭、审美、社交、消闲等生活的各主要方面。通过对以上几方面调查结果的分析，得出了旅游的社会文化影响有利方面占了主导地位，尤以经济方面最为突出和旅游影响具有阶段性等初步结论。

　　1991年以后，当地的旅游业持续高速发展，并由尝试、成长逐步走向成熟。在原有以自然景观为主的基础上，先后开放了建设度假村——苗寨、风情苑、蒙古包等人造景点，并通过实施旅游扶贫工程、举办各种节庆和系列夏令营活动等措施，不断地把旅游开发引向深入。1994年，旅游客流量达50万人次。随着旅游业的蓬勃发展和游客的大量进入，当地的经济迅速增长。与此同时，在风俗习惯、消费观念、人际关系等方面也发生了较大变化。所以，刘振礼教授进行了一次跟踪调查，在与上次调研的结果相比较的基础上，探求旅游深入发展对接待地社会文化的影响机制和实际状况。

　　经过6年的跟踪调查，旅游活动对野三坡的社会、经济、文化等产生了影响，当地的居民生活发生了以下变化：

一、经济状况。旅游的开发带动了当地经济的全面发展，在其他资源较匮乏、经济相对落后的野三坡地区，旅游已经成为当地经济发展的支柱性产业。旅游开发前的1984年，下庄村年人均收入仅70元，1991年的调研结果为800多元，1994年年人均收入上升到1200元。而这次调研，下庄的年人均收入比1994年翻了一番，达到了2400元左右。距景点较近的下庄和苟各庄已成为全县有名的富裕村。随着人们由旅游中获取收入的增加，人们对当地自然资源利用方式的认识有了进一步的变化。开发旅游前，人们只知道将其用于农林、畜牧，上次调研中，有74.5%的人希望将其用于旅游；而在此次调研中，有高达85.9%的人希望将自然资源用于旅游发展。

二、经济意识。在野三坡开发旅游的过程中，当地村民的经济意识也发生了深刻的变化。最初人们不相信当地能发展旅游，在游客来了以后也只是拿他们当亲人相待，食宿均不收报酬，"主客间仿佛是亲戚关系，彼此不计较经济得失"。后来随着经济意识的增强，人们广开脑筋寻找致富门路，或开设家庭旅馆和饭馆，或出租马匹、马车，但与此同时，当地的淳朴之风减弱，出现了不择手段追逐金钱的现象，敲诈勒索时有发生。

跟踪调查发现：一方面，由于当地旅游管理部门会同县里其他管理部门的综合治理，对损害游客的行为进行了严厉打击；另一方面，当地村民在认识上有了新变化，他们在树立市场观念的同时，逐步认识到游客是上帝，"没有游客，就没有财路，自己也就没有了饭碗"。只有通过改善服务环境，提高服务质量和水平，让游客满意，才能吸引更多的游客前来。近年来，当地的饭馆、骑马、乘车的服务水平均有所提高，文明经商、礼貌待客已逐渐形成风气。更可贵的是，当地村民普遍树立起法制观念，即使偶尔与游客发生争执，也学会了主动找旅游管理所的执法人员进行协调处理。

三、消费倾向。在消费倾向方面，发展旅游后带来的影响也可以从上庄、下庄之间的比较中看出。在旅游发达的下庄，多数村民打算把积蓄花费在扩大生产和子女教育两个项目上，与城市居民的观念较为接近。上庄村民则集中在盖房和购买大件用品上。此外，下庄人在满足生活基本需要后有5人提出愿外出旅游，而上庄仅有1人。

四、审美视觉。在旅游开发中，当地居民的审美视觉也发生着巨大的变化。以对服饰的态度为例，越来越多的人开始喜欢城市的流行服饰。从统计结果中看，虽然选择当地一般服饰的人居多数，但考虑到当地居民现今一般服饰与城市居民服饰日趋接近，人们在审美倾向上，逐步摆脱了以往的传统认识。部分年轻人的装束已与外来的城市青年难以区分。但在审美倾向都市化的同时，当地居民对当地的民间艺术依然充满自豪感，所有回答"对当地民间艺术的看法"这一问题的人，都无一例外地选择了"感到自豪"这项内容。

五、人际关系。旅游的发展，特别是旅游带来的经济收益，使得人们对与陌生人交往表现出浓厚的兴趣。与1991年相比，下庄村无大的变化，认为与血缘关系之外的人交往"绝对必要"和"有必要"的占很大比例。上庄这两项虽有较大幅度的波动，但除了由于样本选择的差别造成影响之外，依据在调查中了解的情况，主要反映出被调查者心理个性方面的特点。从调查中可以看出人们对接待游客的积极态度。由于发展旅游后不同家庭间的竞争关系、邻里间协作关系的金钱化以及经营家庭旅馆的村民所接待的游客与不经营旅游的村民间产生的冲突，有部分村民认为发展旅游后，影响了邻里关系，但绝大多数人认为旅游的发展对家庭内部关系及子女没带来任何影响。

六、婚姻家庭。在婚姻目的方面，统计结果与1991年的调查并无大的差别，传宗接代、互相照顾生活仍构成结婚的两个主要目的，出于感情需要结婚的人数比以往有所增加。多数人对自己的婚姻状况较满意，并期望夫妻白头偕老。在1991年的报告中得出了随着旅游发展，婚姻中感情因素比重在增长的结论。但是通过此次调研结果分析可知，旅游对社会结构，特别是家庭与婚姻观念的改变尽管可能产生一些影响，但对彼此做出的判断需要在更长的时间内才能得到检验和确认。夏威夷岛开发初期那种旅游发展威胁到家庭关系、导致离婚率提高的现象，在野三坡并未发生。

七、当地居民对旅游社会影响的综合判断。在此次调查中,增设了当地居民对旅游社会影响的综合判断这项内容,选取了妇女地位、青年地位、社会治安及传统风俗等8个方面,由当地居民做出变好、变坏或不变的选择(旅游开发前后相比较)。此项研究仅局限在旅游较发达的下庄。

从以上调查可以看出,旅游对当地居民社会文明程度、生活质量等方面的影响,多属于积极方面,妇女和青年地位的提高成为明显的事实。对于旅游带来较多的就业机会及促使生活质量和社会文明程度提高方面,也几乎众口一词。对于社会治安方面的影响,人们认识上有较大差异:一部分人认为旅游开发后,当地的青年人大多有了工作,打架的人比以前少了;另一部分人则认为受金钱万能思想的腐蚀,赌博等各种违法现象有所抬头。

20多年来,野三坡的社会经济生活已经发生了深刻的变化。在开发之初,封闭落后的山区百姓尚不知旅游为何物,常常把旅游叫成"流油",看到城里的姑娘身穿泳衣还骂为"伤风败俗",现在他们开办了500多个家庭旅馆、商店,有100多辆私家车、出租车,20多家企业网站,10余个水上游乐项目,8家旅行社。新一代的山里人已变成懂经营会管理的老板、经理,过去朴实的山里人已变成思想前卫的旅游人。

资料来源:刘赵平,再论旅游时接待地的社会文化影响[J],旅游学刊,1998,(1)

Part IV Reading Box
第四部分 阅读与分析

Irridex

阅读分析要点

1. 东道主愤怒的原因
2. 愤怒指数分级
3. 不同群体对游客"愤怒"的程度
4. 愤怒指数的缺陷

Sometimes direct contact and the demonstration effect can result in negative socio-cultural impacts. A case in point is the performance of **oversimplified and commercialized events** for the purpose of displaying traditional crafts and customs, which in fact often brings results contrary to the expectations of the destination and offers little for tourists as far as rich cultural experience is concerned. Negative socio-cultural impacts can also occur due to improper tourism management and the failure to realize the full economic potential.[1] For instance, local residents may feel indignant because most tourism-related jobs, especially some high positions, are taken by foreigners and most investment in tourism projects is also made by foreigners. Furthermore, they may become more irritated and even conflict with tourists for the reason that they are forbidden to enjoy certain tourism facilities such as private beaches and transport services.[2]

The real **difference in wealth** between the tourists and their hosts can be the cause of a major problem. Of course, many tourists are much wealthier than the hosts they encounter. But there are also some tourists who would spend what they have saved in an extravagant way on vacation. This makes the difference more distinct. And it is impossible for the ordinary hosts to learn about the normal spending habits of the tourists and thus a feeling of resentment may arise among them.[3] The following index drawn up by George Doxey can be used to measure **the level of irritation** brought about by direct contact between the tourist and the host:

1. **Euphoria**

The beginning of tourism development often arouses excitement and enthusiasm among the locals who are eager to attract an increasing number of tourists to their community. Tourists are regarded as the honorable guests. The relationship between host and tourists are very good.

2. **Apathy**

When tourism develops and expands to a certain degree, the locals will lose their interest and take it as a way to earn big profits. They tend to contact with tourists on a commercial and formal basis, and try to make as more profits as possible from tourists.

3. **Irritation**

When tourism develops into a stage when further expansion is impossible, hosts have to provide additional facilities to meet the demand of the increasing number of tourists. Contradictions between host and tourists emerge. Some improper tourist behaviors make locals angry.

4. **Antagonism**

At this stage, tourists are regarded as the source of all problems. The hosts express their hatred openly and take it for granted that tourists should be exploited. In some destinations, locals regard tourists as unfriendly "ants"; tourists regard locals as greedy "wolves".

5. **Resignation**

Local residents cannot do anything but resign themselves to the reality and try to get used to the changes of community settings.[4] Tourists who are hurt choose to travel in other destinations, which can lead to a comprehensive and complete impact on the local community.

The irridex is not completely supported by the research based on practical experiences. The point which incurs much criticism is its treatment of the local community as an entity composed of people of the same type.[5] In reality, people react to tourism in very different ways, due to their **socioeconomic status** or whether they work within or outside of the tourism industry. A major factor influencing their attitude is whether they can benefit from the tourists to a certain extent, regardless of the overall effect on the community.[6] Meanwhile, if we can differentiate the tourist "market" in a psychographical way, we can also use this method to classify residents into **allocentrics** and **psychocentrics** who hold very different opinions towards tourists, although this point of view has not yet been proved with evidence.[7]

The assumption of the irridex that local community can only react passively to the changes of tourism market instead of taking the initiative to develop the market has brought about a lot of criticism.[8] In fact, in response to the worsening of the local situation, many communities will try to deal with tourism development with various official or unofficial measures such as staying indoors, slowing down development, introducing or changing zoning, introducing quotas, education programs, and improving infrastructure. In this way an **antagonistic response** can be avoided.

New Words

extravagant	adj.	过度的；奢侈的
irridex	n.	激怒指数
exploit	v.	利用；剥削
index	n.	指标，指数
irritation	n.	激怒，愤怒
apathy	n.	漠不关心，冷淡
euphoria	n.	兴奋，心情愉快
antagonism	n.	对抗，敌对
resignation	n.	放弃，屈从

Notes

1. Negative socio-cultural impacts can also occur due to improper tourism management and the failure to realize the full economic potential.
   旅游管理不当，以及未能充分实现其经济潜力也会导致负面的社会文化影响。

2. They may become more irritated and even conflict with tourists for the reason that they are forbidden to enjoy certain tourism facilities such as private beaches and transport services.
   他们可能变得更加气愤，甚至与旅游者发生冲突，原因是他们被禁止使用某些旅游设施，如私人海滩和交通服务。

3. And it is impossible for the ordinary hosts to learn about the normal spending habits of the tourists and thus a feeling of resentment may arise among them.
   普通的东道主不可能了解旅游者的正常消费习惯，因此会对他们感到不满。

4. Local residents cannot do anything but resign themselves to the reality and try to get used to the changes of the community setting.
   当地居民除了强迫自己接受现实，并努力适应社区环境的巨大变化之外别无选择。

5. The point which incurs much criticism is its treatment of the local community as an entity composed of people of the same type.
   这一理论认为当地社区是由同一类型的人组成的一个主体，因此招致了大量批评。

6. A major factor influencing their attitude is whether they can benefit from the tourists to a certain extent, regardless of the overall effect on the community.
   影响他们态度的一个主要因素是他们能否在某种程度上从游客那里受益，而不管这些游客对社区会产生怎样的整体影响。

7. Meanwhile, if we can differentiate the tourist "market" in a psychographical way, we can also use this method to classify residents into allocentrics and psychocentrics who hold very different opinions towards tourists, although this point of view has not yet been proved with evidence.
   同时，如果我们能从心理和性格分析入手来区分旅游者市场，我们也能用这种方法把居民分为多中心型和自我中心型两种。他们对旅游者持不同的态度，尽管还没有证据来证明这种观点。

8. The assumption of the irridex that local community can only react passively to the changes of tourism market instead of taking the initiative to develop the market has

brought about a lot of criticism.

愤怒指数假设，当地社区对旅游市场的变化只能做出被动反应，而不能主动采取措施发展市场，这一假设招致了大量的批评。

Topic discussion

1. According to the author, what are the causes of negative socio-cultural impacts?
2. What are the indexes used to measure the level of irritation brought about by direct contact between the tourist and the host?
3. At the stage of apathy, what attitude do the local people hold towards tourism?
4. Why is the irridex not completely supported by the research based on practical experience?
5. What measures can be taken to reduce the irridex of the local people and increase the harmony between tourists and the local community?

【即学即用】

With reference to the theory, information or approach applied in the Reading Box, have a case study of the irridex in a resort or a community you know. Make presentation of your study in Chinese or in English using PPT.

【学习资源库】

为了掌握本章更多的相关专业知识，请您登陆 http://sicnu.edu.cn/，点击国家双语教学示范课程《旅游学概论》，进入网络学堂查询相关资料。

Chapter Review 本章小结

This chapter has discussed the benefits and costs that development of tourism bring about on the destination community. However, we should bear in mind that tourism activity exerts the socio-cultural impacts not only on hosts but also on guests. On one hand, tourism activity contributes to cross-cultural understanding, heritage preservation, social well-being and stability; on the other hand, it enhances the commercialization of cultures, lost authenticity, and demonstration effect in the destination. People react to tourism in very different ways because of their socioeconomic status or whether they work within or outside of the tourism sectors. The index drawn up by George Doxey can be used to measure the level of irritation brought about by direct contact between the tourist and the host. The assumption of the irridex that local community can only react passively to the changes of tourism market instead of taking the initiative to develop the market has incurred a lot of criticism.

第十二章 旅游的社会文化影响

Part V　Additional Know-how of Tourism
第五部分　旅游知识扩展

【关键术语】

Culture：the totality of socially transmitted behavior patterns, arts, beliefs, institutions, and all other products of human work and thought that are characteristic of the destination population.

文化：反映一个目的地人口特征的社会行为模式、艺术、信仰、习俗、思想和人造景观的总称。

Built environment：the components or activities within a tourism destination that have been created by humans. These include the infrastructure and superstructure of the destination, as well as the customs of its people, and technology they use, the culture they have developed, and the system of governance that regulates their behaviors.

建成环境：在一个旅游目的地内部,由人类创造的环境组成要素或人类活动。这些要素和活动包括旅游目的地的基础设施和上层建筑,以及当地的习俗,当地人使用的技术、他们的文化,以及规范、他们行为的管理体系。

Commodification：in tourism, the process whereby a destination's culture is gradually converted into a saleable commodity or product in response to the perceived or actual demands of the tourist market

旅游商品化：在旅游业中,为了回应旅游市场已感知到的或实际的需求而将目的地文化逐步转化为可出售商品的过程。

Paradox of resentment：the idea that problems of resentment and tension can result whether tourists are integrated with, or isolated from, the local community

怨恨悖论：无论旅游者融合或孤立于当地社区,都会造成的怨恨和紧张的问题。

Irridex：a theoretical model proposing that resident attitudes evolve from euphoria to apathy, then irritation, antagonism and finally resignation, as the intensity of tourism development increases within a destination

愤怒指数：一种理论模型:随着目的地旅游开发强度不断增加,当地居民的态度会从最开始的兴奋变为冷淡、恼怒、对立,直到最后退出。

【知识链接】

1. 旅游与文化变迁

旅游者和旅游地居民是生活在不同文化范式(cultural paradigm)之下的,其观念形态、生活方式、语言习惯等因素通常带有不同的文化色彩,他们所代表的是两种内质和规则都不尽相同的文化系统。当旅游者进入旅游目的地,其自身所携带的"客位文化"必然会对当地的"主位文化"造成一定的冲击,影响到目的地的生活形态、社会构造等诸方面,由此又带来环境和人的联动变化,即引起文化变迁(cultural variation)。东道主社区或社会的文化变迁实质上可以看做是旅游地原始文化和旅游者外来文化两个相互开放的文化系统之间随着其碰撞发生的持续的交互适应,且在变迁过程中,两个"对峙"系统内部是不断地进行自组织修复的。值得注意的是,旅游所导致的旅游地文化的变迁是不可规避的,要做好旅游文化资源的保护性开发,必须秉承费孝通先生提出的对待"他者"文化"美人之美,美美与共"的文化观。人类学提倡"文化相对观"(cultural relativity),认为每种文化都应该放在该文化的背景中来看待。因此,对待任何文化都不能持民族自我中心的偏见,不能以为某一种文化一定就高于另一种文化,这是文化间相处的基本准则,结合生物多样性问题来考虑,文化相对观实际上又具有保证人类社会持续发展的意义。因此,游客不应居高临下地观光猎奇,而是要设身处地,学会站在文化主位,即以当地人的观点看问题,自觉接受多元文化互补共存的人类现实。只有这样,才能保障旅游及其文化的可持续发展。

2. 旅游与民族认同意识

民族认同,首先表现为对族性(ethnicity)本身即原生要素的认同,就是人们依据各自的语言、文化、血缘、出生地、种族和宗教等来寻求自己属于某一个民族共同体的意识;其次再表现出对族性群体的认同,即在与不同民族的交往过程中形成的族际观念及其相应的行为方式,主要表现为对内维持民族凝聚力及对外区分我族与他族的两个方面。也正是基于这样一种认同,才唤起了人们对本民族的生存发展、荣辱兴衰、利害得失等等方面的认识、关切与维护。由此可见,民族认同是民族的社会存在的反映,是对"周围的可感知的环境的一种意识,是对一个人以外的其他人和其他民族联系的一种意识"。只有意识到别的民族存在,有本民族与别的民族的意识时,才会产生民族认同,而且还随着不同民族接触与交往的广泛深入在一定阶段呈现出增强的趋势。在旅游过程中,接待地的居民肯定自觉不自觉地要与各种各样的国内外游客打交道,而在日益频繁的接触中又往往会唤起他们对自身归属的认识,进而引起他们对自身身份表述的强烈关注。同时,在旅游业迅猛发展和国际交往不断加强的特定情势下,每一个民族一般都会抓住这一难得的契机展示自己、张扬自己,以是其中的一分子而感到自豪和骄傲,并借机树立自我形象,强化民族认同感。

【小思考】

1. 怎样减少旅游对目的居民的地社会文化的不良影响,你认为怎样才能做到游客与东道主和谐相处?

参考阅读:

在旅游目的地,社会文化变迁与社会心理变化是同时存在的。由于许多旅游景区(点)所处的地理位置比较偏僻,经济相对不发达,这种变化本来是缓慢的、渐进的,但是由于旅游业的发展,旅游者的涌入,这种缓慢的进程很快被破坏,取而代之的是急剧的、跳跃式的变化。社会文化和社会心理的变化都容易受到旅游者的示范作用影响。旅游者带来的强势文化与当地的相对弱势文化接触时,当地的弱势文化更多地受到旅游者强势文化的影响。旅游地居民在文化冲击下,自觉、不自觉地将旅游者的行为方式、价值观念融入自身的行为、思想中。这时,当地居民可分为三种类型。第一种是以青年人为代表的进取型居民,他们在社会中起到先锋的作用。他们在文化的各个层面吸收外来的文化,当地文化结构将很快被瓦解。随着对外来文化的不断吸收,他们的个体心理开始发生变化,其中有积极的,也有消极的。第二种是以老年人为代表的守旧型居民。传统的价值观和行为模式在他们身上已经根深蒂固,面对旅游业带来的巨大冲击,采取逃避的态度。他们是传统价值观念最忠实的守卫者,具有怀旧心理。第三种是反社会型居民。他们是不可忽略的一群人。由于对旅游业发展带来的冲击不知如何是好,现有的价值观和生活方式已经行不通了,新的观念却尚未形成或难以形成,思想出现混乱,心里发生变异,对旅游者产生敌对情绪。

2. 旅游文化的功能有哪些?和一般的文化相比,旅游文化的特殊性体现在哪些地方?

参考阅读:

旅游文化是在自然和社会发展进程中所形成的生活方式系统,是旅游者这一旅游主体借助旅游媒介(旅行社、饭店、旅游交通和各类旅游服务中介机构)等外部条件,通过对旅游客体的能动活动而产生的各种旅游文化现象的总和。它包括旅游主体文化、旅游客体文化和旅游介体文化。旅游文化作为文化的一个子系统,除了具有文化的一般功能外,其自身还有特殊功能。

独特的旅游文化是旅游目的地吸引力的源泉。旅游主体的旅游动机是文化驱使的结果。现代旅游本质上是一种高层次的精神需求和审美享受,是旅游者对文化的诉求。文化旅游、科技旅游、教育旅游、工业旅游、农业旅游以及其他各种形式的自助旅游的兴起,充分展现了旅游者主体意识的不断增强和对文化享受的不断追求。

旅游文化指导着旅游资源的开发。旅游资源的开发不仅要以市场为导向,充分满足旅游者的消费需求,更重要的是坚持旅游文化的指导作用。缺乏旅游文化指导的旅游开发,容易造成旅游地资源品位和格调的下降。一味迎合旅游者的消费需求会带来旅游资源开发的庸俗化倾向,使旅游地的文化特色消失。

旅游文化推动国际文化的交流。不同国家或地区的旅游者,虽然自身所处的文化背景不同,但并不影响他们对中国古典园林、古希腊神庙和欧洲哥特式教堂的理解和欣赏。尽管不同的旅游者欣赏水平和理解层次有差别,但是建筑作为一种世界语言理应能够被全世界旅游者所阅读。欣赏有形的旅游文化是我们了解异国文化、促进国际交流的重要内容。我国重要风景区的旅游资源还具有科学、文化和历史价值。可以说,保护当地旅游文化就是保护当地的优良文化传统。

Part VI　Further Readings
第六部分　课外阅读

如果您想进一步学习本章的内容,探讨旅游的社会文化的影响,建议您阅读以下学者的著作和论文。

一、中文部分

[1] 方志远.旅游文化概论[M].广州:华南理工大学出版社,2005.
[2] 张继涛.旅游主体文化的特征分析[J].湖北大学学报(哲学社会科学版),2003(05).
[3] 刘赵平.社会交换理论在旅游社会文化影响研究中的应用[J].旅游科学,1998,(04).
[4] 卢松,张捷,李东和,杨效忠,唐文跃.旅游地居民对旅游影响感知和态度的比较——以西递景区与九寨沟景区为例[J].地理学报,2008,(06).
[5] 李祝舜,蒋艳.欠发达旅游地社会文化变迁与社会心理现代化[J].北京第二外国语学院学报,2003,(6).
[6] 肖佑兴.旅游影响生成机制探析[J].旅游科学,2006,(06).
[7] 刘振礼.旅游对接待地的社会影响及对策[J].旅游学刊,1992,(03).
[8] 刘赵平.旅游对目的地社会文化影响研究结构框架[J].桂林旅游高等专科学校学报,1999,(01).
[9] 朱华,董婷.政府主导下社区参与的民族村寨旅游开发模式——以北川县擂鼓镇吉娜羌寨为例[J].西华大学学报(哲学社会科学版),2011,(06).
[10] 孙九霞,保继刚.社区参与的旅游人类学研究——阳朔世外桃源案例[J].广西民族学院学报(哲学社会科学版),2006,(01).

二、英文部分

[1] Paul Brunt, Paul Courtney. Host perceptions of sociocultural impact [J].

Annals of Tourism Research,1999(26).

[2] Peggy Teo. Assessing socio-cultural impacts: the case of Singapore. [J] Tourism Management,1994(15).

[3] Jan Vidar Haukeland. Sociocultural impacts of tourism in Scandinavia: Studies of three host communities[J]. Tourism Management,1984(5).

[4] Paris Tsartas. Socioeconomic impacts of tourism on two Greek isles. [J] Annals of Tourism Research,1992(19).

[5] Alexis Saveriades. Establishing the social tourism carrying capacity for the tourist resorts of the east coast of the Republic of Cyprus[J]. Tourism Management,2000(21).

[6] Kadir H. Din. Social and cultural impacts of tourism[J]. Annals of Tourism Research,1988(15).

[7] Allen, Long, Perdue, et al. The impact of tourism development on residents' perceptions of community life [J]. Journal of Travel Research,1998(27).

[8] Yooshik Yoon, Dogan Gursoy, Joseph S. Chen. Validating a tourism development theory with structural equation modeling [J]. Tourism Management,2001(22).

[9] Gyan P. Nyaupane, Duarte B. Morais, Lorraine Dowler. The role of community involvement and number/type of visitors on tourism impacts: A controlled comparison of Annapurna, Nepal and Northwest Yunnan, China[J]. Tourism Management,2006(27).

[10] Dong Wan Ko, William P Stewart. A structural equation model of residents attitudes for tourism development [J]. Tourism Management,2002(23).

Chapter 13 Environmental Impact Assessment of Tourism
第十三章 旅游环境影响评估

Learning objects：学习目标

- Appreciate the ecological and environmental impact of tourism on the destination within the tourism system (Leiper's model) 在旅游系统（Leiper 模型）中考察旅游对目的地的生态和环境影响
- Understand the positive and the negative environmental consequences of tourism activity for destinations 了解旅游活动给目的地带来的正面和负面的环境结果
- Describe the costs on environment brought about by tourism development 阐述旅游开发对环境造成的各项成本
- Understand the procedures of environmental impact assessment for any tourism development project 了解任何一项旅游开发项目应当采取的环境影响评估程序
- Take into account both the benefits and costs incurred by tourism activity using the environmental balance sheet 运用环境平衡表考察旅游活动产生的利益和成本
- Identify the variables of checklists which are used to assess environmental impacts 指出检查表中用于环境影响评估的变量
- Appreciate the carrying capacity which is used to measure the physical, environmental, economical, social and cultural thresholds 了解衡量物理、环境、经济以及社会文化影响承载力的阈值

Ability goals：能力目标

- Case Study 案例分析：旅游环境容量的测算——以四川省宜宾地区为例
- Reading Box 阅读分析：Carrying Capacity 承载力

Part I Text
第一部分 课文

Environmental Impact Assessment of Tourism

【教学要点】

知识要点	掌握程度	相关章节
environmental consequence 环境后果	一般了解	本课文与第 1 单元、第 3 单元、第 4 单元、第 5 单元、第 7 单元、第 8 单元、第 10 单元、第 14 单元、第 15 单元相关内容有联系。
environmental impact assessment 环境影响评估	重点掌握	
environmental balance sheet 环境平衡表	重点掌握	
checklist of the environmental impact 环境影响检查表	重点掌握	
performance indicator 成绩衡量指标（绩效指标）	一般了解	
the natural environment and the built environment 自然环境与人造环境	一般了解	

Although the environment, including natural and artificial environment, is one of the most important components of the tourism product, it is vulnerable to change or modification because of tourism activity during various stages of the tourist area life cycle.[1] To select a proper environmental impact assessment requires a deep understanding of the importance of environmental balance. In some areas, tourism/environment balance sheets have been adopted to evaluate the final effects of tourism development in terms of the environment. For example, Scotland has used this approach and has come to the conclusion that in spite of the widespread environmental impacts resulting from tourism activity, tourism still plays a very significant role in the economy, and that these impacts are serious in only a few areas and can be overcome with careful management. Environment balance sheet takes into account both the benefits and costs incurred by tourism activity.

Environmental balance sheet

The specific benefits that the physical environment gets from tourism activity are as follows:
- more beautiful and attractive environment is created owing to the adoption of environmental improvement schemes to attract more visitors, such as urban regeneration, reclamation projects and conservation schemes;[2]
- disused buildings are adapted and restored so that they can be used to receive and entertain visitors;
- an increasing number of recreation and sporting facilities is provided for both locals and visitors;
- historic buildings and ancient sites are restored and revitalized;
- infrastructure including roads, car-parks, footpaths and transport services are built and improved;
- design based on the tourist demand is encouraged and the improvement of environmental quality in the tourism development process is appreciated.

The costs on environment brought about by tourism development were supposed to be:
- **volume pressure**—too many tourists often cause damages to such things as footpaths, wildlife, vegetation, and areas of wilderness and even result in the loss of peace and quiet;
- **traffic pressure**—this is usually brought about by narrow roads, parking problems, too many vehicles (caravans) on main routes and the pollution caused by increased traffic. And it happens at some specific locations;
- **visual pressure**—from point of view of aesthetics, some tourism facilities are not in a high quality because of poor setting, design or inadequate check. Caravan sites and ski centers are good examples here;
- **waste pressure**—the large number of tourists has brought a large quantity of rubbish which threatens wildlife if it is not disposed of properly and adequately;
- **user conflict pressure**—lack of natural resources is bound to result in user conflict. For example, with the rapid growth of the tourists who are interested in such activities as bird watching, walking, climbing and photography, related facilities become insufficient and users are less satisfied with the services offered. More obviously, the same resource is often used competitively to attract tourists and thus causes conflict, such as the competitive use of water between jet-skiing or power boating and fishing or other water-based recreations.

The EIA process

The environment impact assessment is a tool used to identify the potential environmental impacts of any proposed development project before decisions are made.[3] Checklists and network systems are two of a variety of methods used to assess environmental impacts. A checklist of environmental impacts which is composed of fundamental elements such as risk can be made when potential impacts of tourism activity are predicted.[4] This checklist can then be used to evaluate whether the proposed development projects will have no impact, minor impacts, moderate impacts or major impacts on each of the fundamental elements.

Checklist of the environmental impacts

The natural environment
  (a) Changes in the composition of species of animals and plants
  - Disturbance of breeding habits
  - Killing of animals through hunting
  - Killing of animals in order to supply goods for the souvenir trade
  - Migration of animals towards the inside or the outside
  - Ruin of vegetation through the gathering of wood or plants
  - Change in extent and/or nature of vegetation cover through clearance or planting according to the need of building tourism facilities[5]
  - Creation of a wildlife reserve/sanctuary
  (b) Pollution
  - Water pollution through discharges of sewage, spillage of oil/petrol
  - Air pollution from vehicle emissions

- Noise pollution from tourist transportation and activities

(c) Erosion
- Compaction of soils causing increased surface run-off and erosion
- Change in risk of occurrence of land slips/slides
- Change in risk of avalanche occurrence
- Damage to geological features(e. g. caves)
- Damage to river banks

(d) Natural resources
- Exhaustion of ground and surface water supplies
- Exhaustion of fossil fuels to provide energy for tourist activity
- Change in risk of occurrence of fire

(e) Visual impact
- Facilities (e. g. buildings, chairlifts, car parks)
- Rubbish

The built environment

(a) Urban environment
- Land taken out of agricultural production
- Change of hydrological patterns

(b) Visual impact
- Growth of the area covered with buildings
- New architectural styles
- People and belongings

(c) Infrastructure
- Too much infrastructure (roads, railways, car-parking, electricity grid, communications systems, waste disposal, and water supply)
- Provision of new infrastructure
- Environmental management to turn areas to tourist use (e. g. sea walls, land reclamation)

(d) Urban form
- Changes in residential, retail or industrial land uses(move from houses to hotel/boarding house)
- Changes to the urban fabric(e. g. roads, pavements)
- Emergence of contrasts between urban areas developed for the tourist population and those for the host population

(e) Restoration
- Re-use of redundant buildings
- Restoration and preservation of historic buildings and sites
- Restoration of disused buildings as second homes

(f) Competition
- Possible decline of tourist attractions or regions because of the opening of other attractions or a change in tourist habits and preferences

Upon the checklist of the environmental impact the environmental impact assessment could be carried out. The first step is to use the environmental policy document as a **performance indicator** to assess preliminarily a proposed development put forward by a developer.[5] Then the site will be selected and the possible environmental impacts of the proposal will be evaluated. This evaluation can be done with a careful and detailed comparison with the environmental performance indicators recorded in the policy legislation/regulations so that potential conflicts can be found.

After that, the emphasis will be put on evaluating specific environmental costs and benefits by carrying out pre-feasibility study and a detailed EIA.[6] Here the environmental policy is used again to judge the results of the impact assessment. If the proposal will not bring about any serious conflict, **a feasibility study** will be implemented and then necessary modifications will be introduced to reduce its potential negative environmental impacts to the smallest degree and make the proposal consistent with the policy. All of these having been done, the project will be planned and designed and measures to protect the environment in line with environmental policy will be taken,[7] so that when the project is under way, the environmental impact during its development can be monitored.

Now many governments have taken environmental preservation and improvement programs as an indispensable part and such strategy has gained greater respect during the 21st century than it did in the past. Because the environment is bound to become the focus in the future of our world, those tourism projects that may cause environmental problems will continue to be evaluated and modified before proper actions are taken, even though they may bring a big profit to the destination.[8] Anyhow, whether tourism development can be profitable or not will be determined by the attractiveness of the destination. Of course, this needs a long-term planning and a careful study of the environment upon the evaluation of both the benefits and costs incurred by the tourism development.

New Words

moderate	*adj.*	适度的
avalanche	*v.*	雪崩
fundamental	*adj.*	基本的
fossil	*n.*	化石
fabric	*n.*	织物；结构
hydrological	*adj.*	水文学的

Key Terms

environmental impact assessment	环境影响评估
reclamation project	改造工程
tourism/environment balance sheets	旅游/环境平衡表
feasibility study	可行性研究

Notes

1. It is vulnerable to change or modification because of tourism activities during various stages of the tourist area life cycle.
   在旅游地生命周期的各个阶段，由于旅游活动的影响，环境容易发生变化。
2. More beautiful and attractive environment is created owing to the adoption of environmental improvement schemes to attract more visitors, such as urban regeneration, reclamation projects and conservation schemes.
   为吸引更多游客，开发商会实施各种环境改善计划如城市复兴、改造工程和环保项目，于是创造出更加优美、更加吸引人的环境。

3. The Environmental impact assessment is a tool used to identify the potential environmental impacts of any proposed development project before decisions are made.
环境影响评估是一种工具,在做出决定以前,我们依靠它来判断开发项目潜在的环境影响。

4. A checklist of environmental impacts which is composed of fundamental elements such as risk can be made when potential impacts of tourism activity are predicted.
在预测旅游活动的潜在影响时,我们可以拟定一份环境检测清单,它包含风险之类的基本因素。

5. The first step is to use the environmental policy document as a performance indicator to assess preliminarily a proposed development put forward by a developer.
第一步,用环境政策作为绩效指标,对开发商提出的开发方案进行初步评估。

6. After that, the emphasis will be put on evaluating specific environmental costs and benefits by carrying out pre-feasibility study and a detailed EIA.
之后,通过进行前期可行性研究和详细的环境影响评估,重点评估具体的环境成本和收益。

7. All of these having been done, the project will be planned and designed and measures to protect the environment in line with environmental policy will be taken.
所有这些都完成之后,将开展项目的规划和设计,并采用符合环境政策的环保措施。

8. Because the environment is bound to become the focus in the future of our world, those tourism projects that may cause environmental problems will continue to be evaluated and modified before proper actions are taken, even though they may bring a big profit to the destination.
即使它们能给旅游目的地带来巨大收益,但由于环境将成为未来世界关注的焦点,所以,那些可能造成环境问题的旅游开发项目要继续接受评估和整改。

Exercise

1. Fill in the blanks with proper words to complete the following statements.

| indicator | infrastructure | balance | visual | potential |
| artificial | actions | respect | environmental | assess |

(1) Tourism environment includes both natural and _____ environment.
(2) It is important to use environment _____ sheets to evaluate the final effects of tourism development in terms of the environment.
(3) The EIA is a tool used to identify the _____ environmental impacts of any proposed development project before decisions are made.
(4) The first step of environmental impact assessment is to use the destination's environmental policy document as a performance _____ to do a preliminary assessment.
(5) Tourism projects that may cause environmental problems will be evaluated and modified before proper _____ are taken.
(6) In order to attract more visitors, the _____ such as roads, car-parks, footpaths are built and improved.
(7) To select a proper environmental impact assessment requires a deep understanding of

the importance of _____ balance.

(8) Because of poor sitting and design, some tourism facilities may lead to _____ pressure.

(9) Both checklists and network systems are methods used to _____ environmental impacts.

(10) Environmental preservation and improvement programs have gained greater _____ during the 21st century.

2. Questions for discussion

(1) What are tourism/environment balance sheets?
_____

(2) What are the benefits on environment brought about by tourism development?
_____

(3) What are the costs on environment brought about by tourism development?
_____

(4) What is the importance of the checklist of environmental impacts?
_____

(5) Can you describe the typical process of the environmental impact assessment?
_____

Part II Guided Reading
第二部分 课文导读

无论是自然环境还是人造环境，都是旅游产品最基本的组成部分。然而，由于旅游活动的开展，环境不可避免地会发生改变。如今，环境保护和保持得到人们的重视。

环境影响评价是指对规划和建设项目实施后可能造成的环境影响进行分析、预测和评估，提出预防或者减轻不良环境影响的对策和措施，并进行跟踪监测的方法与制度。在做一次详细的环境影响评价前，理解环境平衡的价值非常重要。很多地方尝试构建旅游/环境平衡表，试图评价旅游发展对环境造成的影响。比如，本文中运用"旅游环境平衡表"(tourism/environment balance sheets)评价了苏格兰的旅游项目，得出结论：旅游是苏格兰经济的重要组成部分，尽管旅游活动给苏格兰带来了普遍的环境影响，但只对较少的区域造成严重影响，严格的环境评估和管理可以克服这些不利的环境因素。

旅游环境影响评价有很多种方法，如环境检查法（如本文中的Checklist）和网络法等。要起草环境影响列表，必须确定旅游行为会导致哪些潜在的影响。确定出潜在的环境影响后，将这些环境影响组成评价矩阵，用来评价该方案对环境的影响。旅游环境影响评价结论有以下几种：该方案对环境没有影响、有轻微影响、有中度影响或者严重影响四类。

本文简要地介绍了旅游建设项目从筹建到竣工投产环境影响评估的全过程。首先，开发商提出拟议的开发活动，有关单位根据国家和地方有关法律法规、标准对开发活动进行项目选址，然后进行环境影响因子的筛选和初步评价，最后编写预可行性研究报告。在这个阶段，环境影响评价主要是与政策中规定的环境绩效评价指标进行细致的比较，用以调查潜在的冲突。

初步环境影响评价和预可行性研究报告完成后，紧接着开展详细的环境影响评价，即详细而精确地评价该建设项目对环境的负面影响和积极影响，并再次将环境影响评价的结果与环境法律、法规、政策相比较。如果评价结果与环境法规不相冲突，就可对该建设项目开展进一步的可行性论证。使可行性报告修正后的开发方案起到预防和减免项目建设后可能造成的不良环境影响的作用,并且使该方案与政策法规具有一致性。

旅游建设项目的主体工程与环境保护设施同时设计,使开发活动与环境政策一致。此时,建设项目即可以施工了,环境保护设施也开始施工。环境保护设施,与主体工程同时设计、同时施工、同时投产,一般简称为"三同时"制度。对环境影响较大的建设项目实施后需对其进行监测和跟踪评价,以检验环境保护措施的有效性,并提出有效的补偿措施。

旅游建设项目全过程可以分为项目建议书、可行性研究、设计、建设、生产五个阶段。环境影响评价贯穿于这个过程中,为了更清楚地认识环境影响评价,下面对我国现行的详细环境影响评价过程做一个简单介绍(如图13.1)。

依据中国环境保护总局发布的《环境影响评价技术导则——总纲》,我国建设项目环境影响评价一般分为三个阶段,即准备阶段、正式工作阶段和环境影响报告编制阶段。环境影响评价流程和主要内容见下图。

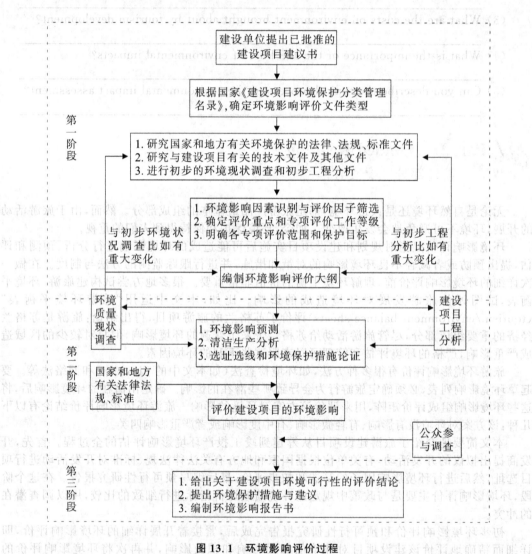

图 13.1 环境影响评价过程

环境影响评价是旅游开发建设项目的重要环节,也是先决条件。环境影响评价对旅建设项目可能造成的环境影响,包括环境污染和生态破坏,也包括对环境的有利影响进行科学分析、论证。环境影响评价不仅要对旅游开发建设项目的选址、设计、施工等过程进行评估,而且还要对运营和生产阶段可能带来的环境影响进行预测和分析,提出相应的预防措施,为项目建成投产后的环境管理提供科学依据,以确保项目有可持续发展的环境条件。因此,根据我国法律规定,任何旅游开发建设项目的立项和实施,都应该首先通过环境影响评价,环境影响评价对旅游开发项目的重要性可见一斑。

旅游知识测试

正误判断:请在正确的选题上划√,错误的选题上划×。

1. 毋庸置疑,所有的旅游活动都会对环境产生不同程度上的破坏性影响,因此环境影响评价是旅游开发建设项目的重要环节,也是先决条件。

2. 旅游环境影响与经济和社会文化影响是相互作用的。环境对旅游目的地的经济和社会文化都会产生影响,反之亦然。

3. 环境平衡表是用于考察旅游活动可能产生的各项成本。根据环境平衡表,可以确定影响生态环境的各种不利因素。

4. 环境影响检查表确定旅游行为会导致哪些潜在的影响,将这些环境影响组成评价矩阵,用以评价旅游项目可能对环境造成的影响。

5. 如果项目环境评价结果与环境法规不相冲突,就可以审批该旅游建设项目,不必再进行可行性论证。

Part III　Case Study
第三部分　案例研究

旅游环境容量的测算——以四川省宜宾地区为例

分析要点

1. 宜宾市生态旅游容量是多少?对发展宜宾市的乡村旅游、生态旅游、户外休闲运动有何意义?

2. 宜宾市旅游空间容量有多大?根据本案例的计算,每天能接待多少游客而不影响其旅游满意度?

3. 请你谈谈如何改善宜宾市的旅游生活容量?列举不少于5项的具体措施。

4. 根据环境影响评价的方法,你认为本案旅游环境容量的分析有什么不妥之处?

5. 在目前无法增加宜宾市旅游环境容量的情况下,你认为应该如何处理旅游淡季、旺季带来的需求波动?

相关理论和问题

1. 环境容量(Environmental capacity)
2. 旅游环境平衡(Tourism environmental balance)
3. 环境审计和保护(Environmental auditing and protection)
4. 旅游的可持续发展(Sustainable development of tourism)

旅游环境容量是指在一定条件下，一定时间、空间范围内所能容纳的游客数量和对旅游行为方式所容忍的程度，其内涵主要包括旅游生态容量、旅游空间容量以及旅游生活环境容量等。

宜宾具有2180多年的历史，是我国国家级历史文化名城。以蜀南竹海、石海洞乡、僰人悬棺等自然文化旅游和五粮液集团的产业旅游为支撑。本文测算了宜宾市旅游环境容量，为宜宾旅游的可持续发展提供参考。

一、旅游环境容量计算

（一）旅游生态容量(Ecological capacity)

旅游生态容量是指在一定时间内旅游地自然生态环境保持平衡所能容纳的旅游活动量，其大小取决于自然生态环境净化、吸收旅游污染物的能力及一定时间内每个游客产生的污染物的量。旅游生态容量计算公式：

$$R_s = \sum_{i=1}^{n} \frac{S_i P_i}{S_a} (i=1, 2, \ldots n)$$

上式中：

R_s——日旅游生态容量，单位：人；

S_i——第 i 个旅游区的面积，单位：m^2；

P_i——第 i 个旅游区的森林覆盖率，用百分数表示；

S_a——人均绿地面积，单位：m^2/人。

宜宾市主要的风景旅游区的总面积为 892.50 km^2，各旅游区的平均森林覆盖率为 45%，人均绿地面积参考国内同类风景区，取值为 40 m^2/人。

求得宜宾市生态旅游容量为：1 004.06 万人/日。

（二）旅游空间容量(Spacious capacity)

旅游空间容量包括面积容量、游道容量、游线容量以及洞穴容量。计算公式为：

$$D_a = \sum_{i=1}^{n} \frac{S_i}{S_a} \cdot \frac{T}{t} (i=1, 2, \ldots n)$$

上式中：

D_a——日旅游空间容量，单位：人；

S_i——第 i 个旅游区的面积，单位：m^2；

S_a——人均合理环境容量面积，单位：m^2；

T——景区每日开放时间，单位：小时；

t——游客平均游览时间，单位：小时。

根据宜宾市实情，参考国内其他景区的情况，公式中 S_a 取 500 m^2/人，景区每日开放与游客平均游览时间都为 8 小时，取周转率为 1。

求得宜宾市旅游空间为：178.5 万人/日。

（三）旅游生活环境容量(Living capacity)

旅游生活环境容量是指旅游区承受游客吃、住、行、乐、购等消费活动的能力。主要包括接待容量、水量和交通量，其大小根据旅游最低量定律，取三项容量中的最小值。

1. 接待容量

接待容量由床位数来表示。目前,宜宾市预计全市共可一次性容纳 5000 人左右。

2. 水量

水量的计算可分为三部分:住宿游客用水量、流动游客用水量和常住工作服务人员用水量。根据有关部门提供的数据,每天共计 650L。由于宜宾市水资源非常丰富。因此,水量不会成为宜宾市旅游生活容量中的最低因子。

3. 交通量

交通量为公路、铁路、水运及航空交通运输量之和。目前宜宾市旅游交通容量为每日 73 395 人。

因此,宜宾市旅游生活容量的大小由接待容量所决定,为 5000 人/日。

二、旅游环境容量分析与评价

表 1　宜宾市旅游环境容量一览表

旅游环境容量类型	旅游生态容量	旅游空间容量	旅游生活容量
日旅游环境容量(万人)	1004.06	178.50	0.50
年旅游环境容量(万人)	366481.90	65152.50	182.50

通过表 1,宜宾市较高的日旅游生态容量和日空间容量表明宜宾旅游资源环境具有良好的自然净化、纳污能力。但是日旅游生活容量为仅 0.50 万人,这说明旅游生活容量的低下限制了宜宾旅游环境容量的提高。

通过环境容量等级系数的计算和等级划分对宜宾市旅游容量进行总体评价,可得出或富余或满足或欠缺的 3 种评价结论。

环境容量等级系数计算公式:

$$Q_d = \frac{Q_i - K_i}{Q_i}$$

上式中:Q_d 为环境容量等级系数,Q_i 为第 i 种环境容量值,K_i 为第 i 种环境现状值。

表 2　环境容量等级标准

容量系数 Capacity coefficient	<0.2	0.2-0.4	0.4-0.6	0.6-0.8	>0.8
容量等级 Capacity rank	1	2	3	4	5
容量评价 Capacity evaluation	极缺 Lacking extremely	欠缺 Deficiency	满足 Sufficiency	富余 Abundance	极富 Ample

表 3　宜宾市旅游环境容量等级评定结果

评价指标体系 Evaluation indexes	旅游环境容量(万人)		
	旅游生态容量	旅游空间容量	旅游生活容量
容量结果 Capacity results	366481.90	65152.50	182.50

容量系数 Capacity coefficient	0.9991	0.9951	-0.7315
容量等级 Capacity rank	5	5	1
容量评价 Capacity evaluation	极富	极富	极缺

由表 3 知,宜宾市旅游生态容量与旅游空间容量都处于"极富"水平,容量等级均为"5",而旅游环境容量的容量等级仅为"1",处于"极缺"状态,容量系数为负值。这与表 1 数据所反映的结果一致,即宜宾旅游生活容量偏低,限制了宜宾旅游环境容量。

环境测量和评估是旅游资源开发的重要前提。宜宾环境容量的测量和分析为当地政府开发旅游资源、发展旅游业提供了数据支持,对于宜宾旅游的建设和管理、推动旅游的可持续发展具有重要的现实意义。

资料来源:周金星.漆良华等.区域旅游环境容量研究——以宜宾地区为例[J].中南林业科技大学学报(社会科学版),2007(7)

Part IV Reading Box
第四部分 阅读与分析

Carrying Capacity

阅读分析要点

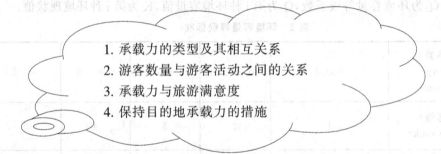

1. 承载力的类型及其相互关系
2. 游客数量与游客活动之间的关系
3. 承载力与旅游满意度
4. 保持目的地承载力的措施

Carrying capacity refers to the greatest number of people who use a site without degrading its physical environment and declining the quality of visitors' experience.[1] Tourism activity has great impacts on the natural environment as well as the social, cultural, economic systems of a destination. And these impacts can be understood in this way. If we think that tourists may bring positive effects on these aspects, we can safely conclude that there are certain **thresholds** which should limit tourist arrivals, otherwise there are not only the environmental, but also social and economic problems in the destination.[2] Once these thresholds are exceeded, problems which have an overall influence on tourism development will arise. These problems can be summarized as follows:

- If physical thresholds are exceeded, tourists' safety will be threatened and the number of tourists will decrease;

- If environmental thresholds are exceeded, some minor problems such as health hazards will arise. What's more, the destination will become less attractive;
- If social and cultural thresholds are exceeded, the host population may feel indignant and hold a hostile and antagonistic attitude towards the tourists;[3]
- If tourist flow thresholds are exceeded, tourists may feel less satisfied and turn to other destinations for better tourism products;
- If economic thresholds are exceeded, resources and factors of production are likely to be allocated in an improper way.[4]

Carrying capacity is not an independent and **fixed value** based on **tourist presence**. It is changeable and can be influenced and altered by the change of other factors, especially the change of the **tolerance levels** of its determinants.

Here the term "tourist presence" instead of "tourist numbers" is used because when the levels of carrying capacity are to be evaluated, focus should be put on the absolute numbers of tourist arrivals which requires the consideration of the following factors:

- The average length of stay;
- The geographical concentration of tourists;
- The degree of seasonality;
- The types of tourism activity;
- The accessibility of specific sites;
- The level of infrastructure use and its spare capacity;
- The extent of spare-capacity amongst the various productive sectors of the economy.

Exceeding the carrying capacity in any of the impact areas will have a strong influence on the tourism development and even hold back the tourism development process and make the development unsustainable. The damage brought by exceeding the carrying capacity may be related to the impact areas or in terms of **tourist satisfaction**, but in the end it will gradually do damage to the regional development.[5] With the decline of the tourism industry in a certain destination, the number of tourists will decrease rapidly because most tourists will search for other better destinations and the mix of tourist arrivals will change. These will make it even more difficult for the destination to realize its planning goals.

Tourist presence exerts a great impact on different destinations and this forms the basis of the acceptable standards that we should observe. The international community, as the World Heritage Convention requires, should work together to make sure that effective measures can be taken to protect and conserve these sites where the management is always carried out in the form of the **access control**. For example, the access provided by Keoladeo National Park in India includes the restricted number of trained guides, bicycles and specified trails built for the tourists. Some other areas adopt more arbitrary and restrictive measures such as the Jiuzhaigou Valley in Sichuan of China where only 10,000 travelers are allowed to visit the place per day during the Golden Week Holidays.[6] There are also other strategies such as the arrangement of tourist visits in different time or the set of specific restrictions for each aspect of a destination so that its overall tourism development can be realized with proper management.

New Words

degrade	v.	降低……的品格(或质量、价值等)
trail	n.	小径
threshold	n.	门槛;限度

antagonistic	adj.	反对的,敌对的
hazard	n.	冒险,冒险的事
indignant	adj.	愤怒的,愤慨的
determinant	n.	决定性因素
arbitrary	adj.	任意的,武断的

Notes

1. Carrying capacity refers to the greatest number of people who use a site without degrading its physical environment and declining the quality of visitors' experience.
   承载能力是指在不降低旅游景点的自然环境和不影响旅游者体验的情况下,景区可以接待的最多人数。

2. If we think that tourists may bring positive effects on these aspects, we can safely conclude that there are certain thresholds which should limit tourist arrivals, otherwise there are not only the environmental, but also social and economic problems in the destination.
   如果我们认为旅游者将在这些方面产生积极影响,那么我们完全可以得出以下结论:应当有若干阈值限制旅游者的数量,否则,不仅是目的地的环境,甚至其社会和经济都会出现问题。

3. If social and cultural thresholds are exceeded, the host population may feel indignant and hold a hostile and antagonistic attitude towards the tourists.
   如果(旅游人数)超过了当地社会和文化生活所能容纳的最大限度,当地居民会感到愤怒,对旅游者产生敌对情绪。

4. If economic thresholds are exceeded, resources and factors of production are likely to be allocated in an improper way.
   如果(旅游人数)超过了经济所能承担的上限,就可能导致资源和生产要素的不合理分配。

5. The damage brought by exceeding the carrying capacity may be related to the impact areas or in terms of tourist satisfaction, but in the end it will gradually do damage to the regional development.
   超过承载能力会对旅游区域或旅游者的满意度产生影响,最终将逐渐损害区域发展。

6. Some other areas adopt more arbitrary and restrictive measures such as the Jiuzhaigou Valley in Sichuan of China where only 10,000 travelers are allowed to visit the place per day during the Golden Week Holidays.
   其他地方采取了更严格的强制性措施,例如中国四川的九寨沟,"黄金周"期间每天只允许一万名游客游览。

Topic discussion

1. What is carrying capacity? What problems will arise if the thresholds set up to limit tourist arrivals are exceeded?

2. What factors should be considered when the absolute numbers of tourist arrivals are to be evaluated?

3. And what effects will be brought to tourists if its carrying capacity of the destination is exceeded? Give examples.

4. What is the the basis of the acceptable standards that we should observe? Give examples.

5. What measures can be taken to realize the overall tourism development of the Jiuzhaigou Valley besides control of tourist arrivals?

【即学即用】

With reference to the theory, information or approach applied in the Reading Box, have a case study of the carrying capacity in a resort you know. Make presentation of your study in Chinese or in English using PPT.

【学习资源库】

为了掌握本章更多的相关专业知识,请您登陆 http://sicnu.edu.cn/,点击国家双语教学示范课程《旅游学概论》,进入网络学堂查询相关资料。

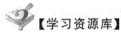

> This chapter has discussed both the positive and the negative environmental consequences of tourism activity. The environment impact assessment is very essential for a tourism project; and any proposed tourism project must be assessed on the basis of environment impact consequences before decisions are made. To develop a tourism project, one should take into account both the benefits and the costs using the environmental balance sheet. The variables of checklists are useful to assess the environmental impacts on the destination community. Whether a destination is sustainable or not depends on reasonable thresholds of the carrying capacity. Of course, this needs a long-term planning and a careful study of the environment upon the evaluation of both the benefits and costs incurred by the tourism development.

Part V Additional Know-how of Tourism
第五部分 旅游知识扩展

【关键术语】

Environment: all of aspects of the surroundings of human beings both cultural, natural and man-made, whether affecting human beings as individuals or in social groupings.

环境:影响人类个体或社会群体生活环境的各个方面,包括文化、自然和人造景观。

Environmental auditing: Environmental auditing are primarily impact studies of particular events or developments, environmental auditing represents a modus operandi, an ongoing process of monitoring and evaluation.

环境监察：环境监察主要研究某些特别的事件和开发对环境的影响，不间断的监督和评估过程是其运作模式。

Carrying capacity: the maximum number of people who can use a site without an unacceptable alteration in the physical environment and without an unacceptable decline in the quality of experience gained by visitors; distinctions can be made between social, cultural and environmental carrying capacity.

旅游承载力：在旅游目的地不至于导致当地环境和旅客旅游体验的质量出现不可接受的下降这一前提之下所能容纳的最大游客数量。承载力可分为社会承载力、文化承载力、环境承载力。

Environmental impact sequence: a four-stage model formulated by the OECD to account for the impacts of tourism on the natural environment:

- **Stressor activities**: activities that initiate the environmental impact sequence; these can be divided into permanent environmental restructuring, the generation of waste residuals, tourist activities and indirect and induced activities
- **Environmental stresses**: the deliberate changes in the environment that are entailed in the stressor activities
- **Environmental responses**: the way that environment reacts to the stresses, both in the short and long term, and both directly and indirectly
- **Social responses**: the reaction of individuals, communities, the tourism industry, tourists, NGOs and governments to the various environmental responses

环境影响过程：经济发展与合作组织制定的一个四步模型，用以解释旅游对自然环境的影响。包括：**压力活动**：引发环境影响序列的活动，这些活动可被分类为永久性的环境重构，废物残余的产生，旅游者活动、间接或诱发的活动；**环境压力**：压力活动给环境造成的故意改变；**环境反应**：环境在短期或长期时间内，直接或间接地表现出对这些压力活动的反应；**社会反应**：个人、社区、旅游业、旅游者、非政府组织和政府对各种环境变化做出的回应。

【知识链接】

1. 累积效应

当一项行动（或活动）的影响与过去、现在，以及可以预见未来的行动（或活动）的各种影响互相合成时对环境所造成的后果，就是累积效应。证据表明，最具有破坏性的旅游环境影响往往是由多项活动的各个较小的影响构成的联合效应随着时间推移造成的，尤其体现在旅游资源与设施的持续使用上。这是由于人类活动对环境的各种扰动在空间上和时间上的密集和拥挤造成的。当人类活动对一个地点的生态系统产生的第一次扰动还没有充分地恢复前，又发生第二次扰动，将这些扰动累积起来，造成累积效应。累积效应的分析重点主要集中在三个方面：

（1）资源（如空气质量、景观与独特资源等）

（2）生态系统，包括自然生态系统、人工生态系统（如城市）及其相互作用系统（如农业生态系统）

（3）人类摄取（指影响生活质量的社会、经济和文化背景条件）

2. 旅游环境容量

旅游环境容量又称为旅游环境承载力，它是指一定时期内，某种状态或某种条件下，不会对旅游地的环境、社会、文化、经济以及旅游者旅游感受质量等方面带来无法接受的不利影响的旅游业规模的最高阈值。

旅游容量是个概念体系，由以下5种基本容量构成：

(1) 旅游者心理容量,又叫旅游感知容量,是在保持最佳旅游状态的条件下,该旅游地所能容纳的旅游活动最大量。

(2) 旅游资源容量,指在保持旅游景观质量的前提下,在一定时间内,某地域旅游资源所能容纳的旅游活动量。

(3) 旅游生态容量,指一定时间内,不会导致地域内自然环境退化或恶化的前提下,某地域旅游资源所能容纳的旅游活动量。

(4) 旅游经济发展容量,指一定时间、一定地域范围内经济发展程度所决定的能容纳的旅游活动量。

(5) 旅游的地域容量,指旅游接待地区的人口构成、宗教信仰、民族风情、生活方式和社会开化程度所决定的当地居民可承受的旅游者数量。

【小思考】

1. 不同旅游开发项目的环境影响评价的目的相同吗?其评价的内容相同吗?

参考阅读:

不同的开发项目,由于所处的地理位置、开发目标等不同,有不同的环境影响评价指标内容。评价指标体系构成的原则是整体上能反映设定的环境目标。

旅游资源开发其评价指标体系应既要反映未来环境质量状况、生态系统稳定性特征,还要能够反映社会、经济、文化的支撑能力;评价指标应具有可操作性,含义明确,方法统一,而且具有普适性;与环境适宜性评价指标吻合;指标要有评价标准,尽量采用现行的各类环境质量指标,以保证标准的相互借鉴作用,一般而言,旅游开发的环境评价指标包括:(1) 社会经济指标:旅游资源开发战略制定的最初动机来源于可以获得相当的经济利益,因此,社会经济指标应是旅游资源战略环境影响评价的主要指标之一。指标体系中应包括区域经济发展指标、社会安定指标和投入产出比指标等;(2) 生态环境指标:科学判定生态环境影响是旅游资源开发战略环境影响评价的核心内容之一。生态环境指标中应包括与动植物种群相关的指标、与生态系统稳定性相关的指标及景观协调性相关的指标等;(3) 自然环境指标:为满足战略实施对自然环境的要求,宏观控制自然环境要素包括水体质量、大气质量、噪声水平等在内的指标也是必不可少的;(4) 可持续性指标:主要以区域环境承载力指标和战略实施系统的协调性、稳定性来考虑战略的可持续性。

2. 我国目前环境影响评价的公众参与程度怎样?你认为哪些地方应当改进和完善?

参考阅读:

公众参与作为环境保护重要内容的思想,由联合国环境规划署(UNEP)于1978年在环境影响评价基本程序中明确提出。

环评中的公众参与(Public participation)是项目方或者环评工作组同公众之间的一种双向交流,其目的是避免政府决策的失误,减少环境污染事故中致害和受害双方的冲突,同时提高了公众的环境保护意识,增强公众环境保护的责任感。

在环境影响评价中主要应考虑的公众参与者包括:(1) 受建设项目直接影响并住在项目建设地点附近的人们;(2) 生态保护主义者和希望保证使开发与环境的需要尽量有效结合的生态学家;(3) 在拟议行动实施后将获益的工商业开发者;(4) 享受高水平生活的一般公众。另外,重要的公众还包括媒体和与项目有关的其他部门。

我国环评中的公众参与始于1991年亚洲开发银行的环评培训项目。目前《中华人民共和国环境影响评价法》规定,对可能造成不良影响的规划或建设项目,应通过举行论证会、听证会、社会调查或其他形式,征求有关单位、专家和公众对环境影响评价报告书的意见。

2006年2月,国家环保部门颁布了《环境影响评价公众参与暂行办法》,详细规定公众参与环境影响评价的范围、程序、组织形式等内容。

Part VI Further Readings
第六部分 课外阅读

如果您想进一步学习旅游环境评价的方法,探讨旅游环境评价的意义,建议您阅读以下学者的著作和论文。

一、中文部分

[1] 颜文洪,张朝枝. 旅游环境学[M]. 北京:科学出版社,2005.
[2] 陆书玉. 旅游影响评价[M]. 北京:高等教育出版社,2001.
[3] 钱益春. 张家界国家森林公园旅游环境质量评价[J]. 东北林业法学学报. 2007,(01).
[4] 赵克军,贺力荃,张勇,赵彤昕. 建设项目实施过程中的可行性研究与环境影响评价[J]. 重庆环境科学,2003,(25).
[5] 薄湘平,唐敏. 旅游对环境影响研究的模糊综合评价[J]. 统计与决策,2007,(22).
[6] 章小平,朱忠福. 九寨沟景区旅游环境容量研究[J]. 旅游学刊,2007,(09).
[7] 李小梅,刘文伟,吴春山;王菲凤;许丽忠. 生态旅游规划环境影响评价的方法和案例[J]. 福建师范大学学报. 2007,(03).
[8] 林明水,谢红彬. VERP对我国风景名胜区旅游环境容量研究的启示[J]. 人文地理,2007,(04).
[9] 汪宇明,赵中华. 基于上海案例的大都市旅游容量及承载力研究[J]. 中国人口资源与环境,2007,(05).
[10] 李小梅,张江山,王菲凤. 生态旅游项目的环境影响评价方法(EIA)与实践——以武夷山大峡谷森林生态旅游区为例[J]. 生态学杂志,2005,(09).

二、英文部分

[1] George Hughes. Environmental Indicators[J]. *Annals of Tourism Research*, 2002(29):457—477.
[2] Morrison-Saunders, Angus;Early, Gerard. What is necessary to ensure natural justice in environmental impact assessment decision-making? [J]. *Impact Assessment and Project Appraisal*. 2008, 26(1):29—42.
[3] Jones, Calvin, Munday, Max. Tourism Satellite Accounts and Impact Assessments: Some Considerations[J]. *Tourism Analysis*, 2008(13).
[4] Maria Berrittella, Andrea Bigano, Roberto Roson, Richard S. J. Tol. A general equilibrium analysis of climate change impacts on tourism [J]. *Tourism Management*, 2006(27):913—924.
[5] Melinda Hillery, Blair Nancarrow, Graham Griffin, Geoff Syme. Tourist perception of environmental impact[J]. *Annals of Tourism Research*, 2001, 28(4):853—867.
[6] Alexis. Establishing the social tourism carrying capacity for the tourist resorts of the east coast of the Republic of Cyprus[J]. *Tourism Management*, 2000,21(2):147—156.
[7] Singh, Sagar; Kuniyal, J C. Vishvakarma, S C; Badola, H K; Jain, A P. Tourism in Kullu Valley: An Environmental Assessment [J]. *Tourism*

Recreation Research，2008，33(1)：119—122.
［8］Gregr，Edward J. Nichol，Linda M. Watson，Jane C. Ford，John K B. Ellis，Graeme M. Estimating Carrying Capacity for Sea Otters in British Columbia[J]. *Journal of Wildlife Management*，2008，72(2)：382—388.
［9］Sayre，Nathan. The Genesis，History，and Limits of Carrying Capacity[J]. *Annals of the Association of American Geographers*，2008，98(1)：120—134.
［10］Moore，Susan A. Smith，Amanda J. Newsome，David N. Environmental Performance Reporting for Natural Area Tourism：Contributions by Visitor Impact Management Frameworks and Their Indicators ［J］. *Journal of Sustainable Tourism*，2003，11(4)：348.

Chapter 14　Utilization and Conservation of the Tourism Resources
第十四章　旅游资源的利用与保护

Learning objects：学习目标

- Study how the government and tourism sectors can utilize and conserve the natural and cultural resources within the tourism system 学习政府和旅游企业如何利用和保护旅游系统中的自然和文化资源
- Appreciate the important relationship between utilization and protection of tourism resources 理解旅游资源的利用和保护二者之间的重要关系
- Describe principles of proper utilization and conservation of tourism resources 阐述合理利用和保护旅游资源的原则
- Appreciate the concrete measures to utilize and conserve tourism resources in a fragile environment 掌握在脆弱的环境中利用和保护旅游资源的具体方法
- Cite examples of increasing the capacity of existing sites, creating new tourism resources and multiple use of the destinations 列举增加旅游景区现有旅游容量、创新旅游资源和扩大目的用途的范例
- Understand how the proper management can resolve potential conflicts between tourism and the environment 了解良好的管理如何解决旅游与环境潜在的矛盾
- Appreciate how tourists can enjoy an authentic, high-quality experience in the national parks 体会旅游者如何在国家公园享受真实的、高品质的旅游体验

Ability goals：能力目标

- Case Study 案例分析：萨尔茨堡旅游资源的开发和保护
- Reading Box 阅读分析：National Parks 国家公园

Part I Text
第一部分 课文

Utilization and Conservation of the Tourism Resources

【教学要点】

知识要点	掌握程度	相关章节
tourist attractions and tourism resources 旅游吸引物与旅游资源	一般了解	
categories of tourism resources 旅游资源的分类	一般了解	
principles of proper utilization of tourism resources 合理利用旅游资源的原则	重点掌握	本课文与第 1 单元、第 3 单元、第 4 单元、第 10 单元、第 13 单元、第 15 单元相关内容有联系。
measures of upgrading the efficiency of utilizing tourism resources 提高旅游资源利用率的方法	重点掌握	
multiple uses of tourism resources 旅游资源的多种使用功能	重点掌握	
management practices of tourist attractions in the destination 旅游目的地管理旅游吸引物的措施	一般了解	

Tourism exerts positive impacts such as enhancement of the environment, provision of funds for conservation, preservation of culture and history, protection of natural attractions, and setting the use limits for further development. However, without proper planning and management, it also brings negative impacts such as destruction of vegetation, creation of trekking areas filled with too many tourists and too much litter, pollution of beaches, elimination of open space with too many buildings, appearance of sewage and housing problems, and neglect of the needs and structure of the host community.

In the twenty-first century, the tourism sectors try to develop and utilize tourism resources and obtain benefits from them. However, an increasing number of people have come to realize that more importance should be attached to **preservation of the tourism resources** and the set of use limits; otherwise, the destination could not develop further.[1] Anyhow, whether tourism can be profitable or not is determined by the attraction people want to see and experience. The quality, quantity, diversity, uniqueness, and accessibility of the attraction are of great importance to the destination.

In some countries, especially in Western countries, researchers use the term "**tourist attraction**" instead of "tourism resource". It falls into two categories in nature: natural and cultural. We can make a further distinction between sites and events. Four categories of attraction are thereby generated: natural sites, natural events, cultural sites and cultural events. In this chapter, we use the term "tourism resource" instead, as most Chinese researchers are used to it. It is necessary to explore the degree of the negative impacts on the tourism resources before we discuss what the best responses of tourism to these impacts should be.[2] While examining the possible effect on tourism, the WTTC paid particular attention to the sharp decrease and pollution of land resources. They state that:

It is obvious that the sharp decrease of resource will have a lasting and extremely serious influence on tourism. Even in the next few decades, the travel & tourism industry could find that it would be impossible to establish new tourism destination and the quality of the existing destination would also decrease rapidly owing to political instability or increased competition for land.[3] Meanwhile, tourists would feel less satisfied with tourism products offered because of the loss of landscape and wildlife, and they would be unwilling to travel in some destination. Furthermore, operational price will also rise because of the increase of fuel prices, which will correspondingly result in falls in the number of tourist arrivals who tend to be sensitive to price.

Now that we have realized the significance of both of the **natural and cultural resources** and the serious impacts of resource depletion, we should take it as an urgent task to find proper ways to utilize and protect them.[4] According to the concept of green tourism development, economic growth and environmental improvement can promote each other. While using the tourism resources, we can also protect the environment by improving the use of resources, controlling waste and restricting visitor flows to limit damage to non-renewable tourism resources.

Proper utilization of the tourism resources will produce better tourist products; save resources and help the public understand the tourism industry better and thus form the basis of a long-term growth. Protection of the tourism resources is essential to the sustainable development which plays a vital role in avoiding the widespread problem—**limits to growth**.[5] The following are some of the important principles that should be used as the guidance of any plan of proper utilization and conservation of tourism resources:

1. to recognize the mutual influence of tourism and the tourism resource and to achieve the aim of resource protection through tourism;
2. to control tourist arrivals in order to reduce environmental pressure;
3. to develop tourism resources properly so that both residents and visitors can benefit from it;
4. to take the environment into consideration while developing tourism so as to maintain and enhance the environment;
5. to carry out responsible management through practices of tourism business to make sure that any development plan will do no harm to ecosystem.

With the increase of tourism demand, some destinations have suffered from degradation because of a growing number of tourists who come to the destination in almost the same short season. Some more fragile destinations have made a response to this by planning and carrying out **management strategies** which are, indeed, of great importance to make sure that the resources in the destination can be utilized more effectively to meet the increasing demand.[6] The healthy development of tourism is determined by both the proper utilization and the conservation of tourism resources in a fragile environment. To achieve the desired goal, the following measures should not be ignored:

1. Increasing the capacity of existing sites

At any place, attention should be paid to improve the capacity of existing resorts to accept more tourists. This requires evaluating again how effectively existing tourism resource has been utilized and what management measures which have been taken are better to develop tourism. The advantage of this approach is that these destinations will be the first to benefit from any increase in demand for tourism, as they are already familiar to the public.[7]

2. Creation of new tourism resources

This can be realized in two ways: (1) reclaim land from water or developing deserted or under-used land. This can be done around the major towns and cities, especially that near the **primary destinations**. Take the recent development of the Chao Tianmen Dock in Chongqing as an example. There, a major development project has been implemented to transform a long stretch of former dockland into a large number of man—made and water—based tourist attractions.[8] Many other resources can also be reused or developed for tourism purposes, such as abandoned mines, former railway beds, deserted canals and airfields. Some of the parks in Britain and France were originally abandoned mines or industrial land. (2) combine tourism with other land uses, especially with water supply, forestation, agriculture and nature conservation. For example, the rural tourism in many places of China is a successful example which integrates the agriculture and sightseeing. It is beneficial to both the agricultural production and recreation of new tourism resources.

3. Multiple uses

As the multiple use of destinations implies, the enterprises can be classified into different groups according to whether they depend upon tourism only, residents only or mix of the two. In fact, only those destinations that are built for particular purpose (such as theme parks) purely aim to serve the tourist. Most destinations combine tourism with other uses; among them, tourism is indeed the last developed and the least respected area.

To use tourism resources in multiple ways, some current reservoirs and their catchments (such as ErTan Reservoir in Panzhihua, Three-Gorge Reservoir of the Yangtze River, etc.) provide other activities such as walking, sailing, camping and fishing while holding themselves as the main attraction for visitors. Tourism has been successfully combined with forestry in many countries in the world and many other activities including scenic drives, picnic sites, camping and fishing have been provided. A case in point is the Netherlands where tourism has been developed in over 10% of the state forest service and roads, camp-sites, viewing platforms and picnic areas have been built for visitors. Similarly, many of the forest areas in the national parks in the United States are also used for tourism purpose and there is no conflict arising between the need for timber supply and provision of amenities for tourists.

Good management is the best and most effective way to resolve potential conflicts between tourism and the environment. While doing so, three aspects should be considered:

1. Traffic management

Car is the most frequently used vehicle in traveling to and within the destination. Therefore a large number of cars, whether they are moving or parked, are one of the most direct causes of the impacts of tourism on the environment. To control the movement and access of vehicles in major towns and cities, it is necessary to implement traffic management. This is true of tourist destinations if they want to minimize the impact of traffic. Traffic management should be carried out in the form of highway engineering and traffic design such as the provision of one-way system, speed limits, and limited access to remote areas. In some areas cars are even completely forbidden. To make up for the inconvenience brought about by these restrictions on motor vehicles, scenic drives, picnic areas and viewpoints at other locations should be provided. In some cases new roads may need to be built to pass around those areas that are easily influenced by the environment.

2. Land management

Design and maintenance are essential to land management which can be achieved by persuading or using financial incentives to stimulate private organizations to provide tourist facilities on their land.[9] A circulation pattern involving the erection of signs, fences and barriers may be necessary so that the flow of visitors through a site can be guided and controlled. It is also significant to change the visitor access points and circulation routes every year in order to minimize the effects of trampling on vegetation, and to maintain the site. The number of visitors is a crucial factor which can reach such a goal. Therefore, estimating and monitoring visitor numbers are very important measures to avoid too much pressure on the services such as car parking, access, water and sewage disposal and to prevent overcrowding or congestion.

3. Visitor management

Visitor management is usually realized by legislation and polite persuasion. It includes two ways. Administrators can prevent or restrict access to those areas in which the environment is easily influenced and broken, or persuade tourists to those areas that can accept them. To control site usage, limiting car parking provision is usually the first choice, even though it may reduce the number of visitors. Controlling the tourist flow by change of the price is another way, particularly for the private sector, such as the change of price according to the season and prevailing visitor numbers.

Now there is a tendency in leisure travel that tourists are less willing to visit polluted environment and this tendency is predicted to have a greater impact for the next ten years. The conservation of the fragile local environment and community must therefore be stressed while considering the use of tourism resource. Tourism, by its very nature, tends to develop very quickly in those unique and fragile parts of the world. These destinations will change or even break because of heavy tourist pressure, especially the fact that a large number of visitors often come in the same season and concentrate at specific popular locations.[10] Hence, the only way to make tourism sustainable is to find proper methods to utilize and conserve the limited tourism resources.

New Words

depletion	n.	损耗
trek	v.	牛拉车,艰苦跋涉
fragile	adj.	易碎的,脆的
correspondingly	adv.	相对地,比照地
hectare	n.	公顷(等于1万平方米)
ecosystem	n.	生态系统
catchment	n.	集水;集水处
prevailing	adj.	占优势的,主要的,流行的
trample	v.	践踏,踩坏;轻视
sewage	n.	下水道;污水

| tendency | n. | 趋向，倾向 |

Key Terms

sustainable development	可持续发展
non-renewable tourism resource	不可恢复的旅游资源
viewing platform	观景台
one-way system	单行道体系

Notes

1. Now an increasing number of people have come to realize that more importance should be attached to preservation of the tourism resources and the set of use limits; otherwise, the destination could not develop further.
现在，越来越多的人已经认识到应当更加注重保护旅游资源和有限度地利用资源，否则，旅游目的地不可能进一步发展。

2. It is necessary to explore the degree of the negative impacts on the tourism resources before we discuss what the best responses of tourism to these impacts should be.
在我们讨论应当采取哪些是最好的应对措施之前，有必要研究一下这些负面影响对旅游资源影响的程度。

3. Even in the next few decades the travel & tourism industry could find that it would be impossible to establish new tourism destination and the quality of the existing destination would also decrease rapidly owing to political instability or increased competition for land.
由于政局不稳定或土地竞争加剧，甚至在今后几十年，旅游业会发现：不太可能开发更多的新的旅游目的地，现有的旅游目的地品质会急剧下降。

4. Now that we have realized the significance of both of the natural and cultural tourism resources and the serious impacts of resource depletion, we should take it as an urgent task to find proper ways to utilize and protect them.
既然我们已经认识到自然和人文旅游资源的重要性，以及资源损耗的严重影响，我们就应当把它视为最紧迫的任务，寻找适当的方法，保护和利用这些资源。

5. Protection of the tourism resources is essential to the sustainable development which plays a vital role in avoiding the widespread problem—limits to growth.
保护旅游资源对可持续发展相当重要，而只有可持续发展才能避免发展瓶颈这个普遍问题。

6. Some more fragile destinations have made a response to this by planning and carrying out management strategies which are, indeed, of great importance to make sure that the resources in the destination can be utilized more effectively to meet the increasing demand.
一些更脆弱的旅游目的地已经通过规划和实施管理策略来应对这一消极影响，正确的规划和管理可以确保有效地利用目的地资源，满足日益增长的需求。

7. The advantage of this approach is that these destinations will be the first to benefit from any increase in demand for tourism, as they are already familiar to the public.
这种方法的优点在于，由于这些目的地已经为大众所知，任何旅游需求的增长都会首先使这些目的地受益。

8. There, a major development project has been implemented to transform a long

stretch of former dockland into a large number of man-made and water-based tourist attractions.

那里已完成一个重点开发项目,以前长长的港区被改造成许多人造水景。

9. Design and maintenance are essential to land management which can be achieved by persuading or using financial incentives to stimulate private organizations to provide tourist facilities on their land.

规划和维护对土地管理是必要的,通过说服或经济刺激,鼓励私有企业在自有土地上为游客提供娱乐设施,就可以有效实现土地管理。

10. These destinations will change or even break because of heavy tourist pressure, especially the fact that a large number of visitors often come in the same season and concentrate at specific popular locations.

由于旅游者带来的沉重压力,特别是大量旅游者往往在同一季节到来,并集中在某些旅游热点,以致这些目的地将会发生改变,甚至消亡。

Exercise

1. *Decide whether the statements are true or false. If it is true, put "T" in the space provided and "F" if it is false.*

   (1) _____ Tourism can exert both positive and negative impacts on the host community.

   (2) _____ It is urgent to find proper ways to utilize and protect tourism resources.

   (3) _____ According to the concept of green tourism development, economic growth and environmental improvement cannot promote each other.

   (4) _____ Most destinations are built only for the purpose to serve the tourist.

   (5) _____ Traffic management can be carried out just in the form of highway engineering.

   (6) _____ Tourism tends to develop quickly in those unique and fragile parts of the world.

2. *Questions for discussion*

   (1) Why should the tourism sectors emphasize the environment protection and try to perfect tourism resources in the 21st century?

   (2) According to WTTC, what effects will the decreasing resources bring to tourism industry?

   (3) What is green tourism development?

   (4) What are the principles that should be used as the guidance of any plan for proper utilization and conservation of tourism resources?

   (5) To develop tourist sites healthily, what measures should be taken?

   (6) What are the two forms used to create new tourism resources? Can you give some

examples?

_____

(7) What are the three aspects that should be considered while trying to resolve potential conflicts between tourist activities and tourist sites through good management?

_____

(8) What suggestions can you put forward to enforce the visitor management?

_____

Part II Guided Reading
第二部分 课文导读

　　旅游资源的开发和保护是环保和可持续发展在旅游业的集中体现,也是旅游与环境关系的必要前提。开发和保护关系贯穿在旅游业的整个发展过程中,并随着旅游业的蓬勃发展而日益显出其重要性。良好的资源环境、生态环境、社会环境是旅游业得以发展的重要前提,而旅游资源与环境的关系也是旅游业能否持续发展的重要依据。

　　本文阐述了旅游资源开发和利用的主要原则,开发和利用旅游资源的主要举措,如增加容量、创新资源、扩大用途等。为了充分利用和保护旅游资源,旅游景区的管理可采取交通管理、景区管理、游客管理等措施。但最重要的是,旅游资源的开发和利用必须遵循旅游可持续发展的原则,做到旅游发展不以牺牲环境为代价,保持旅游资源利用的代际平衡,使旅游业持续不断地健康发展。

　　旅游资源开发和保护既相互联系又相互矛盾,两者是辩证的矛盾统一体,并在辩证联系中共同改善旅游资源与环境的关系,推动旅游业的可持续发展。旅游资源是旅游者进行旅游活动的基础和前提条件,一旦破坏殆尽,旅游业将失去依存的条件,也就无开发可言了。因此,保护是开发的前提。从可持续发展的角度看,资源保护归根到底是为了更好的发展。因此,旅游资源必须经过开发利用,才能发挥其功能和效益,也才具有现实的经济意义和社会意义,资源保护的必要性只有通过开发才能得以体现。

　　随着旅游需求的不断增加,大量涌入的游客必然会对旅游目的地的资源和环境产生负面影响。为了把这种影响降至最低,实现旅游资源保护和旅游目的地可持续发展,很多地方都采取了一系列旅游规划和管理措施。事实上,良性的旅游发展总是有赖于合理的旅游开发和资源保护。

　　旅游资源开发和利用的措施有三种:

　　1. 增加容量

　　旅游景区的容量是有限的,但这个限度并不是固定的。通过引入新技术、新规划方案,可以提高景区的承载力,从而接待更多的游客。

　　2. 创新资源

　　由于旅游资源内涵的广泛性,以及旅游动机和兴趣的多样化,旅游资源可以顺应旅游市场需求的变化,不断更新和再生其吸引力因素,把那些能吸引游客的资源充分利用起来。

　　3. 扩大用途

　　旅游目的地的设施规划不仅要考虑到当地居民的需要,而且也要考虑到旅游者的需要,扩大这些设施的用途。

　　旅游目的地管理包括三个方面:

　　1. 交通管理

　　大量的交通工具进入旅游目的地会对当地的环境产生极大的影响,因此,应当限制游客使用私人交通工具,鼓励他们使用公共交通工具。在一些对环境特别敏感的区域,道路尽量绕开建筑,而不要直接穿越。

2. 景区管理

一方面,每个景区的总体容量是有限的,当游客量已经超过景区的承载力时,景区应当采取措施控制游客进入。另一方面,当景区内某个局域的游客量超过其承载力时,景区应当采取措施分流这个局域的游客。

3. 游客管理

加强各种类型的旅游者行为规范的制定、宣传和实施,加大对旅游者的宣传教育,引导游客的旅游文明行为。

旅游规划和管理措施是缓解旅游与环境之间矛盾的有效方法,但仅仅这些还远远不够。要实现旅游可持续发展,还必须采取一些战略措施。

1. 实施可持续旅游发展战略

在保护资源与环境并最大限度地增加旅游者享受乐趣和给当地带来效益的同时,将旅游开发对所在地区的消极影响限制在最小的范围内,是可持续旅游资源发展的主要指导原则之一。在旅游资源开发与保护中实施可持续发展战略应该对旅游环境承载力、旅游开发的影响等方面进行系统研究,为和谐平衡的旅游资源开发和保护模式提供理论依据。努力开发和推广绿色旅游产品。旅游资源开发的一部分旅游收益应该用于保护旅游资源,改善、美化资源环境。这既是保护资源的需要,又能进一步提高开发的效果,促进更大的发展,符合可持续旅游发展的原则。

2. 导入知识经济内涵

目前旅游开发的粗放型模式、资源保护手段的落后和经营管理技术水平不高都说明旅游业知识含量较低。因此导入知识经济是新时代旅游资源开发和保护的要求。要实行资源开发和保护的"科技兴旅"战略,包括实施科技手段,变盲目的、掠夺式的粗放型开发为集约化的开发,最大限度地减少开发过程中对资源造成的破坏。资源的开发应该在调查基础上应用现代技术进行可行性论证,制定开发总体规则,以保证开发后对资源的合理利用;运用现代高新技术手段对珍贵的自然、人类遗产进行保护,减少旅游资源的自然损耗,延长其生命周期,促进资源的可持续利用;保持并增加旅游资源的文化内涵;培养旅游资源开发和保护的高素质旅游专门人才。

我们应当清醒地认识到,旅游资源开发保护和可持续旅游发展都是一个长期的复杂过程。旅游资源开发和保护中需要政策支持、引导和适度的管理力度,以规范旅游资源的开发和保护。适当的政策和旅游宣传教育,可以使社会形成开发保护的共识,使旅游从业人员成为资源开发和保护的先锋,使旅游者成为旅游资源的保护者。同时,旅游资源环境是社会、自然环境大系统的一个子系统,旅游资源开发和保护有必要与整个旅游大环境协调一致,以形成具有强大凝聚力的整体,在充分利用旅游资源的同时,保护人们赖以生存的自然环境和人文环境,建立环境友好性的旅游景区和旅游目的地。

旅游知识测试

正误判断:请在正确的选题上划√,错误的选题上划×。

1. 旅游资源开发的直接目的就是为了发挥、改善和提高旅游资源的吸引力,其最终目的则是将其潜在的资源优势转化成为现实的旅游吸引物。

2. 世界上有各种类型的旅游资源。旅游资源多样性的特点是客观世界的复杂性决定的,更是与人们旅游动机的多样性分不开的。

3. 很多现实的旅游资源,特别是已为旅游业长期利用的现实旅游资源,不需要进行再生性开发,以避免资源重复开发、旅游项目重复建设。

4. 旅游资源的人为性破坏并不完全是由外来旅游者造成的,还有一类人为性破坏往往是由旅游资源所在地的当地人,甚至是由当地的旅游企业造成的。

5. 旅游资源的开发和建设应遵循以下原则：突出独特性的原则，力求经济的原则，注意保护环境的原则和一次性开发的原则。

Part III Case Study
第三部分 案例研究

萨尔茨堡旅游资源的开发和保护

分析要点

1. 从重视资金转而重视原始自然资源和未被污染的环境，你认为是哪些原因促使萨尔茨堡的旅游管理者产生这种转变？
2. 萨尔茨堡当局更多采用各种优惠措施诱导游客使用公共交通工具，而不是强制性措施，你认为强制性措施还是诱导性措施更为有效？
3. 为调整淡、旺季的游客量，萨尔茨堡旅游管理者采取了一些营销策略，但效果似乎并不明显，你认为问题的关键在哪里？有无更好的建议呢？
4. 为保护环境，萨尔茨堡政府采取了一系列措施，这其中是面向旅游业经营者的措施有效，还是面向游客的措施更为有效呢？政府应当扮演何种角色？
5. 本案例中，萨尔茨堡政府为保护当地的旅游环境和资源所采取的措施，哪些是属于规划措施，哪些是属于管理措施？两类措施的相互关系如何？
6. 萨尔茨堡案例对你所在城市的旅游资源开发和利用有何借鉴意义？结合本案例，列举一景点谈谈你的看法。

相关理论和问题

1. 旅游资源开发（Tourism resource development）
2. 目的地承载力（Bearing capacity of the destination）
3. 旅游规划（Tourism planning）
4. 旅游的可持续发展（Sustainable development of tourism）

一、旅游发展背景

萨尔茨堡州是奥地利国际旅游最发达、对外国游客最有吸引力的旅游目的地之一。近年来，年均接待游客高达 2 500 万人次，而本州居民仅有 50 万人。旅游在这里是一个巨大的产业，有 1/3 的当地人口直接或间接就业于旅游业。旅游业为萨尔茨堡创造了良好的国民收入和就业机会。萨尔茨堡的旅游发展具有悠久的历史。1803 年之前，这里是一个独立的教区。州内的金矿和盐矿给大主教们带来了巨大财富。萨尔茨堡市内富丽堂皇的宫殿和雄伟壮观的大教堂，向人们显示了教皇曾经享受过的荣华富贵。因此，这里也成为人们参观游览，了解奥地利宗教、历史、文化和建筑艺术的地方。萨尔茨堡还是世界著名音乐大师莫扎特的故乡。市区仅有 15 万人口，但却拥有大量引人注目的歌剧院和音乐厅。这里每年都要举行以莫扎特音乐为主题的各种纪念活动，吸引着各国成千上万的音乐爱好者前来游览。

萨尔茨堡市周围的乡村地区又是一番不同的景色。州内 3/4 的地区是峡谷和山地，最高的山峰海拔 3000 多米。20 世纪初期，居住在山区的居民十分贫苦。特别是在冬季，山路经常崩塌,人们无固定的农活可做,缺医少药,食不果腹。50年代之后,山区的年轻人开始跑到城市中找工作,生活环境才有所改善。虽然萨尔茨堡市区的旅游发展由来已久,但山区的旅游是从第二次世界大战后开始发展起来的,而且仅仅开展夏季旅游。山区的冬季旅游是50年代之后才开始发展的,成为向当地农业人口提供就业机会的重要来源。到六七十年代,萨尔茨堡州的夏季和冬季旅游得以迅速发展,年均增长率高达10%。许多新的滑雪道被开通,道路交通更加便利,饭店、餐饮、娱乐场所成倍增长。当地人的生活水平大大提高,当旅游旺季到来时,甚至常常出现劳动力短缺的现象。

旅游开发在萨尔茨堡似乎非常容易。如果谁想来此进行旅游投资,手续既简单,又具有很大的吸引力。由银行提供贷款,政府提供投资补贴和税收优惠政策,投资回报率很高、回收期也很短。建成的饭店经营并不困难,只要在客户的窗户上挂上"房间空闲"的标志,便可招揽客人上门。80年代之前,这里的政府和居民普遍认为,只有资金才是旅游发展最主要的资本。80年代后,萨尔茨堡的旅游管理者们第一次提出了关于旅游发展重要财富的哲学观点,认为一个地区的原始自然资源和未被污染的环境,是旅游发展最基本、最重要的资产。没有人怀疑萨尔茨堡州拥有世界上最丰富、最优良的自然旅游资源,但这些自然财富和资本不但不会增加,而且会迅速减少,甚至消失。

二、旅游发展带来的问题

80年代中期以来,阿尔卑斯山区自然旅游资源受到威胁的情况引起了有关人士的重视。一些学者发表了论文和著作进行评论。1986年由 Jost Kripendor 所著的 *Alpsegen-Alptraum* 一书中,列举了瑞士阿尔卑斯山区旅游发展所带来的正面和负面影响。

1. 旅游发展对社会经济作出的贡献体现在下述方面:
- 旅游提供了就业机会,增加了当地人的收入,使大量的青年人脱离了本地区的贫困;
- 旅游促进了当地基础设施的建设,提高了当地人的生活质量;
- 旅游为农村经济创造了冬季继续发展的条件;
- 旅游保护了农村田园风光;
- 旅游使山区的居民增强了生活的自信心。

2. 旅游发展给阿尔卑斯山区带来了下述一系列问题:
- 旅游造成了当地不合理的经济结构,使当地的经济发展过分依赖旅游这一脆弱的行业,容易引起经济波动和经济危机;
- 旅游发展缺乏合理的规划,使设备设施经常大量闲置;旅游淡季时山区的饭店客房出租率仅有20%左右;
- 旅游发展使部分地区失去了原有的特色,本地区的风貌和风俗习惯被改变;
- 旅游发展使阿尔卑斯山区失去了本地区的独立性,许多重要的旅游决策受到外界的影响;
- 旅游发展给阿尔卑斯山区带来的最严重后果是破坏和污染了这里的自然资源和环境:野生动物和植物减少,土壤被侵蚀,空气和水源被污染,地下水位降低,噪音增大,垃圾废物成堆、难以处理等等,这些都使当地的自然环境质量大大降低;
- 旅游设施的建设占用了大量土地,第二住宅、度假村、娱乐场所、住宿设施和公路等,使山区秀丽的风景和自然空间逐渐减少以致消失,游客成为景观和环境的无情吞噬者。

阿尔卑斯山区给萨尔茨堡州的启示和教训已经足够了。况且在萨尔茨堡州内,这类问题已经发生了许多。例如,夏季萨尔茨堡市区主要的街区和景点经常人满为患,挤得水泄不通;乘汽车而来的游客严重地践踏着区内的自然景观,威胁着珍稀鸟类的生存。然而,一些来自其他旅游区的环境警报更加令人担忧:亚得里亚海区海藻大量而迅速地繁殖;意大利阿尔卑斯山区发生雪崩和泥石流滑坡……严重的环境问题已经成为今后阻碍旅游发展的主要因素。

三、保护旅游资源所采取的措施和步骤

"将未被损害、少受损害的自然资源和环境作为旅游发展的重要财富",这是萨尔茨堡人提出的旅游可持续发展宗旨。开展旅游可持续发展运动,不仅是为了保护自然环境和当地居民的利益,而且是为了保护全人类的利益和地球的未来质量。萨尔茨堡州旅游局正在朝着这个方向努力工作。

1985年,州旅游局重新修订了自己的市场营销目标,确定萨尔茨堡未来的市场营销目标不仅是吸引更多的新游客前来,而且要致力于改善旅游吸引物的质量和内涵,向游客提供一个良好的、有益于身心健康的自然和社会环境。1989年,州旅游局制定了一个"绿色市场营销规划"。其中提出了环境利益优先于经济利益的观点,并要求萨尔茨堡市区和其他各地区都要制定相应的旅游可持续发展原则和措施,作为今后工作的指导方针。"绿色市场营销规划"的主要内容包括以下4个方面:

- 减少使用私人交通工具;
- 控制基础设施、住宿设施和娱乐设施的扩建;
- 调整旅游旺季时的客流量;
- 支持和鼓励具有环境意识的行为。

此规划得到了州政府的批准和支持。在规划发布会上,州旅游局官员还强调政府必须制定限制性旅游发展原则以及相应的政策和法规,支持"旅游市场营销规划"的实施。例如,对旅游住宿实施的建设和新开辟的滑雪区要进行法规性的限制;对提高环境质量、树立环境意识的创举要给予财政支持和物质奖励等。当地许多旅游企业在执行规划中起到了积极作用。以下是对"绿色市场营销规划"主要内容的详细说明。

1. 减少使用私人交通工具

(1) 与国外有关 旅行社达成协议,对乘火车来萨尔茨堡市的游客提供折扣50%的优惠票价;对乘火车到萨尔茨堡州内20个著名景点的游客优惠门票折扣20%。这一举措由奥地利铁路公司和各旅游景点出资赞助。

(2) 调整游客来州内各景点游览的时间,尽量使游客分散在周一至周五之间,减轻周末游客拥挤给交通和环境带来的压力。德国的一家旅行社采纳了这一建议,对周三来旅游的游客提供折扣50%的价格优惠,由此造成的经济损失由该旅行社自行承担。另外几家旅行社也接受了这一建议,取消了周末散客和团队游览线路,只安排周一至周五的游览日程,对周三来的游客给予特别的优惠价格。

(3) 政府在萨尔茨堡市中心区修建了许多步行街和自行车路,还提供了许多廉价有效的公共交通工具,鼓励人们减少使用私人小汽车。

(4) 一些滑雪旅游区为了减少交通阻塞,向游客提供从奥地利各个火车站到滑雪区之间的免费火车票。

(5) 山区的各个景点之间推出了新型的交通工具——电动小轿车,并建立了太阳能夜间充电站,使使用私人小轿车的游客大大减少,产生了良好的环境效益。

2. 控制各类旅游设施的扩建

萨尔茨堡州对新建旅馆和滑雪场制定了严格的综合性法规。80年代之前,政府曾经以提供补贴、低息贷款、信贷担保、降低税收等优惠政策,鼓励各方投资建设更多的旅游设施。80年代中期之后,政府的政策开始转变,采取严格的手段限制旅游设施的建设。1993年颁布的新城镇和乡村规划法规中就包括了限制旅馆建设的条例。目前,在萨尔茨堡州批准建设一座拥有60间客房的小旅馆已经是特例了。政府的目标就是限制旅馆规模的扩大,防止旅游景区旅馆密度增加,保护小型建筑物,将旅馆的床位数保持在2万张之内。此外,政府还决定10年内禁止开发新的滑雪场地,并规定如果建设一条新的滑雪索道,必须取代一条旧的滑雪索道。这一规定有可能延长执行的年限。

3. 调整旅游旺季的游客流量

三月和七八月是萨尔茨堡的旅游高峰季节,给当地的自然和社会环境带来了极大的压

力,同时也给当地的旅游经营者带来了丰厚的利润。"绿色市场营销规划"的目的是增加旅游淡季的吸引力,减轻旅游旺季的压力。为此,一些旅行社推出了秋季自行车团队游、春季滑雪度假游等新产品,并对淡季通过滑雪通道的团队游客给予特别的价格优惠,提供非常低价的住宿设施。这些都大大增加了当地旅游产品的吸引力。

然而,尽管旺季的游客流量被成功地调整,但客源数量却无法更合理地均匀分配。例如,参加自行车团队旅游的客人,使当地9月和1月的客房出租率增加了10%,但旺季的游客数量并没有减少。学生和带着上学孩子的家庭游客是调整旅游旺季压力的主要障碍。

4. 支持和鼓励具有环境意识的行为

政府对旅游的环保投资正在不断增加,前述提供电动公共交通工具、减少私人小轿车的使用就是一例。政府开发的另一个节约能源的项目,是在有条件的乡村地区建立集中供热系统,以当地锯木厂产生的锯木屑为燃料。它具有如下优越性:

- 燃料可以就地取材,运燃料的交通工具精巧简单,可以节约能源,减少空气污染;
- 燃料只在一个锅炉里燃烧,排放的烟尘可以在成本相对较低的情况下得以过滤;
- 锅炉燃烧的温度高,燃料燃烧彻底,可将废气排放量降低到最低程度;
- 一个村庄集中供热系统排放有害气体的数量,仅相当于过去一户居民使用的家用燃油锅炉的排放量。

萨尔茨堡州政府还采取了许多方法促使旅馆业提高环境意识,实施环境保护措施。例如召开各种会议,请旅馆的经理们互相交流意见和经验;组织有意义的竞赛活动;建立环保奖励基金,经过严格的评审,每年奖励两个对环境保护作出贡献的单位和个人。住宿业荣获环保奖励基金的单位必须实行无浪费早餐,安排燃烧锯木屑和供热系统,由农场主经营的青年招待所须向客人提供绿色食品和相关的食品信息。此外,还要求旅馆和各类住宿设施的经营者向前来投宿的客人发放环保宣传品。宣传品的醒目标题是"我是你度假的天堂和我们共同的未来"。许多宣传品中向游客提出了应遵守的环保准则,提醒游客要以实际行动保护萨尔茨堡的"度假天堂"。与宣传品相配合的行动是在旅馆中搞了许多张贴物。例如,在旅馆卫生间里张贴物上建议客人将需要换洗的毛巾放在地板上,不需换洗的则挂起来。这一措施使旅馆洗涤布巾的数量减少了30%。

政府对凡是能造成环境污染的游乐活动也采取措施进行限制。例如,禁止开展直升机运送游客上山滑雪的活动;对山区自行车旅游活动规定线路和区域;游客散步要沿着特定的小路,绕开那些环境易损地区。为了保证自行车旅游活动的刺激性,当地将森林中被砍伐的空地提供给骑自行车的游客使用。旅游局为了鼓励游客结伴步行或骑自行车旅游,推出了步行几日游的活动,即由导游带领一组游客白天长途跋涉穿越全州,夜间在山村的小客栈休息,只带自己的衣物和少量的行李,使游客减少了依赖汽车周游全州的心理。而后旅游局将这些步行和骑自行车旅游者的亲身经历编写成宣传资料,制成广告,以扩大影响,增强吸引力。目前,由于宣传促销的主题有所改变,原来的许多旅游招贴广告已经被更换。例如,原来对自行车旅游的促销主题是"人类可以征服自然",广告画面上展现的是两个偏离了被踏平的山区小路而意欲另辟路径的骑自行车探险旅游者。新更换的广告显示了在一片美丽幽静的森林景色中,一个家庭自行车旅游小组沿着山坡小路翩翩骑来,画面极其美妙地突出了人类与大自然的融合。

四、结论

综上所述,尽管萨尔茨堡州还没有建立一个政府和企业相结合、具有全面责任和利益关系的综合性环境保护工作网络,但这里已经形成了一种可靠的协议,告诉和提醒人们应该如何采取行动保护环境;主持这个协议的是萨尔茨堡州政府和旅游局。在"绿色市场营销规划"中,有关环境保护的内容被修订得更加详细、具体,以便萨尔茨堡的旅游资源得到充分的利用,而当地的生态环境不受破坏。

资料来源:山峰地区—国家公园. Ward,J. 著,曾萍等译.旅游案例分析[M],云南大学出版社,2006.

Part IV Reading Box
第四部分 阅读与分析

National Parks

阅读分析要点

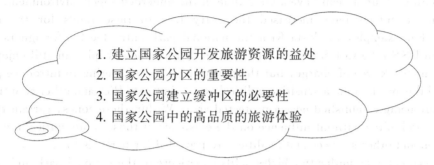

1. 建立国家公园开发旅游资源的益处
2. 国家公园分区的重要性
3. 国家公园建立缓冲区的必要性
4. 国家公园中的高品质的旅游体验

Theoretically, harmful human activities cannot affect the protected areas such as national parks. But in fact, these areas all over the world are faced with increased threat brought about by overpopulation, diminishing resource bases and other human-related stresses. Organizations in some countries doubt whether it is reasonable to establish such reserved spaces. Under such circumstances, tourism may be a good choice to maintain the present state of these endangered spaces if proper measures are taken.

Compared with other land uses, tourism turns out to be a far **more profitable way of resource utilization**. As a research in Kenya shows, an adult lion will bring more profit during its adult life span if it serves as an ecotourism attraction instead of being used as a trophy animal or a source of meat for local residents.[1] It was estimated that ecotourism could bring $65 to a hectare of land in Kenya's Amboseli National Park while agriculture could produce only $1.20. What's more, unlike logging, mining or agriculture the **well-planned tourism** would not bring the negative effect on the destination while helping to earn a big profit. There are beautiful scenery, relatively undisturbed habitat and interesting wildlife in the national park which lie in the fragile areas. Therefore, the tourism industry should try to avoid those activities that may gradually destroy these qualities.

Owing to this argument, park managers try to develop **ecotourism**. They do so not because they believe that they can be successful in tourism but because they confront failure in other businesses and want to have a try. Along with the continuing growth of the tourism sector and the growing interest in the natural environment this has resulted in a sharp increase of tourist arrivals in the protected areas throughout the world.[2] For instance, in the United State there are more than 400 million visits to national park every year, and in Spain, even though its park system only covers 125,000 hectares, there are more than three million visits annually. In addition, according to an estimation based on 1991 data, visitation numbers to Australia's national parks are about 20—25 million each year.

With the rapid growth of tourism demand, congestion has become a serious problem, which proves that tourism can bring as much damage as other activities. However, it is unnecessary to ban tourism totally in those parks where tourism has been set up and accepted for a long time. To solve the above-mentioned problem, park and tourism managers have carried out some strategies that will enhance the integration of tourism and the natural environment so that a greater achievement can be made.³ Among these are **zooming policies** that divide the park into two portions. One is a small site-hardened part in which the large number of soft ecotourists can enjoy themselves with sophisticated services and facilities offered. The other covers the vast majority of park space where those small numbers of hard ecotourists can have a good time in the underdeveloped environment.

Now some countries have increased the entry fees to raise funds for the park management. For example, in Costa Rica the national park entry fee for foreigners was increased from US＄1.50 to US＄15.00 in 1994. In Queensland, people can still enjoy its national park network free of charge, but the government is considering to introduce park entry fees and this has become a sensitive political issue. In Costa Rica and other countries, **buffer zones** are being established near a protected area. Within these zones, certain types of activity are prohibited without influence on the existence of those communities in which accommodation and other services and facilities are provided for park visitors.⁴

Tourists can enjoy an **authentic, high-quality experience** in the national park and other relatively undisturbed natural environments. To their pleasant surprise, they can also enjoy themselves in some modified environments which are under good protection such as reservoirs and farmland which attract interesting birds or mammals. For example, in the Canadian province of Saskatchewan, tourists have a chance of appreciating the beautiful view of migrating waterfowl in the farm fields, while in the town of Churchill, Manitoba (Canada), they can view polar bears.

New Words

overpopulation	n.	人口过剩
ban	v.	禁止,禁运
diminish	v.	逐渐缩小
sophisticated	adj.	精明的,久经世故的
trophy	n.	战利品,奖品
buffer	n.	缓冲器,缓冲物
logging	n.	[美]伐木搬运业
mammal	n.	哺乳动物

Notes

1. As a research in Kenya shows, an adult lion will bring more profit during its adult life span if it serves as an ecotourism attraction instead of being used as a trophy animal or a source of meat for local residents.
在肯尼亚进行的研究表明,比起当作猎人的战利品或当地人餐桌上的佳肴,一头成年狮子作为生态旅游产品在其生存期间可带来更多的利润。

2. Along with the continuing growth of the tourism sector and the growing interest in the natural environment this has resulted in a sharp increase of tourist arrivals in the protected areas throughout the world.
随着旅游业的持续发展和人们对自然环境越来越浓厚的兴趣,到世界各地保护区参观的游客数量有了急剧的增长。

3. To solve the above-mentioned problem, park and tourism managers have carried out some strategies that will enhance the integration of tourism and the natural environment so that a greater achievement can be made.
   为了解决以上问题，公园和旅游经理采取了一些措施，来整合旅游和自然资源，以取得更大成就。

4. Within these zones, certain types of activity are prohibited without influence on the existence of those communities in which accommodation and other services and facilities are provided for park visitors.
   在这些区域，某些类型的活动被禁止。在不影响这些社区的情况下，社区为游客提供住宿和其他服务与设施。

Topic discussion

1. Organizations in some countries suspect whether it is reasonable to establish the national parks. Why do they have such a suspicion?
   _____

2. Why is tourism a good choice to maintain the present state of those endangered protected areas?
   _____

3. Give examples to illustrate that tourism is far more profitable than other land uses.
   _____

4. What kind of tourism do park managers try to develop? Why?
   _____

5. What effects do you think the rapid increase of tourist arrivals may have on the national parks?
   _____

6. What kind of experience do tourists have when they travel in the national park compared with the travel experience in the zoo?
   _____

【即学即用】
With reference to the theory, information or approach applied in the Reading Box, have a case study of a national park you know. Make presentation of your study in Chinese or in English using PPT.

【学习资源库】
为了掌握本章更多的相关专业知识，请您登陆http://sicnu.edu.cn/，点击国家双语教学示范课程《旅游学概论》，进入网络学堂查询相关资料。

Chapter Review 本章小结

This chapter has discussed the important relationship between utilization and protection of tourism resources, and described principles of proper utilization and conservation of tourism resources. In great details, it gives the concrete measures to utilize and conserve tourism resources in a fragile environment. On one hand, we will utilize the tourism resources for the purpose of regional development; on the other hand, we should have responsibilities to protect the resources that are fragile in nature. In a sense, it is a conflict between utilization and protection of the resources, but the proper management of the resources can resolve such a conflict. It is a successful example in the national parks of Kenya, where tourists enjoy an authentic, high-quality experience while the tourism resources have been well preserved.

Part V   Additional Know-how of Tourism
第五部分   旅游知识扩展

【关键术语】

Tourism resources: features of a destination that are valued as attractions by tourists at some particular point in time; a feature that was a tourism resource 100 years ago may not be perceived as such now

旅游资源：旅游资源是旅游目的地的某些特征，它们在某个特定的时间点被旅游者认为是有价值的旅游吸引物。100年前的旅游资源现在不一定被视为旅游资源。

Honey spot: A variety of attractions, shops, restaurants and accommodation are clustered around one or two viewpoints to create a complex capable of absorbing a high population density.

"蜜罐式"场所：各种吸引物、商店、餐厅和住宿场所聚集在一个或两个景点周围所创造的具有可吸纳密集旅游者能力的综合建筑群。

Public goods: The principal feature of such goods or services is that it is not realistically possible to exclude individuals from consumption once they have been made available. Once available, it will be consumed by all individuals; it is open to abuse through over-use.

公共物品：这类产品和服务的主要特点是：一旦有这些产品和服务就会有个人消费。只要能够获取到，所有的个体都会去消费，因此，它们很容易被滥用。

Merit goods: Public facilities made available for the purpose of encouraging consumption are termed merit goods. The facilities are socially needed even if the willingness to pay for them in the market place is limited.

特值产品：为鼓励消费而提供的公用设施被称为"特值产品"。即使市场中有支付意愿的人是有限的，但这些设施也是社会需要的。

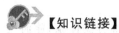【知识链接】

1. 旅游资源的定义

直到目前为止,旅游学术界对于旅游资源的概念还没有形成统一的认识。不同学者的定义各不相同,这里列举几个国内学者对于旅游资源的定义。

"凡是能为人们提供旅游观赏、知识乐趣、度假疗养、娱乐休息、探险猎奇、考察研究以及人民友好往来和消磨闲暇时间的客体和劳务,都可称为旅游资源。"(郭来喜,《人文地理概论》,1985)

"自然界和人类社会凡能对旅游者产生吸引力,可以为旅游业开发所利用,并可产生经济效益、社会效益、环境效益的各种事物和因素都可视为旅游资源。"(国家旅游局资源开发司和中国科学院地理研究所,《中国旅游资源普查规范》,1992)

"旅游资源是指自然界或人类社会中凡能对旅游产生吸引向性、有可能被用来规划开发成旅游消费对象的各种事与物的总合"。(孙文昌,《旅游资源学》,1998)

"指客观地存在于一定地域空间并因其所具有的愉悦价值而使旅游者为之向往的自然存在、历史文化遗产或社会现象"。(谢彦君,《基础旅游学》,2004)

2. 旅游资源的移动性

旅游学界普遍认为旅游资源是不可移动的。旅游资源的不可移动性有三个方面的内容:一是旅游资源的本体不能朝向旅游者移动,否则就将在根本上消灭了旅游者,该资源也不成为旅游资源,而成为可以当地人所利用的普通休闲资源;二是当旅游资源被开发成旅游产品并被出售时,资源乃至产品的所有权不能转移;三是旅游资源个体的小尺度搬迁,如塔、庙等的近距离迁移,并没有在根本上改变旅游资源的不可转移性。

但也有一些人认为自然资源的原生性特点使其表现出位置的不可移动性,但是一些无形的旅游资源和人文资源是可以人造的,也是可以移动的。随着社会经济的发展和科学技术的进步,人们依靠自身的聪明才智,凭借雄厚的财力支持,使得旅游资源移动现象频频发生,如英国伦敦桥被搬迁至美国,安徽黄山市休宁县黄村一座有200多年历史的徽派古民居"荫余堂"被拆散后,远渡重洋被搬到美国波士顿。

随着社会经济的发展,特别是在旅游资源欠缺的地区,会继续出现旅游资源的移动,甚至是旅游资源的"复制品",以满足人们日益增长的精神生活的需要。对于专门的文化旅游者来说,移动后的旅游资源会使其体验的真实性和深度大打折扣,而对于普通的游客来说,这种资源仍然具有很强的吸引力,不会从根本上影响旅游者体验"愉悦"的本质。

【小思考】

1. 旅游资源分类的依据是什么?我国旅游资源国家标准分类体系是如何对旅游资源进行分类的?

参考阅读:

依据不同的原则和角度,旅游资源有不同的分类。比较普遍的分类法是依据旅游资源的基本成因,分为自然旅游资源和人文旅游资源两大类。

自然旅游资源即是依照自然发展规律天然形成的旅游资源,是可供人类旅游享用的自然景观与自然环境,它寓于自然界的一定空间位置、特定的形成条件和历史演变阶段。自然旅游资源一般又分为地文景观类、水域风光类、生物景观类和气候气象景观类。

人文旅游资源则是在人类历史发展和社会进程中由人类社会行为促使形成的具有人类社会文化属性的悦人事物,其形成和分布不仅受历史、民族和意识形态等因素的制约,而且还受自然环境的深刻影响。人文旅游资源一般又分为遗址遗迹类、建筑与居落类、园林类、陵墓类和社会风情类。

根据 2003 年 5 月 1 日实施的《旅游资源分类、调查与评价》国家标准分类体系,旅游资源分成主类、亚类和基本类型三个层次。主类分成地文景观、水域风光、生物景观、天象与气候景观、遗址遗迹、建筑与设施、旅游商品、人文活动八类,主类下再分 31 个亚类,亚类下再分 155 个基本类型。

2. 旅游资源的优劣和区位条件的好坏如何进行评价?比较竞争优势理论如何加以应用?

参考阅读:

旅游资源的开发,不能孤立地就资源论资源,必须将其放置于区域经济的组织结构体系之中进行分析。因此其开发模式的确定,要根据旅游资源自身的状况与区位的配合条件及拟安排相应旅游活动的行为结构来进行。

(1) 风景资源丰富、区位条件良好的地方。既要考虑观光旅游和服务设施建设,又要丰富旅游活动行为所需的各类层次结构,特别要重视开发购物和娱乐设施,提高服务级别。

(2) 区位条件良好,但风景名胜资源不丰富的地方,应注意增建相应的风景资源,努力发挥社会人文资源的吸引力,完善旅游行为结构。

(3) 风景资源突出,而区位条件不佳的地方。这种模式类型应在改善接待服务设施,提高购物和娱乐旅游内容的同时,通过积极的宣传促销活动,树立和塑造区域旅游形象,还要进一步改善交通条件。

(4) 风景资源和区位条件都中等的市镇或旅游区域。要注意对风景资源进行分级评价,重点开发周边市场所缺少且可能受游客欢迎的旅游资源项目,创造区域内的拳头旅游产品,并进一步改善区位交通条件。

Part VI　Further Readings
第六部分　课外阅读

如果您想进一步学习本章的内容,探讨旅游资源的开发和保护,建议您阅读以下学者的著作和论文。

一、中文部分

[1] 肖星,严江平. 旅游资源与开发[M]. 北京:中国旅游出版社,2000.
[2] 王建军. 旅游资源分类与评价问题的新思考[J]. 旅游学刊,2005,(06).
[3] 邢道隆,王玫. 关于旅游资源评价的几个基本问题[J]. 旅游学刊,1987,(03).
[4] 李红玉. 休闲经济时代的旅游资源分类与评价[J]. 旅游学刊,2006,(01).
[5] 杨振之. 论度假旅游资源的分类与评价[J]. 旅游学刊,2005,(06).
[6] 夏赞才. 旅游资源亟须美学价值评价[J]. 旅游学刊,2006,(01).
[7] 刘家明. 从规划实践看旅游资源开发评价[J]. 旅游学刊,2006,(01).
[8] 陈田,钟林生,刘家明. 旅游资源标准应用过程中的几个认识误区[J]. 旅游学刊,2005,(06).
[9] 张红霞,苏勤,王群. 国外有关旅游资源游憩价值评估的研究综述[J]. 旅游学刊,2006,(01).
[10] 王良健. 现行旅游资源评价体系的改进与方法创新[J]. 旅游学刊,2006,(02).

二、英文部分

[1] Sheila J. Backman, Muzaffer Uysal, Kenneth Backman. Regional analysis of

tourism resources[J]. *Annals of Tourism Research*, 1991, 18(2):323—327.

[2] Brian J. Hudson. Waterfalls: Resources for Tourism[J]. *Annals of Tourism Research*, 1998, 25(4):958—973.

[3] Choong-Ki Lee, Sang-Yoel Han. Estimating the use and preservation values of national parks' tourism resources using a contingent valuation method[J]. *Tourism Management*, 2002, 23(5):531—540.

[4] Julianna Priskin. Assessment of natural resources for nature-based tourism: the case of the Central Coast Region of Western Australia[J]. *Tourism Management*, 2001, 22(6):637—648.

[5] Pierre Lainé. Interrelationship between benefits and costs of tourism resources [J]. *Tourism Management*, 1983, 4(1):65—68.

[6] Piero Barucci, Emilio Becheri. Tourism as a resource for developing southern Italy[J]. *Tourism Management*, 1990, 11(3):227—239.

[7] Howard L. Hughes. Culture as a tourist resource—a theoretical consideration [J]. *Tourism Management*, 1987, 8(3):205—216.

[8] Choong-Ki Lee. Valuation of nature-based tourism resources using dichotomous choice contingent valuation method[J]. *Tourism Management*, 1997, 18(8):587—591.

[9] Stephen R. C. Wanhill. Evaluating the resource costs of tourism[J]. *Tourism Management*, 1982, 3(4):208—211.

[10] Xiao-Long Ma, Chris Ryan, Ji-Gang Bao. Chinese national parks: Differences, resource use and tourism product portfolios[J]. *Tourism Management*, 2008.

Chapter 15　The Sustainable Tourism
第十五章　可持续发展旅游

Learning objects：学习目标
- Based on tourism system (Leiper's model), explain the reasons why the sustainable tourism should be adopted in the large-scale and dominant tourism industry 依据旅游系统(模型)，解释为什么要在大规模和占主导地位的旅游业中开展可持续发展旅游
- Appreciate the emergence of the new travelers as an important market segment and the main characteristics of new travelers 领会新旅游者成为市场细分的重要性，以及新旅游者的主要特征
- Cite the sustainable practices taken by larger corporations in tourism industry 列举旅游业中较大的旅游公司采取的可持续发展的措施
- Understand the business ethics code and the social practices taken by tourism sectors to promote sustainable tourism 理解旅游不同部门为促进可持续旅游而采用的商业伦理和社会行为规范
- Appreciate the forms of new tourism and its application in the world 了解新旅游的各种形态以及在世界各地的运用情况
- Differentiate the characteristics of unsustainable mass tourism and deliberate alternative tourism 区分不可持续发展的大众旅游与有计划的替代旅游的不同特征

Ability goals：能力目标
- Case Study 案例分析：生存还是毁灭：大堡礁海洋公园的未来
- Reading Box 阅读分析：New Tourism 新旅游

Part I Text
第一部分 课文

The Sustainable Tourism

【教学要点】

知识要点	掌握程度	相关章节
basic concept of sustainable tourism 可持续发展旅游的基本概念	重点掌握	旅游的可持续发展是旅游的重大问题,本课文是尾篇和结论,与教材所有章节内容有关联。
new travelers 新旅游者	重点掌握	
profitable mode of the sustainable tourism 可持续旅游的盈利模式	重点掌握	
sustainable corporate practices 可持续的公司行为	一般了解	
sustainable social practices 可持续的社会规范	一般了解	
business ethics codes 商业伦理道德	一般了解	
external or environmental systems 外部或环境系统	一般了解	

The concept of **sustainable development** has been recognized with the emergence of the view of the "green" world. Attention had not been paid to this idea before the release of the Brundtland Report entitled *Our Common Future* in 1987, even though this term was already being used in the early 1980s. The Brundtland Report defined sustainable development in the following way: Sustainable development is development that aims to meet the needs of the present while ensuring that future generations will have the ability to meet their own needs. After the release of the Brundtland Report, the term sustainable tourism became very popular. Some argues that the concept of sustainable tourism should include the ability of both tourism and the local community to sustain their own development because without tourism sector, the term would be meaningless.[1]

At the early stage, it was mainly in those small-scale and low intensity situations that sustainable tourism was developed. However, considering the fact that mass tourism takes up the majority of the world's tourism market, the connection between sustainable tourism and mass tourism is reasonably a more important issue. In the following, we will discuss why the industry should focus on sustainability, and briefly summarize the practices and measures that are implemented according to the concept of sustainable tourism.[2]

It is justifiable to adopt sustainable practices within the large-scale, dominant tourism industry. The following are some reasons:
- The growth of the "new traveller" market
- The profitability of sustainability
- The suitability of larger corporations to adopt sustainable practices.

1. Growth of the "new traveller" market

As more and more people realize the importance of environmental protection, they are becoming more judicious, experienced and responsible when they make travel decisions and take the journey. Now the industry has been aware of the significance of the new traveler in the tourist market and is sure that the **new traveler** market will grow rapidly during the next few decades whether it is measured by comparing with other tourist markets or not.[3] If society is indeed attaching much importance to environmental protection while furthering the development, then it is possible for the new traveler to emerge as the most important tourist market and gradually replace the conventional mass tourists.[4] As a result, tourism businesses will have to develop along a more sustainable way; otherwise, they would not survive. Even if this is not the case, to capture this high-spending and growing market is still most beneficial to tourism businesses. We can find the main characteristics of the new traveler, which are regarded as the reflection of the **allocentric** component of Plog's psychographic market profile.

Characteristics of the new traveler
- Green consumer
- Sensitive to local cultures
- Conscious of social justice concerns
- More independent-minded and discerning
- Knowledgeable about environmental issues
- Prefers flexible and spontaneous itineraries
- Carefully assesses tourism products in advance
- In search of authentic and meaningful experiences
- Wishes to have a positive impact on the destination
- Motivated by a desire for self-fulfillment and learning
- Searches for physically and mentally challenging experiences

2. *Profitability of sustainability*

Besides a market concern which encourages tourism businesses to focus on sustainability, another major stimulus for this focus is that many related activities are, by their own nature, profitable.[5] For example, just like the recycling of certain kinds of materials, reducing energy consumption is another way to save cost directly. Meanwhile, there are two ways to realize indirect profits. One is to establish a more efficient organization by downsizing and getting rid of hierarchy in it. The other is to improve the employees' morale which often results from such reforms. In addition, if the community relations can develop positively, the host and the tourist will be able to live in harmony with each other. This will be helpful to leave a good impression of the community and enable the tourist to experience a pleasant vacation, which in turn, will enhance visitation levels because of repeat visitation and the **positive word-of-mouth** about the community widely spread by the tourist.[6]

3. *Suitability of larger corporations to adopt sustainable practices*

Sustainable tourism measures can be better implemented in larger corporations because of their size. Such businesses can raise enough funds to support those specialized jobs working at sustainability-related issues such as environmental officer, community relations officer. They can also support relevant staff training, public education programs and comprehensive environmental audits. What's more, **recycling and reduction programs** can be carried out efficiently with the lowest possible cost because of the high levels of resource and energy consumption. At the same time, the extensively integrated structures of the company allow it to organize its sustainability efforts in a harmonious way through its broad linkages. Because of their big scale of production, these companies can also require external suppliers to "go green"—for instance, a firm may make this as a condition in its bidding process that a certain amount of recycled material and only vegetable dye-based inks should be used in the paper products supplied.

Sustainable **corporate practices** in the tourism sector encompass environmental, societal and organizational categories. Waste reduction involving such components as garbage, sewage, water, packaging and atmospheric emissions is one of the common environmental practices. Some waste products can be recycled, such as metals, glass, paper and plastics, while other materials can be re-used, like the almost unused bars of soap left in hotel rooms.

Besides these, various tourism companies have adopted many other environmental measures. Among them is applying natural substitutes to reduce the use of pesticides, especially in golf course resorts. Other equally important measures include the use of "naturalisation" techniques to beautify corporate grounds such as the substitution of native vegetation for foreign varieties, the use of organic foodstuffs and support for local or national conservation programs. As far as energy conservation is concerned, accommodations can use exhaust heat from its absorption chiller to heat the swimming pool, which has reduced the use of gas. Among major corporations, British Airway has always been the most active and enthusiastic one in adopting sustainability-related measures and in reporting its progress to the public.

Another important sustainable practice is **social practices** because sustainability can be applied not only in the natural environment but also in other aspects. Many measures can be taken such as donation to local charities, establishment of scholarships and community improvement schemes, managerial positions of tourism sectors that give priority to local residents, designs that take into consideration the harmonious co-existence of architecture and local styles, and policies that give special consideration to local suppliers of goods.[7]

Sustainable tourism is an effective way adopted by tourism sectors for long-term benefits. It requires careful planning and management. The continuing and rapid growth of tourism has brought too much pressure on the world's resources and makes it necessary to adopt sustainable development to eliminate the growing negative impact on the planet. It is in tourism rather than in other business sector that to promote and enforce environmental and **business ethics codes** has become the most urgent task. Responsible citizens of the world have come to realize that it is of great significance to examine the tourist activities and their impacts or sustainability in a very critical manner. Carrying out the strategy of the sustainable tourism will be able to protect and develop further those natural and cultural attractions that brought the tourist in the first place.

New Words

criteria	n.	标准
patronage	n.	资助,赞助
variable	n.	变量
judicious	adj.	明智的,审慎的
adherence	n.	信奉,坚持
discerning	adj.	有识别力的
vernacular	n.	本国语,本地话
stimulus	n.	促进因素,刺激物

exotic	adj.	异国风情的
naturalisation	n.	归化,移入
repatriate	v.	遣返
charity	n.	慈善团体

Key Terms

sustainable tourism　　可持续发展旅游　　energy consumption　　能量消耗

Notes

1. Some argues that the concept of sustainable tourism should include the ability of both tourism and the local community to sustain their own development because without tourism sector, the term would be meaningless.
   有些人认为,旅游可持续发展应该包括旅游业和当地社区维持各自发展的能力,因为如果没有旅游部门的参与,这一概念是没有意义的。

2. In the following, we will discuss why the industry should focus on sustainability, and briefly summarize the practices and measures that are implemented according to the concept of sustainable tourism.
   接下来,我们将讨论为什么旅游业要把重点放在可持续发展上,并简单地总结遵循可持续旅游发展思想所采取的规范和措施。

3. Now the industry has been aware of the significance of the new traveler in the tourist market and is sure that the new traveler market will grow rapidly during the next few decades whether it is measured by comparing with other tourist markets or not.
   现在旅游业已经意识到新型旅游者在旅游市场中的重要性,并相信无论是否与其他旅游市场进行比较,在未来几十年里,这一市场都将快速增长。

4. If society is indeed attaching much importance to environmental protection while furthering the development, then it is possible for the new traveler to emerge as the most important tourist market and gradually replace the conventional mass tourists.
   如果社会在进一步发展的同时注重环境保护,那么新型旅游者将可能成为最重要的旅游市场,并逐步取代传统的大众旅游者。

5. Besides a market concern which encourages tourism businesses to focus on sustainability, another major stimulus for this focus is that many related activities are, by their own nature, profitable.
   除了市场关心鼓励旅游的可持续发展,另外一个主要推动力是许多与旅游可持续发展相关的活动本身也是有利可图的。

6. This will be helpful to leave a good impression of the community and enable the tourist to experience a pleasant vacation, which in turn, will enhance visitation levels because of repeat visitation and the positive word-of-mouth about the community widely spread by the tourist.
   这将有助于游客对社区产生良好的印象并享受愉快的假期,同时由于重复旅游和游客对当地社区良好的口碑,旅游人数也会增加。

7. Many measures can be taken such as donation to local charities, establishment of scholarships and community improvement schemes, managerial positions of tourism sectors that give priority to local residents, designs that take into consideration the

harmonious co-existence of architecture and local styles, and policies that give special consideration to local suppliers of goods.

可采取许多促进可持续性发展的措施,如捐赠当地慈善机构、设立奖学金、制定社区发展计划、旅游企业优先招聘当地居民做管理层、设计与当地风格和谐的建筑方案、给予当地供应商特别优惠政策。

Exercise

1. *Fill in the blanks with proper words to complete the following statements.*

| harmony | sustainable | release | mass |
| eliminate | criteria | beneficial | effective |

(1) Attention had not been paid to this idea before the _____ of the Brundtland Report entitled Our Common Future in 1987, even though this term was already being used in the early 1980s.

(2) Once sustainable tourism is properly defined, we should set up some _____ to determine whether the tourism is sustainable or not.

(3) Considering the fact that mass tourism takes up the majority of the world's tourism market, the connection between sustainable tourism and _____ tourism is reasonably a more important issue.

(4) It is justifiable to adopt _____ practices within the large-scale, dominant tourism industry.

(5) Even if this is not the case, to capture this high-spending and growing market is still most _____ to tourism businesses.

(6) In addition, if the community relations can develop positively, the host and the tourist will be able to live in _____ with each other.

(7) Sustainable tourism is a(n) _____ way adopted by tourism sectors for long-term benefits.

(8) The continuing and rapid growth of tourism has brought too much pressure on the world's resources and makes it necessary to adopt sustainable development to _____ the growing negative impact on the planet.

2. *Questions for discussion*

(1) According to the Brundtland Report, what is sustainable development?
_____

(2) Why should the tourism industry focus on the new travelers?
_____

(3) What are the main characteristics of the new travelers?
_____

(4) Why can sustainable tourism measures be better implemented in larger corporations?
_____

(5) What sustainable practices have been adopted by the tourism industry?
_____

Part II Guided Reading
第二部分 课文导读

第二次世界大战结束以后,世界旅游业经过几十年的发展,成为世界最大的产业之一,但繁荣发展的旅游业也存在潜在的危机。人们越来越强烈地意识到那些掠夺性的开发、粗放式的管理、旅游设施的病态扩张等正在损害人类赖以生存的环境,破坏人类的文化,严重影响了旅游业持续稳定发展。在这样的情形下,宏观旅游管理领域中产生了一种全新观念:可持续旅游发展。可持续旅游发展的思想起源于上个世纪的 70 年代,是人们对经济发展和保护环境的关系进行思索的产物。1978 年世界环境与发展委员会(WCED,又称布伦特兰委员会)发表了一篇名为《我们共同的未来》,使得"可持续发展"一词得到广泛应用。

本文阐述了旅游可持续发展的理论,并论证了旅游可持续发展的必要性和可行性。首先,新型旅游者市场已经出现,他们具有良好的环境保护意识,尊重当地民族文化,选择旅游线路更有弹性,不愿意大规模集中旅游;其次,可持续发展旅游节约成本,为旅游企业带来更多的利润和良好的企业形象;第三,许多大公司正在倡导可持续发展的理论,并循环利用能源、使用过的物品等,对旅游地进行资助、捐赠和文化交流,更多地融入当地的社会经济,实现经济目标和社会目标的统一。

由此可见,可持续旅游的观念正深入人心,受到旅游者和旅游企业的重视。可持续旅游发展就是指"在满足当代旅游者和旅游地居民各种需要的同时,又保持和增进未来发展的机会,实现经济目标和社会目标的统一。"那么具体来讲,要实现旅游的可持续发展,人们应当遵循什么样的原则呢?

第一,环境限制性原则。可持续发展的基本原则是实现旅游可持续发展的前提。所以,旅游资源的开发与利用应该保持环境质量不发生恶劣的变化。

第二,综合效益最大化原则。由于旅游产业具有明确的经济属性,所以从经济效益的标准出发,旅游可持续发展的中心原则为"经济持续性",要求实现旅游经济收益的持续性增长。

第三,自然资本的原则。将资源环境视为旅游生产要素的成分之一,作为自然资本参与旅游开发,将旅游资源价值纳入旅游业效益核算体系中,实现旅游"绿色 GDP"核算,建立完善生态环境参量指标体系,为控制与管理旅游业的可持续发展提供技术支持。

第四,公平的原则。它包含三层含义:一是追求当代人的公平,满足全人类旅游基本需要,以消除贫困作为可持续旅游的优先问题加以考虑。二是遵循区域旅游资源与收益分配公平,建立合理的经济结构来调节区域中相关者的利益关系。三是重视代际公平,现代旅游不能以消耗和损害后代旅游资源为代价。

第五,道德伦理原则。人类对赖以生存的自然环境、社会文化环境具有保护的义务,道德观念应该成为人类开发旅游的指导原则。

当前,实现可持续旅游发展战略还需要人类的共同努力。可持续旅游发展与整个国家的社会、经济发展战略紧密联系在一起。因此,加强国际合作、消除贫困、改变消费模式、改善人类居住环境、加强资源管理等宏观目标和战略的实现情况,就成为制约可持续旅游发展的背景因素。那么只有在一个良好的宏观背景之下,可持续旅游发展才能有效地发挥。实现可持续旅游发展的途径主要有以下内容:

第一,重视科学技术在实施可持续旅游发展战略中的作用。最近几个世纪环境的变化非常令人担忧,在下个世纪,随着人类对能源、淡水和其他不可再生的资源消耗的增加,这种变化会更为明显。所以,要想在环境和资源管理方面做到富有成效,要保证人类的日常生存和未来发展,科学知识变得非常重要。科学家所提供的信息有助于长期目标的可持续发展战略的形成,政府部门应该积极支持有关环境问题的科学研究,建立相应的政策机制,完善用以衡量人类生活质量的指标体系,建立改进资源管理的经济刺激机制,鼓励可以减少环境污染和资源消耗技术的开发和应用。

第二,加强法规建设。如果没有法律的约束,旅游活动在满足当前需求和考虑长远利益之间,在寻求旅游发展与保护环境资源之间缺乏行为规范,就会导致对环境和资源的掠夺性使用,所以规范的法律体系是可持续旅游发展战略的必要保证。

第三,积极开展教育和培训,提高公众的环境意识。通过教育和培训,让人们在环境态度、环境行为、环境价值观、环境道德和处理环境问题的技能等方面有所进步。应当提高对环境保护的理解、鼓励社会各界参与环境教育计划等。教育是实施可持续旅游发展的灵魂,只有通过面向全社会环境教育与培训的充分发展,旅游的可持续发展目标才能切实地实现。

第四,从旅游本身来看,可持续的旅游发展目标还要借助于各种符合可持续旅游发展哲学思想的旅游方式来加以实现。这些旅游方式包括:生态旅游、替代旅游、负责任旅游、绿色旅游和软旅游等。

第五,在旅游发展过程中强调各种利益的平衡,积极鼓励旅游目的地社区在旅游发展中积极参与。各国可持续旅游发展追求的目标是"全赢",即旅游者、旅游经营者、目的地社区等旅游活动的参与者在环境不遭受破坏、文化不受到侵害的前提下都能享受旅游带来的利益。所以,在具体实施过程中要把握好公平,权衡各方利益,才能更有效地实施可持续旅游发展。

20世纪90年代,加拿大温哥华Globe'90国际大会上提出了旅游业可持续发展的五个目标:第一,增进人们对旅游所产生的环境影响与经济影响的理解,强化人们的生态意识;第二,促进旅游的公平发展;第三,改善旅游接待地区的生活质量;第四,向旅游者提供高质量的旅游经历;第五,保护未来旅游开发赖以存在的环境质量。从这五点目标可以看出,可持续旅游发展最核心的一点,就是要从长远的观念出发全面认识旅游的影响,在满足当代人发展旅游业和开发旅游活动的同时,实现代际平衡。我们相信,通过旅游各个参与方、各个利益主体的协作,在政府的倡导和组织下,保持旅游目的地持续健康的发展,实现旅游的可持续发展的战略目标是能够实现的。

旅游知识测试

正误判断:请在正确的选题上划√,错误的选题上划×。

1. 旅游可持续发展系统由旅游经济系统、旅游生态系统、旅游社会文化系统、旅游支持保障系统等具有不同属性的子系统构成,是旅游经济、社会文化、资源环境等因素耦合而成的复杂系统。

2. 由于旅游产业具有明确的经济属性,而实现社会福利或实际纯收入的最大化是所有经济活动的最高目标,因此旅游可持续发展的中心原则是经济发展的持续性。

3. "可持续发展"的核心词是"发展",而"发展"必须建立在环境、经济和社会三者和谐统一的基础上,只有这样的发展观才是可持续的发展观,这与科学发展观的核心要旨是高度统一的。

4. 旅游发展要切实满足地方现实的经济发展需要,为旅游者提供高质量的旅游体验,因此地方政府和旅游企业是旅游可持续发展的主体,旅游者不是旅游可持续发展的主要责任人。

5. 道德伦理原则是可持续发展的重大问题,其中基于对人类自然的道德关怀的环境伦理观和基于生物多样性的公平性是其核心内容之一。道德观念应成为人与自然和谐的指导原则。

Part III　Case Study
第三部分　案例研究

生存还是毁灭：大堡礁海洋公园的未来

分析要点

1. 大堡礁海洋公园有什么旅游项目？对生态环境有什么影响？
2. 大堡礁海洋公园管理局为何要采取配额限制？政府为何要划定非捕鱼区？
3. 除了大堡礁海洋公园管理局外，你认为哪些人或哪些部门应该参与大堡礁的管理？为什么？
4. 大堡礁在20年以后会从地球上消失吗？有没有可能挽救这一濒危世界遗产？你有何建议？
5. 大堡礁案例对我国在海南建设"世界旅游岛"有什么借鉴意义？

相关理论和问题

1. 替代旅游（Alternative tourism）
2. 旅游法规（Tourism law）
3. 景区管理（Management of tourist resorts）
4. 旅游的可持续发展（Sustainable development of tourism）

　　澳大利亚东北部昆士兰州的东海岸，珊瑚礁相连，这就是世界七大自然奇景之一的大堡礁（Great Barrier Reef）。大堡礁由2 900个独立的珊瑚礁石群组成，面积有英国和爱尔兰合起来那么大，而大堡礁本身是有史以来世界最大的生物框架，大堡礁堪称为世界上最大的天然海洋公园、珊瑚水族馆。这里生存着400多种不同类型的珊瑚礁，其中有世界上最大的珊瑚礁，鱼类1 500种，软体动物达4 000多种，聚集的鸟类242种，有着得天独厚的科学研究条件，这里还是濒临灭绝的动物物种，如人鱼和巨型绿龟的栖息地。

　　除土著人以外，白澳大利亚人也散居在附近岛屿。这里旅游业十分发达，并成为当地重要的经济来源。从古至今，大堡礁特别是它的北部区域，对居住在西北岸土著人和托雷斯岛屿居民的文化产生了重要的影响，此外，还有供人观赏的石画艺术馆和30多处著名的历史遗址，最早可追溯到1791年。

　　大堡礁是世界上最有活力和最完整的生态系统，但其生态平衡也最脆弱。如在某方面受到威胁，对整个系统将是一种灾难。20世纪，由于开采鸟粪，大量捕鱼捕鲸，大规模海参贸易和捕捞珠母等，已经使大堡礁伤痕累累。现在澳大利亚已把这一地区辟为国家公园，制止了此类活动，并对旅游活动进行了限制。1975年澳大利亚政府颁布的大堡礁海洋公园法，提出了建立、控制、保护和发展大堡礁海洋公园（Great Barrier Reef Marine Park）。海洋公园的建立不仅对保护大堡礁的自然环境，而且对当地文化的保护与传承起到了重要作用。1981年，大堡礁被联合国教科文组织列入《世界遗产名录》。

　　大堡礁有许多吸引游客的旅游项目，同海豚近距离接触是大堡礁旅游热门项目。此外，水肺潜水（Scubadiving）、浮潜（Snorkeling）、海底漫步（Seawalker）、海中骑单车（ScubaDoo）以及乘直升机或乘海上飞机鸟瞰大堡礁都是游客喜爱的娱乐项目。但是，这些活动对大堡礁的环境和海洋资源都会造成一定影响，其长期的生态后果是难以预料的。大堡礁海洋公园管理局打算以可持续发展的方式管理大堡礁海洋公园,其原则是尽可能地适应旅游业和其他活动的发展,并在不破坏环境的完整性的情况下使其更加合理利用,走旅游可持续发展的道路。

1975年的大堡礁海洋公园方案以及有关的规则和区域规划,为管理公园的降灵岛(Whitsundays)和其他景区提供了主要的法律和规章基础。方案是建立在"可以预先告知的原则"之上的,允许管理局通过遵从"最优环境惯例"做出决定,方案内容之一是在规划的暗礁及海滨水域设置一系列装置。这种设置方式是为了完成一个目标,即以一种可持续的方式适应各种不同的用途。装置的五个设计标准几乎完全是以船只为基础的,规定在区内,船只的预定限制为每天20艘船、30艘巡逻舰,而且规定电动船只每年至少有50天禁止通行。白鲸保护区的水域有特殊的规章制度。船只不得靠近白鲸300米之内,在其他旅游区100米之内。

2000年1月,大堡礁旅游休闲咨询委员会成立,委员会会员分别来自与大堡礁有联系的各个行业。会员不定期开会,评估大堡礁的环保现状,向大堡礁海洋公园管理局提出各自对大堡礁资源使用的意见。为了保护大堡礁的生态环境,管理局根据会员们的建议,将大堡礁地区分为四个保护等级,限制游客出入的人数。曾有一段时间,很多游船不敢前往大堡礁降灵岛,害怕抛锚时损伤海底的珊瑚,影响了旅游业的发展。后来管理局和船运业代表共同划定了一片可以安全停泊的地区,在规划的暗礁及海滨水域设置了一系列装置,以解决旅游资源开发与保护的矛盾。

在大堡礁海洋公园的"合作管理"体系中,旅游业是受到政府环保限制最为严格的行业之一。为了确保旅游业避免对大堡礁造成危害,管理局建立了一种与旅行社挂钩的举措:对环保操作不达标的旅行社吊销其许可证,对表现好的旅行社则优先分配旅游资源的使用权。同时,还鼓励各旅行社之间相互监督举报。各个旅行社随时都在提醒游客:不要摘珊瑚,不要随便丢垃圾。旅行社导游也承担了环境监测的职责,一旦发现水质变坏和其他环保问题,他们会立即向管理局报告。在大堡礁从事旅游经营,每年都要向管理局上交数量可观的环保费。

2003年12月3日,澳大利亚政府向该国立法者递交了一份旨在保护大堡礁生态系统的环保计划书。该计划将大堡礁三分之一的地区确定为非捕鱼区。根据该计划,澳大利亚大堡礁海洋公园33%的区域都将被划入非捕鱼区,而之前该公园只有4.5%的区域为非捕鱼区。澳大利亚环境部长大卫·肯普说,该计划将拯救大堡礁的未来,为澳大利亚经济每年带来22.9亿澳元(16.7亿美元)的收益。他说:"这一历史上对大堡礁实行的最大的环保计划将使该地区成为世界上最大的海上保护区。"

但是,2009年公布的一项报告使大堡礁再次亮起海洋生态红灯:在全球变暖和化学径流的双重作用下,被誉为"海中自然生态博物馆"的大堡礁正处于严重的危机当中。作为大多数生物栖息地,珊瑚礁对温度变化极为敏感,大堡礁周边的生态系统因此也极易受到气候变化的影响。另外,由农业化肥和杀虫剂所产生的化学径流则是危害大堡礁的第二个"杀手",其对大堡礁的危害程度目前还是个未知数。大量涌入的各地游客和各种旅游活动,对大堡礁的生态环境也产生了不利影响。

良好的自然资源和环境是旅游业发展的前提和根本保障。没有大堡礁独一无二的自然环境和人文环境,就没有世界各地纷至沓来的游客,就没有大堡礁旅游可持续发展的原动力。美丽的大堡礁的命运何去何从,纠结着人们的心。海洋学家查利·沃隆最近公布的一份报告指出,全球气候变暖和海洋污染或许将在短短20年时间内让大堡礁这一世界自然奇观荡然无存。这一悲剧性的预言再一次提示人们旅游走可持续发展道路的迫切性和重要性。

资料来源:邹统纤.大堡礁——海中仙境.遗产旅游管理经典案例[M],中国旅游出版社,2010.

Part IV Reading Box
第四部分 阅读与分析

New Tourism

阅读分析要点

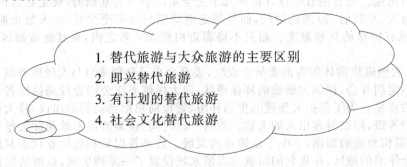

1. 替代旅游与大众旅游的主要区别
2. 即兴替代旅游
3. 有计划的替代旅游
4. 社会文化替代旅游

The development of sustainable tourism focuses on **small-scale tourism** projects and destinations because, as people assume, such tourism is more likely to bring positive environmental, economic and socio-cultural impacts within a destination.[1] As discussed below, this assumption has a sound theoretical basis, and many examples of small-scale sustainable tourism can be found. However, we should not take it for granted that the results are always positive.

Alternative tourism

Some researchers clearly pointed out the problems brought about by mass tourism, and began to provide alternative options in the early 1980s. It was argued that mass tourism was full of problems and could be replaced by small-scale alternatives in most cases. Therefore, the alternative tourism was thought of as substitute for mass tourism rather than other types of tourism.

In Figure 15.2 **mass tourism** and **alternative tourism** are described as sharply contrasting types. Of course, mass tourism is viewed as "bad" model while alternative tourism represents "good" model. For instance, we can find that attractions of mass tourism are regarded as being artificial and unnatural while attractions of alternative tourism are authentic, and that mass tourism tends to be controlled by outside forces which may result in high revenue leakage when they bring their profits back to their original places while alternative tourism encourages local control and close connections with local businesses.[2]

Table 1. A comparative study of mass tourism and alternative tourism

Circumstantial and deliberate alternative tourism

Circumstantial alternative tourism (CAT) and deliberate alternative tourism (DAT) are two types of alternative tourism. CAT refers to the superficial and **unintentional practice** of alternative tourism in the destination, which can be judged from its associated characteristics. These characteristics reflect that the destination is just experiencing the first two stages of the Butler sequence—the exploration and the involvement stage. On the contrary, deliberate alternative tourism is the tourism under administrative controls which retreat to the **backstage.** So this seems equivalent to the circumstantial version. Here the reader should pay attention to the similarities between the situation in which administrative controls withdraw from the front-stage and the exploration stage.[3] It is also important to grasp the distinction between circumstantial and deliberate alternative tourism. This is because a CAT is possible to go astray and develop along an unsustainable path, while a DAT can better maintain a sustainable, low intensity tourism option under the guidance and control of specific policies.[4]

Socio-cultural alternative tourism

Some researchers put emphasis on tourism impacts within social or cultural context. Perhaps due to this, DAT first appeared in these contexts. Similarly, the underdeveloped or "Third World" attracted most of the attention. The "Tourism for Discovery" project in Senegal can serve as one of the pioneering examples. It was established in 1972 and provided tourists with an opportunity to experience an authentic tourism by enjoying real traditional village life in person. Among other countries, Jamaica, India, Tanzania and Mauritius also adopted similar measures during this era. Although a great deal of publicity was given to some of these programs because they were completely new ideas and could create new opportunities, they still made up only a very small proportion of total tourism activity in those countries.[5] For example, in India alternative tourism took up only 0.1 ‰ of all overnight stays by international tourists during the late 1970s.

During the 1980s and 1990s DAT developed and expanded very rapidly. It is estimated that now DAT occupies between 2 and 5 ‰ of all tourism activity, although detailed calculation has not been done. The growth in the **"new traveler" market** has encouraged the development of many socio-cultural DAT products. The following are some distinct ones:

- Cultural villages -*Tourism for Discovery* (Senegal)
- Homestays-*Meet the people* (Jamaica), *Home Visit System* (Japan), *Friendship Force*
- Feminist travel-*Woodswomen*, *Womantrek* (both in the United States)
- Indigenous tourism-*Wanuskewin* (Saskatchewan, Canada), *Tjapukai Aboriginal Cultural Park* (Cairns, Australia)
- Older adult tourism-*Elderhostel* (global)
- Vacation farms
- Social awareness travel-*Center for Global Education*, *Global Exchange*, *Plowshares Institute* (both in the United States)
- Young hostels
- Personal awareness tourism-*ESALEN Institute* (California)
- Religious tourism-monastery retreats
- Educational tourism-*The Humanities Institute* (United States)
- Volunteer activity-*Habitat for Humanity*, *Global Volunteers* (both in the United States)
- Guesthouses

While socio-cultural DAT usually takes place in small communities and rural areas, it does not exclude big communities and urban areas. In Hong Kong, the project "Family Insight Tour" has been carried out, which gives tourists an opportunity to stay with families in the destination's high-density public housing estates. Every year there are about 1,000 tourists who make use of this program.

New Words

deliberate	adj.	深思熟虑的,审慎的
holistic	adj.	整体的,全面的

| contrived | adj. | 人为的,做作的 |
| circumstantial | adj. | 视状况而定的 |

Notes

1. The development of sustainable tourism focuses on small-scale tourism projects and destinations because, as people assume, such tourism is more likely to bring positive environmental, economic and socio-cultural impacts within a destination.
   旅游可持续发展重点在小规模旅游项目和目的地,因为人们认为这样的旅游更有可能为当地的环境、经济和社会文化带来积极影响。

2. For instance, we can find that attractions of mass tourism are regarded as being artificial and unnatural while attractions of alternative tourism are authentic; and that mass tourism tends to be controlled by outside forces which may result in high revenue leakage when they bring their profits back to their original places while alternative tourism encourages local control and close connections with local businesses.
   例如,大众旅游景点被认为是非自然的,而替代旅游景点是真实的;同时,大众旅游往往被外力所控制,当他们将利润带走时就会造成大量收入漏损,而替代旅游鼓励本地控制管理、与地方企业密切联系。

3. Here the reader should pay attention to the similarities between the situation in which administrative controls withdraw from the front-stage and the exploration stage.
   在这里,读者应该注意把握行政管理退出前台和探索阶段二者之间的相似之处。

4. This is because a CAT is possible to go astray and develop along an unsustainable path, while a DAT can better maintain a sustainable, low intensity tourism option under the guidance and control of specific policies.
   这是因为即兴替代旅游有可能沿着不可持续的发展道路误入歧途;而在特定政策的规范和指导下,有计划的替代旅游能更好地保证可持续的、低强度的旅游发展。

5. Although a great deal of publicity was given to some of these programs because they were completely new ideas and could create new opportunities, they still made up only a very small proportion of total tourism activity in those countries.
   由于这些项目体现了全新的理念并能够创造新的机会,人们为它们做了大量宣传,但在这些国家的所有旅游活动中,它们仍然只占很小的比例。

Topic discussion

1. What is alternative tourism?
   _____

2. How can alternative tourism help to promote the development of sustainable tourism?
   _____

3. What are the differences between mass tourism and alternative tourism in terms of food, transport and accommodation?
   _____

4. What are CAT and DAT? Which do you prefer?
   _____

5. What is the significance of socio-cultural alternative tourism? Can you give us some examples of socio-cultural DAT products?

_____

【即学即用】

With reference to the theory, information or approach applied in the Reading Box, have a case study of new tourism. You may take the backpacker or ecotourism in China as an example. Make presentation of your study in Chinese or in English using PPT.

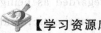【学习资源库】

为了掌握本章更多的相关专业知识,请您登陆 http://sicnu.cn/,点击国家双语教学示范课程《旅游学概论》,进入网络学堂查询相关资料。

Chapter Review 本章小结

This chapter has discussed the emergence of the new travelers as an important market segment and the importance of sustainable development of tourism industry. Tourism sectors must observe the business ethics codes; and social practices should be enforced, too. Both governments and tourism sectors play a key role in promoting the sustainable tourism. Public education and comprehensive environmental audits, recycling and reduction programs, community improvement schemes, and job opportunities that give priority to local residents are important practices that secure the sustainable development of tourism. Alternative tourism is a kind of new tourism that is quite different from the unsustainable mass tourism. At present, various forms of new tourism has been put into practice, and the new traveler's market has become more popular and more profitable in the world.

Part V   Additional Know-how of Tourism
第五部分   旅游知识扩展

【关键术语】

Sustainability: meeting the needs of the present without compromising the ability of future generations to meet their own needs

可持续性:既满足当代人的需求,又不对后代人满足其需求的能力构成危害。

Sustainable Tourism: The concept suggests "economic growth is only acceptable if it can maintain, at a minimum, the stock of tourist assets from one generation to another".

可持续旅游:该理念认为,"只有旅游资产存量能保存到下一代且不低于可接受的程度,经济的增长才是可接受的。"

Ecotourism: A responsible travel in which the visitor is aware of and takes into account the effects of this or her actions on both the host culture and environment.

生态旅游:一种负责任的旅游,游客要充分认识到自己的行为会给东道主的文化及环境造成影响,并在旅游时充分考虑这些影响。

Ecotourism indicators: Applicable to particular ecosystems or types of tourism. Destination-specific indicators are usually used to monitor tourism activities in a tourist resort. These indicators fall into two categories: (1) Supplementary ecosystem – specific indicators for application to particular ecosystems (e.g., coastal areas, parks and protected areas, or mountainous regions). (2) Site-specific indicators that are developed uniquely for the particular site. The use of the indicators helps ensure the economic means to support sustainable ecotourism as well as public support for tourism with a destination.

生态旅游指数：适用于特定的生态系统或特定的旅游类型。特定目的地指数通常用来监测旅游景区的旅游活动,分为二大类:(1)补充性特定生态系统指数,适用于特定的生态系统,如海滨地区、公园和保护区,或山区等。(2)特定景区指数:专门适用于某一特定景区,反映景区的重要因素。使用这些指数有助于保证目的地能从经济手段支持可持续生态旅游,同时还保证了公众对目的地旅游的支持。

【知识链接】

1. 替代旅游

替代旅游可以被称为与大众旅游相对立的各种小规模旅游类型的总称,它的产生基于西方发达国家对大众旅游对环境社会带来负面影响的认识和日益普及的环境意识。小规模是替代旅游的最主要特征,也正由于规模小,替代旅游对目的地环境影响也相应较小。替代旅游是相对于主流形式的旅游而言的,在第二次世界大战后已经被一些少数旅游者所推崇。上个世纪80年代,替代旅游作为一个专有词汇表示一种比大众旅游更具有道德感、更有可持续性的特殊旅游形式。1984年在泰国召开的"第三世界旅游大联合"(ECTWT)的会议上,替代旅游被定义为"一种可以在所有参与者之间达成谅解、团结以及平等的恰当旅游形式的过程"。其主要目标是:提供可以取代大众旅游的剥削和破坏成分的变通旅游方式,保证旅游经济效益得以在目的地国家的所有人民当中公平分配,构筑旅游者与目的地居民之间,以及他们在人的尊严和权利方面的互惠关系,确保对所访问的宗教、文化、社会和自然环境的尊重,激发旅游者和目的地居民之间在旅游之后做出行动上的反应,探索和开发新的替代旅游方式。

2. 可持续旅游的几种名称

可持续旅游是以旅游活动不破坏资源环境为核心目标,关心的是旅游活动的长期生存与发展,强调的是旅游活动的优化行为模式,以传播、培养旅游者具有可持续发展观、伦理观为目的的旅游方式。可持续旅游是在保护和增强未来机会均等的同时,满足现时旅游者和东道主的需要。可持续旅游产品是与当地环境、社区和文化保持协调一致的产品。可持续旅游有以下几种名称：

ecotourism(生态旅游)、green tourism(绿色旅游)、responsible tourism(责任旅游)、low impact tourism(低影响旅游)、nature-based tourism(以自然为基础的旅游)、nature-oriented tourism(自然导向旅游)、nature travel(自然旅行)、nature tourism(自然旅游)、environment-friendly tourism(环境友善旅游)、environmental pilgrimage tourism(环境朝圣旅游)、wildlife tourism(野生动物旅游)、alternative tourism(替代旅游)、ethnical tourism(伦理旅游)、soft tourism(软旅游)、special interest tourism(特定兴趣旅游)、appropriate tourism(适宜旅游)等。

【小思考】

1. 可持续旅游的核心是什么？衡量旅游承载力的主要内容有哪些？

参考阅读：

旅游承载力是指一个旅游目的地在不导致当地环境和来访游客旅游经历的质量出现不可接受的下降这一前提之下，所能吸纳外来游客的最大能力。也就是说，旅游承载力决定着旅游可持续发展的规模极限。旅游目的地的承载力包括旅游设施用地的承载力、物质环境承载力、生态环境承载力和社会心理承载力。旅游承载力决定可持续旅游发展的规模。旅游环境承载力在具体使用中是一个综合概念，它取决于旅游环境要素的分量值大小，这些分量包括环境生态承纳量（大气、水体、固体废弃物、植被等承纳量）、资源空间承纳量（旅游者对资源的占有时间、空间要求在某一时段内的承纳量）、心理承纳量（目的地居民和旅游者心理承纳量）和经济承纳量（旅游地满足游人基本生活条件的承纳量）。旅游承载力在具体的旅游实践中不太被人们所重视，主要是因为环境质量下降到何种程度才不被人们接受，以及旅游经历的质量下降于何时发生等问题是由旅游目的地的管理者和旅游者来决定的。由于环境质量下降到何种程度才是"不可接受的"，以及旅游经历的质量下降于何时发生等问题很难衡量，所以怎样保持旅游的可持续发展仍然是一个有待解决的问题。

2. 传统旅游与可持续旅游的主要区别是什么？联系发展中国家的实际情况，如何开展可持续旅游发展？

参考阅读：

传统旅游与可持续旅游在追求目标、管理方式、受益人、社会环境影响等方面有重大区别，主要差异如下：

对象	传统旅游	可持续旅游
追求目标	利润最大化 价格导向 文化与景观资源的游览	经济效益、生态效益最大化 价值导向 环境资源和文化价值完整性的享受与研究
管理方式	游客第一，有求必应 渲染性的广告 无计划的空间拓展 交通方式不加限制	生态系统承载力第一，有选择地满足游客 温和适中的宣传 有计划的时空安排 有选择的交通方式
受益者	开发商与游客为净受益者 当地社区和居民经济受益但环境损失较大	开发商、游客、当地社区和居民分享利益
正面影响	创造就业机会 刺激区域经济短期增长 获取外汇收入 促进交通、娱乐和基础设施改善	创造持续就业机会 促进经济发展 获取长期外汇收入 交通、娱乐和基础设施的改善与环境保护相协调 经济效益、社会效益和生态效益的融合

| 负面影响 | 旅游对环境的消极作用很容易对旅游区形成污染
旅游活动打扰居民和生物的生活规律 | 旅游对环境的消极作用可以控制在环境的自我调节能力范围内,游客的活动必须以不影响当地居民和生物的生活规律为前提 |

Part VI Further Readings
第六部分 课外阅读

如果您想进一步学习本章的内容,探讨旅游的可持续发展战略,学习不同旅游形式对旅游的影响,建议您阅读以下学者的著作和论文。

一、中文部分

[1] 李长荣. 生态旅游的可持续发展[M]. 北京:中国林业出版社,2004.
[2] 史本林. 论区域旅游可持续发展战略[J]. 江西社会科学,2005,(04).
[3] 朱华,杨怡. 小规模旅游开发模式在少数民族村寨中的运用——以四川省北川县古娜羌寨为例[J]. 成都发展改革研究,2010,(02).
[4] 孙睦优. 旅游环境承载力与旅游业可持续发展[J]. 桂林旅游高等专科学校学报,2004,(03).
[5] 吴楚材,吴章文,郑群明,胡卫华. 生态旅游概念的研究[J]. 旅游学刊,2007,(01).
[6] 张玉萍. 试论旅游资源和旅游环境的现状及可持续发展对策[J]. 国土经济,1999,(05).
[7] 谷明. 旅游经济的可持续发展探讨[J]. 桂林旅游高等专科学校学报,2000,(02).
[8] 崔凤军,许峰,何佳梅. 区域旅游可持续发展评价指标体系的初步研究[J]. 旅游学刊,1999,(04).
[9] 邓明艳. 国外世界遗产保护与旅游管理方法的启示——以澳大利亚大堡礁为例[J]. 生态经济,2005,(12).
[10] 张广瑞. 关于旅游业的21世纪议程——实现与环境相适应的可持续发展[J]. 旅游学刊,1998,(02).

二、英文部分

[1] Ricard Rigall-I-Torrent. Sustainable development in tourism municipalities:The role of public goods[J]. *Tourism Management*,2008,29(5):883—897.
[2] Sara Dolnicar, Friedrich Leisch. Selective marketing for environmentally sustainable tourism[J]. *Tourism Management*,2008,29(4):672—680.
[3] David Leslie. Managing Sustainable Tourism—A Legacy for the Future[J]. *Tourism Management*,2008,29(3):605—606.
[4] E. Sirakaya-Turk. Concurrent Validity of the Sustainable Tourism Attitude Scale[J]. *Annals of Tourism Research*,2007,34(4):1081—1084.
[5] Tanja Mihalič. Cases in Sustainable Tourism. An Experimental Approach to Making Decisions[J]. *Tourism Management*,2007,28(5):1372—1373.
[6] Bill Slee. D. Hall, I. Kirkpatrick and M. Mitchell. Rural Tourism and Sustainable Business, Aspects of Tourism [J]. *Tourism Management*,2007,28(4):1152—1153.
[7] Tanja Mihalič. A. Lanza, A. Markandya and F. Pigliaru. The Economics of

Tourism and Sustainable Development [J]. *Tourism Management*, 2007, 28(3): 924—926.

[8] Colin Hunter, Jon Shaw. The ecological footprint as a key indicator of sustainable tourism[J]. *Tourism Management*, 2007,28(1):46—57.

[9] Ralf C. Buckley C. Buckley. Managing Sustainable Tourism: A Legacy for the Future[J]. *Annals of Tourism Research*, 2006, 33(4):1178—1180.

[10] Regina Scheyvens. T. Sofield, Empowerment for Sustainable Tourism Development, Pergamon. [J]. *Tourism Management*, 2006, 27(4):731—733.

[11] Jeremy Northcote, Jim Macbeth. Conceptualizing yield: Sustainable Tourism Management[J]. *Annals of Tourism Research*, 2006,33(1):199—220.

[12] Sue Beeton. Empowerment for Sustainable Tourism Development[J]. *Annals of Tourism Research*, 2005,32(3):820—822.

[13] Colin Hunter and Jon Shaw. The Ecological Footprint As a Key Indicator of Sustainable Tourism[J]. *Tourism Management*, 2006(01).

Reference

一、中文参考文献

[1] 谢彦君.基础旅游学第二版[M].北京:中国旅游出版社,2004.
[2] 李天元.旅游学第二版[M].北京:高等教育出版社,2006.
[3] 傅云新,蔡晓梅.旅游学[M].广州:中山大学出版社,2007.
[4] 查尔斯·R·戈尔德耐等.旅游业教程:旅游业原理、方法和实践[M].大连:大连理工大学出版社,2003.
[5] 罗明义.旅游管理研究[M].北京:科学出版社,2006.
[6] 李昕.旅游管理学[M].北京:中国旅游出版社,2006.
[7] 崔利.旅游交通管理.[M].北京:清华大学出版社,2007.
[8] 杜学.旅游交通概论.[M].北京:旅游教育出版社,1995.
[9] 李伟.旅游学通论.[M].北京:科学出版社,2006.
[10] 亚德里恩·布尔.旅游经济学(第2版)[M],大连:东北财经大学出版社,2004.
[12] 田里.旅游经济学.[M],北京:高等教育出版社,2002.
[13] Philip Kotler等著.旅游市场营销[M].北京:旅游教育出版社,2002.
[14] 熊元斌.旅游营销策划与理论与实务[M].武汉:武汉大学出版社,2005.
[15] 赵西萍.旅游市场营销学[M].北京:高等教育出版社,2002.
[16] 马勇,毕斗斗.旅游市场营销[M].汕头:汕头大学出版社,2003.
[17] 艾伦·法伊奥.旅游吸引物管理新的方向[M].大连:东北财经大学出版社,2005.
[18] Dimitrios Buhalis.旅游电子商务[M].北京:旅游教育出版社,2004.
[19] 巫宁.旅游信息化与电子商务经典案例[M],北京:旅游教育出版社,2006.
[20] 苟茂兰.孙平.旅行社经营管理[M].山东:山东大学出版社,2005
[21] 杜江等.旅行社经营与管理[M].南京:南京大学出版社,2001.
[22] 何忠诚.旅行社管理[M].广州:广东旅游出版社,2002.
[23] 吕建中.现代旅游饭店管理[M].北京:中国旅游出版社,2004.
[24] 王天佑.饭店管理概论[M].北京:北方交通大学出版社,2006.
[25] 蒋丁新.饭店管理[M].北京:高等教育出版社,2004.
[26] James Keiser.旅游饭店管理概论[M].杭州:浙江摄影出版社,1991.
[27] 邹益民.旅游经济(饭店管理)专业知识与实务[M].北京:中国人事出版社,2000.
[28] 翁刚民.现代饭店管理——理论、方法与案例[M].天津:南开大学出版社,2004.
[29] 肖忠东,黎洁.饭店管理概论[M].南开大学出版社,2005.
[30] 尹隽.旅游目的地形象策划[M],北京:人民邮电出版社,2006.
[31] 李长荣.生态旅游的可持续发展[M].北京:中国林业出版社,2004.
[32] 颜文洪.张朝枝.旅游环境学[M].北京:科学出版社,2005.
[33] 陆书玉.旅游影响评价[M].北京:高等教育出版社,2001.
[34] 张文.旅游影响——理论与实践[M],北京:社会科学文献出版社,2006.
[35] 肖星,严江平.旅游资源与开发[M].北京:中国旅游出版社,2000.
[36] 刘纯.旅游心理学[M].北京:高等教育出版社,2004.

[37] 约翰. 沃德. 旅游案例分析[M]. 昆明：云南大学出版社，2005.

二、外文参考文献

1. Chris Cooper，John Flecher，et al. *Tourism Principles and Practice*. 2nd ed. New York：Addison Wesley Longman Limited，1999.
2. Charles R. Goeldner，J. R. Brent Ritchie，Robert W. McIntosh. *Tourism Principles，Practice，Philosophies*，New York；John & Wiley Inc，2000.
3. Lesley Pender. Marketing Management for Travel and Tourism. London：Stanley Thorns (Publishers) Ltd，2000.
4. J Christopher Holloway. *The Business of Tourism*，Foreign Language & Research Press，Beijing，2004.
5. Milton T. Astroff，James R. Abbey，Ph. D. *Convention Sales and Services*. 6th ed. Las Vegas：Waterbury Press，2002.
6. Trevor C. Atherton，Trudie A. Atherton. *Tourism，Travel and Hospitality*. Sydney：Lawbook Co.，1998.
7. McIntosh，Robert W. et al. *Tourism and Hospitality*，7th edition，Oxford：Butterworth Heinemann Ltd，1995.
8. Medlik，S. *Dictionary of Travel，Tourism and Hospitality*. Oxford：Butterworth Heinemann Ltd. 1993.
9. R. W. McIntosh，*Tourism：Principles，Practices，Philosophies*，6th edition，John Willey & Sons，Inc.，New York，1990.
10. Gee，Chuck Y. *Professional Travel Agency Management*. Englewood Cliffsm. N. J.：Pretice Hall，Inc，1990.
11. Gee，Chuck Y. *International Hotels：Development and Management*. Cincinnati，Ohio：South-Western Publishing Co，1994.
12. Bob McKercher，Hilary Du Cros. *Cultural Tourism：The Partnership Between Tourism and Cultural Heritage Management*，New York：The Haworth Hospitality Press，2002.
13. D. W. Howell，Passport：*An Introduction to the Travel and Tourism Industry*，2nd edition，Cincinnati，Ohio：South-Western Publishing Co.，1993.
14. V. T. C. Middleton，*Marketing in Travel and Tourism*，2nd edition，Heinemann，London，1988.
15. P. L. Pearce，*The Social Psychology of Tourist Behavior*，Pergamon Press，UK，1982.
16. G. Syratt，*Manual of Travel Agency Practice*，Butterworth Heinemann Ltd.，London，1992.
17. Tom Powers，*Introduction to the Hospitality Industry*，3rd edition，John Wiley & Sons，Inc，New York，1995.
18. Clare A. Gunn，*Tourism Planning*，2nd edition，Taylor & Francis，New York，1988.
19. A. J. Burkart & S. Medlik，*The Management of Tourism—A Selection of Readings*，Henemenn，London，1975.
20. Alan A. Lew and Lawrence Yu，*Tourism in China. Geographic Political and Economic Perspectives*，Westview Press Boulder，San Francisco，Oxford，1995.
21. Lavery，Patrick. *Travel and Tourism*. Huntingdon，England：Elm Publication，1996.

22. David Weaver, Martin Oppermann. *Tourism Management*. Sydney: John Wiley & Sons Australia, Ltd, 2000.
23. Biswanath Ghosh. *Tourism and Travel Management*, Vikas Publishing House PVT LTD, 1998.
24. MillRC, A Morrison. *The Tourism System*. Englewood Cliffs, NJ: Prentice-Hall, 1985.
25. Brian G. Boniface, Christopher P. Cooper. *The Geography of Travel and Tourism*. Landon: Heinemann Ltd. 1987.

21世纪旅游英语系列教材

《旅游学概论》(双语)(网络立体化教学,送电子课件)

《旅游英语视听说》(送多媒体电子课件)

《饭店英语》(视听说版)(送多媒体电子课件)

《英语导游听说教程》(送电子课件)

《英语导游实务教程》(送电子课件)

《西南旅游英文基础教程》(送电子课件)

注：为国家双语教学示范课程使用教材,网络课堂教学资源配套。

为普通高等教育"十一五"国家级规划教材

旅游学概论(双语)第二版

尊敬的老师:

您好!

为了方便使用教材,获得理想的教学效果,我们特向使用本教材的老师赠送电子教案、课件、练习答案以及期末考试样题2套。请完整填写"教师信息反馈表"并加盖所在单位系(院)公章,邮寄给我们,以便我们赠送相关教学资料。

祝您教学顺利!

北京大学出版社

教师信息反馈表

书名:	旅游学概论(双语)	版次	第二版
书号:			
所需要的教学资料:			
您的姓名:			
您所在的校(院)、系:	校(院)		系
您所教授的课程名称:			
学生人数:	_____人_____年级 学时		
您的联系地址:			
邮政编码	联系电话		(家) (手机)
E-mail(必填):			
您对本书的建议:		签字: 盖章	

北京市海淀区成府路205号 邮购部电话:010—62534449
北京大学出版社外语编辑部 李颖 编辑部电话:010—62767315
邮政编码:100871 市场营销部:010—62750672
电子邮箱:evalee1770@sina.com;robertszhu@126.com

教材使用说明

《旅游学概论》(双语)由国家双语教学示范课程主持人朱华教授担纲编写,现已建立120万字的教学资源库和网络课堂,课程全程录像。任课教师可以利用国家双语教学示范课程网络化教学平台,采用案例法等教学方法,加强启发式教学和师生之间课内、课后教学互动,提高互动式教学效果。为了更好地使用《旅游学概论》双语教材,提高双语教学质量,建议如下:

一、根据学生的英语语言水平,选择双语教学的比例。如果学生英语水平高,可选择"沉浸式"双语教学方法,全英文授课;如果学生英语水平较差,可选择"过渡式"双语教学方法,50%英文授课。

二、填写《旅游学概论》双语教材"教师信息反馈表",寄到北京大学出版社,以便出版社寄送电子教案、课件和参考答案。也可登陆国家双语教学示范课程《旅游学概论》网站下载。网址:http://zlgc.sicnu.edu.cn/lanmu_5.html。

三、教材每一章已列出本章的教学目标和教学重点。教学应首先理解教学目标,撑握教学重点、难点,以便根据不同教学对象组织教学。

四、雷柏尔模型(Leiper's Model)是本教材教学内容的框架,应将教学内容置于雷柏尔模型中进行分析讨论,做到纲举目张。

五、请注意教材每一章"教学要点"之后列出的相关章节,教学时应注意前后相关知识的有机联系,前后呼应,融会贯通。

六、案例教学时参考"案例矩阵",引导学生运用相关理论进行案例分析,或通过案例分析提升和完善理论。案例"分析要点"仅作为参考,教师或学生可以根据自己的观察和理解寻找切入点进行分析。

七、教材第四部分"阅读与分析"的教学也可引入案例教学法,建议在《旅游学概论》教学资源库案例库中或自己寻找相关案例开展教学。

八、本课程已建立网络化教学平台,有"小知识"、"疑难解答"、"案例分析"、"网上测试"、"本土化教学"等15个栏目,请登陆:http://zlgc.sicnu.edu.cn/lanmu_5.html,或登陆国家精品课程资源网:《旅游学概论》(朱华)。

九、因特网网址经常更新,如果无法访问网站,请使用搜索引擎,先进入四川师范大学网站主页http://sicnu.edu.cn/或国家精品课程网站主页,再寻找相关页面。联系邮箱:ernestzhu@126.com

《旅游学概论》(双语)教材编委会
2012年6月22日